Sales and Marketing
for Travel and Tourism

Sales and Marketing for Travel and Tourism

Second Edition

Philip G. Davidoff
Doris S. Davidoff

 Prentice Hall Career & Technology, Englewood Cliffs, New Jersey 07632

Library of Congress Cataloging-in-Publication Data

Davidoff, Philip G.
    Sales and marketing for travel and tourism/Philip G. Davidoff,
  Doris S. Davidoff.—2nd ed.
      p.   cm.
    Includes index.
    ISBN 0-13-786518-X
    1. Tourist trade—Marketing.   I. Davidoff, Doris S.   II. Title.
  G155.A1D345   1994
  338.4'791—dc20

93-17461
CIP

Editorial production and supervision: **Janet M. DiBlasi**
Interior design: **Greene Communications Design, Inc.**
Copy editor: **Jean Babrick**
Cover design: **Greene Communications Design, Inc.**
Cover art: **©Paolo Curto/The Image Bank**
Manufacturing buyer: **Ed O'Dougherty**
Acquisition editor: **Robin Baliszewski**

 © Davidoff Associates, Inc.

Printed in the United States of America
10   9   8   7   6   5   4   3   2   1

ISBN 0-13-786518-X

Prentice-Hall International (UK) Limited, *London*
Prentice-Hall of Australia Pty. Limited, *Sydney*
Prentice-Hall of Canada Inc., *Toronto*
Prentice-Hall Hispanoamericana, S.A., *Mexico*
Prentice-Hall of India Private Limited, *New Delhi*
Prentice-Hall of Japan, Inc., *Tokyo*
Simon & Schuster Asia Pte. Ltd., *Singapore*
Editora Prentice-Hall do Brasil, Ltda., *Rio de Janeiro*

Contents

Preface

It has been ten years since the first edition of this book was published. Much has happened in the travel and tourism industry during that time. Although most of the theory and practical advice in sales and marketing is similar to what it was in the early 1980s, a number of factors are different today. As we stated in the original edition, the purpose of this book is to provide a practical application of sales and marketing theory for both students and practitioners in the travel and tourism industry. We also want to give persons considering travel and tourism careers an understanding of the real world and a knowledge of specific techniques that can be used on the job, as well as a broad understanding of the interrelationships of the sales and marketing processes in a diverse, segmented, yet interacting industry.

In this new edition, because of changes in the travel and tourism industry as well as changes within our society as a whole, we have added four entirely new chapters. *Pricing* has become a major factor in the marketing of almost all products and services in the American society, so we now devote an entire chapter to a discussion of the marketing implications of pricing.

Relationship Marketing and its importance in the choices made by consumers was not a factor in the early 1980s. It, too, has become important in recent times and is the subject of another new chapter. *Service* is a byword of today's marketing principles and certainly worth an entire chapter in any modern marketing textbook.

The final new chapter examines the advance of *technology* in marketing. Computers, communications and other technologies have had a profound impact on marketing in the 90s.

Within each chapter, we have included "Industry Communiques": examples and readings that provide real-world views of the principles discussed. Readers thus have an opportunity to study the writings and experiences of a variety of people involved in the industry.

Given the dynamic nature of marketing and of the travel industry in particular, we recommend that readers of this book monitor both the trade press and the general press for new information and articles relating to the concepts discussed in this book. In this way, they can remain current on the topic and reinforce the concepts developed in *Sales and Marketing for Travel and Toursim.*

Philip G. Davidoff, CTC
Doris S. Davidoff, CTC

Acknowledgments

This book would not be complete without acknowledging the help given to us by many people in the travel and tourism industry, both in the original edition and in this new edition. Unfortunately, they are too numerous to credit individually, but we would especially like to thank the industry magazines such as Travel Agent, Travel Weekly, and ASTA Agency Management and the consumer publications such as Frequent Flyer that allowed us to reprint pieces from their publications. These real-life industry items allowed us to turn theory into reality.

We would also like to thank the many suppliers in the hotel, airline, cruise, and other travel segments who provided many of the "industry communiques" used in this book. Again, they provided real-life evidence of concepts discussed.

We must also thank Fedele J. Panzarino, New York City Technical College and Roberta L. Long, New York City for their help and comments while reviewing the manuscript.

Last, but certainly not least, we must thank our family and our employees for their patience and the help they have given us over the years that have allowed us the time and opportunity to work on this and other projects.

1

Introduction

buyer's market
consumer-needs strategy
consumer-oriented marketing
marketing
mental-states strategy
problem-solving strategy
product-oriented marketing
seller's market
stimulus-response strategy
tour package
wholesale tour operator

Marketing is a very broad topic, and when travel industry practitioners are asked to explain it, they usually give a wide variety of definitions. Merchandising, advertising, promotion, a plan for selling products, salesmanship, meeting customer needs, media planning are all thought (by various people) to be what the term *marketing* means. Although all of these activities can be considered parts of marketing, no one of them is marketing itself.

Before offering a more inclusive definition, let us point out that two conditions must be met for marketing to be possible. First, there must be a person or company that desires to sell a product or service. Second, there must be potential buyers for this product or service. It is not important which comes first, but both must exist. When both factors do exist, **marketing** *is the total process or series of activities that brings the potential buyer of the product or service together with the product or service.* If a concern can sell its product or service at a profit, its marketing has been successful. If the concern fails to earn a profit, its marketing has failed.

It is important to recognize, then, that marketing is the sum of all the activities related to bringing buyer and seller together profitably. In our exploration of marketing in the tourism and travel industry, we will look closely at the tourism product itself (tourism is, in reality, a combination of products and services), as well as at the potential consumers of tourism—travelers. In addition to examining the needs of the individual traveler, we will look at the travel market, its

1

demographics and segmentation. We will also look at the sellers of travel and at how the image of a selling company or a destination affects how it is marketed. We will concentrate on practical marketing tools that must be understood by anyone planning a career in the field of travel and tourism. We will review advertising and promotion and analyze various media and specific techniques for advertisement planning. We will study the sales function in the travel industry, including all components, and provide a thorough analysis of the sales process, together with a step-by-step method that can and should be applied on the job. Finally, we will look briefly at probable future developments in marketing in tourism and travel.

AN HISTORICAL PERSPECTIVE

This book is a practical approach to the challenge of bringing buyer and product together in the travel industry. However, it is necessary to understand the development of marketing in this century to understand today's processes. We must begin by understanding that manufacturing in the first half of this century basically served a **seller's market**. Consumer demand for goods generally exceeded the ability to produce the goods. With the exception of the Great Depression of the 1930s, when both production and consumption were down, the marketing process was one of developing a product and getting it to the customer.

This **product-oriented marketing** was based on the belief that if you built a better product, people would beat a path to your door. This style of marketing began to fade in the 1950s when supply began to exceed demand and a **buyer's market** developed. Now people had choices. They did not have to buy one type of product—they could choose from many. With the change in supply, the marketing process also changed. Instead of building a better product and hoping people would come to the door, executives began to ask: "What does my customer really want?" Thus began the development of **consumer-oriented marketing**. This style of marketing is very sound economically because, if a producer has accurate information about what customers want before production begins, there is less chance of producing the wrong product. The secret here is accuracy in determining what the consumer wants.

Until the middle of this century, the ancient Latin phrase "caveat emptor" (let the buyer beware) ruled the marketplace. Buyers were expected to educate themselves on what they purchased and were responsible if they bought the wrong thing. Sellers could be much less careful of the safety of the product and of how they represented what the product could do. Caveat emptor was generally the rule until the 60s, when we entered into an era of consumerism in which the seller was responsible for ensuring that the product was safe and was represented truthfully and fully to the purchaser.

Another change over the years was the integration of sales and service in the marketplace. In the early days of retailing in the United States, both local merchants and their customers took service for granted. Products were purchased fully assembled and the proprietor of the store was happy to explain and demonstrate how the product worked. The business was usually a part of the local community and the owner of a retail establishment usually lived in the same community where the store was located.

In the 1970s and 1980s, service diminished. Large retail chains developed where the consumer didn't even know the owner. Managers changed frequently and there was little relationship within the community between many stores and their customers. Large, impersonal malls became popular. Purchases were made that had to be assembled by the purchaser and, in many cases, the person selling the product couldn't explain either how to assemble it or how to use it properly.

This change caused a backlash, and complaints from consumers increased. As we reached the end of the 80s and into the 90s there has been a great emphasis on service as a part of sales and marketing. Unfortunately, in all too many cases, this emphasis on service has been no more than lip service, with employees being given little if any training on how to provide the service. Today, predictions are that consumers will demand greater levels of personal service from the places they choose to patronize during coming years. Businesses that do not provide this service will lose out to those that do and/or to automated methods of purchasing.

SOME TWENTIETH CENTURY MARKET STRATEGIES

The Automobile Industry

In many ways the market strategies in the automobile industry illustrate the points made above—from a seller's to buyer's market. From the 1930s to the 1970s, market strategy changed from product orientation to consumer orientation. Earlier in the century, in the heyday of the famous Model A and Model T Fords, industrialist Henry Ford said, "You can have any color car you want as long as it's black." And people bought black Fords and more black Fords. The producer was clearly in the driver's seat. After World War II, automobile colors began to change, but consumer demand then was so great that almost any car built was sold.

By the early 1950s, automobile production was at a peak. The number of manufacturers was much greater than today. Kaiser-Frazer, Crosley, Studebaker, and Packard automobiles were being produced, along with more familiar names such as Ford, Oldsmobile, Buick, Chrysler, and Plymouth. Supply began to exceed demand, and consumers were able to choose the brands and models that appealed to them most. The V-8 engine gained preference over the straight 8 cylinder engine. Packard, a major producer of straight 8 cars, became history. Other consumer choices governed the survival of some manufacturers and the downfall of others. Companies that were unwilling or unable to change as consumer desires and needs changed, fell by the wayside. See "Industry Communique."

INDUSTRY COMMUNIQUE

From a speech by Sir Colin Marshall, at the time Deputy Chairman and CEO of British Airways, to the American Society of Travel Agents in Taipei, September 1991.

Now and for the future, the consumer around the world is better informed, more knowledgeable, more discerning and much more independent. It is not so long ago that a travel agent sold air travel through the OAG and a telephone. Now travelers have direct access to detailed travel information and understand the booking process.

It is why mutual marketing strategies must now be geared to serving customers consistently well and retaining their support. In a relatively short space of time, we have moved from being order takers to a "can do" industry which is dedicated to providing a style of service which precisely meets the demands of the customer for efficiency, innovation and value for money.

That comes from two key elements: a structured program of research, analysis and dialogue with the consumer; and striving for ultra-professionalism in both the quality of our people and the way they do business.

The most important objective for the industry is a factor which the industry has at times seemed to greet with coyness. That is profitability.

In the face of mounting piles of learned papers and academic addresses on the future path of the travel industry (for which, of course, there is a valued place), I have told a number of similar gatherings that they are all well and good, but what we really need before prop*hets* is pro*fits*. I have no hesitation in repeating it here, confident that we all agree.

Our research tells us that the customer of the 1990s and beyond values quality and convenience, but is clear on how much that added value should cost and is cautious about promises not followed through. The market is telling us that it requires real innovation, efficient and consistent service, value for money and choice. In short, it has no objection to prices that produce a profit for the supplier and the retailer, but the product, service and choice had better be good.

The test therefore, of our marketing abilities lies in the translation of those consumer requirements into services and products. The test of our business abilities lies in their efficient distribution and sale, at a profit.

It also lies in recognition of the part we respectively play in the industry and the way in which our interface is constructed. It is simple to say that airlines and other principals are the wholesalers and the travel agent is the retailer. That is fact and British Airways, for one, has no wish nor need to be in the retail sales side of the business.

As we pursue our strategies, the edges can become blurred and misconceptions arise. Direct marketing, for instance. For carriers, this is a cost-efficient channel of sales promotion designed not to bring customers to our counters, but to drive them to those of the travel agent.

I can only speak directly for airlines and my airline in particular, but I am sure all principals will agree that the travel agency industry, now served with highly-advanced distribution technology, forms probably the most powerful retail force of any industry across the world and we would all be foolish to look away from it.

I have no doubt that our future prosperity lies in harnessing that force to the production power of inventive, efficient travel service manufacturers to create that sought-after partnership in profitability. It is not at all elusive, but with mutual trust, understanding and business commitment, eminently attainable. There is only one way to go towards the year 2000 and that is together.

Togetherness is even more important if we are to break away from the shackles of political constraint which can appear to induce reluctance, even apathy, in our drive for growth and expansion. Undue government involvement and interference has never helped our industry and never will. It is an obstacle to be removed.

However, like the politicians who shape business destiny, we, too, require popular support and need the voters of the world on our side.

Whatever the very real problems of aeropolitics and fiscal discrimination—and the harnessing of the industry's skills needed to counter their adverse effects—there is a constraint far more complex.

I refer to what is no less than the conundrum of the infrastructure. You have all heard a lot, maybe too much, about the problems of slots, airports, ATC systems and how we must achieve expansion if our businesses are not to go into terminal decline.

The easy answer is that all we need are large investments of both cash and political will. The former commodity presents no real problem. The latter is a much more difficult seam to mine.

There is nothing new in recognizing that, alongside the economy and employment, there has emerged a further great ballot-box motivator: Concern for the environment.

You all know what I mean: Reactions summarized in the kind of slogan we have in my country. 'NIMBY'—Not In My Backyard; and 'BANANA'—Build Absolutely Nothing Anywhere Near Anyone.

It is clear, that we will not be able to develop the expanded infrastructure we need desperately and, ironically, that our customers of the future will demand, unless we can demonstrate that transport and tourism development can go hand in hand with environmental care and protection. The problem is, that the person whose vote we seek is schizophrenic. The traveler who complains vigorously about being stuck in an airport for hours on end because of ATC delays, is the same member of the electorate who cries 'NIMBY' at any suggestion of more runways or expansion of the aviation working day in his or her city.

Environmental concern will be an increasingly important factor in our industry. As the manufacturers of cosmetics and detergents and the refiners of gasoline have been forced to go green and present their products accordingly, so too will we. I recall, back in the early 1970s when the State of Washington took the innovative step of banning aerosols, one comic remarked, "Fine—but you can't kill cockroaches with a roll-on." The fact is that the roll-ons have won.

To be environment friendly is much more than just doing good. It's good business sense.

The day will come, if it has not already emerged, when customers will want to see plans of a hotel's sewage disposal system and want to know precisely the sources of food supply. They will want to know about machinery systems and cleaning processes, before making their choices on a convention, vacation or business venue. The same will go for airlines, cruise lines and ground operators.

This is not to say that nothing is not already being done. In the airline industry, IATA has set up an Environmental Task Force. Within British Airways, one of our corporate missions and goals is 'To be a good neighbor, concerned for the community and the environment.' I can promise you these are not just fine words, for we have an active program, under a specially-appointed environmental expert. The objective is that British Airways, in every aspect of our activity, should be environmentally sound within a few years. Our management practices now include environmental disciplines.

The obvious issues are those of engine noise and the emissions of nitrogen oxide from aircraft and carbon dioxide from ground vehicles. But we are also concerned with smaller, more obscure detail. There might, for instance, be a demand to offer more newspapers in our Club cabins on the 15 percent more services we will introduce between the UK and the USA next year. Before, we would probably have responded to customer requests by simply loading more reading material. Now, we stop and think—What are the implications for paper production, the additional fuel needed to carry the extra weight and the disposal of discarded newsprint. We call the process environmental back-charging; and it applies to every area of management.

The central idea is that ERC (Environmental Research Group)—to add yet another acronym to the industry lexicon—should be a clearing house and repository for travel and tourism data in the field of the environment. Its initial task will be to provide a computerized data base on environmentally related activities in all sectors of the industry—transportation, accommodation, catering, leisure facilities and travel services. Not only to catalog and report on what is happening, but to provide a central source of information on much of the good practice that is taking place. ASTA's own guidelines being a shining example. Ultimately, the Center should act as a worldwide environmentally compatible growth.

The operation has been set up in England at the Oxford Centre for Tourism and Leisure Studies, which already has a track record in the environment field. Initial sponsorship comes from a very small core of WTTC members including British Airways and the British Tourist Authority. It has the enthusiastic support of the UK Government. I hasten to add that this is an international operation with a Board of

Governors of eminent individuals and organizations specializing in travel and in the environment. ASTA Past President, Voit Gilmore, has agreed to be a member of this Board, and, of interest to this region, so has PATA President, Neil Plimmer.

Now as vital and progressive as the research and data collation work of ERC will be, it will mean little if the World knows nothing of it, nor if it does not translate into our day-to-day business activities.

I see no reason why this kind of development which ERC will undertake could not lead to very practical research, testing products, services and infrastructure. It would identify standards of environment friendly activity and produce plans and proposals to bring things up to ecological scratch where necessary.

Who knows, perhaps one day an ERC Seal of Good Practice might be seen on aircraft, terminals, maintenance facilities, hotels, tourist attractions, ships, buses and even travel agency premises.

It will form the most vivid and comprehensible demonstration that travel and tourism is a force to be trusted, encouraged and nourished as we go Together Towards 2000. We must show that our most vital objective is that in order to enhance our position as the largest industry *in* the world, we must become the most friendly *to* the world.

From speech to ASTA on September 29, 1991 by Sir Colin Marshall, Deputy Chairman and CEO, British Airways.

Ford Motor Company was one of the first to recognize that consumer choices were affecting the marketplace. As a result, Ford decided to determine what prospective buyers wanted in a car. Ford's management believed that if consumers were given what they wanted, they'd buy it. Thus began the earliest and most primitive market research. Unfortunately, the result was a total failure—the 1957 and 1958 Edsel. According to *Business Week* (Nov. 28, 1959) Ford spent $250 million to bring the Edsel to market, and lost about $200 million more in the two-and-one-half years the car was in production. Ford was the laughing-stock of the automobile industry, but executives recognized what Ford had tried to do. They determined that in this case the execution of market research was faulty, not the concept itself.

The development of market research continued and was refined. It will never be 100% correct, however, because human beings are not predictable. For the last twenty years, no major automobile manufacturing decision has been made without strong attempts to determine what the consumer really wants. By 1970, management consultant and graduate business professor Peter Drucker observed that General Motors was no longer in the business of *manufacturing* motor cars; it was in the business of *marketing* motor cars. Today, successful marketers determine what product or service a client wants before developing the product or service. This approach is valid in all industries, including the travel and tourism industry.

The Airline Industry

Marketing within the airline industry is another parallel in our historical perspective. Through the 1950s, airline marketing was product-centered. Almost all advertising described the features of airplanes, including comfort, safety, and speed. Little was done to recognize the fact that different people travel for different reasons until the 1960s. There are vast differences in the needs and desires of business as opposed to pleasure travelers and within each of these broad categories, there are many subsets of reasons for travel.

Jet airplanes came into use in the late 1950s. By the early 1960s, jets were in widespread use in the United States and overseas. The jet vastly increased the capacity or supply of available airplane seats. It could carry more people per flight than propeller aircraft and fly almost twice as far on a given day. Thus, with supply exceeding demand, the airline industry turned to consumer-oriented marketing.

After World War II, first-class and coach fares developed with differing levels of service. For example, the Boeing Stratocruiser used by Pan American World Airways and others featured a lower deck with sleeping accommodations. It is interesting to note that in 1980 sleeperette seats were reintroduced in the first-class sections of Boeing 747 jumbo jets and are now standard for trans-oceanic travel.

By the 1960s, airline marketers began looking at the reasons why people travel. They determined that business travelers had certain needs (flexibility, speed, and last-minute planning capability) while vacationers had other needs (low cost, reliability, but usually much time for advance planning).

Business and vacation travelers are really purchasing different products. Frequency of service was established to meet business needs. Special excursion fares began to be offered to attract the vacation traveler. Restrictions were placed on these fares so that the business traveler who needed to plan travel at the last minute still paid a higher "regular" fare. Today, passengers on the same flight between two cities may have paid many different fares depending upon the conditions under which they are traveling. The lower fares are established to attract vacationers away from their cars and fill empty seats on the frequent flights that business travelers need.

In the 1970s airlines maketed by promoting an image of luxury and sophistication. They competed on the basis of champagne breakfasts, steak cooked in-flight and designer uniforms. When airlines were regulated by the Civil Aeronautics Board (CAB), changes in price required government approval and competition on the basis of price was virtually impossible.

The Steamship Industry

The steamship and cruise industry provides an interesting contrast in our view of the historical perspective of marketing. From the beginning of the century until the 1960s the steamship was a major form of transportation. The growth of our nation can be traced to immigrants traveling in "steerage" class across the

North Atlantic. Steamships also had other classes of service, including first class. First-class service was exceedingly elegant and expensive and only available to the rich. First-class travelers and immigrants never saw each other because the ships did not permit movement between classes. Shipline marketing was definitely product-oriented through the 1950s.

In the late 1950s, however, something happened that had grave implications for the steamship market—and nobody noticed. This was the time when more people crossed the North Atlantic by airplane than by sea. By the early 1960s, with the introduction of jet airplanes, it appeared that the death knell was sounding for ship transportation.

However, just as the United States Cavalry rides to the rescue in old Western movies, customer orientation rescued the steamship industry. In the 1950s, some steamship lines had experimented with cruises—winter vacation trips where a steamship sails from one city (usually New York at the time), visits a number of ports (Bermuda, Bahamas, or Caribbean Islands), and returns to the city of origin. North Atlantic travel was at a low ebb during the winter because of poor weather and normal vacation patterns. The cruises, which visited such destinations as Bermuda were quite successful and provided some degree of income when ships would otherwise be idle.

With the decline of the steamship transportation market, shiplines introduced cruises on a year-round basis and found almost instant success. With the addition of air/sea packages and special ships designed specifically for cruising (see "Industry Communique"), the cruise market has developed into an

INDUSTRY COMMUNIQUE

From a speech by Dermot McDermott, Chairman of Cunard at Seatrade, January, 1991.

The story of modern cruising goes back only two decades. Before that, ocean liners really existed for the purpose of transportation rather than vacationing. Even though Cunard's *Laconia* inaugurated world cruising in 1922 and Cunard's *Caronia* inaugurated luxury cruising in 1948 on the first ship built solely for the purpose of vacationing at sea, Cunard was mainly a transportation company carrying people across the Atlantic. So were all of her competitors.

During the 1960's, it was clear that the jet airplane would soon make ocean liner transportation obsolete. So for the rest of the decade, there was a rush to sell cruises. The cruise lines were quite busy mounting air conditioners into the hulls of deep-draft ocean liners so we could call them cruise ships. Of course, they were not really cruise ships and were only able to satisfy customers to a certain degree. It was only toward the end of the 60's that it became apparent that purpose built vessels would be needed to create a great cruise experience.

Vessels with smaller drafts, central air conditioning, standardized accommodation and outdoor pools would be required.

At Cunard, we decided to sell off the entire aging fleet of transportation vessels and build *Queen Elizabeth 2*. Because of our own uncertainty, QE2 was built part ocean liner and part modern day cruise ship. She was and still is the only dual purpose vessel ever built.

Quoted from a speech on January 19, 1991, by Dermot McDermott, Chairman of Cunard.

important part of the tourism package. The vast majority of cruises today (especially for consumers who live a distance from the departure port city) are sold as part of a total air/sea program. The development of the cruise was a reaction to changing consumer needs and its continuing development has made cruises the fastest growing segment in the travel industry in the early 90s.

The Hotel Industry

The first hotels of the modern world were inns at critical junctures of stagecoach lines. With the advent of the railroad, hotels developed near (sometimes even in) central city railroad stations in large cities throughout most of the world.

Later, railroads sometimes created cities, as well as other destinations. Henry Flagler, developer of the Florida East Coast Railroad, invested heavily in the development of resorts in Miami Beach. He did this to provide a market for his rail services, and the first wave of winter tourism in Miami Beach, around the turn of the century, was promoted to fill both railway seats and hotel rooms. By the 1920s and 30s the rich routinely traveled to Miami to spend the winter on the beach. Other resorts for the wealthy, such as Greenbrier in Virginia and Asbury Park in New Jersey, were connected to major cities by railroads.

There are also prestigious hotels such as the Waldorf-Astoria in New York City and Palmer House in Chicago that date from the late 1800s and early 1900s. These hotels were patronized by what are known today as "the rich and famous" and have been maintained at their grand scales for those who can afford them. However, as times and consumers' needs changed, other kinds of accommodations were needed.

Shortly after World War II, a Memphis businessman and his family took a trip to Washington, DC and back by car. This man, Kemmons Wilson, was appalled by the lack of facilities for family travelers. The roadside cabins and tourist courts existing at that time were, with few exceptions, very poor in quality. They usually consisted of only a bedroom, a bathroom, and a parking space outside the door. Standards were not consistent and the traveler could not be assured of a pleasant experience. Hotels in cities were expensive, charged high rates for children, and had no parking facilities. Kemmons Wilson decided to do something about this. He and a few fellow investors were the founders of Holiday Inns, which until recently, was the world's largest hotel chain in terms of number of rooms.

Holiday Inn was the first to recognize the needs of the family traveler. Free parking, swimming pools, and no charge for children sharing a room with parents were the initial sales features of the chain. The chain was also one of the first to use franchising as a major method of expansion. Holiday Inn franchises were expected to meet strict operational standards and pass periodic unscheduled inspections. Other hotel chains soon adopted similar methods.

Gradually, the distinctions among hotels, motels, and resorts have faded. Previously, hotels were commercial in nature, offering just rooms and restaurants, and were usually located in cities. Motels (motor hotels) were located near well-traveled highways, provided free parking facilities, and usually had a swimming pool. Resorts emphasized facilities for rest and relaxation, such as pools, tennis, golf, shuffleboard or other activities. They were virtually destinations in themselves.

Today, many downtown hotels offer health clubs, swimming facilities, tennis courts, and other types of recreation. While parking is not always free, it is generally available. Today, downtown hotels compete with resorts and airport hotels for conventions and business meetings. The roadside motel, which previously depended upon vacation travelers, today competes for business travelers—especially where companies have established major facilities in suburban areas. Motels also seek their share of the meetings market.

There has been a growth in the large hotel chains of a variety of brand names within the one company. These brands are used to differentiate among the properties in the chain in terms of price and amenities.

Today all accommodation facilities market to the traveler and also to the local community (see "Industry Communique"). Although the local community does not provide many room nights of business, local residents make hotel restaurants and catering facilities profitable. Such family gatherings as weddings, anniversaries, and bar mitzvahs have helped many hotels to be profitable—especially on weekends when business travelers are not usually on the road.

"In years to come, Margaret, we'll look back on this vacation as one of our happiest moments."

INDUSTRY COMMUNIQUE

GETTING ON TARGET

John Jesitus

HOTEL MARKETERS TO FOCUS ON CUSTOMER, WHOLESALER, AGENT

National Report—Lodging-chain come-ons range from heavy advance-purchase discounts to free slippers. Mouthpieces from Martin Mull to Garfield the cat pitch slogans so formulaic, customers can't tell which chain is which.

Programs like frequent-stay offers and "super-saver"room rates may do more harm than good. The shotgun approach to marketing that many chains seem to favor is off target. But when the guy across the street slashes rates, what's a hotel company to do?

Spend Smart

Survivors of the 1990s' market-share wars will be those companies that target customers cost-effectively.

When asked what's wrong with the way hotels market themselves, Mike Leven, president of Holiday Inn Worldwide's franchise division, said, "I don't think hotels are marketing themselves." Leven said the lodging industry, like the airlines, is in a "me too" mode.

He said that rather than "running after the Superbowl ad," hotel companies must return to a much more closely targeted, regional and local approach to marketing and sales development.

Leven also predicted a "very, very strong" outreach toward travel distributors—travel agents, tour operators, wholesalers and corporate travel departments. He said, "It's not so much who sleeps in your bed, but the person who sends them to your bed that's going to be important."

Marc Yanofsky, executive vice president of marketing for Hyatt International, added that hotel-industry marketing also suffers from an "edifice complex."

This term refers to the lodging industry's habit of advertising buildings. Yanofsky said customers don't care how many rooms a hotel has. "All they care about is that there's a room they like."

Yanofsky said lodging companies must sell a total experience, which begins with the res call and doesn't end until long after check-out. And they must simplify advertising claims and frequent-stay offers. He added, "The customer isn't as interested in our business as we are."

Walk All Over Homewood

One company thinks the way to a guest's heart is through his feet. Memphis-based Homewood Suites found that travelers don't like to walk barefoot in hotel rooms. So, since June, Homewood guests have been getting a free pair of slippers, courtesy of Homewood and American Express, at check-in.

The Totes-style footsies bear the company's colors, khaki and teal. Their non-skid bottoms sport webbed feet reminiscent of Homewood's duck logo.

Promotional goodies like these work best when they're part of an integrated marketing effort. Beth Rooks, Homewood Suites manager of communications, said the Suite Feet program is an effort to reach the consumer market and generate more weekend business. She said they're a big hit with guests.

Consumers love giveaways. They like to feel they're getting a break. The trouble is, the U.S. lodging industry has led them to expect it.

Emphasize Value

Richard Kelleher, president of Boston-based Guest Quarters Suite Hotels, said there's too much "price-led noise" in the hospitality industry, too much advertising focused on price rather than value. Instead, he recommends advertising features, guest benefits and service.

Kelleher said, "We [at Guest Quarters] also believe hotel marketing starts with your own backyard, recognition of your key clients and focusing as much effort as you can on your immediate trade area."

In addition, Kelleher said lodging companies must give international wholesalers and agents the same service U.S. consumers get. Kelleher said he anticipates strong international demand this summer.

If he's right, it couldn't happen at a better time. According to figures from Smith Travel Research, the last two quarters have been the lodging industry's worst ever.

However, a few lodging companies—including Choice and Radisson—went on the offensive during the Gulf War. Barry Smith, senior vice president of marketing for Choice Hotels International, said most companies shelved marketing and advertising efforts during the war for fear of consumer backlash.

In contrast, Choice struck early this year with its Yellow Ribbon campaign, which sends a portion of revenues to the International Red Cross.

Smith said that during February and March, companywide sales jumped 20 percent over the same period last year. He said, "We're beating the socks off our competition."

Choice will intensify its high-impact TV ads during the 1990s. This summer, the company will push its suitcase spots into 97 percent of America's households an average of 32 times during a nine-week period. Smith explained that when you communicate effectively, you need not discount as heavily.

However, it's unclear how many of the discount leaders are getting their message across. Smith said only two lodging companies—his and Motel 6—use consistent advertisements. He said most chains "haven't hit on a strategy that's producing."

Radisson Hotel Corp. also got on the tube in the first half of 1991. Early this year, the company unveiled its first national TV ads in five years.

Tom Storey, Radisson executive vice president of sales and marketing, said that as a result of Choice's ads and summer promotions, chainwide occupancy is up over last year.

John Norlander, president of Radisson, said the company takes a long-term view of marketing. He predicted supply and demand will be in better balance by 1995. As they come into balance, he said, discounting and related marketing fracases will start to subside.

Promote Brand Names

Internationally, however, the market-share battle may be just beginning. Brand names could be an important weapon in selling to visitors from Japan, Asia, Europe and elsewhere. Norlander said, "People are looking for brand names to feel comfortable, and also to identify that they have 'arrived'."

To deliver international reservations, Radisson is counting on advanced technology. The company has learned that you can't use one ad, one language and one phone number internationally. Foreign markets are much more diverse than the states.

Radisson also has learned that international travelers calling for reservations want direct confirmations. Getting these requires data hookups to the company's system. Storey said Radisson will unveil the international version of its Pierre reservation system in early 1992.

With domestic bookings slim in the first half of 1991, it's no wonder U.S. hotel marketers have itchy trigger fingers. But as the industry markets across borders and oceans, it must not overlook potential guests right here at home.

Reprinted with permission from Hotel and Motel Management, July 29, 1991.

The Travel Agency

Thomas Cook began the travel agency industry in England in the 1840s when he organized the first "tour" by escorting a group of people on a one-day train excursion to a temperance meeting. Cook negotiated with the railroads to pay him a commission on tickets he sold to the public. The railroads tried to convince him to add a surcharge, but he prevailed and the concept of commissions to travel agents for their sales, rather than fees paid by the customers, has held to this day. Cook's early tours opened up world travel to the middle class. See "Industry Communique."

By the 1920s, travel agencies had begun to grow and concentrated primarily on selling railroad and steamship travel. Hotel porters also functioned as travel agents, selling railroad tickets to guests of the hotels. ASTA, The American Society of Travel Agents, which is the largest travel industry trade organization in the world, started in 1931 as The American Steamship and Tourist Association. For the most part, travel agencies in the United States in the first half of the 20th century sold international travel to upscale clientele. Plans were customized for each client.

In 1970 there were approximately 7000 travel agencies in the United States, which accounted for sales of less than 50% of domestic airline tickets, but more than 85% of international air and more than 95% of steamship sales. By 1990 there were more than 30,000 such businesses, which sold approximately 80% of domestic air, 95% of international air, and more than 95% of cruise sales. The public had become aware of the existence of travel agents and the help they could provide in complex travel decisions. Most vacations that involve air travel are now booked through travel agents and most business travelers use their help as well.

INDUSTRY COMMUNIQUE

THE COOK'S TOUR: THE BIRTH OF THE MODERN TOURISM INDUSTRY

M. T. Schwartzman

NEW YORK—Thomas Cook did not approve of drinking.

So much so, in fact, that in 1841 he hired a train to bring a group of teetotalers to a temperance meeting.

Thus the modern travel industry was born.

Cook is generally credited with founding organized tourism.

He was the first to package tours—to charter trains, book hotels, provide reduced fares and rates—and to successfully market these tours and make the excursion a universal practice.

He employed agents, who were required to post a bond to join the system.

In return, each agent received a yearly salary and a range of commissions on tickets, hotel coupons, sale of guidebooks and profits on banking services.

Cook knew well the value of commissions; in 1862, after establishing business to North Wales and Scotland, the railroad company terminated his concession, hoping to keep the commission payments.

Thomas Cook was not the only businessman of his time to realize the need for travel services.

He was, however, the most successful, and his innovations shaped the face of the modern tourism industry.

The introduction of the roundtrip, or "circular" ticket as it was called, eliminated the need to buy multiple tickets for the web of private rail lines that crisscrossed Europe.

He introduced Cook's Continental Timetables, and of course, the traveler's check, which Cook first issued in New York in 1872.

Born in Milbourne, England, in 1808, Cook spent the early part of his life as a Baptist preacher.

Later, he became a cabinet maker, a printer and then an active temperance worker.

After his successful temperance excursion, the entrepreneurial spirit gripped him, and that same year he established Cook's Tours.

What made it all possible was the advent of travel by train.

Before railroads were built, long-distance travel was affordable only to the rich.

But for Cook's first excursion, passengers paid a meager one shilling each for a roundtrip rail ticket, and Cook still turned a profit for the Temperance Society.

Travel had become affordable to the middle classes, and there was money to be made organizing group tours.

Cook continued to run temperance tours for the next few years.

In 1845, he conducted his first secular tour, a weekend excursion to the sea resort of Liverpool.

This trip proved enormously popular, attracting 350 people, many of whom had never before seen the sea.

Cook repeated this trip two weeks later, and during the next decade built his business on excursions to seaside resorts and spas along the Irish Sea, North Sea and English Channel.

Scotland, too, became a favorite destination.

Cook personally handled all the advertising and promotion of his tours.

Drawing on his experience as a printer, Cook produced posters, handbills and his first guidebook, "A Handbook of the Trip to Liverpool."

He produced his own newspaper, "The Excursionist," extolling the virtues of Cook's Tours.

In 1855, Cook accompanied a group to Paris.

It was his first tour to the Continent, and it sparked an invasion of British tourists to Europe.

As his itineraries expanded to include Switzerland, Italy and other countries, rail lines were laid and hotels built to meet the growing demand.

He opened an office on London's Fleet Street in 1865 and sent groups of travelers throughout the world.

For those who preferred to travel independently, Cook provided railway tickets and hotel coupons, which could be redeemed for lodging and meals.

In 1866, he sent his first group to the U.S.

As the British Empire grew, so did the reach of Cook's Tours.

In 1869, he sent his first group to the Holy Land, and in the early 1870's began trips to India.

Thomas Cook retired in 1878.

He died 14 years later at the age of 84, leaving behind a legacy of travel services that are familiar to all of us today.

Reprinted courtesy of Travel Weekly, July 22, 1991.

Package Tours and Wholesale Tour Operators

Tour packages are a relatively new marketing strategy within the tourism industry. By definition, a **tour package** is any combination of two or more travel service components put together and sold as single unit. Before the development of packages, travel agents had to make individual arrangements with each service supplier for each client. If a couple traveling to London requested a hotel, transfers to and from the airport, theater tickets, and a city tour, the agent would make separate contracts with the hotel, transfer service operator, theater ticket agency, and sightseeing tour operator. Or else the agent would contact a receptive service operator in London for arrangements. The process would be repeated for each point on the tour itinerary. For overseas destinations, agents would establish "foreign independent tours" (FITs); for domestic destinations the agents established "domestic independent tours" (DITs).

With the development of the jet airplane and the consequent boom in middle-class travel came the need for easy-to-sell vacations. Destinations wishing to encourage development of tourism (such as the Caribbean Islands, Hawaii or Europe) needed inclusive programs that were easy to advertise and promote and easy to book. Travel agents handling the new wave of travelers needed programs that were easier to explain to prospects than FITs and DITs, and also priced lower than the custom-tailored independent programs. The package tour was developed to meet these needs.

The package tour also brought a new class of business operation into the travel and tourism industry—the large **wholesale tour operator**. These companies assemble a range of travel service components into package tours. The programs are described in detail in brochures that are often elaborate and printed in full color. The brochures are distributed to travel agents and airlines for use in soliciting travelers. These folders and brochures have become essential for selling travel, and most prospective travelers expect and want to see them. The brochures help make an intangible service more tangible.

Tour packages are marketed in all sizes and shapes and in all price ranges. The package may be a one-day sightseeing tour, a city or resort package including hotel and transportation, or a long escorted tour with many features to several destinations. Costs may range from a few dollars to thousands of dollars. Several points will be common to all, however. The package will be designed for a target market segment. It will be described in reasonable detail in a brochure, and it can be booked with a single phone call to a tour operator or airline.

SALES VERSUS MARKETING

Some of those who are involved in the sales function in many industries believe that sales alone is marketing. They concentrate their efforts on the skills and techniques of selling and believe that this alone will produce results. Although the sales function may certainly be considered a very important part of the marketing process, it is not a substitute for marketing itself. Sales skills and techniques will help generate sales, but they are best used as part of an overall marketing plan.

Sales is only part of the marketing process. The identification of potential markets, development and pricing of products and services to meet the needs of these markets, and advertising and other promotional efforts are important parts of marketing. When matched with proper sales techniques, this overall marketing process will make all the components of marketing come together as effectively as possible. However, because selling is the marketing component most often confused with marketing itself, a brief consideration of sales strategies may be helpful here.

"And to top off your visit to Paris, my associate, Mr. Quasimodo, will escort you on a personally guided tour of Norte Dame."

Sales Strategies

As marketing concepts have developed, four types of sales strategies have also developed. Stimulus-response, mental-states, consumer-needs, and problem-solving strategies are the primary descriptors of popular sales methods.

Stimulus Response

Most advertising is based on the stimulus-response theory. Originated in the last century by the Russian scientist Ivan Petrovich Pavlov, the basis of the theory is that a person may be conditioned to respond to a stimulus. Pavlov conditioned a dog to begin to salivate (as if food was in front of him) when he heard a bell.

In advertising and sales, **stimulus response** in based upon repetition. Repeat something often enough and, if it has any impact, people will respond to it. "I can't believe I ate the whole thing," conditioned people to think of Alka Seltzer in a famous advertising campaign. "The Friendly Skies" immediately brings to mind United Airlines while "We Love to Fly and It Shows" makes the listener think of Delta. Many sun and fun beach destinations use erotic pictures as the stimulus to invoke the response of desire, hoping that it will lead to the desire to visit that particular destination.

In sales, stimulus-response theory stresses the use of repetitious canned speeches by the salesperson. Although this strategy may be effective in a simple sales process, we do not believe it is an effective sales strategy in the travel industry. It does not consider the needs of the prospective purchaser nor does it provide for much interaction between salesperson and customer.

Mental States

The **mental-states strategy** is based on thorough preparation of the salesperson. This is the preferred strategy of the high-pressure salesperson who can "sell refrigerators to Eskimos." This strategy features a complex, but "canned" presentation technique in which the salesperson convinces the customer to purchase a product or service. Many marketers consider this strategy to be unfair to the consumer. It may generate initial sales, but it rarely creates repeat business because such sales do not meet real consumer needs.

Consumer Needs

The **consumer-needs strategy** emerged in the 1950s and 60s as a byproduct of the customer-oriented marketing system that characterizes current marketing theory. The role of the salesperson under this strategy is to find a need and fill it. This is a highly interactive process in which complex interviews of prospective customers by a salesperson are required to determine the customer's real need. The salesperson then provides the product or service that meets the need. Most successful selling in the travel industry follows this strategy.

Problem Solving

The **problem-solving strategy** is really a refinement of the consumer-needs strategy. It is most often used in the sale of expensive or "high-ticket" items. The strategy requires much preparation on the part of the salesperson to understand the activities of the prospective customer. The salesperson helps the customer identify problems, analyze alternatives to solve the problems, and, of course, provides the products or services necessary to solve the problems.

Chapters 12 and 13 provide detailed discussion of sales processes in the travel industry. These chapters also describe techniques for identifying client needs, making recommendations, overcoming objections and closing travel industry sales. At this point, it is necessary to recognize that selling, while important, is only a part of the larger marketing process.

CONCLUSION

Anyone involved in the tourism industry is involved, somehow, in the marketing process. Understanding the history of marketing in the various segments of the industry will help you to understand this process, as will an awareness of all the components of marketing. This book is intended to help you gain that understanding and awareness.

SUMMARY

The prerequisites of marketing are: a person or company wishing to sell a product or service, and potential buyers for that product or service. When both these prerequisites exist, marketing is the total process that brings these two factors together profitably.

"Thanks for all that information on cruises, dearie—now, which ship has the best table scraps?"

In this century, marketing has generally moved from a product-oriented to a consumer-oriented approach. Examples of this shift can be seen in the history of marketing in the automobile, airline, steamship, and hotel industries. As this shift took place, market research—used first in the automobile industry—has become more and more important. The products, also, have changed.

The tour package is a relatively new marketing strategy that has also created a new class of travel business—the wholesale tour operator who assembles a variety of travel service components into packages.

Although most important, sales is not the sum total of the marketing process. However, knowledge of the four major kinds of sales strategies is necessary. These four are:

- *stimulus response, based on repetition;*
- *mental states, depending on intensive, high-pressure sales presentations;*
- *consumer needs, in which the salesperson interacts with the customer to discover and fill needs (an especially appropriate strategy in the travel industry); and*
- *problem solving, a refinement of the consumer-needs strategy, most often used in selling "high-ticket" items.*

QUESTIONS FOR THOUGHT AND DISCUSSION

1. What is marketing and how does it pertain to the travel industry?
2. Describe the differences between product-oriented and consumer-oriented marketing.
3. Discuss the role of sales or selling in the marketing process.
4. Compare and contrast the histories of the airlines, steamship, and hotel industries.
5. What is a tour package? Discuss the advantages and disadvantages to the traveler of such packages.
6. How has the role of travel agencies changed over the years?
7. Discuss the consumer-needs and problem-solving sales strategies and how they can be used to sell travel.

2

The Nature of the Tourism Product

discretionary travel
intangible
nondiscretionary travel
off-season
on-season
parity product
perishability
quality control
standardization
seasonality
timeliness

Travel is one of the broadest, most diverse products imaginable—it encompasses everything from driving 200 miles to a family event to taking an around-the-world cruise. However, although the travel product encompasses so many activities, it is marketed and sold to two very different primary segments. The motivations of travelers in each of these segments are quite distinct. (Chapter 3 on the psychology of the traveler will discuss these motivations in detail).

NONDISCRETIONARY VERSUS DISCRETIONARY TRAVEL

In discussing the nature of the tourism product, it is necessary to distinguish between nondiscretionary and discretionary travel. **Nondiscretionary travel** is done out of necessity. These travelers go because they have to—not because they want to. The business traveler, the family going home for a wedding or a funeral, the student flying back to college are all examples of nondiscretionary travel. **Discretionary travel**, on the other hand, is a matter of choice. These travelers can choose, for example, among staying home, driving somewhere, or flying to the Caribbean for their vacation.

Because these two segments of travel serve travelers with very different needs and wants, marketing techniques must differ. For example, most of the advertising of low air fares and off-season prices for hotels is directed to the voluntary, discretionary traveler. The discretionary traveler is also the one most influenced by the many advertisements showing the romance of travel. In contrast, most of the frequent flyer and other brand loyalty types of promotion are directed toward the nondiscretionary business traveler. Whether discretionary or nondiscretionary travel is involved, however, the nature of the tourism product is *the purchase of intangible services.*

ASPECTS OF THE TOURISM PRODUCT

Intangibility

When considering the nature of the tourism product, we must remember that travel is different things to different people. Take the purchase of an airline ticket. To business people who must buy a plane ticket to get to a meeting in a distant city, it is a necessary part of getting the job done. These travelers are most interested in the airline's on-time performance and efficiency, and in being able to get their baggage quickly or even carry it on board. All of these factors are **intangibles**. To someone buying a ticket to get home because of a family crisis, buying a plane ticket is a stressful purchase. To make a difficult time easier, this traveler needs such intangibles as understanding, efficiency and a fair price. And the many vacationers, who are deciding how to spend their discretionary income, the airline tickets they purchase are most definitely an intangible—those tickets represent the purchase of a dream.

The 55-Plus Club Hawaii Trip

Before   *After*

For example, a young woman buying a vacation package to Cancun does not get a product—something tangible that she can take home, look at, and enjoy. Instead, she buys the use of some tangible items such as an airplane seat and a hotel bed for a brief time, but, even more important, she buys the culture and friendliness of Mexico, the beautiful beaches, the exposure to new and different things. She buys memories. About the only tangible items left after her vacation may be the pictures she took, some souvenirs, and the receipts for the money she spent. As this example shows, in the purchase of the travel product, we are looking primarily at the purchase of intangible services.

Quality Control and Standardization

The marketing of a service differs from the marketing of a tangible good that can be held and examined. True, there are some similarities, but there are also many differences.

One primary difference is that of quality control capability. At the factory, Black and Decker can institute **quality control** procedures to ensure that all its toasters are identical. These toasters will all carry the same warranty. The price may vary at different stores, but Black and Decker's marketing approach can focus on the quality of the product, which can be kept uniform. Consumers can buy safely at a cash and carry discount store, basing their decisions on price only, because they know Black and Decker will stand behind the toaster if it is defective.

This is not true in a service business. In most businesses within the travel industry, the product is service. You cannot return a defective trip. Nor can human beings ever provide completely standardized service. Travel employees can be trained to perform their jobs in a somewhat similar manner, to reflect the image of the company. However, because the service is so personal, neither **standardization** nor uniform quality control is possible. The same employee can and will act differently on different days.

A hotel can be sure that the rooms have the same furniture and are clean, but the actions of front desk personnel will vary. It is possible for Black and Decker to discard an inferior toaster; it is not possible for the manager of a service business to discard a hasty and inappropriate remark made by a desk clerk to a guest. Any service business must train its people to act in a proper and desired manner all the time, but training is not always remembered, and instructions are not always followed properly.

Similarly, an airline may be able to standardize its aircraft and its food, but it cannot totally standardize its flight attendant crews. Anyone who has flown frequently knows that a flight can be made a very enjoyable experience or a very difficult one by the attitude of the flight crew. The crew is on the front line of the airline's marketing because they influence travelers to continue using that airline or to look for another.

Perishability and Timeliness

Perishability

In addition to the problems of quality control and standardization, service products such as tourism are different from tangible products in other ways. One of these is the **perishability** of the product. A tangible good is manufactured at one time and used at another. It can be warehoused before it is sold. For example, if a dress store does not sell the inventory it has stocked by a certain date, the management has several choices. It may reduce the price of the dress to the level of cost or even below to avoid a total loss; it may keep the dress on the rack for a longer period of time; or it may put the dress away until next season. The store may not make the profit it had hoped to make, and may even lose some money on that item, but at least some money will be recovered. The dress will not be thrown out. Even the so-called perishable products of a produce department in a supermarket have some life and hope left after their ideal date of sale.

Timeliness

A service, on the other hand, is produced as it is used. An airplane, train, or bus seat or a hotel bed must be sold in a timely manner or it will have no value. The product of a seat or a bed for May 10 can only be used on May 10. If it is not sold before that date, it is literally "thrown out." When the plane leaves the gate or the night is over, that May 10th seat or bed can no longer be sold, even at a greatly reduced price. The seat or the room on May 11th is a different product entirely. It can never be put back into the inventory of the company. The company cannot recoup one cent of its cost for that seat or bed. Similarly, the services of a travel agent—consulting, advising, and selling—are produced as the agent talks with the client. They cannot be produced, put on a shelf, and sold later.

This quality of **timeliness** in the travel product explains a practice of the airline and hotel industries that receives much bad publicity—that of overbooking. When a hotel or airline knows that historically some of the people with reservations do not show up on that date, it will sell a number of seats/beds over the number that actually exist. The company is gambling on the historical odds. Usually, this practice works out well and fills seats or beds that would otherwise go empty.

But, occasionally, the airline or hotel misjudges and loses the gamble. Fewer "no shows" occur than expected, and more people arrive than can be accommodated. That is when would-be airline passengers may be "bumped" or hotel guests "walked" to another facility. Perhaps a Florida hotel was counting on a certain number of guests departing on a particular winter day, but a major snowstorm in the north made this impossible. Meanwhile, the expected new guests are arriving. In these cases, the manager has to decide what to do with the overflow. He cannot provide additional beds, so some prospective hotel guests will be "walked." Newspaper reports in early 1983 showed the problems Mexican hotels faced when the devaluation of the peso suddenly made Mexico a travel bargain. Rooms that hotel managers had expected to be empty were suddenly filled and overbookings led to confusion, disappointment, and "walks" to other accommodations for many vacationers. Coping with the perishability of the travel product creates these situations.

A few airlines found a way to handle this problem with minimum disruption for travelers and the method is now required by law. When an airline foresees an overbooking problem on a flight, it is required to request volunteers to take another flight. The airline offers the volunteers some compensation, usually a free ticket on another flight later in the year and transportation on the next flight that day or the next for this trip. In most cases, the airline gets sufficient volunteers who are quite happy with this compensation and the travelers who are not flexible are able to make the planned flight. Only if there are not enough volunteers does it become necessary to involuntarily bump a passenger.

Seasonality

Travel is a product that often suffers from **seasonality.** The beach will attract many visitors when it is warm, but who will come to a northern beach in the winter? The southern beach attracts the northerner who wishes to escape the cold back home, but is not as attractive when the weather improves in the north.

For this reason, destinations, hotels, and airlines have found that they cannot market their product in the same way year-round. Many marketing devices have been developed in an attempt to even out these peaks and valleys of use. One of the most common is that of on-season and off-season prices. In the Caribbean islands, the prices in the summer are usually substantially lower than in the winter. This helps attract the bargain hunter, who would like to visit new places but will sacrifice time of year (and perhaps ideal climate) for price. As another example, because of school vacations some destinations are very crowded in summer. Therefore many bargains are available at other times of year. European prices, for example, are substantially lower in winter.

Another way of improving business during the low part of these cycles is to promote convention business. Because spring and fall were traditionally their slowest travel times, cities began to promote special convention rates and activities in these off-peak times. This practice has been so successful that it has now become very difficult to find rooms in large city hotels or space in good convention facilities during October.

Still another method for promoting off-season business is to develop special activities. Some of the Caribbean islands introduced special summer activities so that visitors in the summer not only get a lower price but actually get more for their money. Nassau has its "Goombay" season; Jamaica its "Boonoonoonoos"; and Bermuda, where the cost in winter is low, its "Rendezvous" season. Hawaii Aloha weeks and Quebec Winter Carnival serve similar purposes. All of these promotional activities have helped to increase business in previously slow seasons. Concerts, parades, and cultural activities are featured during these times. The airlines and hotels cooperate by lowering prices. Commercial hotels and car rental companies frequently offer low "week-end" packages because they do not get many commercial customers during weekends. Therefore, a vacation during the slow season or other off-peak period may cost only one-half to two-thirds as much as an on-season trip.

Airlines develop special "promotional" fares, which encourage the vacation traveler who does not have to fly. However, these promotional fares create other marketing problems with the second segment of travelers—the nondiscretionary travelers. In developing promotional fares aimed at vacationers, the airlines must also establish rules to try to avoid use of these fares by the businessperson who must travel almost regardless of price. That is why many promotional fares require that the traveler remain at the destination over a Saturday night—most business travelers want to come home for the weekend. Advance purchase requirements and penalties such as nonrefundable fares also helps keep away business travelers, because they frequently must make or change plans at the last minute.

The differing needs of business and discretionary travelers can also affect airline fares more directly. On routes that are heavily business oriented, Saturday fares can be quite a value. On the other hand, on routes that are popular for vacations, Saturday fares may carry a surcharge. On vacation routes, Tuesday through Thursday travel may bring the best values, because most vacationers prefer to travel on weekends if there is no price differential.

Another type of seasonality is seen when some resorts raise prices to extremes during special demand periods, such as Christmas vacation. Costs at destinations that offer special attractions, such as Carnival, the Super Bowl, the Olympics or other special events will also rise. In many resorts, special demand periods carry a surcharge and a required minimum stay of varying length. Because the properties will be sold out during that period, they increase prices to help pay for vacancies during the slower periods.

When an airline owns a plane, or a hotel has a certain number of beds, they own them all the time and must try to maximize their use all the time, not only on special days or times of the year. Therefore, the marketing and sales departments must find ways to bring in enough business in the slow times to cover expenses so that the high seasons will bring in a profit. One of the challenges of marketing is to continue to create new approaches to this problem.

PARITY PRODUCTS

In some components of the travel industry, competing companies market what are known as **parity products.** They actually sell the same basic product. The differences among these products are not meaningful. A primary example is the airline industry. All the major airlines fly basically the same equipment, maintain it the same way (government regulations require this), serve the same food (even made in the same kitchens), and train their flight attendants on the same safety procedures. They all have equivalent safety records and virtually the same on-time performance.

With so many features essentially the same, how can one airline get the consumer to choose its product over a competing carrier? To be successful with a parity product, an airline will market small differences that under normal circumstances would not really matter. For example, one airline may advertise beluga caviar in their first-class or business section. Many ads tout less than a 2% difference in on-time performance. The airlines also market minor differences in their frequent flyer/guest programs. Southwest Airlines has been quite successful marketing their "fun and games" on board their flights. Marketing parity products is quite difficult, since the marketer must create a difference in the mind of the consumer when no meaningful difference exists. See the "Industry Communique" for an example of an attempt to do this.

INDUSTRY COMMUNIQUE

WHY HUBS?

Robert L. Crandall

Long before deregulation was even a glint in the Congressional eye, there were a few airline hubs. The largest was in Atlanta, and Southerners often joked that when their time came, whether they headed for Heaven or for Hell, they'd have to change planes in Atlanta.

Today there are 24 hubs in the United States mainland and about two-thirds of all airline passengers pass through a hub to get to their destination. Since most people prefer nonstop service, our customers often ask why so many trips must be made by way of hubs.

The answer lies partly in the preferences of our customers and partly in the economics of the airline business.

As much as customers like nonstop service, they like frequent service and time-of-day choices even more. Thus, when there are many flights from a city to one or more hubs, few people are willing to wait several hours for infrequent nonstop service. As a result, most nonstop service from small and medium-size cities to destinations other than hubs has become uneconomical.

Of course, in large markets, there is non-stop service aplenty. For instance, three carriers operated 17 flights a day between New York/Newark and Los Angeles in 1978. Today [1991], nine carriers offer 22 nonstops.

When a market lacks nonstop service, it is not—as some suggest—because of an absence of competition. In fact, intense competition, between multiple carriers offering frequent service to multiple hubs, tends to drive out nonstop service because it does a better job of providing what customers want most—which airlines are able to provide because hubs are an efficient way to use airplanes, people, and airport facilities.

American's service from Albuquerque to Dallas/Fort Worth offers a good example of how a hub works. On an average day, the typical flight from Albuquerque to DFW carries 123 passengers. Of those, only 43 are bound for DFW. Two are bound for Atlanta, three for Boston, two for London, and 71 for 28 other destinations. In all, 65 percent of the people on all our flights to DFW—are bound for destinations beyond the hub. The important point is that all those people ride between Albuquerque and DFW on the same airplane.

After the plane from Albuquerque and lots of others land at DFW, all within about a half-hour time period, and the folks not staying in Dallas/Fort Worth change planes, our outbound trips begin. A typical flight from DFW to Boston, to cite just one example, carries 158 passengers—61 from DFW, two from Austin, two from Burbank, the three from Albuquerque, and 90 from 27 other points of origin.

The citizens of Albuquerque, although they do most of their traveling via hubs, have a much wider choice of services than they had pre-deregulation. Back in those days, seven airlines offered 88 daily nonstops to 26 destinations; today, nine carriers offer 121 flights—including 74 to 12 airline hubs, where passengers can make connections to virtually anywhere in the world. Competition has given the citizens of Albuquerque lots more air-travel choices than they had when regulators drew the airline map.

People who live in hub cities are particularly fortunate. Raleigh/Durham's experience is a good example. In 1978, six airlines offered 61 daily flights to 23 destinations. In 1987, American launched its Raleigh/Durham hub and today, the airport boasts 251 flights by five airlines to 67 destinations.

Across the country, American has six mainland hubs, as well as one in Puerto Rico—all offering frequent, convenient service to many destinations.

To sum up: Airline hubs provide enormous benefits for the cities that host them, allow airlines to use their assets more efficiently, facilitate competition, and are the means by which we offer our customers the many departure and arrival options they want. For all these reasons, we think hubs make lots of sense.

Reprinted with permission from American Way Magazine, August 15, 1991. This was written at the time when the "hub and spoke" system was at its peak. In the years following the publication of this, mid-sized hub-and-spoke airports lost flights while the major cities continued as major hubs. The recession and financial difficulties of 1991–1993 made the economics of smaller hubs questionable.

Today, airlines, car rental companies, and even hotels are marketing parity products in a different way. They are building brand loyalty in the frequent traveler—a concept which had never really existed in the industry before deregulation. Through frequent-flyer, frequent renter, frequent guest, and other programs, travelers earn free flights or other bonuses. These programs have been extremely successful, although quite expensive.

In the case of hotels, restaurants, destinations, and other travel products, we do not have the same problem of parity products. Here, the differences are actual and sometimes great. A Holiday Inn markets an image of "no surprises," while Intercontinental markets the image of each hotel representing the area in which it is located. The consumer has a choice here of safety and security (but little adventure) or of being able to sample the native spirit (but perhaps not liking it).

The small pension without private bath in Europe is quite different (but in a different way than the Holiday Inn) from the Intercontinental luxury hotel. The location of one hotel, the weather and facilities at one destination, the type of food and price at one restaurant may be quite distinct from that of a competitor. Therefore, in those segments where differences are substantial, the job of marketing is clearer. Marketing managers in those segments can decide which market segment they want to appeal to and develop the appropriate marketing plan. They do not face the challenge of creating differences in the mind of the consumer. However, within each category there are several companies that are viewed as parity products. For hotels offering similar products, small differences may be important in marketing. For instance, hotels are spending substantial sums on constantly upgrading their amenity packages in the rooms. Doubletree Hotels is well known among regular travelers for their chocolate chip cookies in the evening.

COMPETITION FOR THE TRAVEL PRODUCT

There is a tendency on the part of marketing managers in the travel industry to look at other travel products as their primary competition. For example, the airlines look at other airlines and trains as competition and the trains look at buses. One destination sees another destination as its primary competition. Cruise lines tend to see the other cruise lines as their primary competition. A travel agency sees the agency down the street and the attempts at direct sales to consumers by suppliers as its main competition.

Although it is true that one travel product competes with another, there is often far more threatening competition. The real competition is the nontravel product. Consumers have a certain amount of "discretionary" income—that money left over after they have purchased their necessities. Every time they turn around, they see products competing for that discretionary income. The color TV, the video recorder, the home computer, the swimming pool in the backyard, the local country club, the new car—these are the real competition. The travel industry must first market travel as the desired activity for the discretionary dollar. See the "Industry Communique" on page 31.

The travel and tourism industry is currently one of the largest industries in the United States and the world—in terms of both dollars spent and number of jobs created. For this reason, it is important that this industry continue to grow.

There is still much room for growth in this industry. As the desire for travel grows, all travel companies can share in the increase. In addition, since the travel product is so varied, this growth can continue even in times of recession when other industries are retrenching. The growth may slow, but there will still be growth if recent history holds true. This was proven by the continued growth, especially in the cruise industry during the recession in 1991. Even the airline industry and the hotel industry, which was the hardest hit in the recession, had some growth overall. Because of over-expansion before the recession, some individual companies or properties had a downturn, but the travel industry overall still grew. The pie was just split into more pieces, leaving less for many companies that were not positioned properly for the recession. See the "Industry Communique" on page 36.

INDUSTRY COMMUNIQUE

ADAPTING THE CRUISE INDUSTRY TO EVOLVING MARKET TRENDS

Rod McLeod
Executive Vice President
Sales, Marketing, Passenger Services
Royal Caribbean Cruise Line

It's my pleasure to join you at Cruise Op 90 and to have the privilege as well as the opportunity to be today's keynote speaker.

Customarily, and quite naturally given my day-to-day business responsibilities, my speaking engagements take me before gatherings of travel agents throughout the United States, Canada and, on occasion, Europe. These sellers of travel, who account for more than 95% of cruise vacation bookings, are a different audience than I face this morning. Their primary interest is to gain insight as to how they can sell *more* cruises *more* effectively and, importantly, *more* profitably. And the issues that they bring to the table are not, for the most part, your issues or concerns.

The majority of you define yourselves as being involved in the passenger shipping industry, either as ship operators, ship builders, port authorities, ship chandlers, manufacturers of equipment and products used in ship operations, providers of shipboard or shoreside services, consultants, as well as bankers and financial services institutions working with the passenger shipping industry. And, quite naturally, the issues and concerns, and search for information and opportunities, that you bring to the table are quite different than those of travel agents.

In that light, I am eminently *un*qualified to talk to you this morning let alone deliver today's keynote speech. I am *not* a "shipping man"...I'm a "marketing man." And, as I view my company, Royal Caribbean Cruises Ltd. is *not* a shipping company, we're a vacation company—we sell vacations at sea.

Last week I found myself in a somewhat similar situation. I was invited to speak to a gathering of Japanese shipping industry people in Yokohama on the subject of how to develop a cruise vacation market within Japan—another task I was eminently unqualified to perform for I probably know less about the Japanese travel market, let alone the cruise market, than I know about some of the things that you do everyday.

Nonetheless, I want to begin the body of my comments to you this morning with a view, a personal view, that I shared with your shipping industry colleagues in Japan last week. In my opinion:

> No single factor has contributed more to the tremendous growth and development of the cruise industry than the change in perspective of passenger ship owners, operators and managers from *suppliers of ocean-going transportation* to *providers of vacation travel.*

Importantly, this change in perspective has been more than a subtle adjustment in thinking. It has redefined what we do and how we do it. It has sharpened our focus on who our customers are, what they expect from us and a cruise vacation, and how we communicate with them. It has caused us to broaden our view of competition beyond other passenger ship operators so that we now include in our competitive set land-based vacation destinations as well as other discretionary purchases options (for example, a second home, a new car, a high-tech entertainment center). And it is an important determining factor in how we value and balance the day-to-day priorities of running our business.

And, clearly this change in perspective, which began some twenty years ago, continues at work today as the rapidly growing cruise industry changes and adapts to the ever-changing wants and needs of today's consumer within a worldwide environment of economic, political and social change.

One doesn't have to reach too far to find tangible examples of how this change in perspective—or, if you will—this redefinition from a passenger shipping to a cruise vacation industry has impacted us over the past twenty years. There are five main areas I want to address:

- *Ship design, including size, scope and safety*
- *Destinations, such as worldwide expansion and private out-islands developed by the cruise lines*
- *Improvements in and the importance of air/sea availability*
- *The increasingly important role of travel agents*
- *Media advertising and its role in the marketing efforts of cruise lines*

In the area of ship design, we have seen dramatic, precedent-setting evolution that has increased passenger comfort and safety, introduced new and appealing product features and created a true sea-going interpretation of a resort-styled atmosphere.

We are seeing the introduction of grand megaliners like Carnival's Fantasy and Ecstasy, Princess Cruises' Star Princess, Crown Princess, and Regal Princess, and Royal Caribbean's Sovereign of the Seas, Nordic Empress, Monarch of the Seas, and Majesty of the Seas.

And, at the same time, reflecting a well-segmented definition of today's cruise marketplace, we're seeing growth in the number of yacht-like mini-liners such as Renaissance Cruises' fleet of 100-passenger ships, and Seabourn Cruises' Seabourn Spirit and Seabourn Pride. We're seeing ships with sails, ships with spas, ships that carry their own marinas with them. The possibilities appear to be limitless, defined only by the imaginations of ship designers and builders.

A parallel development with these newer ships is an increase in the number, location and types of destinations offered. Recent years have heralded the development of private out-islands which allow individual cruise operators to design and offer new destinations when they would otherwise be unavailable. Royal Caribbean operates two such ports, CocoCay in the Bahamas and Labadee on the north coast of Haiti, and the possibility of additional island developments exists. This leads not only to more construction, provisioning, and service contracts for those islands, but also encourages other areas to enhance their port facilities, tour operations and land transportation systems in order to continue to attract cruise lines. Expansion of this type is likely to continue to ensure quality and variety of ports of call, even as more worldwide destinations become available.

We have also seen the development of a symbiotic relationship between the old nemesis of the passenger shipping industry—airlines—and today's cruise vacation companies. Air/sea packaging has been the cornerstone of the cruise vacation industry's successful effort to reach out to literally millions of potential passengers in cities and towns throughout North America. Literally any place near an airport can be the location where a cruise vacation starts! The growth of the cruise vacation industry has created an on-going demand for air seats—and has meant a substantial growth opportunity for our airline partners on a dependable, expandable basis. But, there is a caveat: as growth continues, so will demand for air seats—but will supply meet demand? Will the terminal facilities for airlines expand? Will terminal facilities at cruise ships' home ports be capable of handling the increasing influx of passengers arriving and departing? As cruise lines look to new cruising areas, will airline and land facilities be capable of handling these new opportunities? These are real concerns—and opportunities—for the passenger shipping industry.

The industry's growth is a direct result of cruise lines penetrating the consciousness of American vacationers and demonstrating cruising's value for the money. These potential passengers are searching for a hassle-free vacation; a way to get away from the pressures of daily life. What better solution than cruising? All-inclusive vacations, including airfare, accommodations, meals, entertainment, and the convenience of having to unpack only once but still visit several different destinations, all in a safe environment, have tremendous appeal to a wide variety of people. The industry has begun to capitalize on this, and is quickly developing new ways to increase consumer awareness of the advantages and value of cruising through media advertising and marketing.

Advertising will also play a major worldwide role in the 90s as cruise lines try to improve consumers' perceptions of cruising's value. Although a lot of attention has been paid to reports that millions of dollars are spent on advertising, the fact is that product identification still remains low. In the near future, we'll see lines trying new and innovative ways of communicating their product as different and distinct from their competitors. This will not only be a challenge, but also a very important factor in the determination of which companies will continue to grow and be successful in an increasingly competitive environment.

What we see occurring with more and more frequency in the cruise industry is operators concentrating on or specializing in particular market segments. There are a number of upscale lines offering cruises to exotic destinations. Crystal Cruises, Windstar Cruises and Seabourn Cruise Line are three prime examples. Then there are a larger number of high quality lines offering distinctive vacations to passengers who cannot afford the highest priced cruises, but still want a quality vacation experience. For example, Royal Caribbean Cruise Line, Princess Cruises, and Holland America Line. Next, cruise lines such as Carnival, NCL, Costa, Premier and Chandris Cruise Lines, appeal to a broad cross-section of the mass market. Smaller lines offering budget conscious consumers a cruise experience that not only satisfies their pocketbooks, but also satisfies their need for a memorable vacation, like Dolphin Cruises, are also operating. All of these are examples of operators who have identified a specific market segment, and who are now catering to the people and groups who fall within this niche.

What does this mean? It indicates worldwide expansion to almost any destination that can be reached by water. Naturally, this must be preceded by development and enhancement of land and port facilities, services, transportation and tour operators. Within each of these areas will be the need for a variety of *choices* depending upon the type of cruise line and passengers visiting the destination. The cruise industry's growth also means your growth.

The acquisition of smaller lines by larger operators, mergers, and consolidations can create international implications for institutions providing funding for such reorganization. The combination of financial support and name-association with a larger parent company may mean that a significant number of smaller lines will be quite successful in the next decade.

On the other hand, there will be some restructuring, intense rethinking and increasing sophistication of marketing techniques, and more attempts by smaller lines to merge. Parallel to these mergers are the growth of new lines creating new products. Consistent flow of orders for new ships has created a bonanza for certain shipyards, their suppliers and subcontractors. Plus, the money sources whose negotiations make such growth possible will have bargaining power and the ability to influence decision makers at the cruise lines.

Perhaps one of the most, if not *the* most, important developments in the coming decade will be the increased use of "user-friendly" technology. The introduction of easy-to-access computer technology, such as real time reservations systems for travel agents, like Royal Caribbean's CruiseMatch 2000, allow almost instantaneous confirmation of travel plans.

In connection with the advent of more user-friendly technology will be an increase in specialization for travel agents. As more products are introduced, agents will have to keep on top of changes in itineraries, vessels, destinations and pricing. The average consumer is bombarded with information from all kinds of sources. They rely on travel agents to make sense of it all. The information explosion could lead to a demand for more specialized travel agents who concentrate on the Caribbean or Europe or the Pacific or particular types of cruises—adventure, exotic, ultimate luxury, etc.

All this increased growth in the size of companies, the number of vessels in their fleets, the investigation of worldwide destinations, expanded itineraries, and specialty and niche products means "trickle-down" effects will impact local, national and international economies. Larger cruise lines mean more jobs for a number of different groups, from building contractors to services to on board personnel to shoreside employees. More vessels translate into increased crew members, from hotel operations to the dining room to entertainment to hospitality. The number of shoreside personnel will also increase, from sales to service to reservations to marketing—throughout the entire organization.

This also leads to an increase in the number of vendors providing shipboard supplies such as food, beverages, linens, paper products, and other services, as well as a demand for machinery for technical marine use and investment in capital expenditures. The industry-wide growth of cruise operators, in terms of both larger, newer vessels and an increase in the number of ships overall, will stimulate the economy, and encourage expansion in affiliated industries.

With a stronger presence in the public arena and in travel industry circles comes increased responsibility. We all know that environmental conservation is a hot topic, and will be for a long time. We must work together and act responsibly to protect our environment by ensuring that federal and international laws are strictly upheld. Efforts should be continued to further develop fuel efficient vessels that are environmentally safe in their cooling and heating systems, air ventilation, and waste disposal, etc. This is an area that will receive increasing amounts of attention and provide additional possibilities for engineers and designers.

What it comes down to is that just like other businesses, the cruise industry will be held more and more environmentally accountable. It's our responsibility to protect the ocean that supports us. We must continue to invest in research and advanced technology that allows us to operate a more environmentally safe and fuel efficient product. The public demands it, environmental interest groups demand it, and we should demand it of ourselves.

An additional concern is safety. Strict Coast Guard and federal and international regulations passed in the last few years clearly show that cruise lines must ensure vessel safety. Tomorrow you will be discussing safety issues in greater detail, so let me just mention it here and say that safety will indeed continue to be an issue.

It's clear that the times are changing, and we in the cruise industry are faced with many challenges. How to improve product design...How to clarify passenger perceptions of the quality and value that cruise vacations offer...How to use technological innovations to our best advantage while ensuring passenger satisfaction and service to travel agents...How to best determine and capitalize on specific market segments...When and where to develop new and exciting worldwide destinations and itineraries...What types of products and services passengers want and need, and how best to supply them...Industry-wide issues...The time to meet these challenges is now, and though it won't be easy, the opportunities are endless and the rewards great. There is a smorgasbord of opportunities for expansion and specialization so that not only will cruise ship operators benefit, but so too will their suppliers, financiers, the port authorities, ship designers and builders, and travel agents. Remember, the potential for success is enormous, the opportunities boundless, the challenges plentiful, and the rewards magnificent. As the cruise vacation industry grows so too will your businesses—as the old saying goes, "A chain is only as strong as its weakest link." We intend to ensure all our "links" are strong, successful, and continue to prosper.

Courtesy of Royal Caribbean Cruise Line from a keynote address by Rod McLeod, Executive Vice President, Sales, Marketing and Passenger Services, "Cruise OP 90" keynote address, November 5, 1990.

INDUSTRY COMMUNIQUE

CRUISE MARKETING IN THE 90S: TIME FOR A CHANGE

Robert H. Dickinson, Senior Vice President
Sales & Marketing, Carnival Cruise Lines

The decade of the 1990s represents a substantial change in the growth pattern of the cruise industry. The 1980s saw an increase of 200% in 1989 (year 10) versus the base year (1979). This was an absolute increase of approximately 2,200,000 passengers annually for year 10.

The cruise industry has an oft-stated goal of 10 million passengers by the year 2000. Assuming a 9 million annual passenger target for 1999, this would translate to a 172% increase of year 10 (1999) over the base year (1989). While this percentage increase is smaller than for the decade of the 1980s, the absolute increase represents 5,700,000 passengers in 1999 alone!

In order to achieve this sales objective, the cruise industry must begin immediately to redirect its sales & marketing strategies. To take a "business as usual" approach will lead, in my opinion, to a much more modest growth curve with 1999 likely to result in a 5 to 6 million annual passengers carrying. Put another way, the failure of the cruise industry to alter its marketing & sales strategies for the 1990s would result in billions of dollars of lost sales.

What changes need to be made? Perhaps most importantly, individual cruise lines must understand that their real competition is not other cruise lines but land-based resorts and sight seeing destinations.

Conventional wisdom has said that the mass market cruise lines should focus on the first timer while the upscale and specialty cruise lines should more appropriately target previous cruisers. The thinking in part being that once somebody has cruised on Carnival or Royal Caribbean they would eventually move up to "something better" such as Holland America or Royal Viking. This is not wisdom. This is fallacy. People who stay at Hyatt or Marriott do not generally move up to L'Hermitage or the Pierre. *Any* cruise line, whether it's positioned in the mass market or the luxury specialty niche, or anywhere in between, is well served to have its primary marketing focus directed to its appropriate non-cruise audience. Past visitors to posh resorts such as Halekulani or the Hotel Du Cap, for example, represent a much larger group of prime prospects for the $700 per diem Sea Goddess product than the past cruise passengers.

Once the industry recognizes the importance of the first-timer as the prime audience, the second major marketing change will evolve: replacing price with product as the prime consumer message. Shouting price may be an appropriate strategy when the prime target is the repeat passenger who already appreciates the product. It is clearly inappropriate as the prime strategy to an audience which has no appreciation of the product. The efficacy of the product must be the prime message to the first-timer. (Marketing widgets at 15% off will not increase widget sales to an audience who has no concept of a widget.)

Moreover, as the virtues of the cruise product begin to be delineated, stressed and emphasized in cruise advertising, the importance of price discounting is diminished. To the extent that each cruise line is able to show the superior desirability of its product versus comparable land based alternatives:

- *the tremendous value of cruising*
- *a hassle free environment*
- *excellent food*
- *the romance of the sea*

- *activities and entertainment choices superior to the targeted land based counterparts*
- *an atmosphere of pampering service*

Then the demand for that product will increase because people will switch from hotels to the more desirable cruise experience. This increase in demand obviates the need for discounting—as long as the brochure prices are reasonable to begin with!

The third change has already begun: the need to develop critical mass...a cruise line has to have sufficient size and scope to meaningfully impact the travel marketplace and to compete more effectively with their land-based counterparts. Larger firms are able to advertise and promote their products far more effectively than smaller companies. This simple fact, in itself, will greatly expand the vacation marketplace, as larger advertising and promotional budgets more effectively dent the consciousness of Consumer America heretofore bombarded with Chevrolets, clothing and real estate! Of equal importance, economies of scale will reduce product costs which will in turn lower selling prices and increase profits. The reduced prices will increase consumer demand while the increased profits will fund necessary capacity expansion. The expanded capacity will, in turn, fuel additional economies of scale to further reduce cost and price. Moreover, the added capacity will support still larger (and more efficient) advertising and marketing budgets. These, in turn, will spur demand by carving out an ever larger share of both the leisure travel market and the vastly larger market for discretionary goods and services. This market expansion strategy demands the best possible value relationship between the price of a cruise vacation and the features and benefits it provides. To the extent that the value of cruise travel is irresistible, it will supplant sales of other vacation alternatives as well as other high-ticket discretionary items.

The final change that needs to occur focuses on the distribution system. Currently the cruise industry relies upon the travel agent as its distribution point for about 95% of its sales. This is a far greater reliance than any other component of the travel industry. This reliance will continue unabated in the 90s. The personal intervention of a travel agent is needed because we are selling an intangible experience, not a commodity like an airline seat or hotel room.

However, during the 90s we have to come to grips with the fact that the agency distribution system is largely inefficient. Rather than complain about it or even joke about it, cruise suppliers must work together and commit the resources to make the system more efficient. Selling leisure travel needs to be recognized as a different business within the agency than servicing commercial accounts and point-to-point travel. We must educate and motivate owners and managers to revamp their businesses to effectively develop vacation sales. In three different samples of travel agent groups this year, it was determined that an average travel counselor converted only 3% and 15% of her daily prospects to a sale! This is highly inefficient!

Owners and managers need to be encouraged to compensate vacation sales counselors on the basis of incentives for sales productivity rather than relying on the traditional, modest fixed salary. There is a small but growing number of travel counselors in this country making $35,000–50,000/year—two to three times the national average—as a result of incentive compensation. Higher compensation will result in more efficient, more productive, more motivated sales people who will in turn make the agency distribution system far more effective as it competes in the overall market for high ticket discretionary goods and services.

A recent ASTA study said that the average agency owner or manager made approximately $20,000 in 1988. We must show these individuals how to restructure their vacation sales business to be productive and profitable so that they, too, may earn many times that amount. Proper compensation at all levels will attract the best sales people, reduce turnover, and make the agency community (at least as far as vacation travel is concerned) happier, more positive, and more productive. If the average agency could close on 40–50% of its *present* vacation sales prospects, the cruise industry sales target for the year 2000 is assured!

Presentation to Seatrade Conference, March 1990.

THE TOURISM PRODUCT AND THE COMMUNITY

The tourism industry must work together—all of its components—to continue to win the discretionary dollar for travel. This cooperation can have benefits for the community, also. When a community realizes the importance of tourism revenue, it will usually improve conditions and facilities for its local residents as it improves itself to attract additional tourism revenue. When local residents understand the benefits of tourism in their area, they will welcome the tourists with behavior that encourages repeat visitors. At times, locals may highly resent the additional traffic and congestion caused by tourism, for example, during the "season" in a resort area. Yet, they do like the revenue and facilities provided. Many years ago, the Ringling Brothers and Barnum and Bailey Circus demonstrated to the community of Sarasota, Florida, the value of having the winter home of the circus located there. For two weeks, the circus paid all its employees in $2 bills, which were quite rare. As members of the community saw these bills popping up everywhere, they began to understand the contribution of the circus visitors to their community, and relations improved.

A welcome reception by the community is an important part of the image of the destination. An excellent example of this is tourism development in the city of Baltimore. Baltimore rebuilt its harbor area into a thriving convention and visitors' center with additional luxury hotels, interesting shopping, and museums in what used to be a decaying waterfront area. This development has brought in

Before (above) and after (right) views of Baltimore's harbor area, transformed from a dilapidated waterfront to an attractive area popular with both tourists and residents. Photographs courtesy of The Rouse Company, Columbia, MD.

many tourists, but it has also proved to be a great attraction for residents within the local area.

Once again, it is necessary to realize that the travel product is broad. Many businesses are included in both the travel sector and also in sectors meeting local needs. Many restaurants, amusement parks, museums, and sports facilities meet both touristic and local recreational needs. When both segments benefit, overall tourism is enhanced and marketing efforts are made easier.

INDUSTRY COMMUNIQUE

Tourism is a multi-functional activity. Seen from the financial point of view, the tourist industry can be described as an "industry without smoke stacks;" from the educational point of view, it is an "education without classrooms." Tourism plays an important role in the increase of international understanding and the promotion of world peace. In this sense, it is "publicity without words," and also "diplomacy without formalities." In reality, tourism really does perform all of these functions, and it has therefore become a very important part of modern life. In every country in the world, no effort is spared in the promotion of tourist activities, and the Republic of China is no exception.

At the same time, we feel that the development of the tourism industry is only one aspect of the development of a modernized nation. A high quality tourist service, apart from reliance on a modernized support system such as transportation, communications, hotels and restaurants, also requires the maintenance of high standards in the preservation of cultural assets, the protection and development of natural resources, and the prevention of environmental pollution. Only then is a country fit for tourism, affording such amenities to foreign visitors.

Speech to the ASTA World Congress in Taiwan, September 1991, by President Lee Teng-hui, President of the Republic of China.

CONCLUSION

The travel product is an intangible, where absolute quality control is impossible, and which has the characteristics of perishability, timeliness, and seasonality. In certain parts of the industry, the challenge of marketing parity products also exists. Knowledge of these characteristics and challenges is essential for the travel professional.

SUMMARY

The travel product can be divided into nondiscretionary and discretionary segments—travelers who travel because they must (for business or personal reasons) or those who travel because they wish to. These segments require differing marketing techniques. Also, the discretionary travel product must compete with other discretionary products, such as color TVs or country club memberships. The basic strategy of the travel industry as a whole must be to market the travel product as a prime contender for the discretionary dollar.

Discretionary travel is an intangible, and as such it is not returnable. This makes the people involved in providing the intangible the most important part of the service. However, quality control over people is virtually impossible. The travel product is also perishable; it cannot be warehoused for later sale. And it is seasonal—a Caribbean beach in December is not the same product as a Caribbean beach in July. Finally the travel product is sometimes a parity product, lacking meaningful differences from one supplier to another.

QUESTIONS FOR THOUGHT AND DISCUSSION

1. Discuss the differences between discretionary and nondiscretionary travel, and how this difference affects marketing.
2. Discuss the four major factors of an intangible product such as travel. How do these affect marketing?
3. Define parity product, give examples within the travel industry, and discuss some of the marketing problems associated with parity products.
4. Based on the comments from Rod McLeod and Robert Dickinson, discuss how the cruise industry has faced changes in the past and the potential changes needed for the 90s.

3

Psychology of the Traveler

allocentric
life stages
Maslow's hierarchy
motivation
motivational segment
need-satisfaction theory
needs
psychocentric

It is impossible to market a product or service effectively without knowing the psychology of the prospective consumer. What motivates potential buyers to take a particular action? What motivates them to avoid a particular activity? Why do they react in certain ways? (See "Industry Communique" for one unusual theory.) What can one do to make them desire a particular product or service? Most of the following discussion of the psychology of the traveler will focus on **motivations—** the forces that cause a person to take a specific action.

The human need for travel has persisted throughout history. However, until the mid-to-late 1800s, most travel was for necessity rather than pleasure. This was true because in early times travel was usually both dangerous and difficult. It is not coincidence that the root word for travel and travail (heavy labor) is the same. Travel was hard. Today, it is pleasurable (or at least it is supposed to be) and looked forward to by most people. Remember, however, that the travel market is extremely broad, and therefore the motivations and needs of various segments of this market will differ and will require different marketing plans.

DIFFERING TYPES OF TRAVEL

Travel is an activity undertaken at every income and educational level within our society. The differences are in the type of travel. In the lower income and educational segments, travel is primarily by automobile or intercity bus transportation, and lodging is primarily with family or friends. As we go up in economic and educational levels, travel increasingly involves air transportation and lodging in hotels. Some segments of the industry, such as airlines and luxury hotels, are primarily interested in marketing to middle- and upper-income groups. Low-priced motels, fast-food restaurants, and intercity bus companies will be more interested in the lower-income groups.

The average business traveler or vacation traveler purchasing a trip involving paid transportation and lodging is an up-scale individual. Members of this group are usually better educated and more affluent than the average. The number of professional or white collar heads of households in this group is also above the average.

INDUSTRY COMMUNIQUE

"How Eggheads Evaluate Tourism" provides additional insight into the psychology and sociology of tourism. The more marketers know about why people travel, the more responsive marketing programs can be to traveler needs. When marketing travel services, it is essential to understand as much as possible about the motivation of prospective buyers.

HOW EGGHEADS EVALUATE TOURISM

Eric Friedheim, Editor

Although there are more than a billion holiday trips every year, this mass migration has been largely ignored by sociologists and anthropologists.

There has been organized tourism for thousands of years: Chinese and early Romans journeyed extensively for pleasure. In Colonial America, there was a thriving trade to spas for health and recreation.

But experts on social behavior and culture, like many governments, seem to have a blind spot when it comes to the significance of travel. The handful of social scientists who have bothered to explore the motivations for vacation trips generally dismiss them as a phenomenon that more often than not fails to meet the participants' expectations.

Their scholarly papers published in obscure academic journals are peppered with unflattering comments about recreational travel. They lament the superficiality of vacations taken by Americans with several arguing that the touristic experience can be meaningless, disappointing or worse.

These pedantic critics of the travel phenomenon obviously are engaged in posturing before their peers; while we have no information about their travel habits, it seems safe to wager that based on what they are writing none would be happy on a package tour or with independent sightseeing which they characterize as a ritual doomed to failure.

Fortunately, this narrow perspective of travel is not shared by all of their own colleagues. We are reminded of this by a splendid rebuttal appearing in the *Annals of Tourism Research*, an internationally recognized publication that covers all aspects of tourism in depth.

An article by Alma Gottlieb, doctor of anthropology at the University of Virginia, contends that what the vacationer experiences is real, valid and fulfilling.

She concedes her conclusions are also theoretical, being based on interviews with both middle class and upper class tourists and from literary, popular and journalistic writing. She says this research has produced "folk" data, which is more likely to produce a realistic appraisal of whether people enjoyed themselves and had rewarding experiences while away from home.

While it has been our admittedly unscientific observation that a tourist is a tourist is a tourist the world over, Dr. Gottlieb confines herself to vacations by Americans. A vacation is defined as an activity that strongly contrasts with what is normally done in the daily life back home.

To dramatize her point, Dr. Gottlieb divides American holiday trippers into two general classes: those who vacation and become "Peasants for the Day" and those who become "Queens (Kings) for the Day."

Those categorized as temporary peasants are upper or upper-middle class Americans who relate to the lower class inhabitants on an equal basis as they never do at home, where they hold authoritative jobs.

They go into local bars, attend folk festivals, revivalist meetings, bullfights, cockfights, see cheap popular movies in native language which they will struggle to understand. At home, they have tickets to the opera and theater and never see such movies and despise local, lower class dialects such as Black English. They adventurously eat in local, cheap and dirty restaurants serving uncontrollable, spicy food at outdoor rickety tables and street stands, although back home they normally dine at expensive immaculate restaurants serving mild or mildly spiced fare.

"In general," says Dr. Gottlieb, "they play at getting with the lower-class natives as they normally don't at home."

"The other type of holiday," she continues, "Queen (King) for a Day, is converse of the Peasant. Here, lower-middle to upper-middle class Americans go on vacation to raise themselves to a position of social *superiority*. While back home they may be extremely practical and keep to stringent budgets, buying only essential goods and even those only on sale, on vacation they become wildly extravagant, paying inflated prices for luxury goods and souvenirs for which they may have little use when they return. But paying such high prices becomes a form of upward mobility, with the vacationers temporarily adopting the buying patterns of the upper class.

"While these vacationers were careful to choose a moderate house or apartment in America, abroad they stay in luxury hotels with features that make them feel like Kings and Queens with breakfast in bed, midnight champagne, perhaps satin sheets. Indeed, a recent vogue has been literally to live the life of royalty by staying overnight in actual castles once inhabited by the noble class and converted to guest houses.

"Back home, the Queen (King) for a Day vacationers are fairly polite to waiters, maids, bus drivers, etc., perhaps even having some of their higher ranks (plumbers, electricians, restaurant managers) in their immediate families and circles of friends. While abroad, however, they are convinced that they are according the host country and its natives the privilege of bringing their tourist money to them and consequently they expect revered guest status. Thus they become embarrassingly aristocratic, ignoring the 'Gentleman/Lady' ideal of such behavior and instead emphasizing the crass privilege of rudely demanding information and special upper class treatment."

Travel agents may not all agree with Dr. Gottlieb's appraisal of how their clients behave but it is interesting to see how some in the scientific and academic community view contemporary travel habits.

Reprinted with permission from Travel Agent magazine, August 30, 1982.

CHARACTERISTICS OF TRAVEL CONSUMERS

Travelers vs Nontravelers

Until recently, it was possible to compare the traveling public (especially that segment that used commercial transportation and/or hotel accommodations) to nontravelers in American society. However, today more than three quarters of the public have traveled by air. A study conducted by the Air Transport Association in 1990 revealed the following facts:

- *78% of men and 72% of women have flown.*
- *31% of adults flew during the past year.*
- *60% of flyers took more than one trip during the year.*
- *The "average" flyer took 3.4 trips in a year.*
- *48% of trips taken were for business; 52% were for personal/pleasure trips.*
- *Frequent flyers (more than 10 trips in a year) were only 6% of flyers but accounted for 38% of the trips taken.*
- *In 1990, 45% of air travelers had incomes above $40,000; 24% had incomes above $60,000.*

TABLE 3-1

CHARACTERISTICS OF VACATION VS BUSINESS TRAVELERS AND TOTAL TRAVELERS

	Vacation Travelers	Business Travelers	Total Travelers
Sex			
Men	49%	61%	53%
Women	51	39	47
Age			
18-24	16	11	15
25-34	26	31	26
35-44	20	29	22
45-54	13	15	15
55 or older	25	14	22
Education			
Some college or less	73	51	70
College graduate or more	27	49	30
Household Income			
Less than $30,000	49	32	47
$30,000-$40,000	20	21	20
$40,000-$50,000	12	17	13
$50,000 or more	19	30	20
Occupation			
Professional or Managerial	13	29	16
Lower Level Technical or Managerial Occupations	16	31	19
Clerical or Sales	14	15	14
Blue Collar	17	14	17

Source: Reed Travel Market Reports, July 1989 (based on 1988 data)

Business and Nonbusiness Travelers

In Table 3-1 we can see that certain characteristics differ significantly when vacation and business travelers are compared. In addition, there are differences between all travelers and either business or vacation travelers. These statistics are from 1988 data. At that time, the percentage of male business travelers was still considerably highly than that of female business travelers (but see the "Industry Communique"). On the other hand, men and women were represented almost equally in vacation travel.

Business travelers are concentrated mostly in the 25- to 44-year-old groups. Vacation travelers, however are more evenly spread, with almost one quarter of them 55 years old or older.

Almost one third of business travelers have incomes above $50,000; less than one third make less than $30,000. On the other hand, almost half of vacation travelers have household incomes of less than $30,000 and less than one fifth earn more than $50,000.

More than twice as many business travelers, as compared to either of the other categories, have occupations considered to be managerial, technical or professional. Only 60 to 66% of vacation travelers or total travelers have jobs classified in the four categories shown (many are either in nonclassified positions or do not hold a paying job). Almost 90% of business travelers have such jobs. This is quite understandable, because people traveling on business would have to be employed and would usually be employed in one of these classifications.

INDUSTRY COMMUNIQUE

"DON'T THROW BOUQUETS AT ME..."

Leslie Dickstein

Years ago, Freud threw his hands in the air as he posed what he saw as an unanswerable question: What do women want? More recently, U.S. hotels did much the same. After years of courting the woman executive by tossing roses, floral bedspreads, women's magazines, and other "feminine touches" her way, hoteliers gave up in frustration.

Finally, someone got the bright idea to ask business women just what it was they were looking for. And wonder of wonders, it turns out that what they really want is a good hotel. Forthwith, U.S. hoteliers began to eschew the all-women's floor concept. With women expected to make up 50 percent of the traveling workforce by the year 2000, according to the American Hotel and Motel Association, there's a lot at stake.

Today's approach is born of common sense: Instead of Lady Hilton rooms, the Los Angeles-based company has integrated hair dryers, bathroom scales, and special soaps into its standard rooms. Likewise, Ramada dropped its Traveling Woman program. A full-fledged women's program at Westin, including a travel-tip booklet giving instructions on safety and packing, didn't take long to fizzle, says Westin public relations manager Dashiel Wham.

It's not that women don't want the added in-room amenities; they objected to the way in which the programs were presented, industry officials say. With the number of female business travelers growing at a rate three times faster than their male counterparts, today's hotel executives are still very serious about courting their business...they've just changed their approach. Most hotels today prefer a subtle advertising technique, perhaps featuring a woman's hand on a briefcase in print ad to suggest that the hotel has both male and female guests in mind.

"Business men and women really want the same thing," says a spokeswoman for the Pickett Company, which ran the briefcase advertisement before the company was acquired by Guest Quarters late last year. "We didn't want to market specifically to women because that would be condescending. But there are some things—like safety—that women are more sensitive to."

In a recently published survey, Pickett reported that 87 percent of the women questioned rated security at their leading concern. Other hotel companies agreed. The nine all-suite L'Hermitage Hotels in West Hollywood installed a system called Digi-lock about eight months ago. The computerized program allowed guests to select a personal, four-digit code, known only to the guest and the hotel's computer. Travelers can also arrange for the front desk to phone their room upon arrival, or have the lights turned on at a specified hour.

Marriott, too, prefers not to promote directly to women, according to director of public relations programs, June Farrell.

A recent study by Hyatt Hotels & Resorts, in conjunction with the New York social research firm, Research & Forecast, concluded that women, who now account for at least 39 percent of business travelers (up from 31 percent last year), experience more stress than men while traveling, have stronger feelings about business travel than men, and find it harder to cope with bad service while on the road. In response to those findings, Adam Aron, senior vice-president of marketing for the Chicago-based company, says the chain has tried to simplify the businesswomen's stay by eliminating some of the petty nuisances of travel like telephone cords that don't reach from desk to bed.

A number of women prefer concierge floors. "I will always stay there if I can," says Wendy Reid Crisp of the National Association of Female Executives. "They save time, they are restful, and they take some of the stress out of traveling. That's the main difference between men and women traveling: women are confined more to their rooms because they can't go down to the lobby bar without appearing like they're lonely. I don't think that's changed one bit."

What has changed is the realization that women business travelers are a powerful and savvy consumer block for the hotel industry. Hotels that can recognize this, plus forward messages on time and have a fax machine at the ready, go a long way toward cornering a lucrative part of the business travel market.

Reprinted from Frequent Flyer magazine 1990.

Recent Growth of Travel in the United States

According to studies by Travel Pulse in 1978, 43% of the adult population of the United States were travelers, defined in this study as one who purchases a roundtrip at least 200 miles from home that includes air fare or paid accommodations for at least one night, or that includes a cruise. By the time the 1980 study was published, this number had risen to 54% of the adult population.

This was a substantial increase in the number of travelers, and the number continues to grow, although at a slower rate. As the general population has increased in the number of college-educated adults and in higher average real incomes, this figure has continued to grow. In 1991 to 1992, there were dips in several areas of travel because of the Persian Gulf war and the economic recession of this period.

As mentioned earlier, by 1990, the percentage of the population traveling by air was up to 78% of men and 72% of women. This means that the market for the travel product is extremely large and still growing. Air travel has become the mode of transportation that is taken for granted—an assumed right rather than a privilege for the elite.

Effects of Income Level and Age Group on Travel

As we can see in Figure 3-1, based on a study in 1988 by American Express Travel Related Services, 63% of the total population were classified as travelers (here defined as an adult who spent at least one night away from home in a paid lodging). Income was a major factor, with only 42% of those with incomes under $20,000 using paid lodging compared to 92% of those earning $50,000 or more. Age only became a major factor in use of paid lodging once the individual reached 65 years of age. From ages 18 to 64, the percentage ranges from 64% to 72%, but drops precipitously after age 65 to only 38%.

Figure 3–1.   Percentage of U.S. adults who are travelers. *Source*: American Express Travel Related Services.

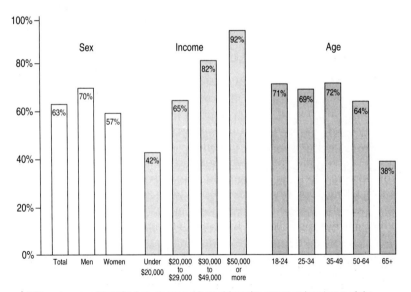

* Travelers are identified as anyone 18 or older who spent at least one night away from home in a paid lodging during 1988.

Choice of Transportation, Accommodations, and Destinations

By far, the most common mode of transportation for travel is still the family automobile. As Table 3-2 shows, more than three quarters of trips are taken in an automobile, truck, or recreation vehicle. The most common trip length is 2 to 3 nights. Visiting friends and relatives (VFR travel) is, by far, the most common reason for travel—accounting for more than one third of all trips. Business and convention travel makes up only 16% of total travel.

It is interesting to note that more travelers stay in a hotel or motel than in the homes of friends or relatives. However, 18% only visit for the day, returning home to spend the night. Almost half (46%) of trips are taken for the weekend.

TABLE 3-2

U.S. TRIP PROFILE—1990
(Base: 1,232.5 million person-trips to places 100 miles or more from home)

Category	Percent of Trips
Round Trip Distances	
200-299 miles	23%
300-399 miles	15
400-599 miles	12
600-999 miles	7
1,000-1,999 miles	15
2,000 miles or more	13
Outside US.	6
	100%
Average distance (miles): 839	
(Domestic travel only)	
Mode of Transportation	
Auto/Truck/RV	79%
Airplane	17
Bus	2
Train	1
Other	1
Trip Duration	
No nights	8%
One night	12
2 or 3 nights	42
4 to 9 nights	30
10 nights or more	10
Average nights	4.4%

Category	Percent of Trips
Type of Lodging	
Friends, relatives homes	40%
Hotel or motel	44
Rented cabin or condo	1
Owned cabin or condo	4
Camper, trailer or RV	3
Other	6
No overnight stay	8
Primary Purpose of Trip	
Visit friends, relatives	41%
Outdoor recreation	13
Entertainment	22
Business	11
Convention	5
Other	7
Vacation Travel	69%
Weekend Travel	46%

Source: U.S. Travel Data Center, Travel Industry World Yearbook, 1991.

Table 3-3 describes the characteristics of travelers from the United States to foreign destinations. For the most part, these travelers are more sophisticated than domestic travelers. They earn higher average incomes (the mean was $68,100 and the median, $64,700), and business travel is a greater percentage of the reason for the trip, accounting for more than one third of all trips (convention attendance is part of business travel).

Almost 70% of these travelers booked their trip through a travel agent, whereas another 10% used a company travel department. Because almost all overseas travelers travel by air rather than in the family car, this use of outside assistance is common.

———

TABLE 3-3

PROFILE OF U.S. RESIDENTS TRAVELING TO OVERSEAS DESTINATIONS—1990

	Percent of Total Overseas Visitors
Purpose of Trip	
Business	30
Attend convention	5
Vacation, holiday	52
Visit friends	31
Study	3

	Percent of Total Overseas Visitors
Other	6
Means of Booking Air Trip	
Travel agent	67
Airline	18
Company travel department	10
Other	6
*Information Sources**	
Airline	23
Travel agency	56
Government sources	5
Company travel department	13
Friends, relatives	25
Newspapers, magazines	8
Published sources	15
Tour company	7
Type of Airline Ticket	
First class	5
Executive, business	16
Economy, coach, tourist	69
Frequent flyer	5
Other	3
Use of Pre-Paid Package/Inclusive Tour	
Yes	27
No (Independent)	73
Type and Size of Traveling Party	
Traveling alone	41
Spouse	31
Family group	18
Business group	7
Tour group	5
Annual Family Income	
Average (mean)	$68,100
Median	$64,700
Number of Countries Visited	
One country	78
Two countries	12
Three or more countries	10
Average number of countries	1.4
Median number of countries	1.0

*Multiple responses.
Source: Travel Industry World Yearbook 1992 from In-flight Survey by U.S. Travel and Tourism Administration.

MOTIVATIONS FOR TRAVEL

Travel has been and continues to be one of the symbols of the good life for many people. It is important that it be marketed properly if this growth is to continue. Several theories have been developed that are useful in understanding consumer motivation, which is essential to successful marketing.

Need-Satisfaction Theory

The **need-satisfaction theory** holds that all consumer purchases are made to satisfy some need of the consumer. An individual has a desire for something. Depending on circumstances, the desire may grow into an actual need. A person doesn't buy a bicycle just to own a bicycle unless he collects bicycles. The purchaser is fulfilling some need that the bicycle can satisfy. Perhaps he needs transportation but is too young to drive, or perhaps he wants to exercise. If the desire becomes strong enough, it becomes a **need**. Perhaps a neighbor just bought a bicycle and there is a desire to keep up with the Joneses. Notice that in all these cases the bicycle was the means to satisfy a particular need.

The same is true of travel. People don't travel just to travel. Travel fulfills some need for each consumer. The needs may differ just as the needs for the bicycle differed, but in each case travel can be the satisfier. Some of the most popular reasons given by people for why they travel are:

- *To visit friends and relatives*
- *To see new places and learn new things*
- *To do things they can't do at home (skiing, for example)*
- *To get away from the weather*
- *To relax*

"The only trips I ever go on are guilt trips!"

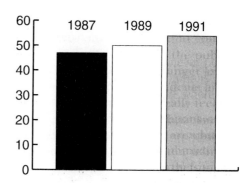

Figure 3-2. The Single Most Important Reason for Not Taking More Trips: "I cannot afford to do so." *Source:* TravelStyles® Surveys, Menlo Consulting Group, Inc.

Reasons For Not Traveling

In addition to knowing why people travel, it is necessary to understand why some people do not travel. There are many reasons. Some of those most commonly heard are: "I can't afford it," (Figure 3-2) or "I don't have the time."

Frequently, these reasons are just excuses. They hide other underlying fears of travel. Fear of flying is quite common and accounts for many people who insist on driving on a vacation or other trip when they could fly. Fear of the unknown keeps many people from leaving their own country or even their own city. Many travelers travel frequently domestically but are afraid to go where they cannot understand the language. Some potential travelers are afraid of the unfamiliar decisions they will have to make in a strange place, such as how much to tip, or how to get around a strange city. All of these fears are valid deterrents to travel. When a seller of travel meets an objection to the purchase of travel, it is necessary to interview the consumer to determine the real reason for the objection. People hesitate to discuss their fears. Frequently, they are unaware, themselves, of their real reasons for resisting a new experience. "Too little money" or "too little time" are convenient, nonembarrassing excuses that can hide the real fears.

Travelers' Expectations

One of the major motivations for travel is the desire to get away from it all for a little while. Thus, travel should be a pleasant experience. If travelers expecting a pleasant experience meet delays in transportation, missed connections, lost baggage, overbooked hotels and conditions different from what brochures show, they will decide that it is better to stay home. Discretionary travel must be enjoyable to be repeated. When problems occur, how they are handled is critical.

Travelers must feel that they are important and that people care about them. They must find travel conditions to be what they were led to expect by the salesperson, the brochures, the advertisements, and all the other components of travel and tourism marketing. If these expectations are not met, travelers will be unlikely to repeat the experience.

Tourism USA Vol. 1 Appraising Tourism Potential (University of Missouri, 1978), a study done for the United States Travel Service of the United States Department of Commerce, described eight different motivational segments of tourism which are still true today. They are:

- *Ethnic tourism—a desire to visit one's roots and learn about the culture from which one has come.*
- *Cultural tourism—a desire to learn about other cultures. This includes the desire to visit museums and other cultural places.*
- *Historical tourism—the desire to learn about the past.*
- *Environmental tourism—the desire to concentrate on the environment, to see beautiful scenery, fall foliage, the ocean, to get away from bad weather. [Note: Today, this has grown beyond just seeing beauty. Eco-tourism has become a major factor in tourism. Tours are now offered that focus on eco-tourism themes.]*
- *Recreational tourism—a desire to participate in activities such as skiing, golfing, or tennis.*
- *Entertainment or sensually indulgent tourism—a desire to be entertained; for example, to see shows, to gamble, or indulge in gourmet dining.*
- *Social status or ego enhancement tourism—the need for recognition, to go where one's friends have been and be able to take part in their discussions of the world. These travelers will usually bring back many souvenirs to prove their status.*
- *Interpersonal tourism—the desire to visit friends or relatives. This travel motivation accounts for the largest number of personal trips.*

As Peter Drucker stated in *Managing for Results* (Harper & Row, 1964), the Cadillac competes for the customer's money with mink coats, jewelry, "the skiing vacation in the luxury resort, and other prestige satisfactions." What this demonstrates is that a purchase satisfies a need—one that could be satisfied in several

"Nervous? What makes you think I'm nervous?"

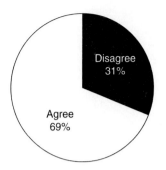

Figure 3-3. "I Am Willing to Cut Back on Other Things in Order to Travel More Frequently." *Source:* TravelStyles® Surveys, Minlo Consulting Group, Inc. 1991.

different ways. Travel, as pointed out in Drucker's example, is a satisfier of general prestige needs. One must understand what is actually motivating the consumer to consider travel and answer that need in selling the travel product.

Drucker also points out that there are actually two consumers. One is the ultimate purchaser—the user of the product or service—and the other is the distribution channel—in the case of the travel product, usually a travel agency. The supplier of the product must convince both of these customers of the product's worth. Frequently, the consumer is not aware of the variety of suppliers available and relies on the travel agent to choose the actual travel service that meets the need.

Therefore, it is necessary for travel producers—airlines, hotels, cruise lines, sightseeing companies, and so forth—to market both to travel agents and their clients. This promoting to the public makes the travel agent's job easier. It is easier to sell something with which the consumer is familiar than a totally unknown product.

In a study conducted by the Menlo Consulting Group, Inc. in 1991, of outbound travelers, travel is shown to be very important. When asked to agree or disagree with the statement: "I am willing to cut back on other things in order to travel more frequently": the results were that 31% disagreed while 69% (more than two thirds of the respondents) agreed (see Figure 3-3).

MASLOW'S HIERARCHY OF NEEDS

A study of travelers' motivations would not be complete without a discussion of Abraham **Maslow's theory of the hierarchy of human needs** as proposed in his book, *Motivation and Personality* (Harper & Row, 1954). This classic theory has been the basis for most modern studies of human behavior and motivation.

Maslow believed that the human being proceeds through five stages of motivation. It is impossible to move to a higher stage until the needs of lower stages are met (see Figure 3-4). Moreover, an individual does not function on just one level at a time, but operates on different levels for different activities at different times. One must be comfortable at a lower level before moving to a higher one.

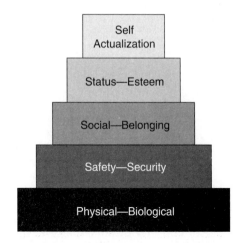

Figure 3-4.   Maslow's Hierarchy of Needs.

Physical and Biological Needs

The lowest level of human needs is physical and biological. These are the needs for food, shelter and clothing sufficient to protect against the elements. Individuals functioning on this level are not generally involved in tourism. They do travel, but usually as refugees seeking shelter and food or escaping from absolute poverty or war.

Safety and Security

The next level of need is that of safety and security. People who prefer escorted tours are looking for security. They do not want to handle their baggage, worry about tipping, or have to find activities on their own. They want the safety of a leader to whom they can turn if a problem arises. They want to be sure that a translator is available if needed.

Another aspect of the human need for safety and security that affects the travel product is that of political conditions at the destination. In 1991, when the Persian Gulf War broke out in the Middle East and terrorism was threatened in a broad area of the world, most travelers chose to stay home rather than risk their safety. When the United States Department of State issues travel

"Perhaps you'd like to re-think your itinerary, Mrs. Simpson—eight of these destinations are having revolutions and four others show signs of political unrest."

advisories warning of problems in particular countries, tourism to those countries from the U.S. drops drastically. Northern Ireland and much of the Middle East suffer from these same problems. People will not travel for pleasure to a location they believe to be unsafe.

Social Needs

The human being has a need to belong, to feel wanted and loved. These are the social needs. Satisfying this level of human needs is a major motivation for choosing a product such as travel. It is one of the main reasons for the popularity of group travel. (See "Industry Communique.") People are more comfortable when they are with others with whom they feel compatible. The success of tour operators who specialize in singles tours focuses on this need. The individual traveling with such a group has both security and social needs met by this product. As another example, cruises also cater to the social needs of people with an abundance of planned activities.

INDUSTRY COMMUNIQUE

WHAT ESCORTED TOUR CLIENTS REALLY WANT

Melinda L. Stovall

One might have called it the escorted tour from hell. Forty-two people traveled by motorcoach from Pennsylvania to Washington, D.C., for the annual springtime Cherry Blossom Festival, and just about everything went wrong once they arrived.

The rains came and temperatures hovered near freezing, leaving the tour group wet and cold at the parade. The group's hotel, marginal at best, botched their breakfast service, so nobody got to eat. And to top it off, the cherry blossoms weren't there because high winds had knocked them off the week before.

After returning home, the tour participants were asked what they thought about the trip. "It was great," they said. On a scale of one to 10, with one being the worst, the participants gave the tour an eight.

That response naturally surprised Margaret Persia, who surveyed the group while a master's degree candidate at Pennsylvania State University in State College, Pennsylvania. "The destination was what got them interested in the tour, but the community of people is what made them satisfied," she says now.

Building on that experience, Persia, now tourism doctoral candidate at Clemson University in Clemson, South Carolina, and a former travel agency owner, has further examined escorted tours. The result is her recently released

"National Escorted Tour Survey"—still in a preliminary stage, but a substantial beginning in determining why people choose escorted tours, what they expect from the experience, how satisfied they are after the tour, and whether there is any connection between their expectations and their level of satisfaction.

DEVELOPING RELATIONSHIPS

"I've been on a few escorted tours myself," says Persia, who likens agent fam trips to a "rigid form" of escorted tour. "You go on one of these things, especially one with a long itinerary, and a community develops among the members on that tour. It's interesting to sit back and view what goes on, how people develop relationships among themselves and with the tour conductor, and the driver if it's a motorcoach tour, and as a group with the destination.

"If you go on a vacation with your family, you don't have to interact with anyone else," she adds. "But on a tour, with the combination of people, there is a special relationship that develops that can enhance or detract from the experience."

Persia intends to explore these social aspects later; early results in the "National Escorted Tour Survey" focus on clients' purchase characteristics. This data is being gathered via a self-administered "pre-experience" questionnaire, whose respondents also will answer a post-experience questionnaire after returning from their tours.

To find her participants, Persia contacted a random sample of agency owner/managers and tour operator executives and asked if they each would forward pre-experience questionnaire packets to five qualified clients—those who had already booked an escorted tour or who had recently inquired about doing so.

Persia is conducting the survey with the cooperation and endorsement of ASTA and the National Tour Foundation, the educational arm of the National Tour Association. She is funding the study with a cash prize she was awarded by the ASTA Scholarship Foundation for her master's thesis.

PREFERRED BY ELDERLY WOMEN

So far, 136 people have responded to the pre-experience questionnaire—64 were clients of tour operators and 72 of travel agencies—and the respondents come from 29 states. The respondents are predominantly female (83 of the participants), older (113 are ages 51 through 80) and educated (75 respondents have some college or more). This dominance by the senior market corresponds with NTA data showing that three out of four escorted travelers in 1989 fell in the 50-plus group.

Escorted tours—long associated with the stereotypical "blue-haired wonders" by those in the travel industry—appeal to older people for particular reasons, notes Janet Hammond, CTC, a member of ASTA's Tour Protection Trust Board of Trustees.

"Older ones like to be with a group," says Hammond, president of Travel Planners/Carlson Travel Network in Miami Lakes, Florida. Chances are the women in the survey are widows; they don't have husbands to make decisions. They can have a circle of people to socialize with, a nice group of people, and don't have to worry about comfort and safety.

"Younger people, on the other hand, don't want to be pinned down today; they are more adventurous," she adds. "They may have a set itinerary, but not down to the hours of that day."

REPUTATION AND DESTINATION

In Persia's pre-experience questionnaire, respondents were asked to rate the importance of 12 features of their escorted tour purchase. A breakdown of the ratings between agency clients and tour operator clients showed only one significant difference—tour operator clients rated "reputation of the tour company" highest, while agency clients cited "destination" as most important.

"A tour operator typically has developed a loyal following." Persia says. "A major reason why someone goes with a tour operator is because of the experience, if it was a good and happy time in the past."

"Now, a travel agency client is not asking for a particular tour operator; their primary interest is in the destination," she continues. "They want to see what it is they want to see. The tour operator is unknown to them, but they have expectations that they will do what they say they want to do."

Hammond believes that more agents have become educated about tour operators and are offering tour protection, but suspects that not all clients share their concern: "Experienced travelers more likely know the reputation of the tour operator or have been taught that by their travel agent, but the average person taking a vacation is thinking of where he wants to go, the cool breezes...He's not thinking about someone's reputation."

Even so, when combining figures for both groups, the most important factors in the tour-purchase decision were reputation of the tour company and then destination—the number-one choice probably reflecting that many of the respondents were experienced travelers. Ninety-six of the survey participants indicated they had been on four or more escorted tours, while 32 had been on one to three such tours. Another seven had never been on an escorted tour.

Inclusion of a tour guide ranked third, followed by scheduled time of the tour, previous experience with the tour company, element of safety in the group setting, ease of booking through a travel agent, and brochures and other advertising matter. These features could be stressed by agents in promotional materials and methods, notes Persia.

Contrary to popular theory, the recommendation of friends or relatives was not rated as particularly important by either tour operator or travel agency clients in this sample. Hammond and Persia speculate that one reason the travel agent's recommendation also rates low for both groups of clients is that these respondents are more knowledgeable, more traveled; they know what they want to do and don't need recommendations.

The idea of looking at expectations versus reactions has been around a while, notes Dr. Charles Duke, a professor of marketing at Clemson and Persia's co-worker on the study, but this comprehensive look at tours and tourism is new. When complete, the data should help tour operators and travel agencies devise the most appropriate and ethical ways of marketing their services so that ultimately they have satisfied escorted-tour clients.

Before this research, "there have been assumptions of what people expect, but no hard research data," Persia says. "We've looked at expectations through a scientific approach, and I chose escorted tours because they have a specific goal in mind." But her interest is also inspired by a trait shared by many travel agents—"I'm just very curious about people."

Reprinted with permission, ASTA Agency Management, January, 1992.

Status or Esteem Needs

This level in the hierarchy of needs is also important in marketing the travel product. When a destination is newly popular, such as China or Eastern Europe, many people will travel there so they can say they have been there. The 1970s movie "If It's Tuesday, This Must Be Belgium," is symbolic of a popular type of trip. See 17 countries in 14 days. Travelers cannot really learn too much about any one country and probably do not remember where they saw what, but they can talk to their friends about seeing 17 countries. Travel is one of the primary status symbols in today's society. This is reflected in the vacation home movies that have been the target of comedians for many years. The home movie is a way to impress one's friends with one's travel experiences and sophistication. It is also

"Hey, Fred! Here's a note from those people who went around the world on a tramp steamer."

demonstrated in the popular use of travel prizes on TV game shows. In the same way, being able to mention one's stay at a popular resort or hotel is important to many people.

Self Actualization

The last and highest level of Maslow's hierarchy refers to the person who is above the level of needing to impress friends and associates. Self actualizers have reached a high level and their motivations are higher yet. They work for such goals as having a hospital named after themselves. The average seller of travel does not often work with people at this level of motivation, because they are a relatively small percentage of society.

Although Maslow's hierarchy is a simplification, as are all models, it does serve an important purpose. It shows that an individual does not operate on one level all the time but on varying levels, depending on circumstances. The businessperson staying at an exclusive hotel to fulfill status needs may drop very suddenly to the safety/security level after calling home and learning that a robbery has taken place. If you are an employee of the hotel, you must now treat this person differently as you help him get in touch with home and take care of the problem. The traveler who is having a great time on a social level and is confronted with hostility in a foreign city will drop quickly to the safety level also. When talking to a potential consumer who is a high level business executive, you may assume a high level on the hierarchy scale, but this executive may be afraid of dealing with a different language in a foreign culture. This traveler must be treated on the security level, just as you would treat the blue-collar worker who doesn't know how much to tip on a cruise ship.

LIFE STAGES

In a study done for the United States Travel Service (*Tourism USA Vol. II Development: Assessing Your Product and the Market*, 1978) nine different **life stages** were depicted. These stages are still applicable today. Each has an effect on travel motivations. These cycles are listed below and illustrated in Figure 3-5:

Stage 1.   *Bachelor stage. Young, single people not living at home*

Stage 2.   *Newly married couple. Young, no children*

Stage 3.   *Full Nest I. Youngest child under 6*

Stage 4.   *Full Nest II. Youngest child 6 or older*

Stage 5.   *Full Nest III. Older couple with dependent children*

Stage 6.   *Empty Nest I. Older couples, no children living with them. Head in labor force.*

Stage 7.   *Empty Nest II. Older couples, no children living at home. Head retired*

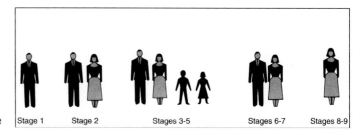

Figure 3-5.   Stages of Life

| Stage 1 | Stage 2 | Stages 3-5 | Stages 6-7 | Stages 8-9 |

Stage 8.   Solitary survivor, in labor force

Stage 9.   Solitary survivor, retired

Some newer categories that do not fit in the stages here because they are not part of the normal progression through life are the newly married older couple without children at home, who may be in a first marriage for both or a remarriage for one or both; the newly married older couple with children at home or with adult children not at home; families with a single parent, and co-habiting unmarried couples of the opposite or same sex. These newer types of households constitute significant target markets and a number of travel suppliers are successfully fulfilling their needs.

Although this list is not the only one for life cycles, it does show some important divisions. Stages 1 and 2 are important elements in the travel market, because they generally have adequate money with few responsibilities competing for those dollars. Stages 3, 4, and 5 have the greatest number of budget items competing for the discretionary dollar. People in these stages of life most often travel by car or camper and visit grandparents or other friends or relatives. They make less use of air travel and paid accommodations for vacations. This age bracket, however, is highly represented in business travel. Some exceptions are those couples with two professional incomes who choose to vacation with their children. This has led to an increase in children's programs in hotels and on cruises.

Stages 6 and 7 frequently return to the pleasure travel market and will buy air transportation or cruises. They are tired of driving from all the years of doing so with the children. Stages 8 and 9 find travel important if health permits in order to meet people and feel less alone. These persons, usually elderly, often prefer to travel with a compatible group.

It is important to realize that the "empty nester," the couple whose children have grown, is different from the "never-nester," the couple who never had children. Given the same age bracket, the couple who never had children is probably much more experienced in travel than the couple who start to travel after the children have grown and usually have more discretionary income. The product that will appeal to each couple, and their levels on Maslow's hierarchy, will differ.

ALLOCENTRIC VS. PSYCHOCENTRIC PERSONALITY

Travelers, like all people, have differing personalties. Some are leaders and some are followers. **Allocentric** personality types are leaders and **psychocentric** personality types are followers. (See "Industry Communique.") The allocentric person is a trend-setter—the first in the community to go to a new destination. The psychocentric person doesn't go anywhere until sure of what the destination is like. The psychocentric waits for friends to go, and then follows what is in fashion. It is necessary to judge a consumer's place on this personality scale to provide the proper travel experience. Most people, of course, fall somewhere in the middle (see Figure 3-6).

Each year, different destinations come and go in popularity. When selling travel to an allocentric person, the salesperson would want to emphasize the new and exciting destination. On the other hand, when a salesperson is working with a psychocentric client, it is necessary to go with the "tried and true" destination. This traveler doesn't want to experiment and is more comfortable with the well-known. Figure 3-7 shows destinations popular with the range of personalties from psychocentric to allocentric in 1974. Figure 3-8 (1991) is a newer version, showing how the status of destinations change over time.

CONCLUSION

Although no two travelers are identical in either their psychological makeup or their motivations, they do fall into certain patterns. It is necessary to understand the consumer's true needs, not just what he or she says they are. It is necessary to

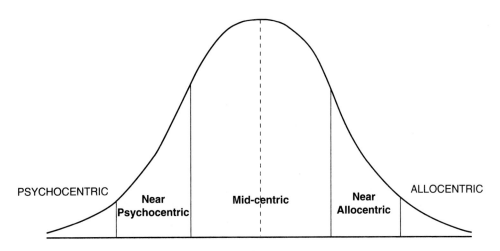

Figure 3-6. Distribution of Psychographic Segments. *Source:* Plog Research, Inc.

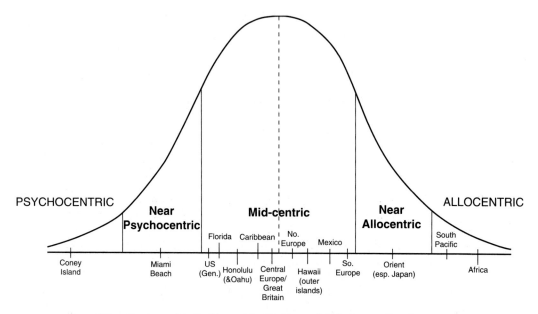

Figure 3-7.   Psychographic Positions of Destinations—1972. *Source:* Plog Research, Inc.

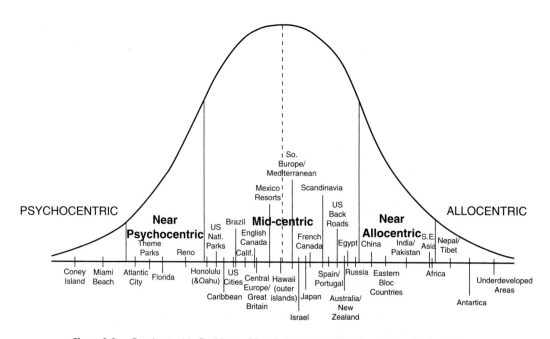

Figure 3-8.   Psychographic Positions of Destinations—1991. *Source:* Plog Research, Inc.

INDUSTRY COMMUNIQUE

DEFINING THE LEISURE MARKET

Buck Banks

The symptoms leading to the current softness in the leisure-travel market began to show long before the war and the recession this year. They were evident in client complaints that travel agents hear frequently: Suppliers make promises they don't keep; destinations are not as pristine as they appear in brochures; planes are late and service is shoddy.

According to Dr. Stanley Plog, who has been studying leisure travel for 25 years, the market's problems are psychological. Travel just isn't as enjoyable, easy or cheap as it used to be, and it's simply not satisfying travelers. To overcome these barriers, Plog says, industry professionals must understand the psychology of the market.

The chairman and CEO of Plog Research Inc. in Los Angeles, Plog (which rhymes with *vogue*) has spend 25 years studying leisure travel, and his new book, *Leisure Travel: Making It a Growth Market...Again!*, is the culmination of that work. Though the book addresses suppliers and destination developers primarily, Plog says his ideas can help agents understand the complexities of the leisure-travel market.

LEISURE THINKING

Over the past 30 years, the basic psychology of the American people has changed. "People who have lived most of their adult years as cautious, conservative, stay-at-home individuals have become venturesome, relaxed, personally expansive, globe-trotting sophisticates," Plog writes.

The historical roots of this change can be traced to the 15 years following World War II. During that period, Americans committed to working hard and saving for the future, a result of living through the deprivations of the war and the Great Depression. They spent little of their disposable income on leisure travel, even after retirement.

In the 1960s, the youth movement took people away from material possessions, emphasizing life's experiences instead. At the same time, the cost of travel was dropping. Lower airfares and economy motels made travel affordable. Plog says the attitudinal changes of that time are summed up in the statement, "I've got to do it while I'm still able to." That inspired what he called the "virus of leisure travel," infecting many Americans.

What followed was phenomenal growth in the travel industry. Now worth about $2.3 trillion annually, according to Plog, travel has become the biggest business anywhere.

TWO TYPES OF TRAVELER

Obviously, though, the travel market is not a single uniform entity. Plog divides leisure travelers into two distinct groups, which he defines as "allocentric" and "psychocentric."

Psychocentric travelers feel unable to control most events in their lives, Plog says. They often have a hard time making decisions and are usually the last to try new products. They prefer close friends to strangers, and they're most comfortable with activities that bring with them a sense of security and familiarity.

Allocentric travelers, on the other hand, are outgoing, self-confident, curious and venturesome. They spend a larger portion of their disposable income on travel than psychocentrics, and they are more likely to risk that income on new destinations or travel products. Leisure travel satisfies a basic need to see and do new things. They are willing to try something novel, even if it may not live up to all the promoter's claims.

Between these two extremes are near-allocentrics and near-psychocentrics. Those in the middle—the largest percentage of the population—are the mid-centrics. The population is distributed across these types in a bell curve, with fewer travelers at either extreme than in the middle.

Pure allocentrics represent only about 5 percent of the total travel market. Near-allocentrics make up about 11 percent, but Plog says this is the most important group, because their preferences match those of almost half of the total market. They follow allocentric ground-breakers to new destinations, and are in turn followed by travelers from the middle portion of the scale. These mid-centrics represent a third of all vacationers, and this is the group that most travel marketers target.

"Agents need to ask themselves what kind of market they are serving," he says. "This can tell them what types of trips to sell by knowing who they are selling to. Are your clients looking for an escorted tour where everything is taken care of, or are they the adventurous type who want uniqueness? Knowing this—as simple as it may sound—can help you set more realistic expectations for your clients."

For instance, Plog says, when trying to sell a travel package to allocentric travelers, sell them airfare, hotel accommodations and a rental car so they can explore on their own. "They also may be more inclined to buy add-ons—allocentric types are the gadget buyers and will spend money to experiment and experience new things," he says. "When selling the same kind of trip to more psychocentric clients, sell them airfare, hotel, city bus tours, and organized guided excursions, and choose destinations that are more commonly known."

Allocentric types may have high expectations and be very demanding travelers, but even if the trip does not live up to their expectations, as long as they experienced something different and unusual, they will usually be satisfied. Psychocentric types have lower expectations, but as long as what you sell meets those expectations, they will be pleased.

Not all allocentrics will want to go on excursions to the Amazon to fish for piranha, and not all psychocentrics will want to go to Disney World. These are not absolute concepts that can be applied to the majority of the population. They are personality tendencies that can only be uncovered through questions and by listening to clients talk about their travel experiences.

"If you are an agent in a middle-class market area, you should do more affinity tour sales where clients travel with a group they are a member of or with a group of friends," Plog says. "That is the last thing allocentrics want to do—unless the tour is smaller, quieter, and caters to an unusual interest or activity."

DESTINATION EVOLUTION

The problem with having two different types of travelers is that they require different types of destination. On the surface, this may not seem to present a problem. You might simply send the allocentric traveler on a hiking tour of Nepal and the psychocentric traveler on an escorted tour to see New England fall foliage. But destinations change as they become better known and more developed.

As this happens, the destination begins to lose its appeal to allocentrics and gains appeal to near-allocentrics. Strip shopping centers and cheap curio shops proliferate, selling souvenirs and tourist products that exploit the very characteristics that made the destination attractive in the first place. Plog calls this "malling."

As the local economy becomes dependent on the tourist trade, the destination inevitably reaches the point where it appeals to mid-centrics and begins to draw from the psychocentric end of the continuum. In short, it has become mass market-oriented and will only continue to deteriorate unless drastic steps are taken.

"Unfortunately, that is the nature of travel markets," Plog says. "It takes tremendous energy, foresight and planning to save destinations from this end."

Amsterdam is an example of a destination that has resisted malling. "Amsterdam has done a lot to protect its quaintness," he says. "If you tear down a building there and rebuild, you have to match the architectural style of the surrounding buildings. This protects the character of the town. Frankfurt is an example of the opposite trend. After World War II, the Germans rebuilt Frankfurt with the most economical design—boxes. It's hard to think of a more boring city than Frankfurt. It is not a tourist center, and it never can be."

Disney World is an example of a destination that has created and maintained a very wide appeal, from the near-allocentrics across to psychocentrics. Plog says that visitors to Disney World almost always comment on how clean and neat everything is.

"The people that work there are neatly dressed and groomed," he says. "They are wholesome, all-American, friendly. What people notice is the attention to detail, the little things, and that is why Disney World, mass-market though it is, remains successful. There is an understanding of the market and what it takes to develop and maintain it."

Travel agents can know when a destination is getting "malled" by listening to returning clients and taking fam trips and talking to other agents. But most travel-agency managers already know what is happening. "Take a dozen experienced travel agents and put them in a room and start asking them questions about popular destinations, and I will bet you they will give you very similar opinions and descriptions," Plog says.

"What destinations don't realize is that crowding the maximum number of tourists into a destination is not a good long-term strategy," he continues. "The idea should be to plan and manage the destination to make travelers happy so they will want to come back, so they will tell their friends, so they will pay a premium price for a high-quality product. People who make the decisions about the hotels and resorts and other components that make up destinations need to realize that it is only by protecting the health and vitality of a place that they can make money over the long term."

THE FUTURE OF LEISURE

For the past six or seven years, the leisure travel market has been called a mature market. "This means that almost everyone in the marketplace that could has bought a travel service or product," he says. "That has brought more suppliers, sensing profit potentials, to compete with the larger, existing suppliers."

There are more entities striving for a slice of the pie, but the pie has not gotten any bigger, so the slices get smaller. Plog predicts a shake-out in the near future.

"The industry has been in decline for a long time," he says. "It has been a steady decline, so there won't be a quick recovery. We haven't seen the consolidation within the industry, except in airlines, that was expected. For example, our model shows that the number of travel agencies in the United States should be between 20,000 and 25,000, not the present 34,000 to 36,000 that are actually vying for the business. And look at the proliferation of car rental companies—I don't see how they can stay in business."

Plog says travel agents are not part of the problems plaguing the leisure travel market but are instead victims of those problems. "Life in a travel agency is not easy," he says. "Agents are the middlemen caught between suppliers and consumers. The suppliers, especially airlines, would rather not have the agents getting their portion of the proceeds, and consumers are quick to blame agents when their expectations are not met."

But by focusing their efforts on developing their local markets, agents can be part of the solution. "People have to get more aggressive," he says. The larger agencies that have been more successful have developed their own tour programs and unique products which they market with the help of advertising support from suppliers." He says direct marketing efforts work best today because they tend to focus the money where it can provide the best yield from the smallest investment.

Small agencies, Plog advises, have to use the same tactics employed by their larger competitors, only on a reduced scale. "Maybe a small agency can't afford an ad in the local newspaper," he says. "But they can afford direct mail to a small mailing list developed from present and past clients. They can afford to make contact with the local PTA and other local groups, and they can give presentations on what they have to offer. It's a tougher market out there, and you have to work harder for the same amount of business you used to get."

Plog suggests that agents think about marketing to their existing customer base. It's less difficult and less expensive than developing new customers. "Contact present and past clients," he says. "Our research has shown that people will take advantage of sudden bargains, and if you can offer something like that, people will buy it."

But before you get comfortable with your knowledge of the leisure market, Plog reminds his audience that leisure travelers, and their preferences, will change. "They will have to be more sensitive to the environment and their impact on its fragile character, more adaptive to local cultures rather than requiring local cultures to adapt to them, and less demanding that their travel experiences be as all-inclusive as they have been in the past." Only then, he says will travel experience by sustainable over the long term.

Reprinted with permission, ASTA Agency Management, December 1991.

know what travel consumers expect to obtain from a travel experience in order to fill their needs adequately. When a salesperson has the ability to judge and properly categorize the consumer, the sale is made much easier and the consumer will ultimately be more satisfied. The marketing manager will also know how to make promotional efforts and advertising appeal to the proper target market.

When all these factors are understood and the proper product is offered, the result will be a satisfied consumer. Any salesperson must be part psychologist to be successful, but the result of a happy consumer is well worth the effort of understanding needs and motivations.

SUMMARY

A knowledge of human motivation is essential for successful marketing. Travel products must be marketed to a wide variety of market segments. As incomes and educational levels rise, so does the possibility of up-scale travel.

Understanding consumer motivation must also include understanding motivations to avoid travel, such as fear of flying or of a strange situations. People who do travel expect pleasant experiences, and every effort should be made by travel professionals to see that the promises made in the marketing process are fulfilled in the actual experience.

Human motivations in general, and motivations for travel in particular, have been described in a number of ways. These include:

- *need-satisfaction theory—needs to be satisfied may range from the desire to see new things to the desire to escape bad weather*
- *Maslow's hierarchy of needs—five stages of motivation, ranging from physical/biological to (successively) safety/security; social; status; and self-actualization*
- *life stages — nine parts of the life cycle that range from the young independent single person to the solitary retired individual.*
- *allocentric/psychocentric personality theory, which divides people into allocentric (leader) and psychocentric (follower) groups*

QUESTIONS FOR THOUGHT AND DISCUSSION

1. Why do some people who can afford to travel choose not to do so?
2. Describe five reasons why people travel, with examples of possible trips for each.
3. Discuss Maslow's hierarchy of needs and relate this concept to travel motivation
4. Choose three of the life stages described in this chapter and discuss their similarities and differences as they relate to travel potential.
5. Describe the characteristics of an allocentric person. What type of travel might appeal to this individual?
6. Discuss Plog's concepts of "the rise and fall" of destinations as their popularity changes.

4

Market Research

demographic information
external market segmentation
focus group
historical research
internal market segmentation
market research
primary research
psychographic information
reliability
questionnaire
secondary research
survey
target market
validity

Market research is the attempt to systematically gather and analyze information about potential consumers to aid in properly understanding and meeting their needs. This research can be very formal and expensive or informal and inexpensive.

Information gained from market research is statistical in nature and describes factors such as income level, attitudes (likes and dislikes), and desires for new products and services.

PRIMARY VS. SECONDARY RESEARCH

There are two sources of market research information. The first is **primary research**. This is new research that you do yourself or have done for you through questionnaires, personal interviews, phone surveys, focus groups, advisory committees, or other similar means.

Secondary research is research that has already been done by someone else. Examples of secondary research are census bureau studies, information from sources such as the Louis Harris Poll, or research published by the United States

Travel Data Center. Secondary research is generally inexpensive to obtain. However, it frequently is not applicable to specific needs. If the product being sold has a broad market, much secondary research can be useful. In almost all cases, it can be used as background for primary research.

Properly used, secondary research can save time and money. For example, census data is broken down into very narrow segments, even as small as specific zip codes. Therefore, if an organization wishes to conduct primary research in a small specialized area, it is a good idea to obtain the census information on that area, which will tell you the income level, the age level, and other such data. There is no reason to take the time and spend the money to rediscover data that already exists.

In most cases, primary data is expensive to obtain. If sophisticated results are necessary for large organizations, the expense may be justified. For organizations such as airlines, hotel chains, steamship companies, amusement parks, and other large enterprises, the information needed generally covers a rather broad area and the results will be used to determine future marketing directions that will involve large expenditures. Therefore, market research is usually conducted by professional market research organizations. See the "Industry Communique" for a description of an airline's market research plan.

On the other hand, this is not normally the case for small organizations in the travel industry, such as travel agencies or independent hotels. A small travel agency does not have the budget to contract for major research. For the small company, research can be as simple as driving around the neighborhood to see the type of people that live there and how they seem to spend their money. A neighborhood with numerous campers and vans in the driveways will signify a neighborhood of families with growing children. Conversely neighborhoods of apartment houses and primarily small cars would signify either a community of young people who have not yet started their families, or of older people whose children are grown, or a combination. Even information as simple as this can be helpful to a company in determining the needs of the market. The travel needs of a family with young children are quite different from the travel needs of the other two groups. See the "Industry Communique" for more suggestions on effective use of market research by travel agencies.

INDUSTRY COMMUNIQUE

PLAN OF ACTION

John Dasburg
President and CEO, Northwest Airlines

Passenger research is one of the most effective tools we use to listen to our customers and measure our performance. Through this research, we are able to statistically measure customer satisfaction with regard to our service and operations. Research also provides us with a profile of our customers and helps us to better understand your travel behavior.

Each and every quarter, we pinpoint a week's worth of flights and ask our Northwest customers a series of questions about their travel experience. In the month of February, for example, we heard feedback from more than 18,000 passengers about all aspects of our service, including the appearance of our check-in counters, the clearness of our gate announcements, and the taste and quality of our in-flight meals. We then took this information and analyzed it as many ways as possible—by location, crew base, catering region, type of aircraft—so that remedial action and feedback could be reported back to everyone at Northwest.

Another measure we use is a quarterly survey that interviews 100 frequent travelers who are located in the country's 12 key markets. The frequent travelers are asked which airlines they most prefer, which they avoid, which they've flown most often. Additionally, they are asked to name the service attributes that are most important to them. From this information, we can measure ourselves against our competitors and study customer perceptions. In many of Northwest's key markets today, we find that Northwest is showing slight improvements in a number of areas.

Northwest is the first carrier in the industry to propose a quality partnership survey, a state-of-the-art call-in customer feedback system that will provide instant reaction to travel experiences. A group of 200 Northwest Gold and Preferred World-Perks members will be recruited to participate in this survey, in which customers will be able to phone an 800 telephone number and record their likes, dislikes and opinions about the service they received. With this program, we can simultaneously recognize our customers' comments and react much more quickly to the feedback we receive.

Another way in which we measure preference and listen to our customers is through district passenger feedback. Our Customer Relations Division and Luggage Service Department receive literally thousands of contacts every month on various aspects of our service—both good and bad. The information is entered into our sophisticated computerized customer response system and compiled into a monthly report. The detailed report is then circulated through every department at Northwest Airlines, and action plans are devised to combat negative trends and problems.

Reprinted courtesy of Northwest Airlines World Traveler Magazine, *August 1992.*

INDUSTRY COMMUNIQUE

DON'T GUESS—INVESTIGATE

Robert W. Joselyn

If you think that marketing research is somewhere between a corporate jet and an executive dining room on the list of likely expenditures for your agency, think again. There are marketing research options open to even the smallest agency that fall within reasonable limits in terms of both finances and expertise.

But why bother? For at least three reasons: Market information will often help a travel agency to plan better; it can lead to better execution of agency plans; and it enables an agency to monitor how well its plans are working.

BETTER PLANNING

Travel agencies are increasingly finding it necessary to "position" themselves relative to direct competitors. Rather than making educated guesses about positioning, it is often beneficial to base such decisions on market research data.

A number of years ago, a brand-new travel agency conducted a market survey profile of area residents before developing its initial marketing plan. It then matched the findings against customer profile data provided by a number of potentially important suppliers. While a number of useful conclusions were drawn from the results, one match jumped off the pages of the analysis.

A significant number of respondents had the same characteristics as the typical Club Med customer of the time. Therefore, this agency established a stated objective to become known in its primary geographic market as the area "Club Med store" within three years. The agency was able to work toward this long-term goal with a degree of confidence that could not have existed without the research.

Another recent example of the value of market research for agency planning involved a commercial travel agency on the West Coast. While agency managers worried about how the Middle East conflict, on top of an already weak economy, would reduce their commercial sales, this agency conducted a number of focus group sessions with its commercial clients to determine what their reactions actually were.

The agency discovered, far sooner than it would have by waiting for negative sales results, that its commercial sales were likely to fall by 40 percent as a result of client restrictions on international travel. It also learned that a number of its commercial accounts were willing to ease their restrictions once they understood the increased security measures being taken by airlines and airports around the world.

The agency responded by preparing a "Travel Security Advisory" that outlined these security measures, and included the agency's own tips for U.S. travelers to international destinations. This "advisory" was then distributed to all of the agency's commercial clients. It also found out which of its own employees were interested in working fewer hours, and reduced their schedules.

Thanks to simple and inexpensive research, this agency was able to reduce commercial sales losses in advance, and to lower its costs quickly in anticipation of lower commercial sales.

EXECUTION AND RESULTS

Market research also can be of tremendous value in the pursuit of agency objectives.

For example, the agency whose goal was to become the area "Club Med store" in the minds of a targeted group made an additional effort to learn more about this group. One discovery was that a sizable percentage of those who fit the Club Med profile belonged to health and athletic clubs.

The agency then approached local health and athletic clubs with the idea of sponsoring "Club Med" events, such as volleyball tournaments, in exchange for promotional exposure at the clubs and access to club mailing lists.

Using research for evaluation also could help the agency pursuing "Club Med store" status. Rather than wait for, or solely depend on, sales results, which may take a long time to show conclusive evidence, the agency could survey a sample of the target customer group from time to time to determine whether its efforts to create an association with Club Med were actually working.

DATA PROCESSED OR RAW

Primary data collection means that you directly collect data from the target source of information. Secondary data collection refers to the acquisition of data which someone else has already collected. Although each of the examples given so far involved the collection of primary data, the general rule should be: "Never collect primary data before determining whether secondary data is available."

There are two good reasons for this: Acquiring secondary data is usually less expensive, and it is usually faster.

On the other hand, great care must be taken to evaluate the data's applicability and accuracy. To be useful, secondary data must answer the questions you are interested in, apply to the target you are interested in, have been collected in a trustworthy manner, and be timely.

All four of these conditions must be met for the secondary data to be perfectly useful. But as long as you are aware of its limitations, even data that doesn't qualify on all four counts may be somewhat helpful.

Consider the agency that wants to identify every business firm within a geographic area that does international business and has its own sales force. It could try to conduct a survey of all businesses in the area—or it could check with the chamber of commerce, which quite probably has such a list and will provide it for a modest fee. Often such organizations will add other details that might be useful in developing a commercial sales call list. While not every relevant firm may belong to the chamber, the agency probably will miss fewer organizations this way than by conducting a survey to which some companies do not respond.

To select appropriate secondary data, as well as to design your own research devices, you should understand two criteria of market research evaluation: validity and reliability.

Validity is a function of whether the data answers the questions it is meant to. For example, suppose questions designed to measure respondents' attitudes about hoping to take a cruise someday actually elicit responses about the respondents' perceived ability to afford a cruise at present. In this case, the results would lack validity.

Reliability is a function of whether the research findings are representative of the population about which the researcher wishes to generalize. If the agency surveying the preferences of potential Club Med customers received responses from individuals whose age, income or lifestyle do not match the Club Med profile characteristics, that survey's reliability could be seriously questioned.

If secondary data is unavailable, you don't have to stop there, no matter what kind of budget you have. There are two useful research techniques every agency can afford: the focus group and the simple survey.

SHARPENING FOCUS GROUPS

A focus group can be described as a data collection session that blends "group interview" and "group brainstorming." Because the number of participants is small, and because participants are seldom selected by random sampling of a defined population, the reliability of focus-group results cannot be guaranteed, even when a number of sessions are involved.

Technically, the focus-group technique is best used to generate ideas rather than to test them. With a full understanding of the risks, however, focus-group research is often used to test ideas and to draw conclusions as well. This typically occurs when the organization doing the research lacks the time or money to conduct more technically correct research, and is usually far better than none at all.

Travel agency focus-group research typically involves gathering a small group of agency customers and/or non-customers together for discussion of one topic or several. Though informal, the discussion is not entirely unstructured. On the contrary, it is recommended that the agency owner, manager or group leader develop guidelines to help keep the conversation on track, and to ensure that all the topics the agency is interested in are at least introduced.

Consider the following possibilities:

- *A focus group of female business travelers to determine whether they have any specific travel needs or desires which the agency can do something about.*
- *A focus group of retired senior citizens to determine whether there is a market for grandparent/grandchild travel in your community.*

- *A focus group of commercial client travel coordinators to determine what your agency might consider doing to help them in their jobs.*
- *A focus group of newcomers to the area to determine how a newcomer selects a travel agency.*

Because focus groups allow interaction, there is less chance that participants will misinterpret questions and reduce the validity of the results. The main validity problem in focus groups is that participants may not express their true feelings because of the other participants' presence. This problem usually can be avoided by staying away from issues that involve personal or socially significant subjects.

A second validity concern with focus groups relates to the dynamics of a group discussion. A natural tendency to want a unanimous conclusion is often fostered by a dominant personality in the group. This problem can be minimized by having participants fill out individual questionnaires before the discussion, and by having the group moderator control the discussion so that no one person dominates.

The final validity concern relates to data recording. People are always somewhat more inhibited when it is obvious that what they say is being recorded.

It is generally best to tape-record sessions rather than take notes. Once it is explained that tape recording enables the focus group moderator to take notes later while paying attention now, the tape recorder can be placed out of view more easily than someone taking notes. In a few minutes, out of sight will be out of mind.

The possibilities for focus-group research are endless. They can be conducted in the office conference room, or after lunch at a quiet restaurant table. And getting participants will probably be the least of your problems. Most people feel that businesses don't ask them for their opinions and ideas nearly enough and are pleased when one does. And, though we all know there is no such thing as a free lunch, being fed just for putting in one's two cents' worth comes close.

SIMPLY SURVEYING

Scientific survey research can be very complex, with the issues ranging from sampling questions design to data analysis and interpretation. But this is no reason for a travel agency to avoid doing simple surveys that can be of great value, such as the telephone survey already mentioned.

Another example of extremely useful travel survey research is the customer-profile survey to be used in developing a customer database, which can be a valuable aid in planning and promotion.

The first task is to determine what information you want to have about your customers. A possible list of desired information might include:

- *Basic information such as name(s), address and phone number.*
- *Place of work (for future cross selling of commercial travel services).*

- *Past travel experiences and future preferences, including type of travel (cruise, escorted group, adventure travel, destination resort, etc.) and destinations (Europe, Hawaii, etc.).*
- *Local publications read, radio stations listened to, etc.*
- *Special interests (golf, tennis, theater, scuba diving, art, classical music, etc.).*
- *Demographic information (age range, marital status, family status, etc.).*

The customer profile involves the development of a questionnaire to be distributed to "qualified" customers of the agency. (Criteria should be established that make customers "earn" their way into your database.)

Some data collection devices, such as following up on customer satisfaction by telephone, may be within your competency and comfort level. But when in doubt, and if at all possible, enlist the help of someone with at least a little training in questionnaire development and design. The wisdom of this investment may be measured by the importance of future decisions to be based on the data collected. And the appropriate talent to design your data collection device may be as close as a local high school teacher or college professor, or a phone call away at an industry consulting firm.

Only a few travel agencies ever give market research more than a passing thought. That's a shame. It is an irony of business that those who can least afford to make a mistake caused by a lack of market knowledge are often the least likely to take preventive action, such as market research. By using existing data, focus groups and simple surveys, your agency can plan smarter, execute better and monitor progress in a more timely manner. No matter what your agency's size, it's never too late to start.

Reprinted courtesy of ASTA Agency Management Magazine, August 1991.

"I don't understand your attitude, sir— our market research indicates you're going to love this car."

The Research Instrument—Surveys and Questionnaires

Many travel organizations conduct primary research. Airlines continually contract for surveys, both of people flying on their airlines (in which case the traveler may be handed a questionnaire to fill out and return by mail) or of people at the airport. An airline may even survey the general public to obtain information on the attitudes of nontravelers as well as travelers. It is important to realize that the information obtained from a person who is at an airport or on an airplane may be quite different from the information returned from a sample of the general community in a shopping center.

If research is to be meaningful, it must meet the test of both **validity** and **reliability**. Research is valid when it provides answers to the questions it is meant to answer and is reliable when it is true of the segment of the population it is researching. For example, if you are trying to find out if people believe traveling is fun, you would not ask questions about whether they can afford it. Answers about cost will not be valid since they do not tell you anything about your goal of discovering if the respondents would like to travel. In terms of reliability, if your market is young singles and you include families in your sample, the results will not be reliable since the interests of families may be quite different from those of young singles.

Hotels also conduct frequent research, as do restaurants. Most hotels leave a form in the room to be filled out by the guest. Restaurants may leave an opinion card on the table, or at the cash register. This is done to obtain the guest's opinion of the service. Here it is important to remember that people fill these forms out and return them primarily when they have something specific to say (in most cases a complaint to make or, in some cases, a compliment over extraordinarily good service). The middle group of people who are satisfied but saw nothing particularly wrong or right generally do not bother to complete these forms. Therefore, the person analyzing the information on these returned forms must keep in mind that it is not a representative sample of all people who have stayed

"Uh—have I got this down right, then? When vacationing, you prefer Palm Springs for the holidays, Rio at Carnival, and Club Med for an occasional weekend?"

in that hotel or eaten in that restaurant. However, these questionnaires do go a long way toward helping an establishment correct problems and continue successful endeavors.

Surveys and **questionnaires** can be very meaningful tools when gathering specialized information. Survey, according to *Webster's Ninth New Collegiate Dictionary*, 1987, is to "examine as to condition, situation or value; to appraise; to query (someone) in order to collect data for the analysis of some aspect of a group or area." A questionnaire, which is one method of surveying, is "a set of questions for obtaining statistically useful or personal information from individuals."

However, it is important to create a valid questionnaire. If the questions are asked in a way that biases the answers, meaningful information will not be obtained. Questions are said to be biased if they are likely to evoke a specific response, rather than the respondents true feelings. Therefore, a questionnaire should either be written professionally or should be tested on a small sample before being sent to a large sample. Ambiguity must be eliminated and questions must be clearly stated.

To save money and increase accuracy, it is a good practice to test a small sample (perhaps up to 10%) before going into a large-scale effort. Thus, you can determine whether the questions are understandable and not ambiguous, whether the answers have any meaning, and whether the questionnaire is achieving reasonable results. After surveying the small sample, make any necessary changes in the survey instrument and go forward to a large, full-scale sample. However, it is important to realize that effective research has been done with fairly small samples and results have been found to be predictable for a larger group. Again, if you are looking for statistically meaningful results, it needs professional personnel expert in statistics. If, however you are just looking for some trends in a given market, it may be sufficient to ask people informally in that area. If research is being conducted in preparation for a large, expensive new marketing effort, it is, of course, advisable to spend more money for more accurate information.

Although market research is helpful and necessary, it is not infallible. We all know the stories of polls that showed the wrong political candidate to be the winner. Good market research, however, is correct most of the time.

Another type of primary research is the use of advisory councils and focus groups. Many travel companies, such as airlines, hotel companies and car rental firms have successfully used advisory panels for many years. For example, some hotel chains have more than one of these groups—one representing travel agencies and one for meeting planners. These groups meet one to three times per year with the company's marketing and sales executives to discuss the viewpoints and needs of the respective market. Potential advertising programs and other potential marketing promotions are shown to these groups and their reactions may cause a change or even a cancellation of the program.

Focus groups can be used when feedback is needed from a variety of potential customers. In a focus group, a specific agenda is planned to get input

HOW DO WE RATE?

Dear Hertz Customer:

Thank you for renting from Hertz.

We want to know how you feel about our service. Was your recent rental satisfactory? Did we measure up to your expectations? Is there some way in which our service could be improved?

If there is any reason why some aspect of our service to you was disappointing, please tell us. Your evaluation is important to us in our effort to improve our performance. Please give us your comments on the attached postage-paid return card.

We value your business as highly as we value your opinion about us. Thank you again for choosing Hertz for your car rental needs... and for taking the time to give us your comments.

Sincerely yours,

Craig R. Koch

Craig R. Koch

Executive Vice President
and General Manager
Rent A Car Division
The Hertz Corporation

HERTZ RENTS FORDS AND OTHER FINE CARS

1. City where car was rented _____

   Date _____ Time _____
   AIRPORT □   DOWNTOWN □   OTHER □

2. City where car was returned _____

   Date _____ Time _____
   AIRPORT □   DOWNTOWN □   OTHER □

3. Rental Agreement number? _____

4. Did you have a reservation? □ Yes □ No

5. How would you rate the courtesy and service of Hertz personnel?

	EXCELLENT	GOOD	FAIR	POOR
At Rental	□	□	□	□
At Return	□	□	□	□
On Courtesy Bus	□	□	□	□

6. If you booked an Express Rental, did it meet your expectations for faster service? How would you rate it in terms of quick service?

	EXCELLENT	GOOD	FAIR	POOR
At Rental	□	□	□	□
The Courtesy Bus	□	□	□	□

7. How long did you wait for the Hertz Courtesy Bus?

2 MINUTES OR LESS	3 TO 5 MINUTES	MORE THAN 5 MINUTES
□	□	□

8. How would you rate your rental vehicle?

	EXCELLENT	GOOD	FAIR	POOR
Cleanliness	□	□	□	□
Mechanical condition	□	□	□	□

9. Do you have any additional comments—good or bad—you would like to make about the service you received or the vehicle you rented?

   _____
   _____
   _____
   _____

   Your name and address (OPTIONAL)

   _____
   _____

   THANK YOU FOR YOUR TIME.
   PLEASE FOLD, SEAL AND MAIL IT TO ME.

TO MAIL: Refold, moisten, seal and drop in the mail. No postage is required.

on the reactions and opinions of the chosen market. For example, an airline might test a program on small groups of consumers representing different interests, such as corporate travelers from small and large corporations, upscale leisure travelers, and middle-income leisure travelers. Because the needs of these groups can differ, it is important to make sure that a program aimed at one will not "turn off" another unintentionally. A domino effect of problems and a waste of a large amount of promotional money can be avoided

WE VALUE YOUR OPINION

At Host we are committed to
providing the highest quality products
and services for our customers.
To help us evaluate our efforts we would
appreciate your telling us about
your visit today by taking a moment to
answer the questions on the
back of this card.
Thank you for being our customer.
We look forward to the opportunity
of serving you again.

Robert M. Dorfman

Robert M. Dorfman
Executive Vice President &
General Manager
Host International, Inc.

1. PLEASE RATE THE FOLLOWING FOR TODAY'S VISIT:

	Excellent	Above Average	Average	Below Average	Poor
Cleanliness	☐	☐	☐	☐	☐
Atmosphere	☐	☐	☐	☐	☐
Speed of service	☐	☐	☐	☐	☐
Friendliness of service	☐	☐	☐	☐	☐
Menu variety	☐	☐	☐	☐	☐
Taste of food	☐	☐	☐	☐	☐
Food quality	☐	☐	☐	☐	☐
Beverage quality	☐	☐	☐	☐	☐
Value for your money	☐	☐	☐	☐	☐
Facility Overall	☐	☐	☐	☐	☐

2. ADDITIONAL COMMENTS OR SUGGESTIONS:

_____

_____

_____

3. REASON FOR BEING AT THE AIRPORT TODAY:

Business trip	Pleasure trip	Meeting/ seeing off travellers	Other
☐	☐	☐	☐

4. IF TRAVELLING, WHAT AIRLINE ARE YOU USING?

_____

5. TODAY'S DATE: _____

6. TIME OF VISIT: _____ A.M. _____ P.M.

7. AIRPORT: _____

8. FACILITY: _____

PLEASE PRINT THE FOLLOWING INFORMATION (OPTIONAL):

Name: _____

Address: _____

City/State: _____ Zip: _____

Thank you very much for your comments. Your opinion will make a
difference. Please drop this card in the Comment Box before
you leave today.

HOST INTERNATIONAL, INC.
DEPARTMENT 928.69
ONE MARRIOTT DRIVE
WASHINGTON, D.C. 20058

if ideas are tested on sample panels representing the groups that will be affected before they are implemented.

Another example would be the planning of a brochure for a product aimed at middle-income senior citizens but which uses only young, glamorous models in the pictures. It will not be successful. A focus group of the target market—middle-income seniors—would have warned the company before it incurred large printing and distribution costs.

TRAVEL RESEARCH SOURCES

Organizations such as the Louis Harris agency run periodic research efforts to determine the habits of the traveling public. Once every two years, the Harris agency runs a survey on the travel agency industry for *Travel Weekly*, an industry newspaper. Another organization that has done some very important research in the field of travel is Menlo Consulting Group. This organization provides a great deal of meaningful information to travel organizations. Most of this information is available only to subscribers; however, some of it appears in publications such as the *Travel Market Yearbook*.

HISTORICAL RESEARCH

Another type of research is **historical**. This is research done by looking over the history of the organization and determining future trends from past practices. The one danger in using historical information is that situations may have changed and, therefore, what was true in the past may not be true (or useful) in the future. However, it is always a good idea to know where a company has been before it can decide where it should go. One example would be the case of an airline deciding whether to add another flight to a given destination. If history shows that they have had to turn away passengers on a regular basis, the time has probably come to add an additional flight for that route.

The same thing holds true for a hotel. If a hotel has consistently been full and had to turn away guests, then the time may have come to add a new wing. A hotel can also obtain meaningful information for market planning by analyzing where its guests have come from for the past year. Registration forms in the hotel's own files provide this data. The information can then be used to determine where to concentrate advertising dollars for the best results.

DEMOGRAPHICS VS. PSYCHOGRAPHIC INFORMATION

Demographics is statistical, objective information about a person, such as age, income, educational level, occupation, religion, family or home structure, or place of residence. This is the type of information usually requested at the beginning or the end of most questionnaires. **Demographic information** allows the researcher to analyze whether the results vary with such factors as different ages, incomes, or educational levels.

EMBARKATION CARD
(Must be completed prior to embarkation)

❏ MV HORIZON   ❏ SS MERIDIAN   ❏ MV ZENITH

SAILING DATE_____/_____/_____ CABIN #_____

LAST NAME_____

FIRST NAME_____MIDDLE INITIAL_____

ADDRESS_____

CITY_____STATE_____ ZIP_____

COUNTRY_____

DATE OF BIRTH_____/____/_____ PLACE OF BIRTH_____

U.S. CUSTOMS: Document provided (check one)

❏ Social Security number_____
(U.S. citizens/resident aliens)

❏ Passport number_____
(non-U.S. citizens)

U.S. IMMIGRATION: (check one)

❏ U.S. Citizen
❏ Alien Green Card holder (complete passport information below)
❏ Non-U.S. Citizen (complete passport information below)

Passport number_____

Passport issuing country_____

❏ MALE   ❏ FEMALE
❏ SINGLE   ❏ MARRIED   ❏ SEPARATED/DIVORCED/WIDOWED

INCOME (Household)   OCCUPATION (Prior occupation if retired)
❏ $75,000 +   ❏ MANAGERIAL / PROFESSIONAL
❏ $50-74,999   ❏ TECHNICAL / SALES
❏ $35-49,999   ❏ TRAVEL INDUSTRY EMPLOYEE
❏ $34,999   ❏ SERVICE ❏ HOMEMAKER
                             ❏ CRAFTSMAN / INDUSTRIAL
ARE YOU   ❏ STUDENT ❏ SELF EMPLOYED
❏ FIRST TIME CRUISER   ❏ RETIRED
❏ EXPERIENCED CRUISER
❏ REPEAT CELEBRITY CRUISER   ARE YOU A CAPTAIN'S CLUB
❏ TRAVELING   MEMBER? ❏ YES ❏ NO
   WITH CHILDREN   MEMBER #_____

HOW DID YOU LEARN   WHAT WAS THE DECIDING
ABOUT CELEBRITY CRUISES?   FACTOR IN TAKING THIS CRUISE?
❏ NEWSPAPER ❏ MAGAZINE   ❏ TRAVEL AGENT RECOMMENDATION
❏ RADIO ❏ BROCHURE   ❏ FRIEND / RELATIVE RECOMMENDATION
❏ OTHER ADVERTISING   ❏ PRICE
❏ TRAVEL AGENT   ❏ ITINERARY
❏ FRIEND / RELATIVE   ❏ OTHER (Specify)_____

SIGNATURE_____

PASSENGER DOCUMENTATION & EMBARKATION INFORMATION

Celebrity cruises is pleased to enclose your documentation. Please check carefully and advise your travel agent of any discrepancy. You must complete the information on the reverse and present this card at embarkation.

RECONFIRM FLIGHTS: If you are flying to the port, call the airline at least 72 hours prior to departure as flight scedules may change. Your return flight will be automatically reconfirmed. Consult airline for check-in times.

BAGGAGE: Fill out the baggage tags completely and securely attach to each piece of luggage, including carry-on bags. This makes it easy for airline and cruise representatives to identify you as our valued client.

PROOF OF CITIZENSHIP: For U.S. Immigration, all U.S. and Canadian citizens require either (1) a valid passport or (2) a certified birth certificate supported by a picture ID such as a driver's license. Non-U.S. citizens (including resident aliens) require a valid passport and necessary visas. Resident aliens should also carry their alien registration card.

U.S. CUSTOMS: For U.S. Customs, all U.S. citizens and resident aliens require their U.S. Social Security number. Canadian and other non-U.S. citizens require a valid passport number. All passengers will be required to clear their baggage through U.S. customs when returning to the United States.

TRANSFERS (Air/Sea passengers only): Roundtrip transfers will be provided on day of embarkation and disembarkation between airport and ship. Representatives will be on hand to assist you.

Thank you for choosing a Celebrity Cruise. You can be sure that we will do our best to make your cruise memorable.

BON VOYAGE!

IN CASE OF EMERGENCY, PLEASE CONTACT

NAME_____

TELEPHONE (   )_____

Psychographic information is more subjective information about the respondent. It includes three types of information—activities, interests, and opinions (AIO). Psychographic questions try to determine what activities respondents enjoy, what their interests are, and what their opinions are. Questions that request a respondent to rate an opinion of something on a scale of 1 to 5 are obtaining psychographic information.

This information is becoming more and more important as the public is given a wider variety of products from which to choose. The danger is that impartial questions are very hard to create, and very often respondents answer as they think the surveyor expects them to, rather than as they really feel. For example, when people are asked what television shows they watch, answers to these questions on surveys differ quite markedly from results that are obtained from recorders attached to their television sets. People very often want the interviewer to believe that they are watching a "classier" show than the situation comedy they are really enjoying. The same thing holds true in travel. People's attitudes toward what they really want to do may be different from what they think they should say. Therefore, psychographic questionnaires or interviews must be very carefully developed if they are to gather accurate, meaningful, useful information.

MARKET SEGMENTATION

Market research makes it possible to analyze a market and divide it into separate parts. The consuming public is made up of many different parts, or segments. Young, single persons comprise quite a different segment from senior citizens or young families. To avoid wasting valuable resources, it is important for a marketing manager to segment this market so that products can be developed that are "right" for each target market, and so that promotional resources can be properly allocated to each specific market.

External Market Segmentation

Travel has a universal appeal, but few travel products themselves are universally appealing. This is because travel is so varied that almost all of the public can find some type of travel that satisfies their needs. However, a specific travel product may have a very limited appeal. For example, a single's tour that appeals to the young bachelor will be quite different from one that appeals to the seventy-year-old widow. When researching a potential market, it is necessary to segment it as much as possible so that products can be developed to appeal to each specific **target market**. This process is called **external market segmentation**.

Once the target market is identified, it is then possible to tailor the product itself. Members of this market may be surveyed concerning their desires and needs for travel, and a product created that answers these needs.

Once these needs have been identified, it becomes important to find a way to inform the members of this target market that the product exists and will meet their needs. This is done by researching what media serves this segment of the public. If, for example, the product is one that will appeal to golfers or tennis players, the marketing manager may advertise in golfing or tennis magazines. Ads for these products would be wasted in another type of publication (an arts and crafts magazine, for example). This does not mean that some readers of an arts and crafts magazine might not also be golfers or tennis players, but rather that the majority of readers will not be in the target market.

Another type of external market segmentation is that of geography. Certain products appeal to people from particular geographic areas. For example, a majority of the visitors to Bermuda comes from the northeast section of the United States; few visitors are from the West. For this reason, Bermuda advertises and promotes its tourism product heavily in the Northeast. Similarly, most United States visitors to New Zealand come from the West Coast, so New Zealand concentrates its marketing efforts there. Thus, the value of promotional expenditures is maximized. Finding a new market and promoting it is extremely expensive, and not always successful. The risks are frequently not worth the potential gain. Market research, carefully and correctly done, can minimize those risks.

Internal Market Segmentation

Within any business, several products are usually marketed. These are known as the product lines of the company. For a hotel, there is the business travel market, the individual or family vacation market, and, perhaps, the business travel meeting or convention market. An airline may have the same type of segmentation. In addition, however, an airline must look at its different destinations and routes as separate market segments. A restaurant might segment its product line into family diners, young singles, and older couples. They also might segment their product into the food segment and the liquor segment. A travel agency might be marketing products such as domestic air, international air, tours, commercial travel, groups, cruises, rail, or bus tours. Cruise lines segment their market into families, singles, senior citizens, wealthy professionals, and so forth. Different marketing techniques and promotional vehicles must be used for different segments, because the motivations and needs of users vary for each segment. This process of tailoring marketing and promotional techniques to fit a specific segment is called **internal market segmentation**. See the "Industry Communiques" for a discussion of growing segments of the travel and tourism market.

For effective management of the marketing effort, it is important to analyze internal market segments and determine the profitability of each one. While a business may be making a profit, certain product lines may be losing money. A marketing manager must determine the profitability of each product line so that unproductive lines may be changed or eliminated. When a hotel finds a particular segment of the market to be more profitable, it should try to increase that segment of its market. See the "Industry Communique" for one example of a market segment. The same is true for other parts of the industry. When an airline finds a particular route unprofitable, it will reduce its service or eliminate that route and replace it with one that it hopes will be more profitable. Any business has a limited amount of resources. These resources should be focused on profitable product segments. This type of market analysis, however, must be ongoing, because conditions in the market change.

Las Vegas is a good example of how a market segment can change. Before the days of Howard Hughes, most Las Vegas hotels lost money on their room and food segments and made all their profit on their gambling segment. When Howard Hughes bought the Dunes hotel, he analyzed this situation and determined that each segment of the operation should be profitable on its own. This resulted in the elimination of extremely inexpensive rooms and food for the small gambler. Room rates went up to the normal rates for luxury hotels. The restaurants in the hotel also began to show a profit. Only the "high roller" gamblers continued to get the benefits of cheap (often free) rooms and food. These rooms were then charged against the operating expenses of the casinos. Each segment of the hotel showed its own profit, and the overall profit of the operations increased.

Today, many travel industry companies have created several brands within their overall product to emphasize the differences to the varied target market segments. Choice Hotels, for example, even changed the name of the company to state that their products provided a "choice" for the consumer. Their brands—Clarion, Quality, Comfort, Sleep, Rodeway, Econo Lodge, and Friendship—are aimed at a continuum of price and amenity desires of the consumer. Their Sleep Inns provide a clean room and bath with few amenities and low price, whereas their Clarion brand provides a much higher-scale product with full capabilities for meetings, upscale restaurants on property, and other up-scale features.

"This vacation was made to order for a travel agent—a cruise to nowhere with Kevin Costner!"

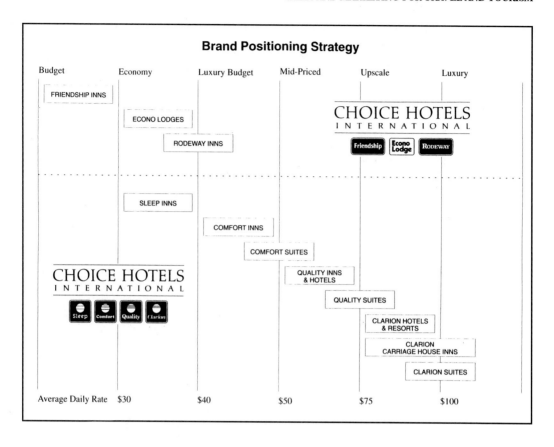

INDUSTRY COMMUNIQUE

A CHOICE MOVE FOR QUALITY

Griffin Miller

Ask Bob Hazard [Chairman and CEO, Choice Hotels] what he feels his greatest achievement is within the hotel industry, and he assuredly says segmentation. Under his guidance, Quality International pioneered the segmentation concept when it brought limited-service Comfort Inn properties on-line in 1981. From that point on, the Choice system has achieved far-reaching growth, going from 339 roadside inns to more than 2,400 inns, hotels, suites, and resorts—all in under 10 years.

"The key is understanding the market," states Hazard. "People don't want or expect a single property to be everything to everybody, which is why I feel the independents are on the way out. Segmentation lets the consumer know exactly what to expect. In the 1990s, I predict segmentation will extend even further until we have more segmentation—super-segmentation!"

Hazard's enthusiasm, as it happens, is well-founded. Today, Choice International has a product to appeal to every level of traveler. The company has divided its now seven brands—having acquired Rodeway Inns, Econo Lodges, and Friendship Inns in the summer of 1990—into two lodging groups. The Sunburst Group consists of Comfort Inns, Quality Inns, Clarion Hotels and Resorts and Sleep Inns. The Economy Group includes Econo Lodges, Rodeway Inns and Friendship Inns. Hazard contends none of the brands is in direct competition, as each offers a different rate scale and has the potential to appeal to different types of customers. From the economy-priced Friendship Inns to luxurious Clarion Resorts, Choice Hotels now offers a brand for virtually every price-point and every consumer taste.

"Our acquisition of Econo Lodges, Rodeway and Friendship Inns came at a good time in terms of the corporate name change," observes [Gerald] Petitt [President and COO, Choice Hotels]. "Because the brands are already recognized as established economy properties with their own brand identities when we brought them in, they fit well with the idea of 'choice.' It emphasizes our desire not to be tied to one brand, as we were when operating under 'Quality International.'"

Adds Frederick W. Mosser, executive vice president of development and an officer of Choice Hotels International: "We're going to be focusing on the Economy Group's brands in terms of image and the public's awareness in the marketplace. Our two lodging groups will generally be marketed separately yet share the same reservation system through Choice Hotels, as well as most other support operations. Of course this means all of our brands now have the marketing clout of a 2,400-plus property chain vs. a 150 or even 600-property chain."

Choice's marketing strategy is obviously paying off. Last year, room sales jumped from $898 million to $1,079 billion over the previous year (up 20.1 percent), and even its Clarion hotels, designed to appeal to upscale leisure and business travelers, managed to do well, *despite* the belt-tightening trend presently taking place in the corporate world. "Our good fortune probably comes from the fact that Clarions are not aimed at the super-luxury market, but rather at the bottom end of the luxury market," says Hazard, noting that the Clarion market is really far more diverse than one might think. "With segmentation there is always the temptation to categorize guests—a Clarion guest, a Comfort guest, and so on. But this is a mistake. A person driving to Florida might stay at Comfort Inns en route, but will stay at a Clarion once they arrive at their destination," observes Hazard. "Conversely, an individual attending a business meeting at a Clarion might turn around and book a Comfort hotel for a family trip."

On the whole, Hazard and Petitt are satisfied with the results of their combined marketing strategies. "We feel strongly about our efforts over the past nine years," says Petitt. "Clearly, we run higher occupancies because of our marketing techniques and we lead the competition in generating business for licensees. Admittedly, it takes some aggression on our part, but in this business that's what's needed most often than not: aggression and a sense of timing. If the rest of the industry is sitting back, playing it cautious, that's our cue to strike. We're going to be the first ones out of the starting gate."

PREDICTIONS

With a new century less than a decade away, Choice Hotels International is looking ahead. Having laid the groundwork for global growth and expanded segmentation, the company is now gearing up for projects that will take it even further into the future.

"Three things are going to shape the hotel market over the next 10 years," forecasts Petitt. "Number one is consolidation. By the year 2000, we'll have 10,000 hotels and a million guest rooms. We're on the way to creating a handful of multi-brand, multi-national chains. Linked together by a mammoth reservation system, these mega-chains will have awesome marketing muscle, so much so that the few independents that do survive will—by necessity—gravitate to the security offered by the superpowers.

"Number two is segmentation, and you'll continue to see clearer definitions of segments because they'll need to be marketed to the 5 billion people who inhabit planet Earth.

"And number three," says Petitt, "is globalization. For those in the lodging industry the choice is pretty clear-cut—go global or go nowhere."

Reprinted courtesy of Hotel & Resort Industry, September 1990.

INDUSTRY COMMUNIQUE

DON'T OVERLOOK THE BUYING POWER OF SENIOR CITIZENS

David C. Dorf, CHSE

The hotel industry has long viewed the senior citizens market as a "last resort" business potential. With some notable exceptions, few hotels include senior citizens in their primary market mix because of the assumption that people over the age of 60 simply sit at home and don't travel.

However, with the number of senior citizens continuing to increase dramatically as we approach the 21st century, society is changing its attitude toward older people. No longer are they considered non-active members of society. They are living longer and leading fuller, richer lives.

With the growth of the senior citizens market, it is now vitally important for hotels to direct more of their sales and marketing efforts toward these people. For a property to acquire more business from senior citizens, it is necessary to consider:

- *The size and scope of the senior citizen market today.*
- *Market projections at the turn of the next century.*
- *How to cultivate this market.*
- *How to sell to it.*
- *How to service it.*
- *How to win referral business.*
- *How to get return business.*

FACTS ABOUT U.S. SENIOR CITIZENS

A statistical look at the senior citizens market will help hotel sales executives make intelligent projections for the future. The four main demographic factors to concentrate on are age, sex, marital status and income. It is also important to note that the United States will be the main supplier of senior citizens traveling throughout the world.

The U.S. Census Bureau reports that one person in 10 in the United States currently is 65 or older. Based on this statistic, it has projected that by 1990, 31.1 million people, or 12.7 percent, will be over 65, and by the year 2000 the number will reach 35 million or 13 percent. Looking farther ahead, by the year 2030, 21.2 percent of the population, or 64.6 million people, will be over the age of 65.

These statistics represent an enormous reserve of people who can bring real dollars into a property.

In a detailed 1983 census bureau breakdown, almost 60 percent of the then 26 million senior citizens in the United States were female. Fifty-seven percent of these 26 million people were married, but of the more than 11 million who were single, (i.e. never married, divorced, or widowed), more than *7.5 million were widowed women.* These women represented 68 percent of the single 65-and-over segment and 30 percent of the entire senior citizen market.

The increase in the average life span has created a new market sub-segment, the super senior citizen, age 85 or older. At the present time, this group represents only a little more than one percent of the total population or about three million people. By the year 2000, the number is expected to increase to almost five million, and by the year 2050, it will jump to 16 million.

With these figures in mind, the questions to ask are, "Will senior citizens travel? Will they use airlines? Will they bring money into hotel and travel destinations?" Obviously not all elderly people will be frequent travelers, but the majority will travel and many will travel extensively.

SENIOR CITIZENS ABROAD

Statistics concerning the senior citizen population of other countries show similar findings. Canadian marketing executives view senior citizens as "the mass market leisure class," and they have high expectations for "affluent free-spending retirees." Canadian figures show that in 1985, 10.3 percent of the population was 65 or older and by the year 2000 it is expected to increase to 13.4 percent. While the number of senior citizens will increase, the number of people ages 25 to 44 is expected to decrease.

In European countries the percentage increases of senior citizens are equally impressive. In 1982, 14 percent of European citizens were over age 65. This will increase to 17 percent by the year 2000.

In France the number of people over 60 is expected to increase from 10 million in 1985 to 12 million by the year 2000. It will jump another three million in seven years, and another two million in three years; bringing the total to 17 million by the year 2020. And the number of super senior citizens in France will be more than one million at the turn of the century.

DISCRETIONARY INCOME: A MARKETING FACTOR

These statistics provide some of the necessary background information on which hoteliers can base their business projections. However, income is probably the most important factor in forecasting how much business senior citizens can provide for hotels. Leisure travelers spend discretionary dollars—that is, the money remaining after necessary expenses are paid for—and of all age categories in the United States, senior citizens have the greatest amount of annual disposable income per person. The yearly per person figure is $5,633 for people 65 or older, almost twice that of any other group under age 40.

MARKETING TO SENIOR CITIZENS

Before hotel sales executives begin to try to attract the senior citizens market, they must decide if they want this type of business, and if so, to what degree. Jim Murray, CHSE, director of marketing at Grossinger's, suggests hoteliers consider the following questions.

1. Is this a desirable market for the property? Are there "off periods" that could be filled, realizing a sacrifice in rate and the possible necessity of physical changes in the property?...This market can be turned on and off to fill the valleys...

2. Can the property afford the "mix" of this market with its other markets? Large numbers of this market (may) influence the desired image of the property.

If a property decides that it wants its share of this market segment, it will need to incorporate it within its marketing plan.

As hotel sales executives develop programs to attract senior citizens to their properties, they must determine whether or not their product will meet the specific needs and requirements of that market. If the property does not meet these needs, they must decide if it is feasible and profitable to invest in capital improvements, if necessary, to accommodate senior citizens properly.

The quality of staff, service, and training are important ingredients of the product. This is especially important in optimizing the satisfaction level of the senior citizens market, particularly for developing both repeat and referral business.

To attract and retain the senior citizens market, hotel sales executives must be constantly aware of changing trends in demographics; psychographics; interests, opinions, and attitudes; and sensation-seeking levels.

Psychographics, which is qualitative lifestyle profiling, is another tool for studying market changes. In the last few years, there has been a dramatic shift in the lifestyle of many senior citizens. They are no longer sedentary, non-active people, but rather those who are seeking a wide variety of highly participative activities.

In addition to being aware of the interests, opinions and attitudes of senior citizens, the hotel sales executive must be sensitive to the sensation-seeking characteristics of the senior citizens market. Previous sales efforts to attract this market centered around the "3.5" comfort syndrome: safety, security and shelter—the psychology of the familiar. Today, however, many senior citizens are seeking something different, challenging or exotic. Destinations being promoted to senior citizens now include Alaska, China, Russia, India and other exotic or adventuresome places.

In general, there are four types of senior citizen travelers—independent self-sufficients, group self-sufficients, social dependents, and physical dependents. As senior citizens become more travel knowledgeable and travel sophisticated, the growth potential will be the strongest in the first two categories.

To attract senior citizen travelers, hotel sales executives must develop strategies that meet their needs and concerns and offer values in terms of benefits and needs satisfaction. The three main categories of needs are: tangible (quantifiable), intangible (perceived), and manufactured (manipulative).

Included under tangible needs are dates, accommodations, food and beverage outlets; special furnishings, services, and amenities; entertainment and sightseeing. Intangible needs include variety, escape, excitement, romance, comfort, relaxation, education, fulfillment, and activity. Needs that are manufactured relate to exclusiveness, trendiness, status, ego, and conformity.

Before a hotel can sell, service, and satisfy the needs of senior citizens, it must determine which are the most critical to them. It must study the trends, note the changes, note significant factors about the market itself, and then utilize this information in its marketing activities.

Reprinted courtesy of HSMAI Marketing Review, Fall 1988.

INDUSTRY COMMUNIQUE

WIN BY UNDERSTANDING THE SPECIAL NEEDS MARKET

Jack B. Ralph

Do you know the personal characteristics and special needs of your market? Do you know how to capitalize on these characteristics and meet these special needs, or do you mistakenly assume that every prospect can be treated the same? To think that everyone can be treated the same is like swimming with alligators— in time you can get bitten.

Many sales departments assume that everyone has 20/20 "normal" vision or has glasses which are corrected to 20/20. Everyone can read any size print with no difficulty. No one is red, green, or blue color deficient ("blind"). The same amount of light or intensity of a reflected printed image reaches the retina, regardless of the reader's age. The amount of contrast between the print and the background does not affect readability. Paper glare from brochures does not reduce readability. No one's vision is affected by cataracts or by one or more of the many visual problems. Everyone is comfortable reading the modern type styles and has no difficulty with italics and cursive. Everyone can read and understand vocabulary rated at about the 11th grade level. Travelers who can afford to stay at the property are not functionally illiterate. They have no difficulty understanding the meaning of "double, double," "packages," and other jargon of the trade.

Of course, they have perfect hearing. No one needs a hearing aid. No one is deaf. They can speak up if they want something. They are not mobility impaired or frail.

If you believe it, you are losing money!

The fastest growing segment of the traveling and meeting market is waiting for you to get and to keep if you satisfy its special needs.

You must ask your sales department some direct questions. To start with, can the CEO of your client organization see and read the brochures you send concerning your room rates and meeting facilities? Have you mistakenly used light blue ink for the text on your brochures? Can the CEO see and read the contracts which must be signed?

How do you book the 21,000,000 deaf or hard of hearing persons in the United States when they call you on the telephone? (Some properties such as the Ramada or Holiday Inn chains have a central reservation number (TDD/TTY) for the deaf.) And, when the deaf person gets into the property, how does he or she receive telephone calls through the switchboard if the call is from outside the property? Do you know how to set up a meeting for the deaf and hard of hearing attendees?

Is your staff trained to reserve a room for and then offer services to people who cannot speak clearly because of a laryngectomy or because they stutter?

Do blind clients make a return visit to your hotel after your housekeeper, with only the best intentions, has moved their personal items from their original place on the wash basin?

Are your health rooms and disco accessible by wheel chair?

Have you installed baseboard lighting in darkened lounges and restaurants to prevent accidents?

Are the front edges of your stairs and staircases tipped with a contrasting color? Have you advised your property engineers to install grab bars in the bath tub to guard against slipping which leads to expensive liability claims?

It is apparent that failure to meet the special needs of hotel guests is the by-product of industry-wide lack of knowledge and sensitivity as well as an undervaluation of the size and potential of the special needs market.

The attitude of many hotel sales and marketing executives is: "It's only a discount market. We don't need it." Even if it is a discount business, which it is not, even discount business is helpful if you are confronted with an off-season 40 percent occupancy.

For example, one hotel chain was able to book over 35,000 deaf clients in a year because they were able to reserve rooms by calling on a special central TDD published phone line.

Very simply stated, when special needs are met and the effort is encouraged by the sales and marketing department, there is an increase in new and repeat business, reduction in printing costs, and liability claims, and more prestige for the property. Hotels and convention centers gain additional business, and convention and visitors bureaus attract more travelers to the community.

Reprinted courtesyof HSMAI Marketing Review, Fall 1988.

CONCLUSION

Market research does not have to be expensive or sophisticated. It is, however, a necessary part of marketing management. When a company is considering introducing a new product or greatly changing an existing one, money spent on research will be very well spent and should result in an ultimate financial savings.

To effectively market any product, it is necessary to segment the market, both externally and internally. Without knowledge of the needs of the potential consumer, much time, effort, and money will be wasted. Only with the ability to determine the profitability of each product line can a business be sure of maximizing its profits.

SUMMARY

Market research is the systematic gathering and analysis of information about potential customers. It can be formal or informal, and cost a great deal or very little. Information may be obtained from two sources:

1. Primary research, done yourself through phone surveys, or questionnaires;
2. Secondary research, in which information is derived from such things as censuses or United States Travel Data Center studies.

Sophisticated primary data is expensive to gather and analyze, and is usually used by large segments of the travel industry, such as airlines or hotel chains. A small company may gather some primary data inexpensively, however, by observing the lifestyle of the surrounding community. In addition, historical research may provide useful information.

Demographic data is statistical and objective. Psychographic data is more subjective in nature, dealing with people's attitudes. This second kind of information has become increasingly important as the number of choices consumers face rises. Psychological questionnaires must be carefully formulated and tested to produce valid results.

Information derived from market research allows the company to segment, or divide, the market into different parts, to decide what portion of it will be most responsive to a specific product. External market segmentation refers to such divisions such as age, interests, or geography. Internal market segmentation refers to such divisions such as, for hotel, the business travel, family vacation, and convention markets.

QUESTIONS FOR THOUGHT AND DISCUSSION

1. Compare primary and secondary research. What are the advantages and disadvantages of each?

2. How can historical research help in marketing decisions within travel? Give three examples of travel businesses that could benefit from this type of research.

3. Define demographics and discuss how this information can be used meaningfully within at least one segment of the travel industry.

4. Define psychographics and describe how this research can help in marketing travel products.

5. Describe the criteria of validity and reliability in terms of market research.

6. Discuss market segmentation—both internal and external—and discuss how a business should use this information.

7. a. If you are in a restaurant, a hotel, or any place where a questionnaire is provided, bring the form in for discussion. Note where you received it and what your own comments would be in completing this form. How can this information help the business?

   b. Design a short questionnaire for a hotel, restaurant, or airline to use to determine customer satisfaction.

5

Image

image
logo
product differentiation
public perception
value judgment

In marketing, image is everything. When the truth differs from the public's perception of a product, it is the public perception—the image—that will determine that product's success or failure. It is critical for any business, in the travel industry or any other industry, to maintain a positive image with the public it is trying to serve. Unfortunately, it takes constant work to maintain a positive image. Negative images, on the other hand, can arise very quickly and are very difficult to overcome.

What is image? Image is nothing more than the mental picture the public has of the company or product. Many times, in the history of the travel industry, an undesired or inappropriate image has hurt a hotel, airline, sightseeing attraction, restaurant, travel agency, or destination.

IMAGE PROBLEMS

Safety

In the 1970s, Jamaica and the Virgin Islands suffered greatly from the American public's perception of those areas as places of danger and political hostility. Local events outside the tourist areas occurred and were featured in United States newspapers. Reports of shootings among the local people and about political unrest appeared. These events were reported in a way that convinced the public that it would be physically dangerous to travel to these destinations. The fact that the tourist areas were quite safe was unimportant. The public, when confronted with potential danger, does not take chances. Hotel occupancy plummeted. As occupancy levels fell, money was not available for necessary improvements to the hotels, and reports of inadequate facilities came back from those willing to chance the destination. The cycle resulted in a downward spiral, and many hotels in both destinations were forced to close. Only in the early 1980s did those destinations begin to make a comeback. The cost of image problems such as these to an area was immeasurable. From the early 1970s to the present, Northern Ireland, in spite of its beauty and wonderful people, cannot attract tourists from the United States in meaningful numbers because of fears of terrorism. In the 1980s, fears of terrorism in Europe and the Middle East occurred. This devastated tourism to those areas several times in the decade. In 1991, the Persian Gulf War kept people home because there were fears of terrorism even in domestic areas. In 1993, a terrorist campaign in Egypt has been specifically directed at tourists, with devastating effects on that country's most important industry. Similar problems exist in many parts of the world where there is political turmoil.

The United States Department of State has, for many years, issued travel advisories on countries that have situations that might cause problems for traveling Americans. Such problems might be anything from a cholera epidemic to political unrest. These travel advisories immediately create uncertainty and fear in potential travelers to such areas and result in a decrease (sometimes slight and sometimes enormous) in such travel. Unfortunately, the State Department does not always make the area of trouble clear and an entire country suffers because of a problem in one remote area. Also, these advisories are not always lifted as soon as they should be. Furthermore, some experts believe that American political agendas may, in some cases, have an unwarranted effect, either positive or negative, on the issuance of such advisories. Therefore, it is critical for companies involved with travel to areas that may be affected by these advisories to be fully knowledgeable about the advisories and to advise consumers traveling to affected areas about any known problems.

Cost

Incorrect perception of costs can be another type of image problem. Some destinations have an image of great cost. For example, many people on the East Coast of the United States perceive Hawaii as a very expensive destination. In fact, it is one of the best values for resort hotels and restaurants. The primary reason for this incorrect image is the relatively high air fare from the East to Hawaii. Most inexperienced travelers assume that the hotels will cost as much as those in the Caribbean and that the overall trip will therefore be too expensive. Hotels in Hawaii must work constantly to correct this image.

Product Differentiation

Airlines, which sell basically identical products, work to sell the public on their image. Both Delta and American Airlines have used advertising promotions emphasizing the care that their employees give to their customers. Studies of the traveling public show that there is actually little difference among major carriers in their service levels, but the advertisements try to promote these slight image differences as much as possible. In 1979, after an accident involving the DC-10 airplane and the subsequent fear of much of the traveling public about flying on this particular aircraft, airlines that did not fly DC-10s promoted the fact. There was a perceived image in the public's mind of greater safety, when, in reality, the carriers promoting the lack of the DC-10 in their fleet had virtually identical safety records to those that flew the aircraft. On-time performances between the number 1 airline in the statistics and the next one may be a fraction of a percent, but it is enough to make a difference in advertising and perception.

It is necessary, in these competitive times, to create a perception of some beneficial difference from competitors. The consumer is confused by the huge number of seemingly similar products and companies. As Bob Hazard, CEO of Choice Hotels, observed in a speech to Choice franchisees in 1991: "Rule number two for success is *develop a competitive point of difference.* What makes your inn or hotel different and better than your competitor down the street? What is your unique sustainable competitive advantage? Why do people buy from you instead of the competition? That's your challenge." This is the challenge to all companies wanting to thrive in a competitive world.

If a hotel has an image as a commercial or convention property, it might find that vacation guests do not visit. On the other hand, if the hotel has a reputation as a vacation hotel for individuals, it will find that business meetings pass it by. It generally takes a great expenditure of both time and promotional funds to change an image. However, some companies have been successful in doing so. Holiday Inns have successfully attracted business and convention visitors, after many years of an image as a family hotel.

Hotel chains have wrestled with the problem of a corporate image for a long time. Some have tried to let the public know of their different levels by using different names, such as Choice Hotels with its seven brands and Marriott with its lower-priced Courtyard and Fairfield Inn brands. Others have tagged on a word for the deluxe line that can differentiate it, such as Hyatt with its Hyatt Regency

"This hotel aims for a homey image."

properties. Some, such as Sheraton, are aware of the inconsistent image their properties have in the consumers' and travel agents' minds and have been working to try to gain more consistency in their product. To set off their truly deluxe properties, such as the St. Regis Hotel in New York, they do not even use "Sheraton" in the hotel's name.

FOSTERING AN IMAGE

It is also important to remember that many images are neither positive or negative. The value judgment differs with the attitudes of differing segments of the public. What is quaint to one may be simply old to another. What one sees as modern and streamlined may seem, to another, cold and "plastic." To one traveler, a nude beach is exciting and modern; to another it is immoral and decadent. The important message here is that few places can promote an image that will appeal to all potential travelers. It is necessary for a hotel, airline, destination or other travel company to decide what type of clientele it wishes to attract and then to be sure that all of its promotional efforts help foster the image that will appeal to that market segment.

EMPLOYEES AND IMAGE

In all too many cases, the image promoted with very expensive advertising budgets is rendered ineffective by employees who do not conform to the intended image. The hotel trying to convince the public that its employees will pamper guest and

"What we have here is an image problem. We need more advertising!"

cater to their every desire will not keep that image for long when guests come home complaining about sullen and uncaring front desk personnel. It is critical for any company to train its personnel to reflect its desired image, and to control the quality of employees as far as possible. Disney is renowned for its "Gracious Hospitality" image and the "Disney Smile." Radisson has, for several years, trained its staff in their "Yes, I Can" philosophy. A pleasant, helpful employee adds greatly to the positive image a business is trying to convey. The front desk person at the hotel, the flight attendant serving the passenger, the guide at the amusement park, the counselor in a travel agency, and all other travel industry front line people are the final controllers of the image the guest will take home. All the advertising in the world will not make up for inadequacies of personnel. Money spent on initial training and regular refresher training is necessary to maintain a positive image. It is not enough to train a new employee in this philosophy and to expect it to last without regular ongoing reminders.

NAMES, LOGOS, AND SIGNS

The name a company chooses and the logo or design symbol it uses is very important to the image conveyed and sometimes to the very success or failure of the company. A name can convey a valuable image: see the "Industry Communiques" on what the name "Ritz" has meant in the hotel industry. Names can convey the very activity that the company provides (the amusement park "Wet 'N' Wild"). The name can help to give an image of security and quality, such as "Quality Inn." On the other hand, a name can be misleading, such as a vacation travel agency named "Sun and Fun Tours" that now decides to market to commercial business. A corporation will not feel too comfortable having its business travel handled by "Sun and Fun Tours".

INDUSTRY COMMUNIQUE

A RITZ BY ANY OTHER NAME

Tom Edmonds

One of the travel industry's better-known competitions features the Ritz-Carlton Hotel Co. versus Four Seasons Hotels and Resorts. An agent might well be puzzled, then, to find that the Ritz-Carlton Chicago is managed by Four Seasons.

"We gave them the name and the license." says a grim Horst H. Schulze, president and COO of the Ritz-Carlton chain. "We can inspect the hotel to assure ourselves that it is run to Ritz-Carlton standards, but we will never let that happen again."

The Chicago situation may be the least of Ritz-Carlton's identity problems, however, given the use of the Ritz name in several other properties. The eight-year-old Ritz-Carlton company is in the unique position of attempting to build a global business with a brand name that is not entirely private property. Because the Ritz name was in the public domain for a number of years, a variety of well-known hospitality companies are operating Ritz hotels today.

"In the beginning there was a lot of confusion," Schulze concedes. "We tried to work it out to avoid clashes, but we did get a bad rap from some travel agents because hotels we have no connection with weren't paying commissions."

Schulze figures, though, that the benefits associated with the Ritz name overwhelm any inconvenience. In almost any case, a Ritz is a five-star property. "Can you imagine the marketing cost to get the kind of image we enjoy?" he asks.

Ritz-Carlton management, which has opened 10 properties in the last 12 months, cannot establish properties all over the globe without resolving the name issue in those local markets where a Ritz or Ritz-Carlton is already established.

FORGING AN IDENTITY

Schulze describes how his company has had to modify its international expansion plans to accommodate competitors who already control the name. Ritz-Carlton is prohibited from using its corporate name in England, Canada, France and Spain. "We have the rights to the name in 140 countries," Schulze says. "That doesn't mean we cannot have a hotel there, but we cannot call it Ritz-Carlton."

The company is getting around that restriction by calling its property now under construction in Barcelona the Hotel Arts by Ritz-Carlton.

According to one independent Ritz operator, identity confusion is a non-issue as long as each property maintains standards that would not disappoint Cesar Ritz, the legendary founder of the old Ritz Hotels. "We all share the same name, but that hasn't been a problem because the majority of the Ritzes, especially in the last few years, have lived up to the name," says Stanley C. Yen, president of the Ritz Asia company, which is based in Taiwan and is unrelated to the Ritz-Carlton management company.

WHO GETS CHOCOLATE COOKIES?

Although this chain is attempting to deliver elegant service in the European tradi-tion, Schulze—European himself—says there's an important distinction between Ritz-Carlton and the traditional European hotel.

"We don't really think the same way," he explains. "We are saying a European hotel is elegance number one. We want to be warm and relaxed first and then elegant. I always say elegance without warmth is arrogance. It really is, and it probably doesn't belong in our industry. Elegance alone probably exists a lot more in European hotels. That's not what we're striving for at all."

ASTA Agency Management, November 1991.

Some companies have been able to overcome an image that their name would be expected to convey and have made their names almost generic. Again, the Holiday Inn chain offers a good example. The name "Holiday Inn" would seem to convey an image of a person or family on vacation or holiday. Although vacation travelers were the original intended customers for Holiday Inns, it has now entered very successfully into the business and commercial market. Since the name has become so well known, it would not be worthwhile to try to change it to one that would describe the broader image. Most people today think of Holiday Inns as a broad type of accommodation facility, good for both vacation and business clientele. The company's advertising has concentrated on making the name "Holiday Inn" synonymous with reliability and consistency. Its "No Surprises" campaign has been in place for almost ten years.

Naming a small company for its geographic area might be perfectly logical. However, this type of name does not allow for future growth. The name loses

"George, is this what 'Homey Highlands' meant to you?"

These examples of the windows of three different travel agencies indicate how image can differ.

The first agency is obviously vacation oriented. The window is decorated elaborately, with the palm trees installed above the window and the shutters added. A client wanting a fun vacation would feel comfortable here. The use of the sun motif and the name "Fun and Sun Travel" indicate specialization in this type of vacation.

The middle window indicates an emphasis completely on price competition. The person wanting the "best" price without consideration of quality might prefer this agency.

The third window, however, indicates a conservative, business oriented agency. Someone wanting a vacation might be uncomfortable here whereas the business traveler would prefer it to the other two.

An agency wanting to handle both commercial and corporate travel would be better served with a neutral name and image.

Holiday Inn's "great sign," a familiar sight near many of the nation's highways for thirty years, was necessary when the chain depended on walk-in tourist trade for most of its business. Marketing personnel at Holiday Inns had suggested changing the sign to suit market conditions, but at first the proposal was resisted, even though the "great sign" turned off certain market segments.

The New Holiday Inns sign responded to both changing market conditions and increased costs. The Familiar Holiday Inn green color as well as the script lettering and a new version of the familiar starburst were retained but in a subdued way, suited to the business traveler who had become a major part of the chain's market. The new sign cost about 34 percent less to construct; about 50 percent less to maintain; and was 69 percent more energy efficient.

meaning as soon as the company expands beyond its original geographic market area. A very good example is USAir. Originally known as Allegheny Airlines, it operated primarily in the region of the Allegheny mountains and was a small regional carrier with all the image problems of a carrier that size. In the late 1970's, with deregulation of the airline industry, Allegheny Airlines decided to expand considerably. The decision was made to change the name of the airline to lose the image of a small regional carrier. See the "Industry Communique" for more about the extent of image changes at USAIR. The second "Industry Communique" shows the image promotion of a new appearance in the late 1980s after the merger with Piedmont and PSA airlines.

INDUSTRY COMMUNIQUE

PRESIDENT'S MESSAGE

Welcome to USAir. As you can see from the date and headline on this inaugural issue of *USAir News*, this is the first day of operation under our new name.

October 28 is a big day for all of us. It is a time for reflection on our history—the growth and development that enabled us to become US Air—and a time for looking ahead to the future of our company. October 28 as the official day of the name change is not the end of our efforts. It marks the beginning of untold opportunities as we do business with a name that more accurately represents us as a national airline.

We have a big task ahead of us—delivering the promise of a major, national airline. And just as the evolution to USAir was made possible through your hard work, so will the success of USAir be made possible through your continued dedication and commitment.

Here's to USAir! Many thanks for making it happen.

THE RANGE OF THE CHANGE

Ever since the intention to change the name of Allegheny Airlines to USAir was announced last Spring, there has been a flurry of activity throughout the company to achieve the change by the October 28 date.

This meant literally changing everything Allegheny to USAir. Every department was involved in this effort.

This effort included changing countless items and documents from things as small as a service pin to something as large as the neon sign on top of the Pittsburgh Central Reservations Office.

Much of the responsibility for the change to USAir in the various areas of corporate identification rested with these departments: purchasing, properties and facilities, advertising, and maintenance.

The first visible sign of change was on June 8, 1979, with the rollout of DC-9-30 #973 in the new USAir livery.

A sampling of the items that had to be changed illustrates their diversity.

- *17,000 signs in 89 locations*
- *17,400 validation cards for travel agents*
- *2,300 telephone book listings*
- *9,200 employee identification cards*
- *1,319 flight attendant wings*
- *2,446 pilot wings and cap emblems*
- *9,200 employee service pins*
- *8,746 seat pocket emergency cards*
- *4,000 decals for ground*

Reprinted with permission from USAir News, October 28, 1979.

INDUSTRY COMMUNIQUE

A NEW LOOK FOR A NEW AIRLINE

May 24, 1989, will be remembered as the day USAir boldly stated to the nation—in an appropriate red-white-and-blue fashion—that it intends to become known as the nation's premier domestic carrier.

On that date, Chairman and President Ed Colodny unveiled USAir's new look for the new airline—a fresh, bright, new color scheme to represent the merged USAir, PSA, and Piedmont, which will all be one airline on August 5.

"We have created with the able assistance of SBG Partners of San Francisco a fresh look that we believe coordinates extremely with our name, USAir. It is not only a new look, but a new wordmark—a look and a wordmark that replaces those that have served us well for many years. Colodny said during unveiling ceremonies at Washington National Airport, Pittsburgh, and Charlotte.

"The past has been good to all of us."

Reprinted from USAir News, May 1989.

USAir Logo

When printing in 4 color process only:
The background is White. "USAir begins
with you": Match Navy Blue PMS 289C.
The large logo. "US": Match Red PMS
200C. "Air": Match Blue PMS 285C.

When Printing with PMS colors only:
The background is White. "USAir begins
with you" prints Navy Blue PMS 289C.
The large logo, "US" prints Red PMS 200C.
"Air" prints Blue PMS 285C.

When printing in one color only:
The backround is white. Print in all black, or
all Navy Blue PMS 289C.

This logo must not be altered in any way.

3/16" **USAir**
      USAir

1/4" **USAir**
    USAir

5/16" **USAir**
    USAir

3/8" **USAir**

USAir Wordmark

The USAir corporate colors are USAir Red and USAir
Blue. The USAir signature is reproduced in two colors:
"US" is red, "Air" is blue

**The proportions and spacing of the wordmark must not be
altered in any way.**

USAir Color Control

The USAir corporate colors are USAir Red, USAir Blue
and USAir Navy. The USAir wordmark is reproduced in
two colors: "US" is red, "Air" is light blue.

**To ensure consistency in color reproduction, samples must
be attached to artwork and visually matched by the supplier.**

This is an example of a logo sheet sent by a company for reproduction. Companies are very
particular about how their logo can be reprinted. They protect them carefully. As shown
above, precise instructions are given for the exact color, spacing, and proportions to use.

Much research was done, and the name USAir was chosen. A name change is an important and expensive undertaking. When a name is changed, very large promotional expenditures are necessary to let the public know that this is not a brand new business but an experienced, larger one. USAir's name change has been an outstanding success story. It was able to lose the negative parts of the image of Allegheny Airlines—the impression of a regional carrier with limited resources—yet keep the positive images it had earned as an old, established line.

The name change of the Ask Mr. Foster travel agency chain to Carlson Travel Network did not work as well. Neither name has had great recognition in the consumer area, and in the corporate world, where it was better known, the complete dropping of the "Foster" part of the name resulted in many companies' believing that Carlson Travel Network was a completely new company. Carlson did not adequately relate the change to a continuation under a different name of a company more than 100 years old. Perhaps they could have modernized the name, given the image of a network of travel companies, and yet maintained the connection to the past by changing to a name such as Foster Travel Network.

The logos and signs used by businesses also convey an image to the viewer. As styles change, it is sometimes necessary to change logos and signs. What worked well ten years ago might be out of date today and make a company appear old fashioned. However, the design choices will also be influenced by the specific image the business wishes to convey. A hotel located in a historical area might intentionally use an old-fashioned style logo to blend in with the atmosphere of the destination. An airline, however, which wants the public to see it as modern and forward-looking, will usually choose styles that convey that impression. Most of the major airline carriers modified their logos during the 1980s.

Hotel logo designs also change as time goes by. When a logo is effective, the public can recognize the company by its logo and does not need to see the name. Hyatt changed its logo and the type style for its name to create a more dynamic and modern image.

When a hotel makes a change such as this, the cost is enormous. Not only do they need to commit the promotional costs to get the change noticed, but they must purchase new equipment for everything that has the logo imprinted. This includes the signage, towels, matchbooks, napkins, plates and glasses in some cases, and hundreds of other items. All the old ones must frequently be discarded and replaced with the new. Only some items can easily be changed to the new image. Therefore, any change in name especially and even in design of logo is not taken lightly. When an airline changes the design on its planes, it can take several years until its entire fleet has been redone. Again, the cost is quite substantial.

COLOR AND STYLE

In addition to logos and signs, the image of a business—whether travel agency, hotel or airline—is also conveyed to its customers by means of the colors and styles

The evolution of American Airlines'
eagle logo is shown above, in versions
dating from 1933 to the present.
Courtesy of American Airlines.

(the decoration) chosen for lobbies, offices, aircraft, and even employees' clothing. One of the most striking examples of an attempt to create image by means of decoration was Braniff's aircraft of the 1970s, painted in designs created by a famous artist. The decorated aircraft did attract a great deal of attention; it is unclear whether or not they contributed to the right kind of images for the airline. Other airlines' use of famous designers to create uniforms for their flight attendants had a similar purpose. (Of course, choice of a famous artist or designer to create image in this way is also an attempt to use the artist's status to create an image of expensiveness and class.)

PSA, a California airline, was well known and loved for the smile painted on the front of their planes. When USAir took over PSA, regular PSA customers

United Airlines' logo has changed significantly over the years since 1934. *Courtesy* of United Airlines.

resented the fact that USAir removed this homey touch. Alaska Airlines gave in to public outcry when they announced that they were going to remove the Eskimo face from the tails of their planes and decided to keep the image.

Color is probably more immediate in its effect on viewers than is style. Colors can be quite effective in conveying emotional images. Blues are generally considered soothing, cool, calm, and secure. Yellows are looked upon as cheerful and active colors. Reds, on the other hand, evoke strong emotional feelings in most people. Travel offices, hotel lobbies, and other public areas frequently use blue/green combinations or yellow/orange/brown combinations for their decor. The blue/green colors seem to give a feeling of visiting tropical paradises and portray colors of the sea, the land, and the sky which increase the desire for travel. The yellow/orange/brown tones are reminiscent of sunsets and warmth on the beach. Bright colors such as red are best used for occasional accents rather than as major parts of a color scheme.

Other colors, such as pink, purple, or gray are not as defined in terms of the images they evoke in the "average" person. A business trying to appeal to a mass public will usually stay with the muted, neutral colors. When a company wants to promote a vivid, different image, it might try an unusual color scheme, but there is potential danger in that attempt.

Something that must also be kept in mind is that different colors have different meanings for various cultures. White may mean either "hospital" or "ultramodern" to a Western viewer (like the white-on-white decorating schemes in decorating magazines). White means death and mourning to some Eastern cultures, however. Similarly, pink has a very different connotation for American and for Japanese viewers. Fad colors may be very popular this year and out of date next. It is best for companies to avoid such colors unless they plan to redecorate every year or two.

CONCLUSION

When an image is positive, part of the job of selling has already been done and marketing becomes much easier. The image that is portrayed should be intentional; it should not be allowed to just happen. Salespeople who must meet with potential customers and defend a business whose previous image has been poor start with two strikes against them, and the chances of a successful sale are greatly reduced. The salesperson coming into a sales situation for a business with a good image, on the other hand, starts with the sale partly made.

SUMMARY

Image—the public perception of a thing, as distinguished from its actuality—is very important to any marketing plan. A good image must be constantly monitored—once lost it is very difficult to regain. Image problems may arise in the travel product over such considerations as safety, cost, and product differentiation.

It must be remembered that many images will be either positive or negative depending on the perceiver, and his or her attitudes. For this reason, no one image will appeal to an entire market.

No matter how well promoted, a good image can be destroyed by employees who do not conform to it. Images also depend for their effectiveness on appropriate business names, signs, and logos. Color and design in such things as uniforms, aircraft, and interior appointments can be very important, because they also contribute to the image the public perceives. A good image, well-supported by well-trained and motivated employees, makes the salesperson's job much easier.

QUESTIONS FOR THOUGHT AND DISCUSSION

1. Obtain business cards from several companies (both travel and others) and discuss the image the card gives you of the business it represents. If you are familiar with the business, discuss if this is the image the business wants to portray.

2. As you shop in different stores (at least three), make notes on the decor, color, and general appearance of the store or business. Write or give a report on your findings.

3. Choose three different destinations and survey five people who have not been to these places (do not use students or employees in travel) on their opinion of the destination. Get information on their view of the cost, the people, the sights, and activities, the weather, and any other images they hold. Then try to find three or more people who have visited each destination, and ask the same questions. Compare the results.

4. Bring in samples (from newspapers, magazines, direct mail pieces, or other sources) of company logos or signs. Do these logos or signs accurately represent the business? What image is conveyed by these designs?

6

The Marketing Mix in Travel and Tourism

communications mix
credit
direct operator
distribution mix
four Ps
marketing mix
marketing plan
multilevel distribution system
product and service mix
publicity
rates of exchange
retailer
terms-of-sale mix
wholesaler

Marketing is, essentially, a planning process. Once you have a target market in mind, you need to develop a strategy to meet the perceived needs of this market. Knowledge and application of the concept of the **marketing mix**—the elements involved in the marketing process—can be very helpful in developing a needed strategy.

The figure on page 118 is a model of the marketing mix. This model will vary in its specifics for different businesses within the travel industry, but the overall structure is the same, regardless of segment. The central focus of all the parts of the marketing mix is a target market segment. The use of the mix is only effective when the buyer power and other demographic characteristics of the target market are known.

COMPOSITION OF THE MARKETING MIX

The marketing mix consists of four separate submixes. Each of these submixes interacts continuously with the other three. In a sense, creating the mix is a juggling act, in which you balance elements of the four submixes to meet the needs of the target market. These four submixes are: product and service, distribution, communications, and terms of sale.

The **product and service mix** is the inventory of products or repertoire of services that the organization is engaged in marketing. The **distribution mix** is the methods or channels through which the products and services are distributed to the consumer. The **communications mix** is the tools or methods used to inform potential customers of the existence of products and services and the ways in which such products and services will benefit the consumer. The **terms of sale mix** consists of the alternative methods of payment that are available to consumers to pay for the organization's products or services and the price charged.

Product and Service Mix

In the travel and tourism industry, the product and service mix is essentially the varied components of tourism. Transportation, accommodations, food service and entertainment, and sightseeing activities can all be considered part of the

Model of the Marketing Mix

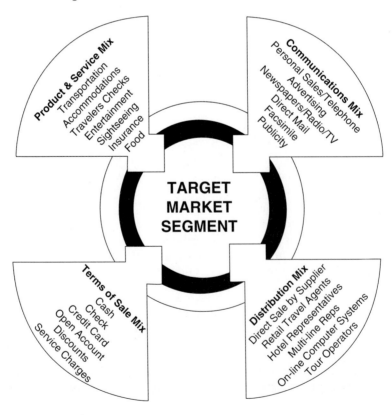

product and service mix. The retail travel agent, the member of the industry who markets the broadest variety of products and services, would have to consider almost all of these things in the market planning process.

Airlines Product and Service Mix

In contrast, organizations that market within a single segment of the industry need only consider the various possibilities within that component. However, that does not always mean that their product and service submix will be simpler. For example, an airline really markets many different services; from one point of view, the various routes served by the airline represent different services. Decisions to expand or contract route structure are based on analyses of how potential travelers will accept new routes, as well as on analyses of how existing routes are doing. Decisions on classes of service (such as first class, coach, or business class) also represent the provision of alternate services to meet differing consumer needs. Not all airlines offer the same classes of service.

There are also niche markets served by a particular airline, such as MGM Grand in the 80s and early 90s and Midwest Express. MGM Grand served the first-class consumer and was quite popular with movie and TV stars. Their routes served popular itineraries for these people such as Los Angeles to New York. Midwest Express is owned by Kimberly Clark and was originally developed to serve routes needed by their executives. They serve a discriminating business clientele with exceptional service.

Furthermore, many carriers do not offer the same selection from the class of service (product) mix on all routes. Most carriers offer first class and coach service on their domestic routes but add a third "business class" on international and long-haul domestic routes. However, the Delta Shuttle between Washington and New York and New York and Boston is an all-coach service. Regional carriers on short-haul routes offer only one class of service. From time to time, some carriers expand their first-class service while others decrease it.

Within the airline industry, basic safety and types of aircraft equipment are the same among all airlines of a similar type (long distance, medium distance, and commuter). As a result, other less important items, such as food service, drinks, and other amenities become part of the service mix.

Hotel Product and Service Mix

In the hotel industry, the product and service mix is far broader than just the differences in room and bath. Location, availability of meeting space, convention services, types of suites, a variety of restaurants and entertainment, recreational facilities, and room amenities such as a nightly turndown service, refrigerators, and candy, are all part of the variety of services available at hotels and resorts. The hotel marketer uses the appropriate mix to meet the needs of the target market.

The differing needs of various classes of travelers will affect the choice of products and services offered by both hotels and airlines. The business traveler looks to an airline for convenience, frequency, and flexibility of schedule, all within a certain expense level, and preferably with an airline from which he or she is collecting frequent flyer credits. This traveler looks for location, availability, and price when deciding on a hotel. Vacationers, who are more flexible in time and destination, will often change destinations or location within a destination based upon budget. Groups also have needs that differ from those of individual travelers. As mentioned earlier, many hotel chains now have developed completely different brand names for different level properties within their product mix.

The Distribution Mix

Establishing a distribution mix for a product or service involves decisions on how to transmit or transport the product or service from producer to consumer. In general the travel and tourism industry features a **multilevel distribution system**. Direct distribution from producer to ultimate consumer is a major method of distribution. For some hotels and car rental firms and for most food service facilities direct distribution is the primary method of reaching the consumer. Airlines also use direct distribution, although it is not their major means of servicing travelers. Cruise lines, however, distribute almost exclusively through travel agencies.

Wholesalers

The wholesale level of distribution, by definition, purchases from the producer and sells to the ultimate consumer through a retail level of distribution. This level does exist in the travel industry, primarily in the category called tour operator. Tour operators secure a variety of travel services (such as hotel rooms, sightseeing, tour services) and promote them by means of brochures and other travel literature through travel agents to the actual traveler. Retail travel agents look to the wholesaler for a variety of packages or services of interest to clients.

"Hey, Martha! Some dummy put mirrors on the ceiling!"

The **wholesaler** or tour operator can keep costs under control through volume purchasing. The convenience of communications with wholesalers and tour operators is very attractive to the retail agent. Otherwise, the retailer would have to participate in extensive and expensive communications with a variety of travel service producers. Through the purchasing and packaging of hotels, transportation, meals, and tours, tour operators create unique travel services (such as hosted and escorted tours) that add to the overall travel and tourism product and service mix. However, because the tour operator secures the travel services from direct operators such as hotels and bus companies, the tour operator can be considered a distributor as well as a direct supplier.

Air ticket consolidators are also essentially wholesalers. Although many sell to the public, retail travel agencies are the prime customers of most of them.

Retailers

The **retailer**, or retail travel agency sells a variety of products and services directly to the traveler (see Table 6-1). Some of the services (airline reservations, car rental reservations) are secured from service producers whereas others (tours and hotel packages) are secured from wholesale sources. With more than 33,000 locations throughout the United States, travel agents are the most accessible suppliers from which a traveler may secure travel services.

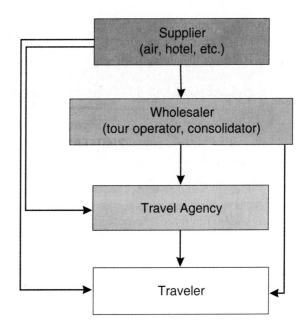

Distribution of the Travel Product

TABLE 6-1

SUPPLIER DEPENDENCE ON U.S. TRAVEL AGENTS
(*Source*: Travel Industry World Yearbook, 1992)

Travel Segment	Estimated % of Volume Booked by Agents
Airlines	80 (domestic)
	85 (international)
Hotels	25 (domestic)
	85 (international)
Cruise Lines	95
Rail	37
Bus	Less than 10
Rental Cars	50
Packaged Tours	90

Mixing of Distribution Channels

Distribution of the travel and tourism product is further confused by a mixing of distribution channels. Although airlines are direct suppliers of their own product as well as suppliers to tour operators and retail travel agents, airlines also serve as a source of securing reservations for other services. Hotel, car rental, and often tour programs can be secured through an airline reservations office. A traveler can do this directly or a travel agent can use an airline reservations system to make hotel and car rental reservations for a traveler.

The multilevel roles played by other organizations add to the confusion in the travel and tourism distribution system. For example, the American Express Company is heavily involved in financial services. Its major programs include international banking, the world-famous credit card ("Don't leave home without it") and the travelers check. However, American Express is also a major wholesaler and tour operator, offering hosted and escorted tours throughout the world, as well as operating the largest chain of retail travel agencies in the United States. Furthermore, American Express has appointed several hundred retail travel agencies throughout the country as "representative agents." These representative agencies sell American Express travelers checks and provide travel assistance as do other American Express offices, but they are independently owned and operated travel agencies.

Establishing a Distribution Mix

The major consideration in establishing a distribution system is to determine the most effective method of profitably providing tourism services to potential travelers. Does a company have the resources to do all its distribution on its own? Will the use of a representation service help a hotel or chain of hotels promote its product and secures bookings? Will the commissions paid to travel agencies be a fair return for the bookings they are providing? Will low group rates fill space that will otherwise be empty? Will cooperation with wholesalers and tour operators help fill seats or rooms? Is a balanced use of the multi-level distribution system an effective method to use? Each travel marketer must answer these questions to help determine the best distribution mix for the product or service offered.

For seventeen years, the Disney Corporation did not pay commissions to travel agents for their hotels. In 1988, when Disney was in a large-scale expansion of their hotel properties, they realized that they would need a bigger and more effective sales force for their hotels. They then began paying commissions to travel agents. By mid-1992, just over half of the bookings in Disney's hotels were being placed by travel agents.

Communications Mix

The communications mix is a marketer's tool kit, providing a variety of ideas and means of informing prospects about various products and services, the benefits of these products and services to the prospects, and the call to action for purchasing.

The most critical form of communications is personal sales. Whether handled over the telephone or in person, in response to inquiries or as outside sales calls, the personal sales effort is the major method for securing commitments from prospective customers. Chapters 12 through 14 in this book provide more detailed information on the sales function in the travel and tourism industry and on specific sales techniques.

Advertising

Advertising is a major communications tool in the tourism industry. Designed to inform, remind, and persuade, advertising is paid one-way communication. The major advertising forms used in the industry are print media (newspapers, magazines, and direct mail) and broadcast media (radio and television). Advertising is an expenditure for large tourism supplier organizations, such as airlines, hotels, tourist boards and steamship companies. Although expenditures for advertising decrease at the wholesale and retail levels, advertising does remain a major method of attracting business. Chapter 8 discusses advertising in the travel and tourism industry in detail.

Sales promotion is another important communications tool. Contests, window displays, and point of purchase displays, posters, slides, and films are all used to support the marketing effort. Many travel agencies run "cruise nights" periodically where they invite the public to hear about cruise programs. In 1991, when travel declined drastically because of the Persian Gulf War and the fears it generated, British Airways promoted a grand-scale giveaway. In a number of countries, people could enter a contest for free tickets to London and other prizes. All seats on a specific day were given over to the winners of the giveaway. Although the promotion cost a great deal of money for promotion and advertising, not to mention the cost to the airline of the free seats, the program was so impressive that it obtained massive amounts of additional publicity as a news happening.

INDUSTRY COMMUNIQUE

PUBLIC RELATIONS IN THE MARKETING MIX

Neal R. McFarland, CHSE

In the last decade, hoteliers have made great strides in becoming better marketers. In the past, the term "marketing" often was misinterpreted to mean "advertising" or "sales." Now most hoteliers understand that they are but two of the tools marketers have at their disposal for generating business....

...The hospitality industry has indeed progressed in its approach to planning. But, one weak link remains in the marketing plans of most hotels even today. That is the failure to include a public relations plan as an integral element of the marketing mix.

Good public relations is powerful. It has a direct influence on buying decisions. Why then is it so often ignored in the marketing planning process? And, why is it so many hoteliers regard the function of public relations as little more than the mailing of an occasional news release or annual contribution to the local charity? Perhaps it is due to their failure to understand its power, its mechanics, and its need for a disciplined approach.

Whatever the reasons for its underutilization, one thing is certain; once a public relations plan becomes a part of the overall marketing plan for a hotel, it can have a very positive impact on both the top and bottom lines of the operating statement. In addition, it can greatly enhance the cost effectiveness of any marketing program.

When the entire world population constitutes a potential customer base for a hotel, the challenge hoteliers face is to target both the marketing plan and the public relations plan to those customer groups that represent the greatest business potential.

It would take volumes to fully address the broad scope of the public relations function. This article then, concentrates basically on (1)the need for planning, and (2)the generation of publicity.

Certainly no marketing effort can be fully effective without addressing the publicity issue, regardless of the size or type of hotel. The only real variable should be the intensity of the publicity effort.

The fundamental difference between publicity and advertising is that publicity is free, whereas advertising is bought. But there are a number of other important differences that must be noted.

Readers, listeners, and viewers expect advertisers to tout benefits. So, creative as an ad may be, it lacks the impact of publicity generated through an outside credible source. Public acceptance of the information received editorially is far more likely when it is presented by a third party.

This is especially true in today's society in which people are better educated and more informed than were past generations. Today's consumer makes more comparisons and weighs options more carefully than the consumer of yesteryear, partly because there are more options available. Since there certainly are more hotel options available than ever before, it is incumbent upon the hotel marketer to furnish the kind of in-depth information the consumer demands and which advertising, in itself, is incapable of delivering.

This is not to say that one should not advertise. Rather, the wise marketer ingeniously uses publicity as positive reinforcement of his or her advertising. And, publicity can certainly help a hotel differentiate itself from its competitors, a common marketing strategy.

There is one more important difference between publicity and advertising. Advertising can be controlled; publicity cannot. In advertising, the advertiser targets the audience, decides the exact message to be delivered, where and when the message is delivered, and (to some extent) the impact to be achieved. With publicity, one has very little control over these variables, though a true public relations professional usually finds ways to overcome these obstacles. Careful planning is one way. Creativity is another.

There are two kinds of publicity; news and features....For the purposes of this article, the proper preparation of news releases is not particularly relevant. What is relevant is the need for professionalism in all facets of the publicity-generating function.

Very often the kind of creativity needed to spark that interest exists within the hotel marketing staff. But, if it doesn't, it is best to leave the job of publicity generation to the true professional, the outside consultant, or agency.

Indeed, the hotelier who takes the public relations function seriously would be well advised to enlist the services of outside counsel.

THE PUBLIC RELATIONS PLAN

Mike Wilson, of Mike Wilson Public Relations in Atlanta, advocates the hiring of outside public relations counsel as does Joe Adams, president of his own advertising and public relations firm in Rockville, Md. He says:

Go for the experience and proven performance if you're serious about getting results month in and month out...you can usually buy the services of a good PR firm—complete with writers, researchers and media—contact specialists—for what it costs to hire one individual.

Sure, these are PR men talking and their remarks may be interpreted as self-serving, but experience has proven time and again that what they say is true; there is no substitute for professionalism.

One is also well-advised to screen firms carefully and to research the track record of those being considered. Are the clients satisfied with their results? Do they follow a plan? Or, do they take a scattergun approach?

Once an outside agency is selected, it is also important to deal with its representatives openly and honestly. Share the marketing plan with them completely so they thoroughly understand your planned objectives. And make them feel as though they are a part of the staff. Better yet, make the PR firm an ex-officio member of the hotel's Executive Committee.

Whether outside counsel is retained or not, the real challenge facing every hotel general manager is to make certain that there is a public relations plan to be followed; consciously designed, scheduled, coordinated, and deliberate program with measurable objectives and trackable results. As with any kind of sound business planning, the public relations program cannot be left to chance. If it is, one thing is certain; it will not happen. There MUST be a plan...that's rule #1!

So, is a public relations program necessary for every hotel? And, how does one design such a program?

The answer to the first question is a resounding "yes," although, as stated previously, its intensity will vary greatly from hotel to hotel.

Author Philip Lesly, offers the following general guidelines and elements of planning in response to the second question:

1. Spell out objectives incisively. Don't have more than a few major objectives so that the focus will be on them.
2. Determine the functions, again by being selective, so the vital ones will get enough attention.
3. Establish a budget.
4. Assign responsibilities to personnel.
5. Retain outside help as needed.
6. Set up a flow chart of the functions, with lead time, relationships, and responsibilities clearly defined.
7. Set up feedback and research points to measure progress and assess trends.
8. Schedule periodic review of plans and functions to assure flexibility.
9. Build in procedures for keeping principals informed and involved.

As with all objectives, PR objectives must be specific, quantifiable, and measurable. They may be as simplistic as stating how often during the course of the year the hotel receives mention in the media, or as sophisticated as measuring total lineage, impressions, or air time that could have been obtained through paid advertising. The important message here is that a value must be placed on the program as a quantifiable return on investment (ROI).

Responsibility must be assigned for development, administration, and execution of the plan. In a small hotel this responsibility may, by necessity, fall on the general manager, though parts of the actual execution may be delegated. In medium and larger hotels, the director of sales or director of marketing is generally charged with the responsibility, while in most large hotels and resorts a full-time director of public relations is in charge of the plan. This does not, however, absolve the general manager from being involved. In fact, in every successful PR-oriented hotel, all employees are involved, from the general manager on down.

THE PR BUDGET

The question of budget very often becomes a sticky one. Joe Adams declares that "a minimum of 15 percent of a hotel advertising budget" should be allocated to public relations. In support of his theory, Adams cites a *Wall Street Journal* survey of major financial advertisers that suggests a shift of as much as 70 percent of their marketing dollars now goes to "other" expenses, including public relations, with only 30 percent earmarked for advertising.

Kenneth Koyen, writing in *Lesly's Public Relations Handbook*, answers the question of budget allocation this way; "The budget should be based on the potential market and the communications media to be employed."

Though Koyen does not suggest that a certain percentage of the marketing budget be allocated to public relations, per se, he does offer an invaluable list of items that need be taken into consideration in budget formulation. They are...

1. Publicists fees. (These include internal employees as well as outside contractors.)
2. Photography.
3. Film or videotape costs.
4. Mats (for newspapers).
5. Distribution of press releases to smaller newspapers. (In some states, the state press association can provide this service.)
6. Mailing costs.
7. Production of copy.
8. Messenger services.
9. Mileage.

10. Entertainment.
11. Models.
12. Clipping Services.

To these costs, printing and reproduction should be added.

Obviously, the final budget will depend a great deal on the type and size of hotel, its location, market mix, distance from major feeder markets, sources of business, need, management's PR-orientation, and a host of other variables.

As the public relations plan evolves, it should be viewed from three different, but integrally related perspectives: (1)by market mix; (2)required scope (local, regional, national, international, etc.); and (3)consumer or intermediary influence (travel agents, tour operators, etc.).

No one of these considerations merits more concern than another. They are all of equal importance.

Once the target audience(s) has been identified, the plan comes down to timing and media selection, much the same as a paid advertising campaign.

REFERENCE SOURCES

There are a number of good reference sources available listing media contacts. Among the better ones is *Editor and Publisher*, which lists every daily newspaper in the United States, news syndicates, and feature story syndicates, along with key staff members. *Ayer's Annual Publications Directory* lists all newspapers and magazines by city and under state headings. *Printers Ink* publishes a list of business publications while three sources are available listing major radio and television media. They are: *Broadcasting, Broadcast Advertising,* and *Variety Radio Directory.*

There are two less comprehensive but more focused publications worth mentioning: *Guide to Travel, Leisure, and Entertainment* and *Florida News Media Directory.*

Three often overlooked sources for hotel publicity are special interest, trade, and business publications read by a well-defined audience, such as bankers, scuba divers, architects, and the like. The mention of a hotel in these kinds of publications automatically enhances a hotel's image, and establishes its credibility among the magazine readers.

The thing that makes trade journals such an effective publicity vehicle is the fact that they devote 100 percent of their space to the field they cover.

There are several good sources of trade magazines available for compilation of a media list. A few are: *IMS Directory of Publications, The Standard Periodical Directory,* and *Standard Rate & Data Service* (Business Publication Division).

One additional specialized publicity source that should be mentioned is the *International Association of Business Communicators Membership Directory.*

IABC members are responsible for publishing newsletters, magazines, and other "house organs" for the companies and corporations by whom they are employed; consequently, mention of a hotel in these publications has an impact on the company's employees who travel on business or for pleasure.

The business of publicity is a people business, one in which personal relationships must be cultivated and nurtured over a long period of time. Successful public relations does not occur instantly, as an advisory note in the introduction of the *Guide To Travel, Leisure and Entertainment Media* warns; "Media listings can be prepared wholesale, but successful media placements are won only by the painstaking accumulation of individual transactions and contacts over the years."

CONCLUSION

In conclusion, public relations involves a great deal more than "being a good neighbor." It requires careful planning in a calculating and deliberate process. To be effective, it must be designed in concert with the overall marketing objectives of the hotel. Its timing, delivery, and focus must be in sync with all the other functions of the marketing mix: direct sales, advertising, special promotions, internal merchandising, and research before it can even begin to approach optimum effectiveness.

Perhaps as much as any other marketing function, it requires creativity; the ability to make ordinary events newsworthy and major newsworthy events even more so.

While responsibility for public relations in a hotel must be specifically defined, it is incumbent upon the general manager to create a climate among all employees, a PR mentality, if you will, that will encourage them to take interest and pride in the hotel's public relations program, so that no publicity-generating opportunities are missed.

The public relations program demands the allocation of resources: time, personnel, money, and effort, in proportion to the results desired.

Finally, good public relations demands the patient cultivation of personal relationships: with the media, with the community, with the industry, with employees, and last, but most importantly, with every guest who enters the hotel.

A marketing plan without a public relations plan is like a prize-fighter in the ring with one arm tied behind his back; he may succeed with a lucky punch, but the odds are against it.

Reprinted courtesy of HSMAI Marketing Review, Fall 1988.

Public Relations

Publicity is unpaid or free coverage in the media or other free promotional activities. Much money is spent on public relations efforts designed to influence the media and generate favorable stories, articles, pictures, and presentations on behalf of travel and tourism organizations. The advantage of publicity over advertising is that a news article or picture is usually perceived by the general public as being impartial and therefore more credible than a paid advertisement. This is true even though many articles and pictures were developed by the organizations they describe. Publicity articles and photographs are often used by media hungry to fill space. Speeches and presentations before civic organizations represent another way of gaining publicity in a positive and impartial manner.

Many promotional activities are a combination of advertising and public relations. For example, the British Airways giveaway mentioned previously had to be advertised to advise consumers to enter the drawing but was a newsworthy event in itself and was given substantial time on newscasts around the world. The opening of a major new attraction such as Disney-MGM Studios or Universal Studios in central Florida is a newsworthy event and generates a lot of publicity. It does, however, also have to be advertised heavily to successfully get the word out. Advertising and publicity feed off each other and maximize the results from either method. See the Industry Communique on page 124.

The Terms of Sale Mix

Basic pricing is critical to any marketing effort. Generally speaking, pricing should relate to costs of production and produce some degree of profit. However, varying degrees of competition in the transportation industry often result in fares unrelated to actual costs, with travel to some far-away destinations available at a lower cost to the traveler than fares to nearer destinations. Although the overall amount of discretionary travel may not be affected by specific prices, the choice of destinations by vacation travelers and the length of stay is often directly related to pricing. The volume of travel to many destinations (for instance, Hawaii or the Caribbean) has often risen and fallen as a result of pricing cycles. When more distant destinations become available at a lower price or at a price as low as closer destinations, the more distant destinations are perceived as a better value. Tourism to those further destinations will generally grow. The development of special promotional airfares to many destinations has had great impact on the growth of tourism to those places. Because pricing has become such a critical factor in the marketing mix of most travel companies in recent years, the subject will be discussed in depth in Chapter 7.

Credit

The availability of credit has had a positive influence on the growth of the tourism industry. Beginning with travel and entertainment (T&E) charge cards such as American Express and Diners Club, through the development of airline credit cards designed to encourage flying on a given airline, through the growth of local bank-supported credit cards such as Visa and Master Card, credit is now available to almost all levels of the working population.

The credit card makes it possible to buy a high-cost item and pay over time without getting a specific bank loan. Even when used on a 30-day basis, the credit card has made the ability to purchase without cash a reality. In addition to credit cards, tourism services are often provided by one company to another on a billing, or open account, basis. For example, the availability of an open account is often a requirement when a company decides to give its travel business to a travel agent. On the other hand, the limited availability of credit from the airline to the travel agent (approximately two weeks on the average from the writing of an air ticket to the requirement to pay the airline) means that travel agents must be exceedingly careful in granting open accounts to business clients.

Rates of Exchange

The rate of exchange (the fluctuation of currency rates on the international scene) is another terms of sale factor that must be considered when dealing in international travel. Foreign destinations rise and fall in popularity as the relationship between their currency and the United States dollar changes. Obviously, each party to a transaction seeks the terms most favorable to itself. For example, the drastic drop in the value of the Mexican peso against the United States dollar in the early 1980s led to turmoil in the Mexican tourism industry, as hotels there attempted to recoup some of their losses and travelers appeared in record numbers at overbooked facilities. Several tour operators who offered Mexican packages withdrew from the market because of this confusion.

From the mid-1980s through the early 1990s, the dollar was not worth much in Western Europe. This meant fewer Americans traveling to Europe, but, on the other hand, led to an increase in Europeans traveling to the United States. During the recession of the early 1990s, inbound travel was one of the few positive items in our country's balance of trade.

USING THE MIX

The factors in the marketing mix can be used as the basis for the development of an operational marketing program. Once information about the lifestyle of the target market (information gained by market research, see Chapter 4) is obtained, the tourism products and services most needed by the segment can be selected. The tourism organization can design the most effective distribution system for the target market and determine the proper mix of communications through sales representatives, advertising and promotion to meet the needs of the market segment. Pricing and credit arrangements must also meet the needs of the market segment, provide a profit to the company, and be competitive in the field.

The marketing mix should only be considered a framework and general model. Real world activities will require substantial flexibility, with the need to make continuing adjustments as competitive factors change. The philosophy of the marketing mix should not be slavishly followed as the only methodology. Rather, it should be a guide for planning marketing activities. Effective use of the marketing mix will satisfy consumers and create a strong competitive impact.

THE 4 PS OF MARKETING

Many writers on the subject of marketing recommend that marketing programs be developed focusing on the FOUR Ps—product, price, place, and promotion. All planning and action should take these factors into consideration.

There are great similarities between this approach and the marketing mix model. All four Ps can be found in specific parts of the marketing mix. Product, obviously, is covered in depth in the product and service mix. Price is also a major factor in the terms of sale mix. Place refers to the relative position of the company and its marketing program within a given industry and to the convenience of its geographical location. In addition, place includes the choice of distribution channel. This might be direct sales, through travel agents, wholesalers, and so forth. Promotion is equivalent to the communications segment of the mix.

In the model of the four Ps, additional forces affecting marketing are shown. These are all factors that are beyond the control of the company itself. However, it is important for anyone responsible for marketing to be aware of current trends and changes in any of these sectors and to take these into account in planning marketing. Changes in these areas can also necessitate changes in the plan after it is created, because the business operates within the changing environment around it.

The factors affecting all businesses are:

- *Government—Government has an effect through laws passed and through economic actions taken by federal and/or state, or even by local, governments.*
- *Social forces—the sociological factors within our society are constantly changing and marketing must change with them. In the 1980s, for example, ostentatious, status purchasing of travel was popular. In the 1990s, however, individuals, as well as corporations, are very concerned with and motivated by price and value considerations. Status is not as important as it was.*
- *Economy—The economy, obviously, has a great impact on marketing decisions. The recessions of the early 1980s and again in the early 1990s put great stress on most segments of the travel industry. The economy, in turn, has its own effect on social forces, as indicated previously.*
- *Competition—All businesses must keep aware of what the competition is doing and determine how to compete effectively. Copying is not necessarily the best way. Only by keeping up with what the competition is doing can a business be sure of its competitive*

The 4 Ps

points of difference or unique selling propositions. Companies should not market from a position of fear of competition, but from a position of knowledge, confidence, and careful analysis.

THE MARKETING PLAN

As noted earlier, the marketing mix can be used as a decision-making guide when developing a marketing plan. The **marketing plan** is a blueprint for action. The development of a simple but logical marketing plan provides a road map that can direct activities with a minimum of wasted effort. Use the following six steps when developing and operating a marketing plan:

1. Analyze the present situation.
2. Establish measurable goals and objectives.
3. Determine strategies to achieve the objectives.
4. Allocate resources to achieve the strategies.
5. Implement the plan.
6. Evaluate results and adjust goals, strategies, and budgets.

The starting point of any plan is to determine where you are now. What are the current business climate, competition, potential client needs? What are the existing resources of the company? Needless to say, this six-step program is not finite—it is circular. When you reach step 6, you go back to step 1 and reanalyze the present situation and continue forward.

Establishing Goals

Establishing goals and objectives answers the question, "Where do you want the company to be, and by when?" Based on the present situation, a determination is made of the business to be accomplished: specific objectives are established for each phase of the business; and, most importantly, a timeframe is established for achievement of the goals and objectives. Without the time frame and without specific objectives, there are no criteria or standards that can be evaluated to determine success or failure.

Determining Strategy

The marketing mix can be applied most successfully to the strategy section of the marketing plan. In establishing strategies to achieve objectives, it is necessary to consider the target market segment and choose the proper mix of products and services, distribution methods, communications tools, and terms of sale to best achieve the objectives. As a marketer, you are tailoring your recipe of ingredients to meet the needs of both your company and your target market.

Allocating Resources

The allocation and budgeting of resources to achieve strategies is the final phase that must be accomplished before implementing the plan. The current status of resources (manpower, money, and material—the three Ms) was evaluated when determining the present situation. These resources (especially time and money) must be allocated reasonably to reach desired results. The balanced use of time and money will go a long way toward a successful final product.

Implementing and Evaluating the Plan

After reviewing the previous processes and determining that together they form a reasonable, workable marketing plan, it is time to implement the plan.

Earlier, when developing objectives and strategies, specific timeframes were established to measure results. Proper management of the marketing process requires that evaluations be made of progress at the times specified. The evaluation will allow necessary midcourse adjustments because plans rarely go exactly as designed.

If results are not being achieved as planned, try to determine why. Is the advertising and promotion not effective? Have economic conditions changed so that projected results are no longer achievable? Were you not realistic in determining objectives? The goals, objectives, strategies, and budgets should be adjusted as needed. If sales are not as strong as expected, some budget cuts can be made. It is also possible to reallocate resources to other, more profitable activities. Evaluation is also necessary if results are better than planned. Perhaps assigning additional personnel or doing promotion will increase sales and profits even more.

Proper evaluation and feedback is often the most neglected phase of the marketing plan. It is an ongoing process that should be conducted regularly through the implementation of the plan—not just a function performed at the end. Adjustments of goals, objectives and strategies based upon continual evaluation results in a marketing plan managed by the company—not a company managed by a marketing plan.

CONCLUSION

Knowledge of the submixes that make up the total marketing mix is necessary before a successful marketing effort can be planned. Once the submixes are identified and marketing goals and strategies are established, an effective marketing plan can be put into operation.

SUMMARY

The marketing mix is composed of four submixes:

- *Product and service—in the tourism industry as a whole, such components as transportation, accommodations, food service, entertainment, and sightseeing. A retail travel agent would probably need to consider all these components, whereas an airline would be concerned with corporate vs leisure. However, one component may have many aspects—classes of service and various routes might each need to be considered separately by an airline, as well as a division of corporate vs leisure air travel.*
- *Distribution—in tourism, a multilevel system. Some organizations, such as hotels and car rental firms, use direct distribution as a major factor. Wholesalers, while not common, also exist such as tour packagers. Retail travel agents form the third part of the distribution mix. In addition, some organizations may act as direct suppliers, wholesalers, and also secure reservations for such other services as hotels and car rentals.*
- *Communications, which includes personal sales, advertising, sales promotion, and public relations.*
- *Terms of sale—including pricing, credit and rate of exchange.*

The components of the marketing mix identified above are similar to the four Ps of marketing: product, price, place, and promotion. These factors must all be considered in developing a marketing plan. The plan is developed in the following steps:

1. analyze the situation
2. establish measurable goals
3. determine strategies
4. allocate resources
5. implement the plan
6. evaluate results and adjust the plan as necessary.

QUESTIONS FOR THOUGHT AND DISCUSSION

1. List the four parts of the marketing mix, describe them, and give examples of each part.
2. List and describe the four Ps and explain how they relate to travel industry marketing.
3. What are the six steps in the marketing planning process? List and explain.
4. Discuss the differences between a retailer and a wholesaler in the travel industry.

7

Pricing

consolidator
discounting
fee-based pricing
guaranteed group
inelastic
overrides
price elasticity of demand
rebate
service charge
yield management

Everybody wants a bargain. Buying at discount prices has become the rule rather than the exception. Although this mentality began in the automotive industry many years ago (no one pays full list price for a car), and spread to electronics, clothing and other goods, discounting has most recently become prevalent in service industries—including travel and tourism.

The recession of the early 1990s created substantial pricing pressures on all segments of the travel industry. As travel demand growth slowed, airlines, cruise lines, hotels, and car rental companies were left with an overabundance of inventory. Their marketing strategies turned to lowering prices as the prime method of generating additional sales.

The way pricing decisions are made is a major factor in the marketing process. Increasing competition among travel suppliers combined with increased buyer sophistication has made the pricing process a most complex issue. An understanding of pricing issues in each travel market segment is essential.

PRICE ELASTICITY OF DEMAND

An economic principle, **price elasticity of demand**, is an inherent factor in the pricing process. This principle states that a product or service is considered to be either elastic or inelastic, depending upon whether lowering its price would increase its sales. The degree to which a product or service is price elastic will determine the degree to which pricing policies are important within the marketing process in the absence of limiting factors such as government price controls.

Table salt is an example of a product that is totally price inelastic. The cost of salt has no effect on its purchase for the home. Salt prices could double, triple, or be cut in half with little effect on sales.

On the other hand, sirloin steak is more price elastic. Some steak will be sold regardless of price. However, the quantity of steak which is sold increases greatly when the product is featured "on sale" at the supermarket. Some people will only buy steak when it is on sale; others stock their freezers with steak purchased on sale for use at other times.

A truly elastic product or service will generate more total revenues when prices are lowered than at original higher levels. The increased volume sold will more than compensate for the lower per unit price. Furthermore, a profit-oriented company will only be satisfied when total profits are higher from sales at lower prices than they were when the product or service was sold at higher rates.

To see how this works, consider the following scenario about sales of tickets at the "Funtime Amusement Park." At $20.00 per ticket, Funtime can sell 10,000 tickets. However, by lowering the price to $14.00, Funtime can sell 20,000 tickets. If the price were lowered even more, to $8.00 per ticket, sales would skyrocket to 40,000. It appears that tickets are price elastic because both sales and total revenues increase from $200,000 to $280,000 when the price is lowered to $14.00. Total revenues increase to $320,000 at the $8.00 price.

The real marketing question should center on profits. Assuming a cost of $10.00 to service each ticket, Funtime's profit will drop from $100,000 (10,000 tickets at $10.00 profit per ticket) to $80,000 (20,000 tickets at $4.00 profit per ticket) even though the ticket is price elastic enough to double sales when the price is reduced 30%. Sales quadruple at the $8.00 price—but Funtime would lose

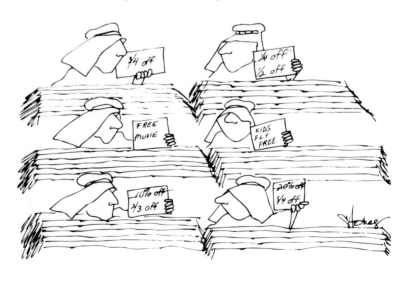

The Flying Carpet Bazaar

$2.00 per ticket or $80,000 total. There is a great difference between volume and profitability.

Spring 1992 was a prime example of price elasticity in terms of airline tickets and profitability. When American Airlines announced a half-price sale on already highly discounted airline tickets for the prime summer season (and was followed by the other airlines), all records were broken on number of tickets sold. Unfortunately, so were all records on profitability of a normally profitable quarter broken. All the airlines involved had the lowest profit or greatest loss for that season, because of the huge volume of low-priced tickets sold. Because of the finite number of seats available, the airlines had record high load factors with record low financial results. This was a disastrous use of price elasticity marketing.

There is no magic formula for determining price elasticity of demand. It is mostly a trial and error process with judgments made based upon observations and experience.

The degree of price elasticity of travel products is directly related to whether the travel situation is discretionary and how flexible the traveler's plans are. Business travel and travel for family emergencies is far less price elastic than vacation travel. Leisure travelers will frequently change days and time of travel to take advantage of lower fares. (See Industry Communique.) Often the choice of destination, hotel and/or cruise ship is affected by price. In fact, if the price is too high, they might decide not to travel at all.

INDUSTRY COMMUNIQUE

TRAFALGAR OFFICIAL URGES CLOSER AIRLINE-TOUR TIES

New York—Air fares are the key to Europe tour sales, and there is a need for closer cooperation between airlines and tour operators, said Nigel Osborne, vice-president of sales and marketing for Trafalgar Tours.

"We are seeing changed consumer booking patterns with people, conditioned by last-minute air fare specials shopping around for the best prices," Osborne said.

"There is no doubt that price and destination are the hot selling points."

Since the end of the gulf war, he said, Trafalgar's reservations lines have received up to 1,000 calls a day.

"Our reservations lines ring in direct proportion to the number of promotional air fares available on a given day.

"When new, low fares are announced, our phone volume surges. The minute fares increase, our phone volume decreases.

"I'm certain that other major operators are seeing the same correlation," he said.

Osborne is calling for zone fares as the best marketing stimulus in encouraging European travel.

"Fares of $599 from New York, $699 from the Midwest and $799 from the West will help generate increased bookings in this era of localized gateways and hub-and-spoke systems," he said.

Given the price sensitivity of today's travel marketplace, Osborne voiced concern over the tour operator-airline relationship.

"Tour operators enhance the Europe product, providing airlines with attractive packages to strengthen sales," he said, "but the airlines are expecting tour operators to generate the market.

"We can't generate the market alone, without cooperation from the airlines," he said.

Illustrating a common problem, Osborne noted that airlines often offer consolidators considerably lower prices than they are willing to negotiate with tour operators.

"We cannot compete effectively and put together an attractive air-land package when a client or travel agent can go to a consolidator and book the same air ticket for $200 less than our net," Osborne said.

"By working closer together and negotiating, tour operators can be an effective sales and marketing partner for the airlines. But it's a two-way street," he said.

Reprinted with permission from Travel Weekly, July 11, 1991.

TRAVEL INDUSTRY PRICING PRACTICES

Airlines

Before deregulation airline pricing was much less complex. All fares required approval by the Civil Aeronautics Board (CAB) and securing a change was time consuming. If one airline's fare was changed, so were all others operating in the same market. Travel agencies were also required to charge official tariff fares and could not legally rebate commission or add service charges on airline ticket transactions. Airlines and travel agencies were specifically granted immunity from antitrust limitations on cooperative pricing activities.

CAB approval was also required if an airline wanted to serve new cities or to cease service to any cities. Securing new route authorities could take years. Many routes were only served by one airline.

Thus, before the 1980s, innovations in pricing were few and far between. Airlines were satisfied with first class and economy fares, a single excursion fare which required a minimum length of stay and could not be used on flights departing at certain peak times, a children's fare, and a family plan providing discounts when family members accompanied a passenger paying full fare.

Until deregulation was accomplished, there was little incentive and even less opportunity for true price competition within the airline industry. With the demise of the CAB on January 1, 1985, antitrust immunity ended as well. Airlines were given full flexibility to adjust fares whenever they wished.

Yield Management

Just as a dress store does not want to lower prices if it can sell its inventory at higher prices, an airline does not want to sell a seat at a low excursion fare if it can get a higher fare for it. The technique airlines have developed to try to maximize income from each flight is called **yield management**.

Yield management requires sophisticated computer programming to establish the "mix" of seats allocated to specific fare levels and to monitor seat sales so that allocation changes can be made when conditions warrant. The initial fare mix is established after analysis of historical data showing how specific flights on specific dates, days of the week and times have filled. As the date of the flight approaches, sales are monitored regularly with daily and even more frequent review taking place during the two to three weeks closest to departure.

The airline's computer is programmed to identify sales performance of each flight on a daily basis and advise yield management personnel when conditions appear to support a change in the fare mix. Lowest fare excursion seats could be added, for example, when sales are slow or reduced when sales are more brisk than anticipated.

The frequent adjustments as departure day approaches explains why a low cost fare may not be available Monday morning, for example, but becomes available the same evening or the next day. Unfortunately, travelers lose confidence in their travel agents when told on one day that a flight is not available at a low excursion fare and they call the airline from home at night and are given seats.

"Would you like the sunrise special fare...the early morning fare...the midafternoon fare...the midmorning fare...the early afternoon fare...the high-noon fare...the late afternoon fare...the early supper fare...the supper super fare...the dinner fare...the deluxe dessert fare...the late night fare...the late late night fare...the midnight fare...the super-duper excursion fare...the dawn fare...the ...?"

INDUSTRY COMMUNIQUE

AIRLINE PASSENGERS FACE BAFFLING PRICING TRENDS

Martha M. Hamilton
Washington Post Staff Writer

If you paid full fare for your airline seat, you probably paid too much.

Discounting has become so deeply embedded in the industry that last year only nine out of every 100 airline passengers paid full fare.

That makes sorting out the trends in fares—in an industry where more than 200,000 fare changes a day may be fed into the industry's computer clearinghouse—a bewildering exercise. Adding to that confusion, advertised discount fares may come and go with increasingly litttle relation to changes in full fares.

Full fare yields (revenue per passenger miles traveled) are up 63.9 percent since 1981, including a 6.7 percent increase in 1989, according to Salomon Brothers airline analyst Julius Maldutis. But Maldutis also notes that discounts from full fares have been getting deeper. In 1981, when discounting was in its infancy, the average discount from full fare was 46.2 percent, compared with 66.5 percent in October, 1989. Discount fares are up only 6.3 percent since 1981, with only a 1.2 percent increase in 1989, Maldutis said. Instead of moving in tandem, the spread between full fares and discounts has widened.

At the same time, the percentage of traffic flying on discount has also increased—from 70.6 percent in 1981 industry-wide to 91 percent in 1988, although it declined slightly this year. "In 1978, 47.9 percent of our passengers traveled on a discount," said Bob Coggin, vice president of marketing development for Delta Airlines. "In the first six months of 1989, 88.4 percent traveled on some kind of discount fares. That's the product of the pricing freedom the airlines have enjoyed as a result of deregulation."

To obtain discounts, passengers usually must fulfill various conditions, such as advance purchase, and discounted tickets often are non-refundable. But for passengers paying their own way, and increasingly, for business travelers too, the search for discount fares has become a way of life.

Discounts are currently helping to keep the overall increase in airline fares roughly in line with inflation. George James of Airline Economics, an airline research and forecasting group, estimates that fares increased by 5 percent last year and will rise by approximately 3 percent this year.

"We may see some downward movement and we may see some upward movement, but the general trend will be—and has to be—upward," he said. "The airlines have to improve profitability to take care of the increased cost of fuel, growing labor costs and $130 billion worth of equipment on order and option."

> Increasing fuel costs have been the biggest factor in recent price increase announcements with some airlines facing costs at least 30 percent higher than the price they paid for fuel a year ago. Every penny increase in the cost of fuel costs the airline industry $150 million annually, so fuel increases have put serious pressure on airlines to raise fares, said James.
>
> Even in the face of a slowdown in the demand for airline travel, airlines have found that they sometimes benefit from increasing fares, even if traffic declines.
>
> For instance, Airline Economics found that during February through May 1989, major U.S. airlines' yields (which generally reflect fares) increased by an average of 13.1 percent. As a result, they lost 4.6 percent of traffic but increased revenue by 9 percent. In contrast, in June through August, 1989, yields were only 2 percent higher than a year before. Traffic was up 1.2 percent, but revenue increased by only 3.2 percent. "In that situation, if you were a business, which way would you price?" asked James.
>
> *Washington Post, January 4, 1990.*

Free market competition has produced an exceedingly complex industry fare structure. Many low fare roundtrip prices are lower than the lowest one way fare between two cities. Advance purchase and Saturday night stay restrictions are designed to prevent business travelers from using the lowest excursion fares. Yet, for many years, most airlines established "meeting fares" and negotiated city-pair fares with commercial accounts and travel agencies which substantially undercut the basic fare structure. Actions often defied logic.

Airlines are so concerned with maintaining their market share in almost every city-pair market that their marketing decisions are clearly made without consideration of profitability. Almost any time that a carrier lowers a fare in an attempt to gain market share, it is matched within hours by competing airlines who fear losing market share. The end result is usually little change in market share and increased loss or less profit for all.

Override Commissions

Before deregulation, commissions paid to travel agents were fixed and any changes required CAB approval. Since deregulation, a basic commission level (10%) is paid by almost all airlines. However, travel agents can qualify for additional commission—**overrides**—with many airlines. Overrides are usually negotiated on a one-on-one basis between a travel agency and an airline. Antitrust regulations prevent group action.

Free air tickets for use by agency staff and/or for promotional purposes are also used by many airlines to encourage travel agencies to increase sales on the specific airlines. Sometimes free ticket incentives are combined with cash overrides.

Although some overrides are based on meeting specific sales volume goals, most are based on the travel agent's "peer market share." This method compares the percentage of Agency A's sales on Airline A with other agencies in the agency's peer group (usually a specifically defined geographic area). For example, if all agencies in a peer group sell, on average, 15% of their total air sales on Airline A, and Agency A sells 16% on Airline A, the agency may receive additional commission if that level exceeds Airline A's requirements. In the above example, overrides would rarely be paid to agencies producing less than 15% of sales on Airline A.

Consolidators

The airline ticket consolidator is an additional level of distribution between the airline and the travel agent or traveler used by some airlines to increase sales primarily of international tickets. International air fares require the bilateral agreement of the governments of both the countries of departure and destination. **Consolidators** provide a method of lowering seat prices without seeking formal government approval.

Airlines provide seats to consolidators either at low net prices or with an exceedingly high commission rate (25% to 40% levels are not unusual). Consolidators, in return, commit to sell large numbers of seats for the supplying airline. The result is the sale of tickets to the public at rates lower than the lowest fare available from the airline directly or written by an appointed travel agent.

Travel agencies avoided the use of consolidators for many years, but most now recognize the need to meet the traveler's desire for air tickets at the lowest possible fare levels. Thus, while few will advertise consolidator fares, most will check to see if a consolidator ticket is available for the destination and dates their clients require.

Cruise Lines

The normal price of a cruise varies with the level of quality of the ship (budget to deluxe), as well as the size and location of cabins within specific ships. Prices obviously increase with the length of the cruise as well.

Cruise pricing is based upon the use of almost all cabins by at least two persons. Thus, cruise rates are per person rates based upon double occupancy of cabins. Some cabins can hold additional persons. The cost for a third, fourth (and in some cases, a fifth) person is considerably less per person.

Single rates, however, are much higher. Some ships have a few single cabins that are available for about 125% of half of a double cabin in an equivalent location on the ship. To book a double cabin for a single person can cost as much as 200% of the double occupancy rate so that the cabin will generate as much income from one person as from two. To lessen the cost for the single traveler, some cruise lines and some travel agencies will either provide a guaranteed share rate or at least try to help a single person find a shared cabin.

For many years, the pricing of cruises was fixed—by the prices stated in cruise brochures. As the cruise product grew in popularity, more ships were added to cruise fleets and competition increased. In 1970 about 400,000 United States travelers sailed on cruises. By 1990, their numbers had increased to 4,000,000. Estimates for the year 2000 range from 8,000,000 to 10,000,000. As ship and line competition increased, price competition became a major factor as well.

Some lines quickly gained reputations for inflating brochure prices and substantially discounting all rates on all cruises. Others kept greater control of the pricing of their product through selective discounting based upon sailing dates and destinations. Upgrading is another form of discounting. Travelers pay the rate for a lower price cabin and receive a higher price cabin.

Traditionally, groups have received discounts on cruises. Levels vary with ship and season. On many sailings, cruise lines establish "guaranteed group" or "GG" sailing dates and allow preferred travel agencies to sell individual cabins at group rates. "Early bird" discounts are provided by many lines to induce travelers to book well ahead of sailing (generally 4 to 6 months in advance).

The economies of the cruise industry require that ships sail at levels as close to full as possible. Commitments to the service crew (salary and tips) and other fixed costs encourage ship lines to sell cabins at nearly give-away rates rather than sailing with many empty cabins. Thus, even two-for-one prices may be offered when sailing dates are weak.

In 1992, led by Royal Caribbean Cruise Lines (RCCL), major cruise lines instituted pricing policies designed to encourage early bookings. Instead of cutting rates as sailing dates approach, the cruise lines adopted a yield management approach which provides the highest discounts to those who book first. Early booking passengers are promised a refund if prices are lowered later. As bookings increase, the discount levels decrease, providing greater yields for the cruise lines and a more stable sales environment for travel agencies.

Cruise line discounting practices have contributed to the traveler's belief in the great value of the cruise product. Cruise discounts abound for all cruises except the most deluxe and for all except the most popular sailing dates (for example, Christmas and New Year's). Some travel agencies provide added discounts through rebates and shipboard credits for bar and shop charges.

Hotels

Pricing is a major marketing strategy throughout the hotel industry. Like the cruise brochure price, the hotel brochure or "rack" rate is often discounted. Like the cruise ship, rates within specific hotels and resorts vary with season, and size and location of room. From there, discounting begins.

Because of varying travel demand, many hotels' weekday rates are different from weekend rates. Major city and airport hotels promote substantially discounted weekend rates because their prime users, the business travelers, avoid weekend travel. Some resorts, however, have lower weekday rates because of greater demand on the weekends.

Lower group and convention/meeting rates are standard practice within the hotel industry. A variety of corporate rates are offered by most hotels, with the lowest rates being granted to those companies that book the largest number of room nights per year. Special government rates are established for persons traveling on official government business. Because of the perishability of the hotel room night (no income for last night's empty room), many hotels permit front desk personnel to substantially discount rooms to walk-in guests after a certain hour of the day.

Newer pricing techniques include advance purchase discounts and nonrefundable discount rates patterned after the airline industry. These, of course, are aimed at the leisure traveler. See the Industry Communique for another point of view on pricing in the hotel industry.

The commissionability of hotel rates to travel agencies is another pricing issue among hotel companies. Some, like Choice and Hilton, clearly state that all individual room rates are commissionable. Other hotel chains and many independent hotels do not pay commissions on certain corporate and other discounted room rates.

INDUSTRY COMMUNIQUE

SELL VALUE, NOT PRICE

Robert C. Hazard, Jr.
President and CEO, Choice Hotels

So what is better *value*? It is the improvement in quality of product, quality of service and quality of attitude per dollar of price. For value to rise, quality and service satisfaction have to rise faster than price.

Value is guest satisfaction per dollar. Creating value is tricky. If we create more value and satisfy guests, but don't earn a profit, we are out of business. If we earn a profit (or even if we don't) but fail to reinvest the proceeds to satisfy guests, we will soon be out of customers.

Decreasing value and losing competitiveness is an issue that does not hit you overnight with full force. It's more like being nibbled to death.

Car Rental Companies

Pricing is as major a marketing function among highly competitive car rental companies as in other sectors of the travel industry. Like airlines and hotels, car rental companies use different strategies for marketing to commercial and leisure travelers.

Most car rental companies offer special contract rates to businesses in addition to general corporate rates. Space available upgrades to larger (and more expensive) cars are also offered to frequent users. Upgrade certificates are frequently given to travel agencies as an incentive to book a specific car rental company.

Weekly and weekend rates are primarily offered to attract leisure travelers. With some companies, the rate for a weekly rental could be less than the rate for renting the same car for 4 or 5 days based upon daily rates. To avoid use of these rates by business travelers, a minimum use of 6 days might be required to qualify for weekly rates. Thus, a 5-day renter could be paying more than a 7-day renter for the same car.

Some car rental firms offer discounts to members of organizations (for example, American Association of Retired Persons (AARP)) based solely on membership. The discounts are promoted by the organizations as member benefits.

Competition on the basis of commission levels paid for specific types of business is a pricing technique used by car rental companies. The policy of Hertz and Avis is 10% for leisure and 5% for corporate rentals, for example, whereas Alamo and Thrifty pay 10% on all rentals. Another, smaller rental company pays 10% of the rental or $10.00, whichever is more.

Extra charges are additional factors in the pricing mix. Collision or limited damage waivers (CDW or LDW) can cost as much as the car rental itself for small cars in Florida or Hawaii, the most competitive areas for leisure car rentals. Some companies also charge extra for additional drivers or for drivers under age 25 (Some won't even rent at all to people under 25.). Extra taxes and airport use charges also increase the cost of car rentals.

Tour Operators

Competitive considerations, actual cost of tour components, and promotion costs are the primary factors affecting the costing of tour programs. Discounting is not prevalent, at least at present. Thus, there are rarely situations when two travelers are paying different prices for the same travel program.

Travel Agencies

In the years before deregulation, travel agencies never considered pricing either a problem or a benefit. Agencies simply charged the prices established by their suppliers. Only when developing travel programs for groups or complex, personalized independent tours did agencies make pricing decisions.

In those years discounting of supplier prices was a dirty word. Rebating of air ticket fares was illegal and enforcement action was taken against those who discounted international air tickets. But the 1978 Airline Deregulation Act and activities of the 1980s changed the industry. As late as 1987, the American Society of Travel Agents urged the Department of Transportation to enforce existing regulations against rebating commissions on the sale of international air tickets but was rebuffed by the government which encouraged the discounted fares.

Today's travel agency owner and manager must consider pricing strategies when establishing marketing plans. Essentially there are three choices:

- *charge the prices established by suppliers*
- *rebate all or a portion of commission income*
- *add a service charge to supplement commission income or to provide income when there is no commission*

Different policies can be established for different products and clients.

REBATES

Rebating is the practice of giving back all or a portion of the commission income earned from the sale of a travel product to a client. Through this practice, a travel agency can provide a travel product at a price less than the retail price established by a supplier.

Rebating has become a way of life with respect to the handling of large commercial accounts by travel agencies. When bidding to secure these accounts, agencies often must respond to questions about potential "revenue sharing" or rebating. Agencies often agree to rebate hotel and car rental commissions completely and a portion of their air ticket commissions (usually 1% to 3%).

Producing a profit while rebating commission income is a strong challenge to a travel agency. Before offering rebates, an agency must fully understand both the agency's own operating costs and the nature of the travel done by the potential account. Often the amount of air ticket rebate is keyed to specific ticket prices or the average ticket price on a monthly or quarterly basis. The higher the ticket price, the more affordable the rebate.

Fee-based pricing is a commercial account pricing strategy developed in the 1980s that is used by some large travel agencies for their largest commercial accounts. Under this concept, all commissions are rebated to the account and set fees are paid by the account for specific services including making reservations, changing reservations, writing tickets, delivering documents, and so forth. When this strategy was first developed, its promoters predicted that it would become the primary method of pricing. Although this has not and probably will not occur, fee-based pricing will remain a valid pricing alternative.

Discounting, rather than rebating, is the term used when a travel agency sells a leisure product at a price lower than that established by the supplier. Discounting is used on a limited basis by some travel agencies to attract new business and to remain competitive with other agencies who use this pricing strategy. Agencies that earn override commissions from preferred suppliers are in a better position to provide discounts to clients and still be profitable than agencies which do not. Most suppliers will not permit travel agencies to advertise discounted prices using the specific supplier name in print or broadcast media.

SERVICE CHARGES

Some travel agencies charge clients **service charges** for functions that either do not generate commission income or do not generate enough income to cover agency costs. Such activities as making hotel reservations at pensions and other hotels that do not pay travel agency commission and writing airline or rail tickets at prices below a specified amount are the kinds of services for which some agencies have established service charges.

Establishing service charges is a valid pricing strategy as long as agencies inform their clients of the charges before performing the requested work. To do otherwise could be considered fraudulent.

A service charge policy does not always produce additional income. Often, clients will either go elsewhere or perform the function themselves rather than pay extra charges.

Establishing service charges is a better marketing strategy than telling a client that the agency will not perform the service. At least the client gets an alternative and if he or she agrees to pay the charge, the travel agency will receive sufficient income for providing the requested service. By having a service charge policy a travel agency can avoid either saying "no" to clients or performing work without income.

CONCLUSION

Pricing has become one of the most critical considerations in the travel and tourism marketing process. The discount mentality of the American public has forced all segments of the industry to focus on price more than ever before. Even the travel agency, which was protected from concern about pricing when airline prices were regulated, must now make pricing decisions.

SUMMARY

The degree to which a product or service is price elastic will determine the degree to which pricing policies are important. Prices will be lowered in those situations where marketers believe that increase volume at lower price will increase total revenues and, hopefully, increased profit.

The combination of deregulation and increased sophistication of computer technology has led to the development of the technique of yield management in the airline industry. Through yield management, airlines continuously adjust the number of seats on a specific flight available at different fare levels to maximize potential revenue. Payments of override commissions to travel agents and the use of consolidators are other price-related techniques airlines use to increase total sales.

The organization and economics of the cruise industry requires pricing to be based on sailing with a virtually full ship. Increased competition has forced almost all cruise lines to provide either discounts on existing rates for most sailings or upgrades to higher level cabins without extra charge. Guaranteed group rates provide another method of organized discounting in the cruise industry.

Hotels and car rental firms use a variety of pricing techniques to increase sales. Weekday rates are higher than weekend rates, especially in business-oriented locations. Special meeting and convention and tour package rates also are part of the pricing mix. Advance purchase savings, based on the airline model, are becoming a factor in these segments as well.

Major discounting practices are not yet a factor among tour operators. It is rare to find travelers paying different rates for the same tour product unless they received a rebate from a travel agency.

Pricing decisions are relatively new to the travel agency segment of the industry. Travel agency owners and managers have three choices:

1. Charge the prices established by suppliers
2. Rebate all or a part of commission income
3. Add a service charge to supplement commission income.

QUESTIONS FOR THOUGHT AND DISCUSSION

1. What is price elasticity of demand and how does it affect the travel and tourism industry?
2. How is the yield management technique used by airlines?
3. What types of pricing decisions must be made by cruise lines?
4. How do different days of the week and seasonality affect travel and tourism pricing decisions?
5. How do car rental firms apply pricing decisions to commercial accounts?
6. What pricing choices must travel agencies make?

8

Communication

communication
customer relations
feedback
jargon
nonverbal communication
one-way communication
two-way communication
verbal communication

Communication is at the heart of all of marketing. All marketing efforts are aimed at bringing supplier and consumer together, and without some form of communication, this would not be possible.

COMPONENTS OF COMMUNICATION

Communication consists of three parts—a message, a sender, and a receiver. All three are equally important to the act of communicating. The message is what is being communicated. This can be something as simple as the greeting, "Hello," or as complex as a lengthy report. The sender is the individual from whom the message originates. The receiver is the one to whom the message is directed.

In addition, all communication is transmitted through a channel or medium. There is a wide variety of media from which to choose, such as face-to-face, via telephone, over radio or TV, by letter, or in the newspaper. The medium used will affect the overall process and should be carefully chosen.

Feedback is the other crucial step in most communications situations. **Feedback** goes from the receiver back to the sender. It can let the sender know that the message has simply been received, that it has been received and accepted, or that there is confusion. Feedback may be a direct answer to a question, a shrug of the shoulders or shake of the head, or even silence. In fact, sometimes no feedback is, in itself, powerful feedback. Being ignored after sending a message can result in strong reactions. A great percentage of problems

151

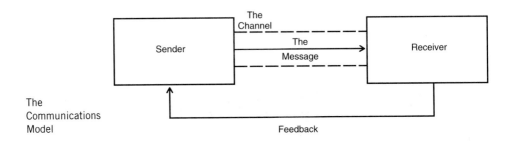

The
Communications
Model

among human beings results from poor communications and misunderstandings due to improper feedback.

Verbal and Nonverbal Communication

Communication can be either verbal or nonverbal. Both forms are equally important. **Verbal communication** uses spoken or written words. **Nonverbal communication** uses such unspoken forms as a nod, shrug, or a tone of voice. Even facial expressions can send a message, and qualify as nonverbal communication. See the Industry Communique for more on the importance of nonverbal communication.

Frequently, nonverbal communication may contradict the verbal message the sender is trying to transmit. When this happens, the receiver will get a confused message, and may take either signal as the "true" one. For this reason, tone of voice is a particularly important nonverbal means of communication. As an example, sarcasm depends on the contradiction between verbal and nonverbal messages. In sarcasm, the words say one thing while the tone makes it clear that the message really means quite the opposite. Similarly, a friendly smile and warm tone of voice make a hotel clerk's "Welcome," mean one thing. A cold stare and an icy tone of voice can change that meaning drastically, even when the word—"Welcome"—is identical.

It is extremely important to remember that you are sending nonverbal as well as verbal messages. Be sure that the total message (verbal and nonverbal) is the one really intended for the receiver.

Ome-Way and Two-Way Communications

Communication can be either one way or two way. Examples of **one-way communications** are advertising by newspaper, radio, or TV, writing a letter or sending a fax. In one-way communication, a message is transmitted but the sender cannot get an immediate response from the receiver. The sender hopes that the message

The examples show how important nonverbal communication can be. In the first, the client is restrained, with arms folded in a protective shielding manner. He is not yet convinced that he wants to be part of this. on the other hand, in the second illustration, the client is highly involved. He is even displaying the brochures that interest him and asking questions. The first agent still has a lot of work to do and should be concentrating on getting the client involved rather than on the product itself. The second agent should already be trying to close the sale.

INDUSTRY COMMUNIQUE

COMMUNICATIONS

John F. Kelly

So I'm at this seminar and the speaker, Richard Greene, asks us how people communicate. And I think, what a stupid question; with words, of course. That's one thing that separates man from beast, right? But Richard continues to probe, and we finally come up with words, voice tone, and what he calls "physiology" and we call "looks." Then he wants us to identify what percentage of communication each represents. Words are number one, of course. That's our language, after all.

Next, he gives us a word we should all be familiar with—executive—and asks us to each write 10 words that mean or describe "executive" to us. Then we get into groups of six and find out how many words match. Amazingly, in my group there isn't one word that every one of us has on our lists. One group has one out of 10 words match, the rest are all goose eggs. Perhaps words aren't the end-all in communication.

When Richard reveals that words represent only 7 percent of a communication, voice tone 38 percent and physiology 55 percent, we are shocked, even after our experiment with defining executive. To think that 55 percent of communication comes from gestures, body language, appearance, eye contact and the like is a real revelation.

But just think about saying the word "fire" in a quiet monotone. It's just a word that way. Add voice tone—FIRE—and it becomes more alarming and more of a call-to-action. Do the same thing and run out of the room with fear in your eyes and it takes on ultimate urgency.

A week after Richard's seminar, I was flying to Portland to attend a new flight-attendant training class, and I was watching our flight attendant very aptly performing her duties. Then it hit me: Everything she was doing involved communication, yet very little of it had to do with words. Her smile, her eye contact and her appearance were all communicating strongly and very positively. As was the tone of her voice as she greeted us, made announcements and served us. Very clearly, her physiology and voice tone were the keys to how we perceived the service.

So when I got to the training session, I decided to try Richard's approach, only I had the class come up with 10 words that mean or describe "flight attendant." The results were the same as from our session, with only one group coming up with even a single word that matched with all six people. Not surprising to me, but a real eye-opener to them.

Then we had an in-depth discussion about how physiology and voice tone could have a strong impact on our customers. For instance, we got talking about how we have always maintained appearance standards, but never could really explain why. Knowing the importance physiology plays in communication, though, it becomes very understandable. A flight attendant who does a fine job but has a rumpled, ill-fitting or otherwise conspicuous uniform cannot communicate the professional, caring service image that is so important to us. No matter how nice the flight attendant is, he or she cannot totally overcome the negative image from the uniform. So maintaining uniform standards is not a small detail, but rather a major portion of our communication.

Or think about the communication that is made when you are onboard an aircraft when it's dark outside, you are reading the morning paper, and all of a sudden, the flight attendant turns out the light to prepare for taxiing. No warning, the lights are just all turned off. How rude, you think, as you reach up to find your overhead reading light. We use this example now in our training classes, and have even put the correct procedures into our manual: Make an announcement and let people know you are about to dim the lights and make them aware of their overhead reading lights, in advance. It communicates we care.

This discussion about communication has become an ongoing part of my presentation to flight-attendant training classes. Together, we have come up with a long list of items we can focus on to ensure our actions continue to speak louder than our words. We have recognized that communication is the prime job of a flight attendant, whether it be through safety briefings or showing how much we care through our service. In fact, we have recognized that all areas of our business can be improved through improved communication—not words, but full communication.

Reprinted with permission from Horizon Air Magazine, March 1991.

is received and understood, but it is not possible to discuss what is in the message at the time it is given.

Advertising communication—one-way communication—will be discussed fully in the next chapter. Here, we are considering only two-way forms of communication. A sales conversation is a good example of **two-way communication**. In these situations, a receiver as well as a sender is immediately involved. Sometimes the salesperson is the sender, with the customer acting as the receiver, and sometimes it is the reverse, but there is always one in each function. Of course, there is always also a message. In this example of two-way communications the salesperson has the opportunity to study the buyer and to adapt what is being said to the buyer's reactions. The salesperson should be alert and look for nonverbal signs of agreement, disagreement, or even confusion, so that the presentation can be altered as necessary.

This is true in a face-to-face sales conversation as well as a telephone conversation. In telephone communication, nonverbal signs are greatly diminished, but they are still there. Tone of voice is the primary nonverbal communication on a telephone conversation. The tone of voice says a great deal, if one is listening carefully. Pauses can also be significant.

It should be noted that a scripted telemarketing phone call is, for all practical purposes, one-way communication. Although a sender and a receiver are taking part, the sender is not looking for and reacting to the receiver. In fact, if the receiver should interrupt the caller with a question, more often than not, the sender gets confused. The sender is merely reading a script and asking at the end for a "yes" or "no" response.

FAILURES IN COMMUNICATIONS

Most problems in marketing, if not in much of life, are due to miscommunication. Misunderstandings usually arise from differences between what the sender meant to communicate and what the receiver understood. In business situations, especially those relating to sales efforts, the ethical professional knows that it is important to be sure that the sender and receiver are getting the same message.

Making Things Clear

In business communications, it is wise to use basic expressions that are clear in meaning. Current fad or slang expressions may be easily misunderstood. The use of simple words is also advisable. It is more important to convey a meaning clearly than to impress your customer with the extent of your vocabulary. Your receiver may be too embarrassed to admit that he or she does not understand the meaning of a word, and fail to ask for clarification. As a result, your client may make an incorrect assumption of meaning.

Jargon

Another dangerous form of communication is the use of jargon. Every industry has its own jargon—words that have a particular meaning for a given group of people, but that are not in common use elsewhere. For example, it would be better to tell a potential consumer that the price of the hotel includes breakfast and dinner rather than to say that the price includes MAP. When it is necessary to use jargon in talking with a customer, it is important to define the jargon as it is being used. For example, a salesperson could say, "This price is MAP—modified American plan. Breakfast and dinner included." The consumer is then introduced to a term used in the industry, but because it is defined, there is no chance for misunderstanding. It is also important to assure that the consumer understands industry accepted differences such as "adjoining" vs "connecting" rooms in a hotel or

"What do you mean, the seasons are reversed down here?"

"nonstop" vs "direct" vs "connecting" airline flights. Always assume that special words are not understood and define them. It is better to define unnecessarily than to assume understanding that may not exist.

Listening

A good communicator is a good listener. Remember, listening is part of communicating. It has been said that because humans have two ears and only one mouth, they should listen twice as often as they speak. Unfortunately, many people talk without listening. All too often, each member of the communication effort concentrates on sending. Then, instead of listening carefully so as to respond correctly, the other party spends time that should be receiving time on planning a response. Neither participant is really sure just what the other said, and each is answering based on the message that he or she expected to receive. Many arguments could be settled quickly or would be avoided altogether if people learned to listen. The technique of listening—of really receiving—is a very important technique for a salesperson. Look at the other person and concentrate on what that person is saying.

Effective listening is hard work. We can hear and assimilate verbal communications at a rate two to four times that of normal speech. This discrepancy leaves gaps when our mind can become distracted, or wander, losing track of what the speaker has said. Thus, it is easy to become distracted. Most salespeople believe they are better listeners than they really are. You will do well to underestimate your own listening ability, and to work hard on sharpening this critical skill.

The best way to listen effectively is to practice "active listening." Look right at the person who is speaking to you if possible. Maintain eye contact. Take notes on what they are saying. Not only does this make them feel you consider them important, but it forces you to focus on what they are saying. It slows down your listening to your note-taking speed, and assures that you will hear everything said. It also lets

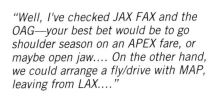

"Well, I've checked JAX FAX and the OAG—your best bet would be to go shoulder season on an APEX fare, or maybe open jaw.... On the other hand, we could arrange a fly/drive with MAP, leaving from LAX...."

you pull out the important items from the extraneous material being communicated. Ask questions where necessary and make appropriate responses where expected.

Confirming Messages

It is advisable to confirm important items in writing to avoid misunderstandings later. Much of the communication in the travel industry is oral only. In most cases this is sufficient, but where a misunderstanding could result in a serious problem, put all agreements in writing. Thus, there will be no argument later about whether baggage handling expenses were included in the price or whether the meeting room was complimentary in price for the group at the hotel. Where arrangements are complex, written itineraries should be provided, with all prices and features spelled out.

When sending complex and lengthy written communications, it is also advisable to have someone else in the company read them before they go out. In this way, you can be sure that what you said is what you meant. Frequently, a person who knows what he or she meant to say may be ambiguous without realizing it. Another person, who reads the communication without knowing what was meant, will be more likely to question what was said. If this happens, the original sender can clarify the meaning before it is too late.

MISLEADING ADVERTISING

Misleading advertising deliberately sends an inherently false message with the hope that the receiver will believe the false message, although nothing provably false has actually been said. This type of intentional miscommunication can be dangerous, and it is eventually unprofitable. The first sale may be made, but the customer will not return, nor will referral business be created.

CUSTOMER RELATIONS

Customer relations, of course, is communication, and any business that hopes to grow through repeat and referral business must be concerned with communicating its concern for its clients' well-being and satisfaction. Advertising, low prices, or unique products may get the first-time customer, but unless the customer is satisfied, the repeat sale will not be made. Because there is a limit to the number of first-time customers in an area, it is important to keep the customers you get. Customers are kept by strict attention to effective communication.

Importance to Repeat Sales

It is much easier and less expensive to make a sale to a repeat customer than to a new one. When selling to the new customer, part of the sales process is first selling the customer on using this company's service as well as trust in the salesperson—that is, communicating the desirability and reliability of the service and the service provider. The customer must be convinced that the business is reputable and knowledgeable and safe to use. The salesperson must also build trust in the consumer for himself or herself as the best one to provide the service.

When a customer comes back as a repeat sale, this part of the sale is already made. Thus, the salesperson can concentrate on selling the particular product that will meet the customer's needs. This is also true of the referral customer. When a buyer has been referred to a business by someone he or she knows, the sale is partially made.

Because repeat business is so important, all businesspeople must be concerned with customer relations. Customer relations is that part of the marketing process that helps to ensure satisfied customers. When everything goes as expected, customer relations should be an easy process. Pleasant personnel, good communications, efficient service, and products that are as advertised will help with the greater part of the task of maintaining good customer relations.

Ways of Handling Problems

The true measure of a business's ability to promote good customer relations, however, comes when there is a problem. Unfortunately, problems do arise in some transactions. If complaints are too frequent, the underlying reasons for the problems need to be discovered. Perhaps personnel need more training. Or perhaps more up-to-date reference materials are needed. In a properly managed business, problems will be infrequent, but they are important when they do occur. The way in which these problems are handled will determine the business's success or failure in gaining repeat clientele.

INDUSTRY COMMUNIQUE

CAPITALIZING ON COMPLAINTS

Perry W. Buffington, Ph.D.

Preliminary research is suggesting that being the recipient of complaints may contribute to excessive worry, burnout, and perhaps physical ailments. Yet, inherent in the simple complaint is a wealth of information. As a result, forward-thinking corporations are choosing to risk the "dis-ease" which may result from complaints.

It is possible to maintain one's composure, minimize physical discomfort, and concomitantly learn a great deal while facing a complainer. To do this effectively takes three things: training in problem-solving, a change of mind, and future thinking. When these are present, then the basic complaint is seen as information rather than criticism; an opportunity for product refinement; a displeasure with the product rather than a personal attack; and most important of all, a chance to redeem a customer.

As regards training, imagine the following. A group of 20 students who had experience in problem-solving were matched with an equal number who had no specific training in this area. The study was conducted at a local television station so that the students could be observed. In this experiment, they were given a real-life problem to solve: develop a plan which would bring in more guests during the off-season at a seasonal hotel.

According to Roger L. Firestien, Ph.D., acting director at the Center for Studies in Creativity, Buffalo State University (New York): "After we analyzed the videotapes, we found that the groups who were trained in creative problem-solving smiled more, supported others' ideas more, criticized ideas significantly less, and generated more useful ideas. To take it a step further, when we analyzed the ideas for quality, we found that the groups who were trained in creative problem-solving outperformed untrained groups about three to one on the number of high-quality ideas."

Firestien, who has been studying problem-solving in the workplace for over ten years, explains that this study "generated a massive insight." Now he wanted to know: "What happens when we train people to turn a complaint into a problem statement?"

"The results are the same, if not better," says Firestien. "With a little problem-solving or complaint-handling training, they learned how to come up with 20 or 30 possible ideas in the same time that it took the untrained groups to come up with five or six. They had better solutions to pick from by which to solve the complaints."

Training appears to remove the problems associated with complaints. "Without training, recipients of complaints bottom out when they feel unskilled. What we are giving them [front-line staff] is a little mental confidence. Plus, we are giving them a way to distance themselves from the complaint, set it up like a problem statement, remove the negative energy, and focus their minds for gathering information and effectively dealing with the complaints," adds Firestien.

Summarizes Firestien: "Listen to complaints; turn them into problem statements (that's to skip the negative energy); then generate some ideas to solve them; and finally, implement those ideas."

After this, complaints take on a different timbre. "There is information in complaints, powerful information," adds Firestien. "It is the proactive organization that looks at those complaints as stepping-stones to success. A complaint is not necessarily a crisis. It can tip you off to an impending one."

Not every organization sees complaints in this light. But there is a trend which reflects a change of mind is underway.

According to Oren Harari, Ph.D., professor of Management at the University of San Francisco and consultant with the Tom Peters Group (Palo Alto): "Let's just say that in many companies, customers' complaints are treated like a disease; you want to avoid them, or you treat the complainer as if he or she were the criminal."

However, striking new research is causing more and more corporations to take complaints to heart, scrutinize them carefully, and respond proactively. "Most well-run companies know that most customers do not complain," says Harari. "The problem here is those who do not complain, but quietly look for the first opportunity to go elsewhere. When this happens, many explain the loss of revenue on all sorts of things like soft markets, unfair international competition, and, of course, the competition in general. The smart companies look to their complaints for answers."

"Well-run companies," explains Harari, "know that for every customer who complains, on the average there are 26 customers who have similar complaints, similar dissatisfactions, but who do not complain."

In fact, some companies strive to make it easy for people to complain. Several reasons justify this tactic. First, Harari says, "The research indicates that if the organization which receives a customer complaint responds really well to the issue, the company seals an even tighter relationship between company and consumer than they had before the phone call.

Another reason companies are listening to complaints has to do with the concept of complimentary advice. Whereas consulting companies charge high fees to find out what the public really thinks about a product, each complainer who calls or writes is giving it to you for free. Companies who realize this see complaints as a "strategic weapon" in modifying products and taking the corporate image steps beyond the competition.

Probably the most cogent reason why companies make it easy to complain is based on the following information. "Research suggests that if a company prevents just five percent of its customers from defecting to the competition, the bottom line can be impacted significantly," says Harari. In fact, the figures concerning that positive impact range from 25 percent to 85 percent. Harari specifically adds that this is most effective in service companies like dry cleaning, credit cards, car dealerships, and retailers.

"It's a five-step process," says Janis Cannon, director of Sales and Marketing, Swissotel (Atlanta). Cannon, whose procedure has met with acclaim, acknowledges that this plan of attack developed after years of experience working with "big-group houses" (hotels where 65 percent or more of the business is represented by groups).

Says Cannon: "The very first thing that you do, and this dawns on me immediately: don't promise what you can't deliver. Set realistic expectations for your customer." She acknowledges that, often, print, radio, or video advertising implies the optimal or perfect aspects of consumer services. To cope with the illusion of perfection, Cannon counters, "Just be sure that what you say is going to happen."

Next, acknowledge that there is a reason why the client complained. "Don't deny it: the customer is always right; at least their perception is always right," admits Cannon. "Accept what they say at face value, and in accepting it, what you do is recognize that this is different from every other complaint. Treat them all [complaints] as unique."

Cannon says that the third point is the key: "After accepting the uniqueness, then explore. Why did it happen, and is it a symptom of a bigger problem?" The rule here is to get the consumer talking.

Cannon's fourth step is the obvious one: react. "Of course, you must do your best to fix what is perceived as wrong. You must also ask yourself what is to be accomplished with the solution. Listen as if it were a real problem, then evaluate for yourself."

If you concur that the problem is one that must be resolved, Cannon offers the following advice: "Get the person who is responsible for the development of the product or service integrally involved with solving the problem."

Occasionally, the difficulty doesn't lie in the product, but with the individual who is complaining. Cannon expects that two percent of complainers will never be happy.

Finally, and most important of all: follow up. Cannon firmly believes that follow-up has two purposes. First, check to see if the problem has been solved and if the individual who complained is content. Next, follow up and verify that the organization has used the information provided by the complainer so that the problem will not occur again.

Is it possible to stop complaints and complainers? Firestien, Harari, and Cannon say, "No." Is it possible to plan so that complaints are minimized? The researchers say, "Yes."

To do this requires training in problem-solving, whereby employees are empowered to fix a problem on the first complaint; a change of mind which views complaints as research and information rather than personal attacks; and future thinking, which prevents complaints found in the present from affecting a future consumer.

When this happens, as Harari says, "The customer is given what he or she wants, and a promise is kept."

Reprinted with permission from Sky Magazine, June 1991.

Many companies, including airlines, restaurants, hotels, car rental companies, and travel agencies regularly provide comment cards for the customer to complete (see Chapter 4 for examples). These cards provide an ongoing ability to measure the success of customer relations. If patterns start showing up for particular problems, remedial action can be taken before the company starts losing customers.

Compensating for Errors

First and foremost, it is important to remember to remain pleasant and sympathetic when a complaining customer confronts you. Even if the problem was completely of the customer's own making, you must offer sympathy and friendliness—you must communicate your concern. When the problem resulted from your company's mistake, it is necessary to admit the error and compensate the customer as needed. Of course, this is difficult to do in the travel business. One cannot give back the lost time from a ruined vacation. However, out-of-pocket expenses can be reimbursed.

For this reason, airlines have traditionally been quite generous about compensating travelers for meal or accommodation expenses caused by missed connections even where the fault was not of the airline's own making. Unfortunately, airlines have gotten much less generous in recent years on such compensation. The cost of such reimbursement will be more than recovered by the promotional value of this instance of positive customer relations. The traveler taken care of in this manner will tell friends, and encourage them to use the carrier's service. On the other hand, a traveler on an airline that did not take such care may very well return from the trip, telling friends of horrendous experiences where no one cared and suggesting that friends avoid that carrier. The same is true when a hotel overbooks and must move a guest to another hotel. The manner in which the customer is cared for will determine how that person feels about the supplier. Most people are reasonable (even when they are angry) and a smile goes a long way to diffuse the anger. It is hard to stay angry with someone who is sympathizing with you and saying "I'm sorry" with a reasonable offer of help.

It is critical to keep people informed whenever possible. Nothing makes people feel more insecure, frustrated and angry than to be kept in the dark, wondering what is happening. They will think of everything that could be happening and get themselves all worked up over the worst possible scenarios. If there is a delay in their flight, or construction at their hotel, it is better for them to know the truth. When people feel knowledgeable, they become part of the solution rather than of the problem. Make them feel like partners and you will win their cooperation instead of their anger.

Helping with Other Problems

In some cases, the client is angry because something happened that is not the fault of the company receiving the complaint. Retail travel agents must often handle complaints of this type. Once the agency sells the product, it cannot control the delivery of the product. The agent may have done everything possible to assure the client of a happy experience and then an airline, hotel, car rental company, sightseeing company, or even Mother Nature (in the form of poor weather) spoils part of the plan. In such cases, a sure way to guarantee an unhappy customer is to refuse involvement and refer the complainant to the supplier that was truly responsible for the problem. It is important, again, to sympathize and listen to the customer and to offer to help in any reasonable way.

Frequently, just listening as the customer verbalizes the complaint is enough, and nothing further is needed. In other cases it is advisable to ask the customer to put the complaint in writing. Offer to send their complaint along with a cover letter of your own to the supplier. Even if you know that nothing can be done, the interest you show by spending a little of your own time to help the customer goes a long way toward making you a friend. This feeling of care and friendship can often help avoid a potential lawsuit. Where the customer is due compensation, it is important to use the resources of the agency to help the customer obtain it.

Unfortunately, a service as complex as travel cannot always be provided without problems. The mark of a good salesperson and a good business is handling problems without losing potential repeat business—so important to a business's growth.

CONCLUSION

The travel professional must be aware of the importance of both verbal and non-verbal communications in marketing the travel product. He or she needs good listening skills as well as the ability to communicate clearly and accurately, so that misunderstandings do not arise, and so that problems can be handled effectively.

"So it's my fault it rained on his vacation?"

SUMMARY

Communication involves a message, a sender, and a receiver. It may be either verbal (spoken or written words) or nonverbal (tone of voice, facial expressions, or movements). It can also be either one-way (newspapers, TV commercials) or two-way, as in a face-to-face or telephone sales conversation.

Communication failures are usually not planned, and result from poor choice of words (use of slang or jargon) or failure to listen carefully. At times, however, a false message may be sent deliberately, as in misleading advertising.

Customer relations is an extension of communication that is vital to developing repeat sales. Handling problems and compensating for errors pleasantly and efficiently communicates concern and professionalism.

QUESTIONS FOR THOUGHT AND DISCUSSION

1. List and describe the functions of the three components of any communication.
2. Give examples of nonverbal communication as they might occur in a travel industry situation.
3. Describe and give two examples each of one-way and two-way communications. Use travel industry examples.
4. Define jargon and give six travel industry examples.
5. Discuss the importance of customer relations. How is this part of a company's marketing effort?

9

Relationship Marketing

core values
customer-oriented marketing
interactive relationships
personalization
preferred suppliers
product orientation

Clearly, the marketing function has evolved over time. As discussed in the intro-duction, the earliest marketers focused on the product itself, believing that the best products would attract the most buyers. The operative cliche was "Build a better mousetrap and people will beat a path to your door." The importance of identifying and meeting customer needs was recognized later, and by the 1980s, marketing focused on a problem-solving and customer-oriented approach. During the last 10 years, a new marketing concept has emerged, one best charac-terized as "relationship marketing."

RELATIONSHIP MARKETING IN THE TRAVEL AND TOURISM INDUSTRY

Whereas customer orientation displaced **product orientation** as a focus, **relation-ship marketing** complements the process of identifying and meeting customer needs, rather than replacing it. This kind of marketing recognizes that relation-ships develop between buyers and sellers of products and services. The stronger the relationship between a product or service provider and a customer, the more likely that the customer will purchase from the provider—as long as the provider's product or service meets the customer's need.

Relationship marketing is an important process within the travel and tourism industry. For example, the relationship between travel agency management and supplier management is critical when establishing or changing preferred supplier relationships. The continuing relationship is more important than most other fac-tors. As companies within the travel industry have become more sophisticated and competition has become keener, it is no longer enough to build a better mouse-trap. Nor is it enough just to identify and meet consumer needs.

Interactive Relationships: Travel Agency, Supplier, Traveler

For relationship marketing to be effective, **interactive relationships** must be developed by both buyer and seller. But the typical relationships in the travel industry involve two distinct relationships for each party.

Whereas a travel agency and a tour operator, for example, must develop relationships with each other, both must also develop relationships with the ultimate consumer of the travel product—the traveler (see Figure 9-1). The travel agent is, in essence, a buyer from the tour operator and seller to the traveler. The tour operator is a seller to both. To add complexity to the entire situation, the ultimate success of the relationships (and thus the marketing efforts) will depend upon how effectively the tour operator provides travel services to the traveler as well as to the travel agency.

Relationships and personalized services are more important in the travel industry than in many others because of the intangible nature of travel products. Because we are not providing physical objects such as desks, cars, or clothes, our customers cannot focus on the product itself. The travel agency's only product is service, while suppliers produce the travel experience itself. Both before and after the travel experience, travelers can only relate to their hopes and experiences and the service they have received. On the trip itself, although the plane, car, or hotel room is tangible, the experience is not. The travelers' primary memories will be of the services they received and the experiences they had. Thus, sometimes the relationships are more important than the products themselves.

Identifying Customers

Obviously, the first step in the development of relationships is knowing who your customers really are. Without this knowledge, no relationship is possible.

Although travel service providers (airlines, cruise lines, hotels, car rental companies, and so forth) know the ultimate user—the traveler—there is often an

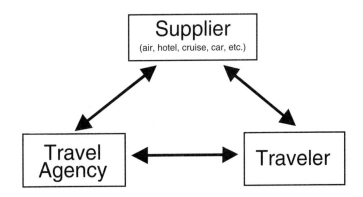

Figure 9-1 Two-way Marketing Relationships

important missing and unidentified link when the traveler purchases from a travel agency. For example, Mr. and Mrs. Jones purchase a one-week package to Aruba from ABC Travel. The package includes air transportation, hotel, and use of a rental car.

For reasons of economy (lower costs for the Joneses) and efficiency of booking for the agency (one call does all), ABC books the trip through XYZ Tours. The travel agency recommended the Sunshine Hotel to the Joneses. Mr. and Mrs. Jones pay ABC Travel for the package. ABC Travel pays XYZ Tours and XYZ pays the airline, the Sunshine Hotel and the rental car company. XYZ sends vouchers for the Joneses to ABC. The vouchers, which Mr. and Mrs Jones present for each component identify the tour operator, but not the travel agency.

As a result, the Sunshine Hotel never knows that ABC Travel generated the sale and a relationship between the hotel and the travel agency, which actually recommended it to Mr. and Mrs. Jones, cannot be developed. ABC also fails to receive sales credit in most cases from the airline and car rental company used by XYZ Tours. In reality, a travel industry supplier has two customers—the travelers themselves and the agencies who book them. See the "Industry Communique" for more discussion of the most beneficial supplier-agency relationship.

INDUSTRY COMMUNIQUE

AGENTS AND SALES REPS—A TWO-WAY STREET

Doris S. Davidoff

In a world of parity products, with so many suppliers to choose from, the relationship between the travel agent and the local sales representative is frequently the deciding factor. The subject of sales reps, however, evokes conflicting reactions. Some agency managers look at these people as their most critical source of information and assistance. Others see them as a waste of time.

On the flip side, sales reps have their own ideas about travel agents. Some consider agents the backbone of their company's sales efforts. Others look at agents as nothing more than freeloaders who don't know what they are doing.

When both sides understand each other and work together with respect and consideration, there is no better system for selling the travel product. Effective relationships with the sales reps of primary suppliers is essential to an agency's success and profitability. These same relationships are also key to the success and profitability of suppliers.

NO LONGER ROUTINE

During the past 20 years, the number of travel agency locations has more than quadrupled. The sales staff of the suppliers has not increased proportionately, though. Some carriers have had only small increases in sales staffs, and many supplier sales staffs are actually smaller than they were 20 years ago.

One exception is the growth in the number of sales reps for cruise lines. These companies expanded their sales forces during the explosion in available berths. Some lines have done better than others in this regard, and the results are obvious.

Because of the dwindling agent-rep ratio outside the cruise industry, the frequency of personal sales calls to any one agency has declined substantially. No longer does every agency on the Airlines Reporting Corporation list get regular sales calls from all major airlines and other suppliers. Some agencies don't see any sales reps in their offices for months at a time.

Suppliers tend to limit sales calls only to their largest accounts. The routine sales call is a thing of the past. It is too expensive—a field sales call can cost more than $200—to visit an agency without a specific objective.

Many agents believe that sales volume is all that counts with a supplier. While volume is important, it is not everything. Many owners and managers of small and medium-size agencies have developed strong professional relationships with suppliers and their reps. Their agencies receive marketing support and problem-solving service at levels equal to or better than those of much larger agencies. By learning how to deal with sales reps, any agency can get the same kind of support.

First, invest the time to develop or improve contacts with reps of suppliers important to your agency's product mix. Make the initial contact if necessary. Attend functions sponsored by these suppliers and talk with your assigned rep before or after the presentation.

For suppliers, membership in an organization such as ASTA [American Society of Travel Agents] can pay off when it comes to developing sales relationships. For $125 or less per year, a supplier can enroll its district sales managers and sales reps as associate members of ASTA. The associate members can then attend ASTA [American Society of Travel Agents] chapter meetings where they can make the equivalent of a large number of sales calls in one evening or weekend. And typically the sales relationship created in the informal atmosphere of the meeting over cocktails or at a dinner table is more meaningful than an official call in a busy office.

COURTESY COUNTS

Once the relationship is established, agents should invite the reps to their office. Make a specific appointment. Take them out to lunch and pick up the check.

This will be a pleasant surprise to the rep, because so many agents expect suppliers to treat them all the time.

Reps can take the initiative too, but they should make appointments with agents before they visit the office so the agency can make sure that the proper staff member will be there. The agency can also determine if the rep's services are needed or if there are outstanding questions or problems that need the rep's assistance. When no appointment is made, invariably some of these preparations are not made, and time is wasted.

Agency managers should train two or three staff members to know what information is needed from sales reps and have those staff members meet with reps. If the total office staff exceeds four, sales time is wasted if the rep meets with every member of the staff individually. Not all agents need all information, and not all information a sales rep has is important to your agency.

STAFF MEETING

If, however, a topic is important enough to require meeting with the entire staff, invite the rep to a staff meeting. Schedule the meeting before or after regular office hours and ask the sales rep to make a presentation. Coffee and doughnuts or wine and cheese are in order.

The staff meeting can be more effective than bits and pieces of time one-on-one between the rep and staff members. Also, when presentations are made at a staff meeting, everyone receives the same information.

Agents should help reps understand their agency and its needs. Explain the business mix and the areas where you are planning for growth. Reps, on the other hand, should only discuss the information that would pertain to the needs of the specific agency.

They should know the agent's clients just as the agent does. Just as an agent would not discuss the Bahamas with a client who only travels to Europe, a sales rep should not discuss the new programs for corporate travelers with an agency that does only leisure business.

A good sales rep is a resource for creative marketing ideas. Reps see many programs in the field that have worked for others. And while it would be unethical to give one agency ideas generated by another agency in the same general market area, it is good business to share an idea that comes from a rep in another city.

Managers should ask for ideas that might help attract additional business or serve existing clients better. Many sales reps have broad experience, and they are more than willing to assist interested agency owners and managers.

USE, DON'T ABUSE

Sales reps can provide many privileges to our agencies and our clients. We should not, however, abuse those privileges. Save requests for clearance of space or other special services for important items. Suppliers tire of agents who request clearance of space (or free drink chits, etc.) for every traveler who walks in the door.

Fam trip privileges can also be easily abused. Be sure to send only staff members who are in a position to sell the destination. These trips are designed to increase sales, not to reward staff.

Teach your staff that they are representing your agency when on a fam trip. They should know how to act and should attend all functions.

Unfortunately, travel agents sometimes make reservations to attend supplier presentations and never show up. Usually the supplier must guarantee a minimum number for food-and-beverage service. No-shows result in wasted money. When you or your agents tell a supplier you will attend a function, either attend or cancel two or more days in advance. If an emergency forces a last-minute cancellation, call afterward to explain and apologize.

Travel agents should treat their sales reps with respect and understanding and should expect the same in return. When both parties meet this standard, both benefit from one of the most rewarding relationships in the industry.

ASTA Agency Management, December 1991.

PHASES OF RELATIONSHIP MARKETING

Westin Hotels was one of the first major companies in the travel industry to formalize the application of relationship marketing techniques into their overall marketing plans. According to Fletch Waller, a Westin marketing executive at the time of its implementation, relationship marketing in Westin involved four phases:

- *Core Values*
- *Augmentation of Core Values*
- *Rewarding Frequent Customers*
- *Personalization.*

Figure 9-2 illustrates these four phases.

Phase 1

Core values are the understanding of the needs, wants, and expectations of the target markets. A traveler, for example, requires an assured reservation, fast check-in, a clean room, security, some good food, and quick check-out. A travel

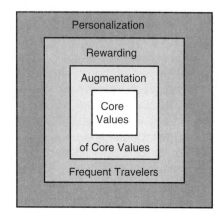

Figure 9-2   Phases of Relationship Marketing

agent requires information about the hotel chain, reservations accessibility, firm confirmation of reservations, confidence in the product (the traveler, in the end, must be satisfied), and prompt payment of commissions.

These core value services are, in reality, the basic services expected by each target market segment. They are the end product of **customer-oriented marketing**. But they are just the beginning of a true relationship. The hotel chain that does not provide these core value services will find that neither the traveler nor the travel agent will use them in the future.

Phase 2

Augmentation of core values is the second step in the relationship marketing process. In this phase, a company tries to provide something special that differentiates itself from the competition. A hotel might provide a special restaurant, extra amenities such as a small box of candy to take home, or even a free newspaper. It is the extra something that gives the guest a pleasant feeling or something to remember.

Premier Cruise Lines, for example, augments its basic 3- and 4-day cruises with chocolate "ship" cookies for the kids (family travel represents Premier's core market segment), and with the use of official Disney characters on board. Doubletree Hotels is known for their chocolate chip cookies every evening.

In relationships with travel agents, for example, hotels might provide augmentation of core values through central commission payments, familiarization trips, special travel agent rates, or other special services. Augmentation of core values gives the traveler or travel agent a rationale for choosing one product over a similar, competitive product.

Food service is sometimes used by airlines as a means of augmenting core services in a competitive market. Special meals for kids (United Airlines, in 1992, offered meals from McDonald's), international cuisine, and upgrading of meal service for business class and first class travelers are but a small sample of this technique.

Cruise lines, tour operators and other travel suppliers provide travel agencies with seminars and fam (familiarization) trips.

Phase 3

Rewarding frequent travelers (or clients) is the third phase in relationship marketing. Airline frequent traveler, hotel frequent guest, and car rental frequent renter programs are the most prominent examples of this concept. Airline frequent flyer programs were among the first industry attempts to reward frequent travelers. Within a short time they were very successful in developing brand loyalty among consumers of basically similar competitive services. Today some travel agencies even have their own frequent traveler programs awarding points toward gifts for regular customers.

Travel suppliers often reward travel agencies that use their services frequently with overrides, free flights, rooms, cruises, or tours and other special services. These programs have been effective in developing preferred relationships between agents and suppliers in segments with relatively equally perceived competitors.

Phase 4

The fourth step—**personalization**—is the most critical phase of the relationship marketing concept. Personalization is the glue of the concept. Without it there are no relationships. To Westin, personalization is knowing names and guest preferences before the frequent guest arrives. It is knowing who the guest really is. The truly important relationship is not between Westin management and the guest, but between front line personnel and the guest. Information on a frequent guest's background and room preferences is stored in Westin's computer and is at the fingertips of the front desk receptionist. Recognition makes travelers feel at home and less likely to try the new hotel across the street.

Records kept by some of the world's best hotels even include beverage preferences of their regular guests. Hotels in the Orient are especially known for high degrees of personalization. Their employees are trained to anticipate the needs and desires of their guests. A concierge who has been with one of these hotels for many years helps bring back repeat guests.

Client profiles are also used extensively by travel agencies for their frequent clients. Preferences for meals, smoking/nonsmoking seating as well as preferred airlines, hotels, and car rental companies are routinely stored within the agency's computer reservations system (CRS). Special seating and meal preferences are automatically transferred into the traveler's reservation record (PNR or passenger name record) when bookings are made. Credit card payment or billing information as well as delivery information is also stored in the CRS.

Most travel agencies maintain client histories with details of vacation preferences and past activities. This information encourages a more personal approach when meeting with clients and also permits target marketing to the clients who would be most interested in specific types of travel.

Remembering birthdays and anniversaries is yet another way to cement personal relationships. Cruise lines, airline frequent traveler programs, hotels, and travel agencies have used this personalization technique successfully.

PREFERRED SUPPLIERS

In the travel agency segment of the industry, the personal relationship factor is, by far, the most important factor to consider when establishing **preferred supplier** relationships. Core values such as product quality, competitive price, and ease of booking must, of course, be present. Augmentation of core values (for example, seminars and fam trips) and frequent user awards (for example, co-op advertising and overrides based on sales) are also present.

But the most important question to be answered before establishing preferences is "What level of support will my agency receive if a problem develops?" Most suppliers are the same if all goes well. But when problems develop, support levels depend on strong marketing relationships. Many travel agencies' choice of automation systems over the years, for example, has been based primarily on their relationship with the computer reservations system vendor. The best systems available are, to many agencies, quite similar. The vendor chosen is perceived to provide the highest level of problem-solving support.

Choices of preferred car rental companies, hotels, cruise lines, tour operators, and other suppliers are often based upon similar considerations. The recommendations that travel agents make are frequently based upon their personal relationships with specific suppliers, especially with the sales representative calling on them. This provides assurance that problems will be minimal, but if they occur, they will be solved easily.

Preferred supplier relations do not benefit only the supplier and the travel agency. They benefit the traveler as well. Because of the strong relationships between agency and service provider, travelers are assured of the highest levels of service. If problems develop, they can be solved most efficiently and to the benefit of the traveler. Travel agents are most familiar with the travel products of their preferred suppliers and can be sure that the products truly fit the needs of their clients. The Industry Communique further explains this.

Carnival Cruise Lines has developed into the largest and most successful company within its industry. It has, for many years, had the largest and most active sales force calling on travel agents. With 95% plus of its business coming from

---
INDUSTRY COMMUNIQUE

SELECTING PREFERRED SUPPLIERS

Doris S. Davidoff

THE SELECTION PROCESS

What should you look for when choosing preferred suppliers? The first and most important consideration is whether the supplier provides a high-quality product. Supplying a high-quality, dependable product will help you keep a satisfied client. No supplier can pay a high enough commission to repay us for handling client complaints about its product.

Another consideration when choosing a preferred supplier is to look for one that will provide better service to the agency and the client. In addition to having a good product, it is critical that the supplier adequately services its customers as well. Service-related questions to ask about are the timeliness and accuracy of documents and whether the supplier will try to accommodate emergency requests and whether your agency is given priority for breaking space, when necessary.

One of the most important factors in any relationship, but especially in a business relationship where forgiveness may not be automatic, is what happens when something goes wrong. In an industry as complex as ours, it is impossible to eliminate mistakes and problems. Unforeseeable things happen sometimes that are simply beyond anyone's control. When a client has a problem it becomes a test of the relationship. Will the supplier help to resolve the problem in a friendly, helpful manner that will help the agency keep the client or will the supplier get defensive and try to avoid taking any responsibility for the situation?

A third factor in a preferred relationship—increased commissions—is by far the least important. The first two considerations are far more important, since they will ultimately bring in additional profits. A good product and excellent service delivery save the agency time (thereby saving money) and provide happy clients who will return in the future and will also refer business to the agency.

In an industry that works on such tight margins, however, any additional commission that can be generated is important. It goes directly to the bottom line, since no additional expenses are involved in generating it. Where several suppliers provide similar products, as well as the same level of quality and service, it simply makes sense for an agency to recommend the one that will pay the highest commission.

Within each market segment, an agency should have a preferred supplier. For example, in the cruise segment, an agency might need a budget and a moderate- and also a deluxe-priced line. There might be a need for a line for each variety of destination products, such as Caribbean, Alaska, and Mediterranean, and that may influence the choice of preferred supplier.

EXPECTATIONS

Once an agency has chosen two or three cruise lines that meet a variety of its needs, what can reasonably be expected of them, and what do they expect of the agency? First, there must be a true preferred relationship. That means more than just promising fidelity—it means practicing it. If an agency has designated three or four moderately priced Caribbean cruise lines as "preferred," then there actually is no true preferred relationship. In the stable of preferred suppliers, there should be no more than two cruise lines which compete directly with each other.

Cruise lines in a preferred relationship expect their partner agency to offer that line's product to the appropriate client as the first choice. The agency staff should be well versed in the preferred lines and know their brochures well. When the agency is promoting travel in its ads or newsletters, it should focus its marketing efforts on its preferred suppliers. When groups are booked, first opportunity to provide the space at the desired cost should be given to preferred suppliers.

The agency, on the other hand, has the right to expect certain things from its preferred suppliers. There should be promotional cooperation. Preferred cruise lines should provide their preferred agencies with guaranteed group dates so they can compete with other agencies in the very price-sensitive market of today.

Sales representatives should call on preferred agencies regularly to make sure they have what they need to sell the line's products, A good sales rep will, in fact, become a partner with the agency's manager in developing marketing plans. Training should be provided to assure that the agents are completely familiar with the line's products and policies. A preferred agency also should be given preference for familiarization trips and seminars given by the line. Nothing helps an agent sell a product better than having experienced it.

CONVINCING THE STAFF

Once the relationship between preferred supplier and agency is established, how do you get your staff to remember to sell the line and thereby help your agency make more money?

The most effective way to get employees to sell the products you want them to sell is to provide more training on those products. Agents like to appear knowledgeable to a client, and this can only happen when the agent can explain the product fully and is familiar with the brochure. By training agents on preferred products, you will find that they will automatically tend to mention those products to clients first.

It is also a good idea to store the brochures of preferred suppliers in a convenient and prominent place. Make sure that there is always a sufficient stock of these brochures, and never put non-preferred suppliers' brochures where clients can easily get to them.

Send agents on cruises on preferred lines. Again, the more familiar they are with these products, the more likely it is that they will recommend them first.

All travel agents know that when we sell preferred suppliers, we make more money. If override commissions are involved, the additional earnings are obvious. However, a more important source of additional bottom line income is less obvious. I am talking about the earnings that come from the time saved by agents familiar with the preferred product who can sell it easily and efficiently. It also comes from time saved by dealing with friends and partners with whom we have developed a true preferred supplier relationship, and who know and respect us.

ASTA Agency Management, February 1992.

travel agencies, the use of sales representatives is no accident. The relationships developed by Carnival's sales reps with the travel agency community are a major factor in Carnival's success. Many other cruise lines have followed Carnival's lead and have expanded their field sales forces.

Relationships become even more important in hard economic times than when money is flowing. The most successful travel suppliers during the 1990 to 1992 recession were those who had developed strong personal links with both travel agencies and the traveling public.

Relationship marketing is important in all sectors of the travel industry. The cruise line, travel agency, and traveler situations described above are only examples. See the following Industry Communique for an in-depth discussion of the travel-agent–hotel relationship. This Industry Communique is a report of a meeting Hyatt Hotels and Resorts held with its Travel Industry Advisory Group on February 21, 1991 in Chicago. The purpose of this meeting was to have Hyatt's corporate staff understand and interact with a market which their President, Darryl Hartley-Leonard, considers vital to the ultimate success of Hyatt in the 90s. The four phases of the concept can and should be applied when developing a marketing plan. Determine and meet basic needs (core values). Provide some value-added services (augmentation) and reward frequent clients. Most important, develop personal relationships to keep customers from crossing the street.

The Marketing Hierarchy

As we have seen, three different marketing theories have evolved over the past half century. Early marketers focused on products and services themselves.

INDUSTRY COMMUNIQUE

BUILDING PRODUCTIVE RELATIONSHIPS...

Susan Gawriluk
Director of Travel Industry Sales, Hyatt Hotel Corporation

"Our attitudes have really changed, and we have a distinct and very, very clear mission that right now we want to be known as the hotel company that has the best relationship with the travel industry."

Jim Evans, Senior Vice President of Sales

One of the main questions the group [Hyatt's First Advisory Group] set out to answer was: What exactly is the relationship between travel agencies and hotels? While each individual differed in his or her approach, the main message was effective partnership. Here's what they had to say.

According to Ed Peters of IVI Travel, "98% of the time when a hotel contacts an agency it is for the purpose of getting business for that property." Hotels, comments the advisory group, need to learn more about how to build relationships with the agency that are seen as productive from the vantage point of both parties.

"On the average, I receive thirty calls a week from hotel people," says Peters. "I'm responsible for strategic planning for hotels, and they want to tell me about the new carpeting in the ballroom or the new restaurant that's going up." As a results-driven executive, Peters doesn't have time for those calls. "But when a caller says, 'I've got a sales proposition for you that's going to help you build your business', I'll stop whatever I'm doing and listen."

But the fact still remains, Peters says, that "if you're going to try to get business from somebody, you have to make it good for them. You have to make it exciting...show them ways they can build their business too. That's what's missing on most approaches."

EFFECTIVE NETWORKING...

So what makes it "good" for agencies? At minimum, it helps for the agencies to meet the hotel staff—as long as you are meeting the right people.

The right people to meet are those with whom both parties will have a chance to work in the future. "This promotes a kind of bonding process," states Marianne Toldalagi of Thomas Cook. "At one point, we had a lot of people from a lot of properties coming through. They were in town, they made appointments, and they came in. Our meetings' staff, our tour division, agents, they were all there, and I got good feedback from people. Periodically that kind of thing is very effective."

However, on the whole, the group felt that shotgun calls, sometimes called blitzes, did not constitute "quality calls." Jim Smith of GEM feels that blitzes are generally "ineffectual." You have salespeople out there running around like chickens without heads wondering if they're going to make their quota for the day." And Doris Davidoff of Belair Travel was quick to note that these are generally people with whom "there's no relationship already. You know what's better than a blitz today? A fax message." All agreed that a creative, short and to-the-point fax would generate as much attention at less expense to suppliers.

Once a key decision-maker has contacted Irene McDermott of American Express, she likes to sit down and plan what he/she wants to accomplish. This involves asking such questions as: What does his/her network look like? What kind of commitments can we make to each other and how can I help you to get more of what you want?

The entire travel industry may possibly have grown too large for suppliers to "put their arms around," commented Bernice Rosmarin of VTS Travel. Her suggestion is to "target where most of your business is coming from. Is it out of twenty single offices, or is it out of the other 16,000 that are part of a consortium or marketing group?" Having done so, spend proportionate amounts of time with those select agencies.

Davidoff agreed with the group that tradeshows remain an important factor for reaching the large marketplace. "Since Hyatt is of fairly good size, with broad product lines in both the corporate and leisure sides, you need a broad exposure." However, she wisely pointed out that "one problem that a lot of suppliers have is they concentrate on (only) the tradeshow and forget that the tradeshow is almost secondary to the real exposure...which is in the networking (at the seminars and social events)."

The caliber of the booth staff is critical as well. Toldalagi wants to meet someone "at our level" with whom we can either be negotiating or planning. That's when it is "worth her while." Davidoff concurs. "Americans as a whole don't go to tradeshows to buy. They go for information and networking and then they go home and make the deal and buy. If this is an important show with an important group of agents attending, you're going to have to have at least mid-level or upper mid-level people attending."

Evans took this opportunity to ask about Hyatt's travel industry account team. Mike Boland of Maritz feels that "what you've done in our case of assigning an individual who can represent Hyatt across some different departments within our company, bring in resources when needed, and deal with our different kinds of business, is very good. And, frankly, I think we're just beginning to see that pay off."

EDUCATION...

Davidoff continued, "The hotel area is just beginning to learn that there is a distribution network out there that can work for them. So you're in on the ground floor. But one thing that has always surprised me, is that the vast majority of agents, something like 92%, are now $5M (in sales) or less, and there are a number of things, ASTA meetings of chapters, Bons Vivants, SKAL, places where groups of these agents get together at meetings. It would seem to me to be effective for your people to be there. Take some of your General Managers, have them represent more than their own hotel—have them go to those dinner meetings. That's going to be fifty or sixty sales calls they make in a night and it actually has more power than a real sales call because it's informal. They become friends. 'Oh, I know John Smith. I'm going to give him a call and see what he can do.' Your GM's are a sales force all over the country."

In the area of education, while the group agreed that our product was outstanding, Rosmarin encourages us (Hyatt) to train our GM's and the operations people as well as our sales staffs. "You've got to reinforce the message that you really want to work closely with the travel agency community...from the top level down." Peters suggested that one of the most effective forms of training would be to have a GM listen to the phone calls that the agents are having with customers. "What I want him to do is put a headset on and listen to what the agent goes through when the customer calls up, and then he'll start to figure out why we do or don't book as many Hyatt hotels."

In addition, Davidoff believes the front desk's handling of a customer is critical to a smooth agent-hotel relationship. "An education has to be done on the front line people that there are good and bad travel agents like there are good and bad front desk people. But the travel agent is a distribution system and never under any circumstances, even if the travel agent was wrong, should that be said to the client. Take that problem up after the fact."

Rosmarin adds, "Get the client in a room; let them be happy." And Davidoff said, "It's very easy to blame the one that isn't there. So there's education needed on both sides and again, none of these relationships can come overnight. You cannot make one sales call and form a relationship. It really takes time to build. The cruise lines have done it probably better than any other part of the industry." Evans' comment at that point: "That's because they've concentrated on it. They understood it before we did. But we plan to change all that."

Evans continues, "What we have to do is to get our General Managers to understand who our best travel agent customers are and that when those agencies have people in their hotels, the front office managers must be aware that these are very special customers. And it's education and exposure (that will take us there)."

SECURING CORPORATE BUSINESS...

McDermott believes that chains and agencies should visit corporations together. "I think you will get tremendous mileage and we will as well...we all have to understand what it's going to take." Evans points out that "Hyatt's national account directors don't go to the company until they've gone through the company's agency. Because we agree it takes that team effort."

Boland added, "Agencies live much closer to the airline programs. The airlines will sometimes provide X number of miles or cards as a way of beginning to build some brand loyalty or offset another brand loyalty. So if part of your program is to derive some complimentary Gold Passport benefits, then it can be a shared process in making it work." As Rosmarin explains, "It's the same thing as an airline giving you drink chits. What does a drink chit mean? And yet, you hand that to a client and, boy, are they happy and you look like a big hero to them." As Jodrey points out, "Don't exclude us in the sales process. Let's make it a triangle."

Even with Hyatt's new program, "Gold Passport at Leisure," designed for the repeat Hyatt resort guest, Davidoff assures us that the good agent "can identify people that are potential Hyatt-level customers because we know our clients. So, if we have an incentive (upgrade, champagne, etc.) to get them to go to Waikoloa instead of Mauna Kea, then that is money worth spending. Because that extra time it takes to sell them the first time is our time, not yours. In fact, getting that person to change and come to a Hyatt resort is sometimes even more important than the person who has already experienced it and already knows what it is."

Davidoff brought up the age-old question of "To what extent does the agency influence the sale?" and her point is well-taken. "The interesting thing is surveys. I remember a McCall's survey which said travel agents only determine where travelers go in 11% of the cases. Well, I'd say that's 11% where agents didn't do their jobs. Because, if I've done my job right, 100% of my clients would tell any researcher that they themselves made the decision of where to go. Of course, they made the decision based on where I directed them, but I never want them to think I made the decision."

AUTOMATION...

Efficiency of Hyatt's 1-800 number service at the Omaha Reservations Center was also discussed. Boland agreed with the rest of the group that Hyatt really had no problems but "the ultimate goal has got to be to get (all your rates) in the CRS [computer reservation system] because that's the tool and frankly, no offense, we would rather never talk to the 800 number." Jay Risher with Uniglobe Travel International feels that "the only reason we should ever call the 800 number is for major problem-solving. Not to book...we don't want to touch a phone."

Speaking on Quality Assurance, Mike Sarvady of Best Travel stated, "80% of the complaints that come in concern the no-show factor or 'I don't have you in the records, sir." Risher agreed. "Let's talk about the customer, the ultimate guy we've got to please. The problem they have when they walk in is they're, for the most part, in no-man's land. You're in control, they're out of control. The difference on the air side is they've got the ticket." All of this points to the need for automation flexibility and more thorough training at the front desk.

COMMISSIONS...

An additional operations issue which we wanted to address with the group was commissions. Risher feels that "there should be no reason in the world why there should not be a commission paid to a travel agency. If you can cut your hotel rate from $110 down to $59, then you can afford to charge $6 more and pay the travel agent."

Gawriluk at this point explained that Hyatt does pay 10% commission on all published rates: rack, corporate, weekend, senior citizens, and packages. On the subject of agencies tracking commissions, Davidoff's agency does track and maintains that as more and more agencies are becoming adequately automated, they track as well. "Put it this way—Well-managed agencies track commissions." Smith with GEM agrees. "Even for the small to mid-size shops, back-office automation alternatives—cost-effective alternatives—have come in that allow agencies to be well-managed where formerly they didn't have the recourse."

When asked about the desirability of commission "hotlines," Smith said that even if you cannot solve a problem, "the very fact that someone knows that you're taking the time and you have the concern to at least address their problem is 90% of the battle." Davidoff believes, however, "It's got to be interactive. There are times when it has to be a personal contact because the question is too complex to take the time to write it up and really you need to know something so you've got to talk back and forth."

All agreed that this special problem-solving hotline would be another step forward in "building the bridge" between agents and hotels. Risher commented, "I prefer to think you're keeping 90% of what I've earned for you by putting a body in your hotel room." He believes that when hotels understand this, "we'll no longer have a communication problem."

Synergy...Travel Agencies and Hyatt Working Together, Spring 1991.

They stressed the features and functions of their wares. As we ended the 1960s, the focus shifted to identifying the needs of customers and filling them. The importance of personalization and the development of relationships between buyer and seller is the newest concept and has not yet fully matured.

Analyses of product and service development as well as marketing programs shows that the three concepts operate in a hierarchy. Just as Maslow's Hierarchy of Human Needs requires that the lowest level of need must be fulfilled before one can operate at a higher level, the Marketing Hierarchy (Figure 9-3) requires that the most basic market concept must have followed its full course before the next higher level marketing concept takes hold.

As shown in Figure 9-3, product-oriented marketing is the most basic level. It is followed by customer-oriented marketing. Relationship marketing is the highest level marketing concept.

Consumer demand and levels of competition are the prime determinants of which type of marketing orientation is necessary for successful product or service development and sale. Product orientation is effective only when there is little or no competition in the marketplace.

For example, after World War II, the demand for private automobiles was so high that their mere availability was sufficient for successful sales. Product orientation was the operational marketing concept. As basic demand was met, competition among manufacturers developed and those who identified and served consumer needs were effective while others closed their doors. Today, car makers and dealers try to develop personal relationships with car buyers in an era of increased competition.

On occasion, new inventions can be marketed in a product oriented manner with great success. Because they are protected by patents, direct competition is difficult until the patents expire, they are licensed to other producers, or parallel technology results in the development of competitive products. Velcro had no competition until its patents expired. Leasing a Xerox copier was the only way to get a plain paper copier for several years until parallel technology produced competitors. Both Velcro and Xerox could market any way they wanted to—they were the only games in town.

A similar example in the travel industry is China as a destination. When the Chinese mainland was reopened to tourists in the 1970s, demand was such that any trip at any price was salable. Inadequate rooms, lack of air conditioning or adequate heat, and other shortcomings were accepted by travelers who would not accept such conditions in other destinations.

Tour operator competition based on meeting customer needs only developed after the initial demand for travel to China had run its course and there

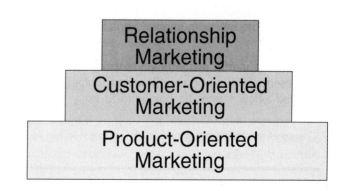

Figure 9-3 Marketing Hierarchy

were sufficient facilities for choice. Today, the marketing of relatively equal, competitive products depends heavily on the relationships between tour operators and travel agents as well as the relationships between travel agencies and their clients.

In the travel industry, the increased sophistication and knowledge of the traveling public has resulted in the application of relationship marketing techniques. Both frequent traveler rewards and the high degree of personalization implemented by both travel suppliers and travel agents goes many steps beyond basic customer-oriented marketing techniques because of the increased competition within most segments of the industry. As the Industry Communique points out, this new breed of travelers has greater expectations that must be met.

The high levels of competition for the traveler's dollar will surely continue through this decade and beyond. As a result, we can expect to see continuing sophistication of the traveler as well as the advancement of relationship marketing concepts as the preferred and most successful marketing system in our industry.

INDUSTRY COMMUNIQUE

TRAVEL MARKETING:
INDUSTRY RELATIONSHIPS AND BENEFITS

Andrew Vladimir

NEW BREED OF TRAVELERS EMERGES

A whole new breed of travelers with a different set of needs and perceptions has thus emerged.

Robert Shulman, president of Yankelovich, Clancy, Shulman, in discussing changing consumer values said, "We're not a bunch of country bumpkins any more willing to settle for bad service because we're away from home. We have greater expectations because we have more experience."

J. W. Marriott, Jr. in his closing comments on managing change in the travel industry echoes the same theme: "Today's travelers are not equal any more. They are better educated, more well-trained about the mechanics of traveling and less likely to accept standardization in what they consume. They're not interested in having their needs and expectations filled nearly; they expect their needs and wants to be met exactly."

Shulman's company, which regularly issues the *Monitor* reports that track lifestyle trends, has called this new group "strategic travelers": "Rather than searching for the lowest price, today's (and probably tomorrow's) strategic traveler is looking for the best value. *Monitor* shows that the strategic traveler is a more information-oriented consumer."

Andrew Vladimir, The Complete Travel Marketing Handbook, 1988, NTC Business Books, Lincolnwood, IL.

CONCLUSION

Relationship marketing has evolved during the past decade into the newest and most advanced form of the marketing process. Built upon the product-oriented and customer-oriented marketing concepts, relationship marketing adds recognition of the strong, interactive relationships that develop between buyers and sellers of products and services. The stronger the relationship between a product or service provider and the customer, the more likely the customer will purchase from that provider—as long as the provider's product or service meets the customer's needs.

SUMMARY

As competition within the travel and tourism industry has become stronger, merely developing a new product or identifying customer needs is not enough to assure sales. Strong interactive relationships between buyer and seller must also be developed. Relationships are especially important in this industry because of the intangible nature of the tourism product.

Understanding the needs, wants, and expectations of target markets form the core values and first phase of relationship marketing. Product or service differentiation by providing something special to customers augments the core and becomes the second phase of the process. Rewarding frequent travelers or clients is the third phase in development, followed by the most important fourth phase—personalization.

The three marketing theories that have been developed over the past 50 years form a hierarchy. Most basic is product orientation, a theory that operates well when demand far exceeds supply. As the supply of competitive products increases, meeting customer needs becomes more important. And in the most competitive marketing environments where many products potentially meet customer needs, the four phases of relationship marketing become determining factors.

QUESTIONS FOR THOUGHT AND DISCUSSION

1. Describe and differentiate the three major marketing theories?.
2. Why have relationships within the travel industry marketing become important?
3. What are the four phases of relationship marketing? Describe a travel marketing example demonstrating the four phases.
4. Describe the marketing hierarchy as it pertains to the travel industry.
5. Describe examples of personalization in different segments of the travel and tourism industry.

10

Advertising, Publicity, and Promotion

advertising
area of dominant influence (ADI)
broadcast media
brochure
circulation
cost per thousand
direct mail
directional advertising
ethics
intrusive advertising
legality
media
print media
public relations
publicity
sales promotion
shell

Advertising, publicity, and promotion are the major communication activities designed to attract potential customers. This chapter will discuss these activities in broad terms; the next chapter will give specific information on the use of print and broadcast media in advertising.

ADVERTISING

By definition, **advertising** is paid communications. It has three primary uses: to inform, to remind, and to persuade. The main limitation of advertising is the one-way nature of the communication. Although effective advertising may direct prospective customers to action, the give and take of personal communication is lacking. Unless and until the prospective customer comes into an office or makes a telephone call, there is no opportunity for in-depth discussion.

There are two primary types of advertising—directional and intrusive. **Directional advertising** emphasizes where to buy a product or service whereas **intrusive advertising** emphasizes what to buy. In general, the prospective customer seeks out directional advertising, while intrusive advertising, on the other hand, seeks out the customer.

The yellow pages of the telephone book are a prime example of directional advertising. Prospects responding to directional advertising are already interested in a product or service. Advertising in a specific section of the newspaper (for example, the travel section) is also basically directional, even though products and services are featured. People with no interest in travel rarely look through the travel section of a paper.

The broadcast media—radio and television—are the best examples of intrusive advertising. TV commercials and radio spot announcements literally intrude on the viewer or listener during regular programming. People tune in for the program, not the ads, but cannot easily escape the exposure without risking missing part of the program they want to see. To be effective, intrusive advertising must be heavily repetitive. Because prospects are not looking for the information conveyed by intrusive advertising, frequent repetition is needed to create a lasting impression. For example, United Airlines' "Friendly Skies" slogan has earned lasting identity as has Carnival Cruise Lines' "Fun Ships" because of continued repetition.

PRINT MEDIA

Newspapers, magazines, and direct mail are the major types of **print media** advertising. All are used extensively in the travel industry and each has its own characteristics. An analysis of the characteristics of print media will help you understand proper usage, which will be discussed in more detail in the next chapter.

Newspapers

Newspapers can be categorized into two types: the large circulation city or metropolitan area daily newspaper, and smaller local newspapers usually issued on a weekly or twice-weekly basis. The daily newspaper is a very transient medium—it has a very short use life. Readers get it delivered to their door or buy it on a daily basis. They usually discard it with the same regularity.

Only the largest organizations advertise in the daily newspaper effectively. For example, airlines often announce new fares and schedules through large, expensive newspaper advertisements. However, many large city dailies have Sunday editions that include special features, such as a travel section. Smaller travel and tourism organizations can use this medium effectively. A smaller advertisement will be noticed in a travel section more easily than elsewhere in the paper because the reader of that section has travel in mind and is often looking for destination ideas, comparative prices, or other information.

Small-town and suburban semiweekly and weekly newspapers are rarely used by national or international travel organizations. However, these newspapers are not as transient as the daily paper. Often they are kept for several days or even a full week. These newspapers are often leafed through several times before being discarded. An advertisement in such a newspaper does not have to be huge in size to be noticed. Local travel organizations, such as retail travel agencies, find the local newspaper an important means of telling prospective clients about their services, as well as of reminding regular clients that the agency is still in business.

Magazines

Magazines represent a most interesting advertising potential for the travel and tourism industry. Magazines are more lasting publications than newspapers. Because they are smaller, printed on better paper, and come out less frequently, people tend to save magazines for varying periods of time. The vast majority of magazines are published on a monthly basis, although a substantial number of weekly and quarterly publications are available for advertising.

The major feature of a magazine for the potential advertiser is the degree of specialization available. Magazines are available for almost every special interest imaginable. Most organizations and special interest groups publish monthly or quarterly magazines. Whereas the general circulation type of magazine (for example, *Newsweek, Better Homes and Gardens,* and *Sports Illustrated*) is an attractive

The commercial says I can do everything...or nothing...and I am parked for the duration.

marketplace for large national advertisers, including airline and hotel chains, travel-oriented magazines (for example, *Holiday, Travel and Leisure,* and airline in-flight magazines) offer advertising opportunities to a broad range of travel interests, including tour operators and steamship lines as well as airlines and hotel chains. Special interest magazines are excellent, also, for the promotion of special interest tours. For example, tours to the Galapagos Islands (noted for wildlife) are often advertised in Audubon Society publications. Every hobby, such as gardening, stamp collecting, diving, golf, or crafts has one or more magazines aimed at its constituency.

BROADCAST MEDIA

Advertising in the **broadcast media** is the most transient and intrusive of all. Both television and radio rely on the ability to produce images in the mind of the listener that will be retained and remembered. Repetition—using the same commercial or message again and again and again—is required for effectiveness in these media, because broadcast advertising leaves no hard copy that the recipient can keep for minutes, let alone days, weeks, or months.

Television

Television is the most influential form of advertising in America. It is also the most costly. A one-minute commercial during prime time on a national network can cost hundreds of thousands of dollars. Thus, a full television campaign can be quite an expensive proposition. Television does combine video and audio in a moving format so that it is possible to see and hear activity. A travel destination or organization can show a destination's beautiful beaches. Airlines can show deluxe meal service and smiling cabin attendants. Properly used, television can make far deeper impressions on the viewer than any other form of advertising medium. Because of cost, however, only the larger components of the travel industry, such as airlines, cruise lines, destinations, hotel/motel chains, and car rental companies can afford network time. See the Industry Communique for more on the importance of television advertising for cruise lines. However, in recent years some smaller businesses, such as travel agencies, have begun using less expensive local cable TV channels.

Radio

Whereas television often holds the complete attention of the viewer, radio is generally a background medium. As a result, it is easier to ignore or not even notice

INDUSTRY COMMUNIQUE

REMARKS AT THE SEATRADE CRUISE SHIPPING '90 CONFERENCE, MIAMI, FLORIDA, MARCH 21, 1990

Kirk Lanterman, President and CEO, Holland America Line—
Westours, Inc. and Chairman, Cruise Lines International Association

...The 1980s also saw a tremendous growth in marketing efforts as competition heated up and the industry became more savvy and sophisticated. Most notably, we saw a marked increase in television advertising. According to a study done for the advertising firm of Ogilvy and Mather, *spending* by the [cruise] industry on *television* commercials *more than doubled* in *1988* alone—to *$43.9* million—and has increased *fivefold since 1984.* And more companies continue to jump on the television bandwagon. Television now comprises *26* percent of *all cruise advertising expenditures*, which are projected to approach half a billion dollars by 1992.

a commercial. It is possible, however, to make a commercial impact using radio at relatively reasonable costs. For this reason, radio is preferred by some large and many smaller advertisers. Although most radio commercials tend to be straightforward, and some commercials are actually simply the sound tracks of television commercials, radio does provide the opportunity for creativity. With radio there is the opportunity to play on the mind and the imagination of the listener.

As with magazines compared to newspapers, radio presents an opportunity for concentrating an advertising message to specialized markets. In addition to generally-oriented radio stations, many specialized programming stations can be found. Specialized formats include all news, contemporary music, top 40 record sellers, hard rock, progressive, easy listening, classical music, and country and western. Each station has listening audiences with separate demographics characteristics. It is thus possible to use radio in a highly targeted fashion.

DIRECT MAIL

Newspapers, magazines, television, and radio are media that have primary purposes other than providing advertising. Most people read newspapers and magazines for the information contained in them. People view television and listen to radio primarily for the program content and entertainment. Advertising, as far as the reader, viewer, or listener is concerned, is secondary. Direct mail, on the other hand, is a medium dedicated to advertising. The only purpose of a direct mail piece is to inform a reader of a product or service and, hopefully, persuade the reader to take some action.

Advantages and Disadvantages of Direct Mail

One of the greatest advantages of direct mail advertising is its ability to pinpoint mailings to an exact target market. It is possible to compile a mailing to meet any need. A second important advantage of direct mail is the wide latitude of control in both the content and amount of information that can be sent. As a disadvantage, direct mail is the most expensive form of advertising on a per potential reader basis. In addition, direct mail pieces compete with other pieces of mail received at the same time.

The question is often asked: Will a given direct mail advertisement even be opened? Surveys, however, have shown relatively positive results. Contrary to popular belief, the vast majority of so-called "junk" mail is opened. As a general rule of thumb, it can be said that the more specialized the product or service being offered, the more chance a mail advertisement will be read and acted upon if the advertisement is sent to truly potential users. Thus, a properly matched direct mail campaign and mailing list can produce very positive results.

THE TRAVEL BROCHURE

Because of the intangible nature of the travel product, some relatively inexpensive mechanism had to be developed to capture, even for a fleeting moment, some of the features and benefits of travel products and services. The mechanism that has evolved is the travel brochure. Travel brochures are issued by almost all types of tourism enterprises. Government tourist offices spend vast sums of money to develop full-color brochures and booklets describing the features and advantages of tourism in the host country. Every state in the United States has a tourism office and a brochure promoting tourism in the state. Some counties or other regional areas produce such brochures and distribute them as well.

Almost every hotel in the world has issued a brochure of some sort describing its facilities. Most are in full color. Tour operators and cruise companies depend on travel brochures as the primary means of describing their services. Even airlines have issued a variety of brochures describing equipment and service. Travel brochures are thus both an advertising medium and important support material for those selling travel.

Many airlines, hotels, and tourist offices can provide "shell" brochures to tour operators, travel agencies, or groups to help promote a tour. These shells are brochures containing full-color pictures of the destination, but not copy. They may then be customized to the needs of the user, and printed by the tour operator or the travel agency. This allows a personalized full-color brochure to be offered by a small group at a reasonable cost.

To those considering the purchase of travel, the travel brochure offers a means of analyzing the alternatives in the choice of such products as tours, cruises, or hotels. To the travel agent selling the travel service, the tour brochure is a way to show prospects what they will be getting for their money. To the people who have purchased a tour or cruise but have not yet departed, the travel brochure is a promise of what is to come. To the traveler who has returned from a trip, the tour brochure is a souvenir and record of the travel experience.

CHOOSING THE RIGHT ADVERTISING MEDIUM

No single advertising medium can ever meet the total communications needs of any part of the travel industry. The combined use of two or more media usually has a multiplier effect over the use of one medium alone. Thus, we often see the same travel producer using a variety of print and broadcast media for different purposes.

For example, when an airline is introducing a new destination or new fare, it will use newspaper advertising for several purposes. Newspaper advertising can be done on short notice, which is very important for a new fare proposal, and present more information on rules and restrictions than other forms of advertising. This campaign will then be followed by radio and TV advertising to encourage public awareness. This combination of media takes advantage of the best features of each. If well done, it leads to the highest possible level of public awareness of and desire for the new product.

"Little Markie had such fun with your brochures!"

The object of any advertising campaign is to get a message to as many truly potential users as is possible at the lowest possible cost. Vital to this is choosing the media that are read, viewed, or listened to by those potential users, while avoiding paying for advertising that is in media read, viewed, or listened to by nonusers. This is the critical factor of media choice.

Because of the popularity of television, the use of famous spokespersons has become very popular among travel companies. Carnival Cruise Lines has used Kathy Lee Gifford for many years, and Princess Cruises has ridden on the popularity of the well-loved series "The Love Boat," by using "Captain Stuebing," better known as Gavin MacLeod. Hertz has used famous sport stars such as O.J. Simpson and Arnold Palmer to portray the image of winners for their product. Walt Disney World and Disneyland have made their statement "I'm going to Disneyworld (or Disneyland, depending on where the ad is being shown)," a household phrase by having the winners of many sports events use it in television and print ads. This campaign is meant to show that going on a Disney vacation is the best prize of all after hard work.

Area of Dominant Influence

One concept that is often useful in choosing media—especially on a regional or local basis—is the area of dominant influence (ADI). Every newspaper, magazine, television, and radio station, as well as every mailing list broker, publishes demographic information on readers, viewers, and listeners. The primary areas of service, readership, and reception in terms of geographic location, as well as population characteristics including age, sex, education, and income can be described for the area of dominant influence of each of the advertising media.

Proper marketing requires that the demographic characteristics of the target market segment must also be defined. It should be possible to make media decisions by matching the ADI characteristics of potential advertising media with the demographic characteristics of the target market. The closer the ADI matches the demographic characteristics of the target market segment, the more effective the media should be. The advertising message in these cases will be read, viewed, or listened to by more real potential purchasers than media whose ADI do not match the target market segment as well.

For example, if a target market segment is comprised of people in a limited geographic area, the best media buys would probably be those print and broadcast media whose ADI characteristics cover the geographic area desired and no more. If the ADI of a newspaper, magazine, television, or radio station covers an area much broader than that identified with the target market segment, the extended coverage would, of course, be included in the cost of the medium but would not benefit the travel-producing organization. Because the cost of advertising is governed by the number reached, the cost per actual potential buyer would be higher than necessary.

Thus, it makes little sense for a travel agency in a suburb on the edge of a metropolitan area to use the large metropolitan daily newspaper. Although the target market segment would be included in the newspaper's coverage, the agency would also be paying for coverage of a wide area not likely to contain potential clients. Greater value would be achieved by using the suburban area weekly newspaper. It is important to note that many national magazines, such as *Time, TV Guide,* and others have regional issues that make advertising for regional suppliers effective.

Circulation

An important factor affecting both newspaper and magazine advertising rates is circulation, or the number of readers that will probably see the newspaper. The circulation of the large city daily newspaper may range from 50,000 to more than 200,000 copies per issue. The circulation of a suburban or small-town weekly is usually only a small fraction of that (from two or three thousand to twenty thousand). Obviously, the higher the circulation, the more expensive the advertisement.

However, one must also consider the concept of cost per thousand, or CPT. Cost per thousand refers to the cost of an ad appearing in 1,000 copies of the publication. Normally, the larger the overall circulation of a newspaper the lower the cost per thousand copies from an advertising standpoint. For example, a large city daily newspaper issuing, on the average, 100,000 copies per day may have an advertising cost of $75.00 per column inch. On a cost per thousand basis, this translates

"Alice, let me see that air-sea brochure again!"

into seventy-five cents per thousand issues. On the other hand, a suburban weekly may have a circulation of 10,000 and an advertising cost of $12.00 per column inch. This translates into $1.20 per thousand copies. The cost of advertising in the daily newspaper has a higher dollar amount but lower cost per thousand copies.

LEGAL AND ETHICAL ISSUES

As well as choosing the correct medium for the marketing message, those involved in marketing travel must be concerned with the content of the message. Although, from the point of view of legality, only the most blatantly improper types of advertising are truly illegal, many others may be considered unethical. It is illegal, for example, to advertise a product that does not exist or a price which is rarely, if ever, available. Federal Trade Commission regulations can be invoked when advertising is completely misleading. United States Postal Service regulations govern illegal activities conducted through the mail. Thus, direct mail advertising of a tour that does not exist would subject the advertiser to charges of mail fraud. In recent years, the attorneys general of several states have investigated advertising practices of car rental and airline firms. Because travel is growing in both volume and importance, it is getting closer scrutiny from local, state, and national regulatory concerns.

"He promised good circulation for our ad, but this isn't what I had in mind."

The ethics of travel service advertising is a much broader area. One of the main functions of advertising is to persuade. Persuasion requires that travel be shown in its most positive light. Good travel advertising describes a dream that can come true. Problems arise, however, at least in the mind of the traveler or potential traveler, when what is presented is somewhat tricky or when the dream is one that can only almost come true.

For example, a cruise is advertised with rates beginning at a certain level. Out of several hundred cabins on the ship only one or two percent are priced at that rate and the next rate is substantially higher. There is nothing actually misleading or deceptive in this advertising, at least from a legal point of view, but does the price advertising of this type really represent the product for what it is? Resort hotels with very small numbers of minimum rate rooms can fall into the same category if they feature the minimum rate in their advertising.

Overzealous promotional efforts in travel brochures are another source of potential ethical problems. Are the rooms pictured in the hotel brochure characteristic of the hotel, or are they just the large suites? Does the picture of the hotel make it appear to be on the beach when really it is not? Is the swimming pool shown at an angle that makes it look much larger and more inviting than it really is?

Satisfied travelers will return again and again to their favorite spots. However, if travelers are led to believe that a resort or a ship is something that it is not, dissatisfaction will be rampant. Abe Lincoln's adage: "You may fool all of the people some of the time; you can even fool some of the people all the time; but you can't fool all of the people all the time," will certainly apply. Those responsible for travel and tourism advertising should consider long-range implications as well as short-term needs when they are deciding how to present products and services.

PUBLICITY AND PUBLIC RELATIONS

The real distinction between publicity and advertising is cost. Advertising, as defined earlier, involves payment for printed space or broadcast time. Publicity, on the other hand, involves the securing of free space in print media or free time in broadcast media. This space and time is usually found within the program content of the particular medium.

While it may sound contradictory, many organizations in the tourism industry spend considerable amounts of money to generate free publicity. Public relations departments and consultants specialize in securing coverage in print and broadcast media for their employers or clients.

Publicity appears in print media as part of the news or feature sections of the newspaper or magazine. In broadcast media, publicity is generated through guest appearances on talk shows as well as the reading of releases on news and feature programs.

Most readers and listeners do not view publicity content with the same skepticism as they do advertising. Advertising is seen by consumers as paid content, showing only the point of view of the advertiser. Publicity, on the other hand, is usually viewed as "truth." Few realize the efforts of a company and its public relations personnel to place such information in the media.

Favorable publicity and public relations can be generated by positive relationships with three primary groups—the media themselves, the business community, and the entire public community served by the organization. Special events and activities, such as travel shows, inaugural flights, and the opening of new facilities will often generate press coverage. The more spectacular the event or the more localized the medium, the greater the opportunity for free publicity.

For example, any time Disney has opened a new park, such as Epcot or MGM Disney Studios, the organization has attracted thousands of media people and generated great amounts of publicity in both broadcast and print media. When a television show such as "Today" or "Good Morning America" broadcasts from a remote location such as Hawaii or a cruise, the destination gets priceless publicity. The old television series, "The Love Boat," provided a tremendous boost to the cruise industry. "Hawaii 5-O" spurred travel to Hawaii.

On the positive side, the placement of a press release or photograph can greatly enhance a company's image and therefore its business opportunities. However, publicity is not always positive. When a problem occurs (for example, an airplane crash, political unrest at a tourism destination, or a hotel fire), the negative publicity that is generated can take a long time to overcome. As an example of this point, the president of Lounge Car Tours sent a letter to performer Johnny Carson, asking him to stop his joking references to the bad weather California experienced several years ago. These references, he claimed, were adversely affecting tourist reactions to California as a destination. In 1992, Los Angeles' tourism industry suffered greatly from riots, which were followed by a couple of major earthquakes. Terrorism has devastated tourism in many countries.

As with all marketing efforts, a planned campaign for publicity and public relations will achieve better results than a hit-or-miss approach. A publicity campaign should be planned as carefully and precisely as all the other phases of marketing. See the Industry Communique for some examples of successful campaigns.

SALES PROMOTION

The Committee on Definitions of the American Marketing Association states that **sales promotion** includes "those marketing activities other than personal selling and advertising and publicity that stimulate consumer purchasing and dealer effectiveness, such as displays, shows and exhibitions, demonstrations, and various non-recurrent selling efforts not in the ordinary routine." These promotion efforts are generally one-time activities that attempt to encourage communication between the selling organization and prospective buyers.

INDUSTRY COMMUNIQUE

CREATIVE PUBLIC RELATIONS INCREASES PROFITS

Richard Bassini

The most dynamic side of the public relations function is creating excitement and harnessing the energies of the entire staff toward building new business.

In many cases, creative ideas come from the employees themselves, and a properly functioning public relations office should be constantly on the lookout for employees with an inventive flair for attracting attention to the hotel. Indeed, in the most progressive hotels, periodic creative sessions are held in which a select group of employees are invited to share ideas with other staff members. Many has been the time when a smashing idea came from the bellman or front office clerk, the ones who constantly get feedback from the guests. Ideas are there to be recognized, and it is the public relations executive who must probe and set the proper stage for creativity to blossom. Such ideas produce room nights and internal sales, much to the delight of the general managers and owners.

In addition, special events can be designed to create an awareness of the hotel or, in some cases, be the first step in changing the hotel's entire image. Once a special event is conceptualized, the public relations office becomes the catalyst that promotes the event internally, seeking cooperation and creative input from every department. Every department should be involved in special promotions including the comptroller and the head of security. These departments are often overlooked, but should be considered vital members of the creative team.

Two examples of well thought out promotions and processes which produced significant revenues, both short and long term, show how to tap this creative well.

THREE EXAMPLES OF CREATIVE PUBLIC RELATIONS

A 220-room Ramada Inn in Southern New Jersey was having trouble with its luncheon business. Indeed, the problem was that there was no luncheon business at all.

A creative consultant, called in from the holding company, made the following analysis after the first day.

1. The dining room was too formal, giving the impression that it was too expensive.
2. The dinner business was adequate because the guests tended to stay in the property and didn't mind the formal decor.

3. The property was surrounded by a huge industrial complex. None of the workers in this complex came in for lunch, yet the surrounding restaurants were crowded at lunch time.

4. The chef and staff were young and eager to create activity and sales.

A meeting with the consultant and a marketing team was called by the general manager and held in a suite to heighten the sense of importance of the work. The marketing team soon recognized that the dining room could not be redecorated and that they had to work with what they had. After three meetings, the team formulated a plan.

On the next payday, a dozen high school seniors blitzed the industrial complex, putting a promotional leaflet under the windshield wiper of every car in the parking lot. The leaflet announced that there was a new chef—Chef Ben—at the restaurant and he was offering a special "All You Can Eat" soup and salad buffet lunch at a very low price.

Chef Ben prepared the buffet and the marketing team waited in anticipation. At noon the lobby became flooded with people who were promptly taken to the dining room. All had the leaflet in their hands.

The room soon filled and the marketing team was ecstatic. However, the initial joy was mild compared with what they learned when their new guests left to return to work.

Chef Ben announced that not one person went to the buffet, but instead ordered a drink and then proceeded to order a la carte from the menu. The captain of the room said that no matter how he pushed the soup and salad buffet, the new customers relaxed with a drink, thought the room a perfect setting for payday, and ordered expensive lunches from the menu.

The local newspaper was sent a story and photo, which it printed, with a most complimentary write-up. The article was then blown up, mounted on an easel, and put in the most conspicuous part of the lobby.

Fortified by their success, the marketing team reprinted the article on leaflets announcing a surprise the next payday. Again the students blitzed the parking lots with leaflets. Again, the crowds came through the doors. This time they knew where to go.

All guests found a blank press release and pencil on their plates. The general manager told them that if they filled out the release, it would be printed by the next Thursday, at which time they could read their own news. Information was then jotted down about promotions, births, engagements, bowling trophies won, etc. And the next week, the same people arrived to read their news printed in a newsletter.

The restaurant now enjoys a good following of steady customers who see it as the place to celebrate almost any occasion. It is also always filled on payday. Chef Ben has long since given up the buffet and instead is in the kitchen cooking steaks, chops, and house specialties.

The once prestigious Barclay Hotel in New York City acquired, over the years, a reputation for being stodgy, staid, and "too white glove" for young executives. These executives had healthy expense accounts, entertained frequently, and often suggested where people should stay when they came to the Big Apple. In addition, meeting planners had long forgotten the hotel because the competition offered planners a potpourri of promotions, benefits, and packages.

Shortly after the management of the Barclay changed, the new marketing team began to assess customer perception of the hotel. The public relations department and the balance of the marketing team put their heads together and came up with a dynamic promotion designed to be the first step in changing the image of the hotel.

A gala, week-long Mardi Gras festival was planned after a few "brainstorming sessions, "and the staff adopted the idea with great enthusiasm. A fixed package was established at $50.00 per person. One thousand dollars in bogus money was given to each guest as he or she entered the party. Auctions were held, music played throughout the night, and as the word spread, more and more singles, couples, and parties filled the hotel.

Ads were placed in local newspapers announcing the week-long celebration, and a mailing went to every possible source of new business.

The press was invited each evening and the public relations staff followed up by telephone the next day. Each public relations person told of the activities of the night before and who, of note, would be there that evening. As a result, a representative of every newspaper came to at least one night's festivities (some returned on their own to have fun) and they all wrote favorable stories.

As a result, the hotel repositioned itself in the market as an active, vibrant, and fashionable hotel to stay and entertain in. The various articles were reprinted as a composite in the newsletter which was given out in the lobby, used by the sales force with great success, and mailed to prospective customers through a mail order house.

This productive strategy is a clear example of how to properly use marketing tools available at their highest efficiency:

- *The advertising department designed provocative ads that reached the correct audience and persuaded them to join the celebration.*
- *The public relations executives persistently kept after the press and got their story printed in every paper.*
- *The team then regrouped and used the newspaper articles as promotional material and effectively got it to the hands of the consumer and meeting planners, which was the ultimate goal.*

The result was that the hotel enjoys an entirely new universe of guests which, in turn, has raised occupancy to unprecedented levels.

As stated earlier, the public relations office/agency usually is responsible for initiating the creative process for the marketing team. It must take the first step in identifying the need, then orchestrate the process which will create the promotion, act as the catalyst to get the most out of the staff, and finally put the plan into action. Once completed, it must get the story printed by successfully engaging the press in the activity and then reprint and distribute that coverage. Once it is in the hands of the consumer, the hotel will experience higher levels of occupancy, enhanced internal business, and ultimately significantly increased profits.

HSMAI Marketing Review, Fall 1986.

Sales promotions may be directed toward the ultimate consumer, the trade, or the salesperson. Activities such as special displays, contests, and product demonstrations characterize the promotion process. Airlines have been unbelievably successful with their frequent flyer programs and were copied by hotel chains with their frequent guest programs. These programs have established a measure of brand loyalty in industries that had never had such loyalty in the past. CLIA (Cruise Lines International Association) supports a very successful National Cruise Vacation Month that has helped gain recognition for the industry. Successful sales promotion is part of the overall marketing plan, and promotion efforts are highly integrated with advertising.

In the airline industry, sales contests represent a type of promotion activity. Airlines commonly promote special bonus commissions for travel agencies selling tickets on routes where the airline wants to encourage additional traffic. Airlines also become "the official airline..." of organizations that can give them substantial publicity in the public media. For example, Delta Airlines pays a considerable sum of money to Disney (as do National Car Rental and Premier Cruises) to be the "Official Airline (or car rental or cruise company) of Walt Disney World" because this tie-in provides an exposure they would be unable to obtain any other way. There is also frequently an "official" airline of the Olympics, the Special Olympics and other large charitable organizations that will get the attention of the media. See the Industry Communique for one unique airline promotion.

Hotels are major participants in trade shows, especially those involving travel agents and associations. These promotional activities enable hotel sales representatives to make many contacts and "sales calls" in a short period of time.

Tour wholesalers engage in a variety of promotional activities to attract the attention of retail travel agents. One example is that of a company offering escorted motorcoach tours, which sent coupons for free ice cream cones to 30,000 travel agents because they wanted agents "to get to know us better."

Travel agents often volunteer to provide programs about destinations and travel services at meetings of local clubs and service groups. Contests and free gifts with purchase are other promotional activities often found in travel agencies. Cruise nights generate interest in cruise vacations.

Destinations, of course, also engage in promotion. The New York Convention and Visitors Bureau produced a 19-minute film that highlighted the attractions of New York City. The color film used theater and movie personalities, and was available for rental or sale to retail travel agents, tour operators, and incentive travel planners. Most countries and states produce such films or videos.

No matter what segment of the industry uses it, sales promotion must be controlled if it is to build sales without cutting profits. It is easy to fall into the trap of using low-profit promotional activities as the normal way of doing business. Managers must recognize the dangers as well as the opportunities involved in the sales promotion process. Once again, proper planning is essential.

INDUSTRY COMMUNIQUE

SPEECH DELIVERED IN TAMPA, FLORIDA ON MARCH 22, 1991

Sir Colin Marshall
Deputy Chairman & Chief Executive
British Airways PLC

I like to think that we in British Airways have a determination to succeed which is encompassed in three, very short words, "Go For It."

Now, I am sure you will agree that "going for it" gives license to plug and promote a business or endeavor at every opportunity. So I will not apologize for bringing to your attention a small promotional activity which we have just unveiled. I hope you may have already heard about it through the media and in advertisements which appeared this morning.

For those still in the dark, we in British Airways have decided to give away the world.

On April 23, we will be giving away free, every one of our 50,000 seats, on routes across the world, in every class of service, in every aircraft we fly. Of course, it includes our services from Florida, as well as all other US gateways. We are modestly calling it "The World's Biggest Offer," from the World's Favorite Airline.

It is the spearhead of a comprehensive campaign involving a long-running package of special arrangements and supremely attractive deals for both the business and leisure traveler in which we are investing millions of dollars.

Some may think we've gone crazy. Others—those who will receive the free tickets—will delight in our philanthropy.

Altruism, however, has not been the guiding force behind our campaign.

The motivation is, the need to get the world on the move and our business back in shape after the slump caused by ongoing recession in many major markets; and the effects of the Gulf war.

Perceptions of terrorist activity and expenditure cutbacks within commerce and industry; and an attitude of 'wait-and-see-what-happens' among leisure travelers have produced a plethora of empty airline seats and cut-price deals over the last few months. Our own carryings dropped by 25 percent in February. We cut back flights and instituted rigorous cost-saving strategies to compensate.

Conservative estimates for the industry, as a whole, in January indicate that there were more than 15,000 flights cancelled.

The estimated financial loss for the month was $1 billion, of which $600 million was for European airlines and $200 million for North American companies.

The results for February are still being calculated, but are expected to be worse.

Now, thank goodness, the war is successfully over. But that does not mean lost business will come flooding back automatically. The airline and tourism industries were dealt a heavy business blow and economic downturn is still with us. The process of recovery will not be easy—certainly no bed of roses. Some, in our industry, may not recover at all. A European travel agency organization predicted recently that up to one million jobs in tourism would be lost this year.

So, what do we do? Beat our breasts in remorse, or get up and go for it?

The question is, of course, rhetorical. There is only one way we in British Airways will go. We are after business and we'll go through all the barriers to get it. To quote a certain military gentleman, we'll go through the middle, over, under, around and any damned way we can!

Our "World's Biggest Offer" campaign is the manifestation of our determination to get the world back on the move again. It is the biggest, single promotional drive we have ever undertaken. Our own troops have been mobilized for some weeks and yesterday crossed the start line with more than 100 news conferences and launch events everywhere from Sydney to Stockholm to San Francisco. It has attracted the support of tourism and travel organizations around the world, including those here in Florida.

The campaign will rank as the greatest travel event the world has ever seen. It represents a major investment in—and a massive commitment to—the future development of travel and tourism as the world's number one industry.

So, don't forget to clip the newspaper coupons and get in line for a trip with us to London. There will be a welcome you and many thousands of other Americans won't forget.

CONCLUSION

Advertising, publicity, and sales promotion together constitute one of the most important components in the communications mix. They are a primary way of bringing a potential customer to the point where personal selling efforts may close a sale. For this reason it is important to understand the various choices available and to make use of a combination that will be effective. To do this, the marketing manager must plan the advertising and promotion campaign carefully. Planning must be done with full understanding of the needs of the target market and the resources of the business.

SUMMARY

Advertising—paid communication—is designed to inform, remind, and to persuade. It is a one-way method of communication that may be divided into directional and intrusive. Directional advertising, as seen in the yellow pages, emphasizes where to buy something; intrusive advertising, such as in TV or radio commercials, emphasizes what to buy by means of repetition. Publicity is, essentially, unpaid advertising, placed by public relations specialists to enhance an image and promote awareness of a product or service or occurring because of a newsworthy happening. Sales promotion involves a variety of one-time activities, excluding advertising, that stimulates interest in a product.

The media used in advertising include print (newspapers, magazines, direct mail, brochures) and broadcast (radio, TV). Each of these has its own advantages and disadvantages, as well as a specific range of costs and a series of techniques for effective use. A medium must be chosen that will reach the target market as effectively and inexpensively as possible. One useful concept in selecting a medium is to determine the area of dominant influence, which can be done by studying the demographic information on readers, viewers, and listeners that the various media provide. In developing any advertising campaign, ethical and legal standards must be maintained for the ultimate good of the company.

QUESTIONS FOR THOUGHT AND DISCUSSION

1. Define advertising, promotion, and publicity. How are they similar and how are they different?
2. Discuss and give examples of directional and intrusive advertising.
3. What are the three primary purposes of advertising?
4. Discuss the advantages and disadvantages of different advertising media
5. Discuss some of the legal and ethical issues of advertising. Bring in examples of ads that you feel violate these principles.

11

Using Print and Broadcast Media Effectively

copy
headline
institutional advertising
layout
mailing list
newsletter
prime time
spot announcements
teaser copy
white space

DESIGNING EFFECTIVE ADVERTISING

Two questions are often asked about advertising. First, what is good advertising? Second, what is effective advertising? The second question is the most important. What is good and what is effective are often not the same. Good advertising is aesthetically attractive and pleasant. Effective advertising brings in results. The best advertising, perhaps, should be pleasant and bring results. But results—sales—are what is required from effective advertising.

According to a *Wall Street Journal* source, one of the most effective advertisements in the detergent industry was the "ring around the collar" ad for Wisk liquid detergent. Some Madison Avenue professionals maintain that it was also one of the most obnoxious advertising campaigns on television. Critics said it was irritating, insulted women, and even damaged the credibility of advertising in general. But it can also be argued that "ring around the collar" was one of the best advertising campaigns ever. It lasted more than twenty years (far longer than most) and outscored dozens of alternatives in terms of results at the supermarket. (You may be wondering why we have not used an example from travel advertising. However, by the nature of the product that travel advertising sells—dreams—it is difficult to find truly obnoxious travel ads.)

PRINT MEDIA

In using print media, whether newspaper, magazine, telephone directory or direct mail, effectively, it is essential to know specifics about media. It is also essential to be aware of the tricks of the trade—the techniques of handling the verbal and visual aspects of the advertisement. These techniques are the same for both kinds of print media.

Ad Size

Two important measures of newspaper ad size are the agate line and the column inch. Advertising rates are based upon these measures. A column inch is a unit of newspaper space 1 inch high (from top to bottom) and one column wide (from left to right). One column inch contains 14 agate lines. Space contracts with newspapers offer lower unit rates for larger users. The lowest unit rate goes to the advertiser using the most space on a daily or weekly basis over a full year. The rates are designed to encourage the use of more space. It is usually a good idea to buy the maximum contract rate that you might possibly use. If you actually use less than that number of inches in the year, the paper will charge you back for the shortfall. However, if you do use that number of inches and did not contract at the lower rate for more inches, the paper will not reimburse you for the difference in rate between your contract and your actual usage. You will end up paying more than was necessary.

Magazine advertising is generally sold by the portion of a page (for example, 1/16 to a full page). Because of the lower frequency of issue of magazines and the better quality of printing as compared to newspapers, more advance planning is needed when considering magazine advertising. The deadline for advertising for newspapers may be as short as a day or two before publication, but many magazines have advertising deadlines 1 month or even 2 months before publication.

PRINT MEDIA TECHNIQUES

Layout

A number of basic techniques can be used when developing effective print media advertising. Newspaper specialists believe the following elements of advertising setup or "layout" will increase the effectiveness and readership of the ads:

1. *Make the advertisement distinctive and consistent.* Newspaper advertising, especially in the travel section, puts competing organizations face to face with each other. Each ad vies for the reader's attention with other travel advertisements. When used outside the travel section, the ad competes with ads that are not travel related at all. The primary objective should be to make an advertisement stand out from the others. Use distinctive artwork, borders, or typefaces. Stay consistent with the image of your organization and keep promoting this image.

Be sure to be consistent with the use of your logo so that even a glance at the ad will create an image of your company in the reader's mind. If you are running a current theme, use that theme throughout your advertising. The sample ads from Hertz are examples of the use of the cute life-like, almost human bus they have been using to promote leisure travelers to rent Hertz cars.

2. *Target your ad to your target market as much as possible.* Try to use pictures or copy that will appeal to that particular segment of the market. If the readers are senior citizens, then use pictures of mature people enjoying your product, not twenty-something models in bikinis. The Nintendo ad shown here that ran in airline inflight magazines is a perfect example of this. This ad would have made no sense in any other type of magazine, but it was certainly appropriate for the bored airline traveler who has already read everything available. The headline is catchy and grabs even the casual reader.

The Hertz ads also show the targeting of ads to a specific market. The first ad is targeted to travel agents and discusses how using Hertz will make the agent's life easier. The second ad is targeted at the consumer who is encouraged to rent a car from Hertz.

3. *Keep the layout—the arrangement of the type, white space, and illustrations—simple.* The advertisement should be well organized and uncluttered. It should be easy for the reader to understand. Keep the demands on the reader simple. If more than one service is advertised, divide the total space into segments and separate the items with lines, boxes, or white space. The reader's eye should flow through the message easily and in sequence. The headline or illustration should make the first impression, followed by explanatory detail. Avoid the use of too many different typefaces and sizes. Overly fancy borders tend to confuse readers. Reverses (white type on black background) should be used only for headlines; they can be hard to read if the print is small. When distracting elements are eliminated, readership will be increased.

4. *Use a dominant element in the advertisement.* A large **headline** or a photo or drawing will capture the reader's attention and arouse interest. Any illustration that is used should be clean, simple, and large enough for the reader to understand. Photographs of people, action, and destinations are very successful—although somewhat expensive. If a photo of people is used, a release must be obtained for permission to use their picture. When an illustration is not available, make the headline dominant enough to attract attention. When pictures are not available, the use of clip art (black and white line drawings ready for reproduction, usually sold by category) can be very effective. Several companies specialize in the

With Hertz Freedom Rates, anything's possible.

Nationwide Subcompact

$19
per day
Free Unlimited Mileage
(When kept over a Saturday night)
Optional LDW $12 a day or less.

Low Rates & Flexibility

Hertz Freedom Rates will make your life a lot easier. Offer your clients low rates with the flexibility to take off for as long as they want. All they have to do is keep the car over a Saturday night.

Free Unlimited Mileage

These rates are available nationwide, by the day, and include Free Unlimited Mileage. So now your clients can afford to take off on weekends and vacations of any length. And to suit their particular needs, we offer Freedom Rates on a wide range of other cars.
For your information: These rates are available at participating airport locations and may be higher in some metro areas. Blackout periods apply and availability is limited especially in peak periods. There are advance reservation and minimum keep requirements. Standard rental qualifications apply. Minimum rental age is 25. Cars must be returned to renting location or higher rates apply. Taxes and optional items, such as refueling, are extra.
So give your clients a taste of freedom. Access keyword PROM or call Hertz at 1-800-654-3131 for details.

Hertz

Hertz rents Fords and other fine cars.
⊛ REG. U.S. PAT. OFF © HERTZ SYSTEMS INC. 1991

Introducing our Low Cal Special.

$19^{99}
a day.
Subcompact
Cars must be kept
over Saturday night.
Optional LDW
$9 a day.

Hertz reduces the rates for Escorts with Free Unlimited Mileage in California.

Rent from Hertz in California for just $19.99 a day-any day of the week! All you have to do is keep the car over Saturday night.

So whether you're taking off for a long awaited vacation or slipping away for a long romantic weekend, Hertz helps make it possible with low rates and Free Unlimited Mileage throughout California.

This offer also gives you greater flexibility to extend our already low weekly rentals a day or two.

For your information: Rates are available at participating California airport locations. Availability is limited, especially during periods of peak demand, and may not be available at some other times. Advance reservations are required. Cars must be returned to the renting location or higher rates apply. Taxes and optional items, such as refueling, are extra.

Call your travel agent or Hertz at 1-800-654-3131 and ask for our Low Cal Special.

GUARANTEED
FREE MILEAGE
GUARANTEED

Hertz rents Fords and other fine cars.
® REG. U.S. PAT. OFF © HERTZ SYSTEMS INC. 1991

Hertz
AMERICA'S WHEELS

As long as you're up here, why not zap a few aliens?

If you're reading this ad, you're very bored. You've mastered the safety instructions in every language, and the flight attendant won't give you any more almonds. Now what? ▶ Why not travel to another galaxy, seek out alien life forms, and destroy them? Or, for that matter, how does a couple of rounds of golf sound? If you had a Game Boy, you could do both, without leaving that seat you're wedged into. ▶ Game Boy is the personal game-playing system from Nintendo, with over a hundred sports, puzzle and adventure game cartridges to choose from. And the

first cartridge is on us. It's Tetris, the jigsaw puzzle that fights back. No matter how crowded the flight, as long as you can move your thumbs, you're golden. Remember, the secret to a successful journey is choosing the right traveling companion.

Game Boy won't ask you for your dessert, and fits just as neatly into the mouth of that screaming child† beside you, as it does into your briefcase.

If, however, you prefer playing "go-fish" with strangers, a **Nintendo** Game Boy system is the perfect gift for travel-weary loved ones who aren't as easily amused.

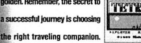

Game Boy won't ask you for your dessert, and fits just as neatly into the mouth of that screaming child† beside you, as it does into your briefcase.

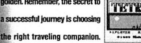

™ and © Ekorg. Licensed by B.PS. sublicensed by Nintendo. © 1989 B.PS./Nintendo. Original concept, design and program by Alexey Pazhitnov. ® & TM Nintendo © 1992 Nintendo
†(Just kidding about the child.)

sale of clip art in both printed and computer formats. Shown above are two examples of clip art:

5. *Use white space and borders effectively.* Use white space to make illustrations and headlines stand out, and also to separate different items in the ad. White space can also separate the advertisement from others on the page. Simple black borders around an advertisement (especially a small one under 1/8 of a page) increase readership. Don't crowd advertisement.

6. *Use color if available at a reasonable price.* Today's telephone directories usually have the capability of adding one or two colors to display ads. The most popular color for such ads is red, followed by blue or green. Direct mail coupon mailings usually offer a second color at little, if any, additional cost. Even newspapers have started using much more color in both the editorial as well as the display advertising segments. The use of color adds to the appearance of the advertisement, but can also add to the cost of both creation and insertion. The Industry Communique gives additional advise on creating effective advertisements.

INDUSTRY COMMUNIQUE

HOW TO CREATE AN AD
THAT SELLS

Ever notice how some ads pop right out at you while others just seem to sit there or get lost in the newspaper? This is no coincidence. This is professional ad-making at work.

Whether you're selling Sitmar Cruises or peanut butter, there are certain basic rules for creating ads that get noticed. In this Partnership newsletter, we'd like to review some ad-making fundamentals and look at ways you can improve the overall effectiveness of your agency's print advertising.

FIRST QUESTION, HOW BIG AN AD?

How big is your pocketbook? Your decision, however, should be based on factors other than just cost. How big are your competitors' ads? Do you plan to maintain a regular schedule of advertising? Is the ad you are planning a special, one-time-only event? Does your message require a great deal of body copy or a coupon?

Remember, it takes more space if you plan to feature a photo or illustration. It takes more space if you're going to include descriptive information on the ports of call. And it takes even more space if you want to include other information. The point is, be realistic when you choose your ad size. Don't over extend yourself. The job of your ad is to generate an interested buyer.

Unless you have an established presence in the travel section or some other section of the paper where people expect to see your ad, try to run at least a quarter page.

With smaller ads, you run the risk of being positioned amid a clutter of busy ads and disappearing from sight. You may also run the risk of having your ad positioned on a page with a larger, more dominant ad that steals the reader's eye away from your message.

If the cost of a quarter page is still prohibitive, then it's still possible for a smaller ad to work. Just remember to keep your small ad clean, simple and well designed. Focus your message, shorten your headline and reduce your copy to the bare bones. Depending on where your ad runs, you might consider a border or, at least, enough "white space" to let the headline "pop."

Before you start the actual production of your ad, get exact size requirements from the publication. It's much easier to produce an ad to size and shape specifications, than to first create the ad and then try to adapt it to a publication's requirements.

WHAT ARE YOU GOING TO SAY?

A good ad has a strategy, a focus...a message. You must decide what that message is before you advertise.

For instance, suppose you want to promote Sitmar 7-day Mexico sailings. Consider what Sitmar has to offer and try to match those advantages with the needs and desires of your clients or target audience. Maybe the message is that Sitmar Mexico sailings are booking fast and cruisers should make their reservations. Maybe Sitmar's Air/Sea program is important to your clients. Or perhaps Sitmar's Early Booking Discount makes these particular cruises especially attractive. Whatever you decide, keep the thrust of your ad single-focused with a clear benefit to your target audience. Remember, the purpose of the ad is to get you a "lead."

THE HEADLINE

Your ad begins with a headline. The headline should convey your message in a way that's fresh and provocative without losing sight of the all important reader benefit. In your attempt to grab attention, however, don't mislead or fool your reader. Deception, however light hearted, creates a negative response.

Keep in mind that even the type style you choose will influence the way your message is perceived. It's important to select your headline type carefully and order from a quality conscious typesetter. Something as subtle as letter spacing or the use of upper and lower case type can noticeably improve the readability of your headline. Research shows that all cap headlines are harder to read than upper case/lower case headlines.

THE VISUAL

The visual is the graphic element in your ad. For best results it should work hand in hand with your headline to convey the basic message.

Like your headline, it should be both provocative and include some reference to a reader benefit.

In selling a cruise, you may want to include people in your visuals that your potential clients can identify with. You may also want to consider using a photo of a Sitmar ship in an inviting location. Ship photos reassure cruise shoppers that Sitmar has large, modern, luxurious ships. Interesting maps that detail destinations also work well to involve readers with your cruise message.

At some point, you will decide whether your visual should be a photograph or an illustration. There are pros and cons to either choice. Photography is considered more realistic and trustworthy, but it also reproduces less dependably than an illustration in the newspaper. This is especially true for ads with small visuals.

If you opt for an illustration, the quality of that illustration should reflect your professional image. Be as quality conscious in selecting your illustration as in selecting your typography.

THE BODY COPY

If you manage to catch your reader's attention with your headline and visual, then you must provide the what, where, when, why and how of your message with body copy. Make these important facts easy to uncover by using short sentences, short paragraphs, familiar words and a conversational tone.

The best way to write copy is to pretend that you are speaking directly to one person in particular. Convince that person, one-to-one, why he or she should respond to your offer. Don't skimp on information or use vague generalities. When people are spending money for their vacation, they want as much information as possible. Include dates, destinations and some price reference. Telephone numbers are a definite must.

One last point on copy. Include captions under your visuals whenever possible. Captions are read five times more frequently than body copy. Captions give you an opportunity to communicate an important idea and set it apart where it's most apt to be noticed.

THE LAYOUT

Now you have a headline, a visual, a caption or two and your body copy. When you arrange these elements within your space, you will have a layout.

Research shows that readers look first at the visual, then the headline, then the copy. As you assemble your ad, keep these priorities in mind.

It may help you to keep a file on ads that have successfully attracted your attention. Analyze why these ads work and how the different elements contribute to their success.

Then last, but not least, your layout should include your agency name, phone number, address and/or logo. At just a glance, the reader should understand what your offer is and where it is available.

TO SUMMARIZE

Here is an easy to follow outline for preparing a travel ad that will help bring business through your door.

1. Pick a size that's large enough to do the job.
2. Get the exact size requirements.
3. Focus on a specific sales message.
4. Write a strong, benefit oriented headline.
5. Choose a visual that works with the headline.
6. Write copy that tells who, what, where, when and why.
7. Arrange the elements giving priority to visual, headline and copy, in that order.
8. Make sure your agency's logo, address and phone number are prominently featured.

A clean, well-designed ad can be an extremely effective Sitmar cruise sales tool. Each time you advertise, keep track of how well your ad pulls. By measuring the results, you can determine what kind of offer and ad format works best for you. Good selling!

Reprinted from Sitmar Cruise Lines (now part of Princess Cruises); Partnership Newsletter for travel agents.

Copy

In addition to the general layout, certain elements make the content or "**copy**" of an advertisement more effective. There are three primary elements that should be considered.

First, a major benefit headline should be used. Put the number one product or service benefit in the headline. And remember, factual benefits are important but emotional benefits are equally significant. For example, a major benefit of a trip to the islands in January is to get away from cold weather. Saying "The Caribbean—$250.00" is not as effective as saying "Give your cold away in the sunny Caribbean—$250.00." The Cunard ad is a good example of this. The headline must answer the first question of any reader—"What's in it for me?"

When the advertisement promotes more than one item, use an overall headline for focus and to hold the ad together. For special interest groups use selective headlines. For example, say "For the SCUBA diver…" or "Golf away today." A headline that asks a question or announces a new program attracts attention.

A second major point in copywriting is to be direct, simple, and complete. Amplify the headline in the rest of the advertisement. Give all relevant information including prices in simple, clear language. Do not generalize and do not make excessive claims. Also do not forget the name of your organization and its address and telephone number so that a reader can take action.

Taking action should be the result of the third element. Urge action! Tell the readers what they should do—call, write, or complete and return a coupon. If a coupon is included, it should be large enough to be filled out. It should be next to one of the ad borders where it can be clipped without destroying the rest of the ad. If choice location in the newspaper is available, place an ad with a coupon near the border of the page so that the page is not totally destroyed and the coupon can be clipped easily.

HELP IN ADVERTISING FOR THE SMALL ORGANIZATION

An advertising agency can be of great help in developing layout and copy for print advertising. However, many small organizations in the travel and tourism industry do not have a large enough advertising budget to make use of an advertising agency worthwhile. In these situations the advertising medium itself can help.

A good working relationship with the newspaper's or magazine's advertising representative can be a great benefit. The representative can assist with almost every aspect of advertising. The newspaper's advertising department will often be able to do the layout of the actual advertisement. Most newspapers use offset printing, and "camera ready" copy is what is used to make the printing plate. Many newspapers today are created through desktop publishing which allows easy creation and editing. It can often put the ad together from your design. The newspaper can also suggest free-lance artists who, for a reasonable fee, can help you. They

LIFE IS SHORT.

And four other reasons to cross the Atlantic on the QE2.

You only live once. Between now and December, Queen Elizabeth 2 sails regularly between New York and Europe, each voyage an opportunity for you to travel aboard this 13-story legend at sea. For five days and five nights, travel in old world elegance that recalls how the jet set traveled before there were jets. Surely, it is the ultimate luxury that everyone should experience at least once in a lifetime.

Variety is the spice of life. Dine in world class restaurants, then dance the night away. Or take a chance in our European casino. Shop at the only Harrods afloat. Maybe a few laps in one of four swimming pools, followed by paddle tennis. Or just treat yourself to a relaxing massage in the Golden Door Spa at Sea®. The choice of activities is endless on the only 24-hour city to cross the Atlantic.

A little too much is just about right. Your life of luxury continues even after your crossing. Because you also receive a free return trip in British Airways' exclusive World Traveller™ Class, where you'll be pampered as only British Airways can. Enjoy fine wines, free in-flight entertainment,

gourmet cuisine, even eyeshades for napping, and world renowned service. Or for $1,095 extra, break the sound barrier on a specially reserved British Airways' Concorde®.

Where there's a will, there's a way. Sail to or from Europe for $1,480 to $9,640. Or take advantage of our low standby fares. You can even combine your crossing with a QE2 European cruise and save 35% on the cruise fare. If that's not enough, we also offer all-inclusive land, sea and air vacations throughout Europe. Take your pick.

Life is short. So make it sweet. Treat yourself to the grandeur of a transatlantic voyage on the QE2. See your travel agent or Cunard for details. For a free brochure or $8.95 videotape of life aboard the QE2, call Cunard at 1-800-352-3800.

Rates are per person, double occupancy, dependent upon departure date; taxes extra. Registry: QE2-Great Britain. ©Cunard 1991.

BRITISH AIRWAYS
The world's favourite airline®

CUNARD
We're Not The Best Because We're The Oldest.
We're The Oldest Because We're The Best.

may even have an artist on staff. Working with an artist for a short time may be worth the cost and may help establish a direction so that an organization can produce its own effective layouts in the future. Most newspapers maintain a wide library of clip art for many types of businesses. If you advertise with them, they will make their library available to you.

PREPARING EFFECTIVE DIRECT MAIL PIECES

The guidelines provided above for preparing effective newspaper advertisements are just as important when preparing direct mail presentations. Because more space is available for direct mail, the guidelines should be easier to apply. However, it is easy to get carried away with direct mail and provide too much information. Care must be used to choose the proper information to print and to assure an even flow for the reader. Keep direct mail presentations simple and eye-catching.

Although direct mail advertising allows for the preparation of brochures and flyers that should be developed in accordance with the above guidelines, there are some additional types of presentation pieces that differ from other print media. First is the letter and the second is the newsletter.

Letters

Letters are the most widely used of all direct mail forms. Often, they are used alone as sales letters or thank-you letters. They can also be used to transmit flyers, brochures, invoices, or other material. Letters can be either individualized or printed form letters. The individually prepared letter is most effective because the reader will consider it more personal than a printed form letter. Today, the use of word processors, along with computerized mailing lists, make it possible to produce an individually-prepared letter at a fraction of the cost of individually hand-typed letters.

With direct mail, the sender can control the amount of copy and the space it takes to say what it is necessary to say. The benefits of a travel service should be described in glowing (but not repetitive) detail. A balance is needed without making the mistake of saying too little or being too repetitive. The content of the letter should be direct and basically simple.

Ample margins should be used on the letter to make it more attractive and readable. A personally-signed letter is quite impressive. This, of course, is not possible in mass mailings. Individually addressed or hand-typed envelopes will help to personalize direct mail—but they, too, have a higher cost than the use of labels. However, labels are substantially better than the use of "occupant" as part of the address.

The use of good quality paper stock for letters and envelopes will make them more attractive. The organization's name, logo, or symbol, as well as its complete address and telephone number, should appear on the letter.

Teaser copy on the envelope (for example, "Important information enclosed") or other information can increase the chance of letters being opened. Postage stamps rather than metered or printed postage make a letter more likely to be opened. The use of commemorative stamps attracts even more attention.

Postal Cards

Postal cards are another form of direct mail "letter" that should not be forgotten. They are well suited to short, direct messages and they are less costly to mail and print than letters. A postal service study found that 83% of people who received postcards actually read them. Postage costs are one-third less than first-class letters.

Newsletters

All kinds of **newsletters** are mailed by almost all elements of the travel and tourism industry. They range from multipage, professionally prepared magazines to one-sheet typed and duplicated pieces. Airline clubs and frequent flyer programs (for example, United's Mileage Plus or American's AAdvantage program) send regular newsletters to their members, as do steamship lines to their previous passengers, hotels to their frequent visitors and club members (for example, Hyatt Hotels' Gold Passport), and travel agencies to present and prospective clients. In addition to sending newsletters to past customers, many travel industry suppliers frequently send newsletters to travel agencies. More and more companies are using newsletters now because they can be produced at a much lower cost in-house with today's desktop publishing capability.

The newsletter is an excellent way to provide both sales promotion and institutional messages. (**Institutional advertising** is designed to convey the overall image of an organization and create an awareness in the reader's mind, rather than selling a particular product or service.) Providing "nonselling" articles that directly benefit the audience demonstrates the company's concern for the traveler's needs. Examples of such articles are those giving information on customs regulations, how to pack a suitcase, or what to do when certain problems arise during travel.

Product messages should be handled as in a letter. Give all the pertinent information and elaborate on it, including details that emphasize the emotional benefits to the traveler. Details that might not fit into newspaper advertising or would be too expensive to include in the broadcast media can be added. Flyers or brochures can also be inserted with the newsletter.

The audience of a newsletter should be invited to take action on at least one item within the newsletter. Coupons to return can also be effective.

Copy for Newsletters

As for newspapers and letters, copy for newsletters should be simple, informal, and briefly convey information to the readers. Clear and interesting communication of the main idea of each item should appear near its beginning. Gain the reader's attention and keep it. After conveying the main idea, build it up in future paragraphs and sentences. Again, avoid using overly pompous words or superlatives. Show benefits, but make them accurate and believable.

Format for Newsletters

The format of a newsletter should be designed for easy reading. The print and type should be large, dark, and clear so that even older readers who may be a bit farsighted can read it. The same rule applies to illustrations and photographs. White space aids in clarity and readability. Ample margins on all sides and ample space between paragraphs and articles adds to readability. Don't crowd copy. It is better to leave out an item or shorten it than to crowd the material.

Clean and simple lines or borders around special items draw attention to the items and make the page look clean and orderly. Borders should not be fancy or ornate. Colored paper or colored ink can often be used to attract attention. Black ink and white paper, however, are the least expensive.

Flyers, Brochures, and Other Printed Material

The guidelines provided for newspaper and direct mail advertising copy and layout apply as well to flyers and brochures. Keep the copy content simple and clear so that the reader will be attracted and will understand.

COSTS OF DIRECT MAIL MAILING LISTS

Buying a List

Several costs must be considered when planning direct mail advertising. First among these is the cost of a **mailing list**. Many retail travel agencies maintain lists of their clients and of people who have requested information. Cruise lines and tour operators also maintain lists of previous customers. Airlines and hotels have use of the names and addresses on their frequent flyer/guest programs. For the solicitation of new business, mailing list brokers offer lists of categories of people of all types. The lists may be subscribers to certain magazines, members of certain types of organizations, or specific businesses. They may also be lists of people who meet a certain profile, such as income level, net worth, education, or special interests. The general cost of a list varies from $40.00 to $100.00 per thousand names, with some highly-specialized lists costing even more. When using a broker's list, the advertiser is actually renting a one-time use only. Mailing lists are generally sold on labels that can be affixed directly to an envelope or self-mailer. See the Industry Communique for advise on choosing the right direct mail list.

INDUSTRY COMMUNIQUE

THE RIGHT LIST

Don Bohlin

For sheer frustration it's hard to beat having an expensive direct mail offer come back marked, "Not at this address—return to sender." Non-deliverables are called "nixies," and when he got 1,000 of them recently, one direct mail marketer called his list company to complain.

Brooks Gentleman at Dun's Marketing Services (A Dun & Bradstreet company) understands the frustration felt by new direct mailers. "A thousand returned envelopes do make a pretty impressive looking pile in your office," he says. But nixies are only part of what makes one mailing list better than another.

Selecting the right list is the most important thing a direct mail marketer does. The choice ranks right up there with advertisers picking the correct magazine for a print campaign or betting on the success of a new TV series. Yet most companies are product driven, Gentleman says. New mailers tend to focus on the Three P's—product, price, and purchase offer—and a good looking creative package to carry them. But the best conceived package will fail if it goes to the wrong people using the wrong list or doesn't arrive at all.

So how do you pick the right list? Today's direct mail marketers are faced with a wide range of prices, sizes, and collection methodologies. You can rent lists (less frequently a list may be purchased outright) from literally hundreds of brokers, list compilers, publishers, and big direct mail operations.

Some lists offer the mailer lots of information, some very little beyond address and Zip Code. To get a handle on the subject, we called on two top companies with very different products to find out where lists originate, what features and failings to look out for, and how much you can expect to pay.

Dun's, with headquarters in Mountain Lakes, New Jersey, specializes in business-to-business lists organized by United States Standard Industrial

Classification (SIC) codes and bolstered by info from Dun & Bradstreet credit reporters.

National Demographics and Lifestyles Inc. (NDL) based in Denver, Colorado, supplies consumer lists of home addresses selected by demographic and psychographic criteria gathered from in-product questionnaires, the kind a buyer fills out along with the warranty card in many retail purchases.

BUSINESS OR CONSUMER LIST? BUYING A SUIT AT THE OFFICE

Business-to-business lists are most frequently used to market products and services to industrial buyers at the wholesale or manufacturing levels, while lists of home addresses are used to sell finished consumer goods to the general public. But there are applications that cross over between business and consumer lists. Manufacturers can by-pass the retail level and appeal directly to consumers at home by mail. And certain consumer products can be sold using business lists. At Dun's, both custom tailored clothing and portfolio investment services have been marketed successfully through mailings to high status individuals at work.

A business list constructed by title and company size to reach highly paid executives at the office can circumvent competition in the mailbox at home. The apparel maker, for example, uses Dun's lists to identify prospects and offer pattern samples, after which a tailor actually goes to the customer's office to take measurements. But not all consumer product mailings will be considered appropriate in the office, and only the most creative will make it past the executive secretary who opens the CEO's mail.

SELECTION CRITERIA: HOW MUCH IS ENOUGH?

A directory compiled list might limit your selection to gender, location, and age group. An expensive response list or house file should be made up of recent direct mail purchasers, but it may not be particularly adaptable to another kind of mailing simply because the type of purchase is unrelated to the new product or service.

Merging several lists is an effective, though often an expensive, method of locating prospects who have more than one desired characteristic. A list based on auto registration can yield owners of late model cars. A homeowners list can provide prospects within a prescribed geographic area and price range. A list of people who have purchased high-ticket sporting goods, combined with the first two, might help you market recreational property to people who have the interest and the means to drive to the site on weekends.

The more original research a list company does, the more demographic and psychographic choice it can offer the mailer using a single data base. For examples of selection criteria, let's look at NDL's "hybrid" list. Containing 17,105,800 consumer names as of February 1988, this is one of the largest lists of it's kind available. NDL currently offers:

- *Gender, including preference among Mrs., Miss or Ms.*
- *Nine age groups.*
- *Fourteen income levels.*
- *Marital status.*
- *Home owner or renter.*
- *Eleven occupation groups.*
- *Children at home, by age.*
- *Credit cards in use.*
- *Location by State, County, and Zip Code.*
- *Fifty-nine hobby and interest categories such as bicycling, camping, fashion clothing, grandchildren, golf, running, sailing, and wines.*

Business-to-business list selection is based primarily on industry type and geography, and since most business lists are directory compiled, yellow pages business headings are often used as categories. Dun's and some other business list compilers use the U.S. Government's SIC (Standard Industrial Classification) code instead of yellow page headings. SIC codes can be an advantage, especially to a marketing director who taps industry data bases or looks to government generated reports for help in planning a campaign.

Dun also offers six geographical selections from state to Zip Code, company size by number of employees or annual sales, and seven "status" selections (i.e., headquarters, branch, manufacturing or non-manufacturing location, etc.) A special list focusing on the computer market is also available which provides information on the number and type of computers in use at listed companies.

WHAT DOES IT COST?

Mailing lists are usually rented, not bought. Charges increase with the number of "sort" selections, that is how many demographic or psychographic criteria are applied in selecting a mailer's list from the supplier's data base. In general the cost per thousand should vary inversely with list size, decreasing as the list grows larger.

NDL's base price is $60 per 1,000 names including one demographic selection. Each additional choice adds $7 per 1,000. Seventy dollars to $75 is the average cost per 1,000 for an NDL list, according to a company spokesperson but a more strictly defined list would obviously cost more. Females, interested in skiing and real estate investments, with income over $45,000 would cost $81 per 1,000 by that formula.

All list companies have minimum purchase requirements. The smallest number to effectively test a consumer list is considered to be 10,000. If tests generate enough response to justify proceeding with the offer, the subsequent mailings are always much larger.

Dun's top price (from the Dun & Bradstreet credit data base) is $80 per 1,000 names for one time rental, according to Gentleman. There is a minimum $450 purchase requirement. Sort options included are choice of industry by SIC, geography, company size, and company status.

A mailer must pay for each use of a list. An additional mailing to the same Dun's list costs one half the price of the first mailing. For twice the original rents per 1,000, you may order a list on magnetic tape and use it for multiple mailings up to one year.

Most companies keep close tabs on the names they rent to others. To insure there's no cheating they "seed" the lists with names of employees who monitor the number of mailings they get from each source.

WHO SHOULD BE ON IT?

Before you go shopping for a mailing list, look at one you already have—your sales records. A consumer list that you rent should match the demographic profile of your best customer. For a new business or a new product the only way to achieve that match is with good market analysis.

At this point you'll be faced with the choice of mailing to selected job titles within companies or to individuals—real people—by name and job title. A name-and-title list will cost more, but if it is current and accurate it should bring better results. You can include a request for the correct name and title in any title-only mailing. Many companies are happy to help route mail to the correct decision maker. Remember, you pay every time you use a rented list, but anyone responding to the mailing becomes a legitimate member of your own house file.

WHAT DOES A LIST LOOK LIKE?

Larger mailings, mailers using several different lists or renting for multiple uses often require lists on magnetic tape. A computer fulfillment house can then merge the lists, purge duplicate names (or names that don't fit the profile), and print and attach labels using automated equipment. List companies will also provide preprinted pressure sensitive or "cheshire" labels which can be handed over to a fulfillment house and attached by machine.

Lists on computer disc are available from some sources, making it possible to create theme copy in the mailing piece with a different message for executives within certain functions or job titles. Consumer mailings customized by inserting the recipient's name and community into letter copy are becoming commonplace with the growing use of PC's to handle lists.

TESTING

Direct mail is often claimed to be the only really testable marketing method and with good reason. Other forms of market research may ask for consumer reactions, opinions, or stated preferences; but direct mail asks for action. People may say they like a product, but you don't really know if a marketing program will work until someone pays money in response to an offer. And every answer that comes back from a test mailing helps pay the research. You can estimate in advance whether a commitment of major resources has a good chance of paying off.

Every aspect of a mailing is susceptible to testing: the design of a brochure; the product; the postage rate; the time of year; the price and terms of the offer. The list is an especially prime candidate for testing. Business reply mail should be coded to determine how well each list performs as well as to separate returns from different offers or different creative packages.

SET REALISTIC GOALS

No list supplier will guarantee the rate of return that you can expect from a mailing, but a knowledgeable one can help with examples of how well similar mailings have done and what in the list selection contributed to their success or failure. The rate of return needed to break even or show a profit will vary with the offer. Some mailers are satisfied and profitable with a fraction of a percentage point.

The "magic number" that experienced mailers look for when they test a list is 1 percent or better, Gentleman says. "I've encountered first time mailers who expected a 50 percent rate of return. I think you could offer a free $100 bill and not get 50 percent."

You can't sell everything by direct mail, he cautions. New marketers get into trouble with prices that are too low or margins too slim to pay for the program. "You have to know the rate of return you'll need to break even."

"People will try direct mail without understanding list selection," Gentleman says. "The man who called me, disturbed about 1,000 nondeliverables, was really working a very low nixie rate—less than 1 percent. It depends on the list source of course, but for directory-compiled lists a 10 to 15 percent nixie rate is fairly common."

Reprinted from HSMAI Marketing Review, Fall 1988.

Other Costs

Postage is one of the highest costs of direct mail. Current costs vary from $160.00 per thousand pieces of bulk mail up to almost $300.00 per thousand for first-class (based upon a 1 ounce mailing). To these costs must be added the costs of creating the advertising piece, plus printing, folding, and often stuffing and sealing costs if envelopes are used. Thus, the cost of a 1-ounce mailing can vary from a minimum of about $.35 per piece to $.50 or $.60 per piece. On a cost per thousand basis this translates to $350 to $600 per thousand pieces mailed. Some complex mailings may cost even more.

YELLOW PAGES AND OTHER TELEPHONE DIRECTORIES

Advertising in the yellow pages or in other private local telephone directories is a major method of effective directional advertising. Sales representatives of the publisher can help in developing effective copy.

Several basic elements should be kept in mind when developing telephone directory advertising. Along with the organization's name, complete address and phone number, include the organization's logo and office hours. As in other printed media, use a headline or illustration to attract the reader's attention. Line illustrations reproduce far better than photographs in the yellow pages.

Because this type of advertising lasts for an extended period, it is not wise to try to advertise timely products. This form of advertising is best suited to institutional advertising—informing the reader of what services you offer and where to locate you.

Because your yellow pages ad will be competing with ads for other similar organizations, any special feature your product or service offers should be included in the body of the copy. Conveniences such as delivery service, ability to take appointments during off times, credit cards accepted or other features should be included to give you a competitive edge. Don't forget to urge the reader to action. "Call for fast friendly service..." or "Come in and visit..." can be effective.

BROADCAST MEDIA

As with print media, cost and placement (timing) of broadcast media advertising are important factors that must be considered when planning an advertisement. The techniques used in creating advertisements for broadcast media are specialized. In most cases, the travel professional will be wise to turn to other professionals in these fields for help in planning effective use of the media.

Television

Television time is sold on the basis of length of commercial and time of airing. **Prime time** is the time of highest viewing and also highest advertising cost—8:00 P.M. to 11:00 P.M. in the East and West and 7:00 pm to 10:00 pm in the Midwest. Weekend special events such as professional football games also carry a prime rate. The lowest cost television times are after the late news and on non-network stations.

Since the mid-1980s, there has been a growing choice of cable stations and programs in many areas. These frequently have very attractive rates and reach specialized audiences.

In addition to air time, the production of television commercials can be an expensive proposition. It is necessary to consider both the cost of creation as well as actors, camera, crew, and film or tape production or editing. For these reasons, television advertising will not be cost-effective for many components of the travel industry, but is used extensively by larger companies such as airlines, cruise lines, hotels, and car rental firms. A few tour companies also use television.

Guidelines for Television Advertising

It is not advisable for an inexperienced person to try to develop television advertising without professional help. Organizations wishing to use television advertising, even on a local level, should consider working with people who are knowledgeable about TV commercial production. This may be someone from an advertising agency, an employee of a TV station, or a public relations professional who has worked in the medium.

Just as with radio and print media, it is important to work closely with the sales department of the television station. The TV advertising account executive can give valuable information about production as well as placement of the commercial.

Radio

Radio, unlike television, can be used effectively even by smaller components of the travel industry, if timing and station selection are chosen carefully. The prime time of radio listenership is the morning rush hour (approximately 6:00 to 9:00 am). This is the most productive radio time because people are freshest and most alert at the beginning of the day. Thus, they are least likely to ignore commercial announcements. The next most popular and most expensive time is the afternoon rush hour (4:00 to 7:00 pm). Evening time (television prime time) is relatively inexpensive.

Radio commercials, usually called **spot announcements**, are generally sold on a per-spot announcement basis. While it is possible to sponsor short programs (for example, newscasts) and segments of programs such as traffic reports, most

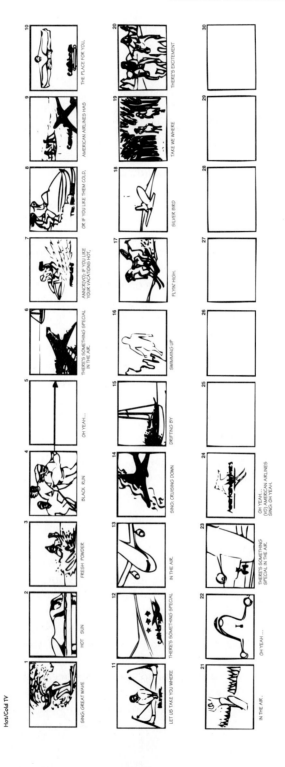

Storybook for American Airlines television ad "Hot and Cold," preliminary step before filming, 1992.

COMMERCIAL: HERTZ RENTAL CARS, "Unlimited Bus"

LENGTH: 30 seconds   DATE: 12/19/90

1. (Musical Background) When you rent from Hertz in Florida,

2. you get more than a great car at a great rate.

3. The real bargain is the company behind the car . . .

4. because whatever it takes to make your vacation go smoothly,

5. Hertz is there to make it happen -

6. from emergency road service that's . . .

7. as close as a phone to free unlimited mileage.

8. Wherever you roam . . .

9. next time you're in Florida, . . .

10. wouldn't you feel better with Hertz behind you?

11. M/SINGERS: Hertz.

12. We're America's Wheels.

Storyboard for a Hertz 30-second television ad, carrying through the theme of the friendly Hertz bus.

advertising is on a run-of-the-show basis. Substantial cost savings can be obtained for a long-term contract and for contracts using some of the less popular times.

Most radio programs run from 1 to 4 hours with the same host or disk jockey. As a result, regular audiences develop varying degrees of identity with radio personalities. Because the radio personalities have personal followings, a successful travel advertising technique has been to offer tour programs led by the radio personality. This often means that the travel agency, airline, tour operator, or hotel involved buys the commercial time on the radio station, and provides free travel and often fees to the radio personalities as well.

Effective Radio Advertisements

Preparation of material for radio advertising can be done in two ways. First, radio ads can be taped or written in advance. Second, fact sheets about the service can be given to a station announcer or personality (for example, the disc jockey) who uses them as a basis for informal discussion. The only real advantage of the latter form lies in the selling ability of the personality. The same selling ability can be used if the voice of a well-known personality is used on tape.

A radio station sales department will be quite helpful in advertising development. An advertising agency can also be used. However, a number of points should be kept in mind when developing or helping to develop radio advertising.

First, the number of facts in a radio advertisement should be kept to a minimum. Give only the essentials. Radio is a background medium and radio listeners are only half listeners. They do not absorb detail. Second, important words should be repeated. The name of the service, the price, and where to go to take action should be emphasized.

Third, a radio ad should attract attention immediately. If listeners are caught at the very beginning, they'll probably listen to the whole message. Sound effects, music or other special techniques should not be saved for the middle or the end of the advertisement. Capture attention as early as possible and try to hold it throughout the ad.

As with print media, copy should be simple, informal, and believable. Superlatives and generalizations usually miss the mark. A radio ad should be written as if it were part of an informal conversation.

The ad should end with a call for action. Do not leave the listener wondering what to do. Give a phone number, location, or some other way the listener can order the product or service or at least get more information.

CONCLUSION

A knowledge of the costs, vocabulary, and techniques in both print and broadcast media is necessary to make the right decisions in using them for effective advertising.

SUMMARY

Good and effective are not always synonymous in advertising because what is effective may not always be pleasant. However, the nature of travel products makes it easy to produce advertising that is both good and effective.

Circulation and ad size, as well as the nature of the publication, will govern the cost of advertising in newspapers and magazines. In direct mail, important costs include the price of renting a mailing list and the cost of postage. Timing, frequency, and production costs are important factors in the advertising budget for broadcast media. In both print and broadcast media, the advice and help of professionals can increase advertising effectiveness. In advertising in any one of these media, however, clarity, simplicity, and concern for communicating a message and suggesting action are essential.

QUESTIONS FOR THOUGHT AND DISCUSSION

1. a. Collect samples of advertisements (particularly in travel) from newspapers or magazines. Discuss the good and bad points of each.

    b. Discuss good and bad points of some travel ads from radio or television.
2. Create an advertisement for a hotel, airline, or travel agency. Use whatever features you wish to create for this company.
3. Write a 30 or 60-second radio spot for a travel business (hotel, airline, destination, or other).

12

The Sales Function in the Travel Industry

dual distribution
inside sales
order taking
outside sales
sales presentation
supplier

The question is often asked: "How do you differentiate sales from marketing?" Earlier, we defined marketing as the total process of bringing buyer and product or service together. Later, in the discussion of the marketing mix in travel, personal sales was described as a major part of the overall marketing process. A complete marketing plan will include sales, and effective sales are part of any successful marketing effort. Although the sales function might be able to exist apart from other marketing functions, using the sales function as a part of the marketing effort definitely multiplies its effectiveness.

DUAL DISTRIBUTION

As we noted earlier, most components of the travel and tourism industry are characterized by a dual distribution system. Travel services generally have three distribution levels—producer, wholesaler, and retailer. In other industries, the producer sells to wholesalers (and often directly to retailers); wholesalers sell to retailers; and the retail establishment is the prime distributor to the general market of individual purchasers. For example, in the food industry, Dole grows and cans pineapples. Its place in the distribution system is that of producer. Dole sells canned pineapple to food jobbers (wholesalers) and also directly to large supermarket chains (retailers). Food jobbers sell to smaller retail food markets, which also sell to the general public. In the automobile industry, the manufacturers such as General Motors, Ford, or Chrysler produce the cars and then sell them to their dealers. They do not sell directly to consumers. When consumers want to purchase automobiles, they must buy them through a dealer.

In travel and tourism both the producer and the retailer sell to the general public. Airlines, hotels, car rental companies , railroads, and most other service producers sell directly to the general public. However, these producers also sell their services through wholesalers and through retail travel agents. Most cruise lines and some tour operators are the only suppliers that have chosen a virtually unitary system—through the retail travel agent.

BUYING AS A LEARNING EXPERIENCE

Anyone in sales has a continuing opportunity to improve his or her ability to sell effectively. Salespersons are also consumers, constantly experiencing both good and bad selling efforts. As they experience these selling efforts, true professionals will analyze them, and use the examples, both good and bad, to improve their own sales abilities. As John Zeeman, former Senior Vice President, Marketing, of United Airlines stated:

> One of the most valuable sales experiences is as a 'buyer.' In my career with United, I started in advertising where, obviously, it is important to make significant media purchases…both because of the importance of media to carry messages as well as the magnitude of dollars involved. When one is in a buying environment one has the opportunity to clinically evaluate sales presentations. How well did the salespeople understand my needs? How well did the salespeople fit the product or services to those needs? How persuasively did the salesperson present and explain this fit?
>
> I think travel counselors could learn a lot about selling if they would evaluate the mistakes suppliers make in their presentations and to extract the strong selling points that are likewise made. In addition, they should give some thought as to how they, as consumers, react to sales people. How do they choose both merchandise and services? How do they quantify among differing values of importance to them in making purchases?

Tourism professionals should use personal experience as an aid to on-the-job effectiveness if they are in any of the categories of sales positions found in the industry. The Industry Communiques identify eight other qualities of a professional salesperson, and point out how challenges for the professional salesperson will change in the 1990s.

TRAVEL AGENT VS SUPPLIER

Under the dual distribution system, consumers have a choice. They can purchase travel services directly from the producer or through one of the more than 33,000 travel agency offices currently open in the United States.

INDUSTRY COMMUNIQUE

EIGHT QUALITIES OF A PROFESSIONAL SALESPERSON

Tony Alessandra

Talk to people all over the United States, and you will find that the term "salesperson" generates many responses. A few of the most common are: pushy, high pressure, dishonest, huckster, hard sell...and it deteriorates from there.

The answers are quite different when you ask for a description of a *professional* salesperson. Then you hear responses that are a big improvement: thorough, honest, friendly, polite, competent, and sincere.

The questions are what can you do to develop the qualities of a professional and how do you convey to others that you now possess or are developing those traits? The answers are simple, although not always easy. The first step is knowledge, becoming aware of the qualities of a professional. The second step is action—making a commitment to apply this knowledge and follow through with your commitment.

No matter how nice a person we are, some of us still need to work on one or more traits which will help us be more professional. Let's consider the key traits which will make your contact with a client more conducive to a long-term business relationship.

IMAGE

It has been said that you never get a second chance to overcome a bad first impression. The first few minutes of a relationship are often the most important. People like to be right about how they "size up" others so it takes a lot more work to change a negative first impression to a positive impression in the first place. You will probably agree that those first few moments can often make or break a sales call. Creating a positive impression increases the probability that you and your products will be accepted.

Dress and grooming are only one aspect that forms first impressions. Equally important are voice inflection, posture, personality, style, and attitude.

YOUR ATTITUDE IS SHOWING

Our attitudes are reflected in everything we do, including relationships with our clients. Our attitudes elicit different responses from our clients, so if we see them as jerks who can be manipulated, their responses will be entirely different than if we see them as fellow businesspeople with whom we have a lot in common.

We can never be truly professional salespeople unless we develop a sincere respect for—and healthy attitude toward—our clients. Try thinking of them as valves through which your energy flows rather than as dams (obstacles) who will stop your progress. Only your positive attitude toward them will ensure the mutual trust which is so vital to doing business successfully.

DEPTH OF KNOWLEDGE

In all hotel sales positions, the property has the obligation to educate you about the specific product you are selling. This knowledge, however, rarely goes beyond that required to describe competently the product to a client, so you should set aside time on a regular basis during which you can deepen your knowledge (and hopefully your enthusiasm) for your hotel.

If someone were to say to you, "Tell me about the property that you are working in," could you give them an interesting, in-depth explanation of how it started and where it is today? Perhaps you think that knowing the history or philosophy of your hotel is not necessary for your day-to-day selling. The fact is that with an increase in knowledge comes an increase in confidence and authority. The result: longer lasting client relationships and more sales.

BREADTH OF KNOWLEDGE

It's also important to develop your ability to discuss a broad spectrum of subjects. Having a depth of knowledge in your field without knowledge in a wide variety of topics puts an automatic limit on the number of people you can relate to and who in turn can relate to you. This is a serious handicap for a salesperson.

It is not necessary for you to have an opinion on all the issues, but being informed on them and keeping up to date by scanning a good daily newspaper will give you confidence and expand your conversational effectiveness.

SENSITIVITY

No matter how great your conversational skills may be, your efforts will be completely wasted if you are not sensitive to your clients' needs. It is crucial to be aware of your clients' "silent messages" which often reveal the real meaning behind the verbal ones.

Study body language and try to be empathetic. Observe what people do with their bodies in different situations. Put yourself in their shoes so that you can be open to what's happening with them, but do it intellectually rather than emotionally.

ENTHUSIASM

It is literally impossible to be a top seller in your field without a contagious sense of enthusiasm. To prove this to yourself, try to think of top hotel salespeople you know or have heard about who do not have a genuine enthusiasm for themselves and their properties.

Enthusiasm shows the client that *you* are sold on the product. Your enthusiasm, good eye contact, and your overall sincerity will also tell your clients that you're an honest person. This will motivate them to establish or continue a business relationship with you. They will become interested in you as a person. This is what you want, both for yourself and your hotel.

MATURITY

Maturity is a rather nebulous quality. It combines all the positive character traits we have already mentioned.

One of the things that distinguishes a mature person is the ability to recognize the need to do things whether liking them or not. In addition, mature people accept responsibility for their actions. The result is they are willing to admit mistakes and suffer consequences as well as reap rewards.

Maturity means handling disappointments and setbacks without becoming self-destructive. These people know there are times when things won't go right and they know that those times won't last forever.

PROFESSIONALISM

Professionalism is a state of mind and conduct. It is not *what* you do, it is *how* you do it. There are many highly paid incompetents as well as many very professional volunteers in every field.

Pride is the sense of satisfaction you have from knowing that you are important, worthwhile, in control of your destiny, and aware of and acting on your potential. Pride will make you stand tall even when surrounded by giants. Professionalism recognizes potential and is, therefore, not stung by small disappointments or undermined by larger ones.

Taking pride in yourself and what you do is the seed from which professionalism grows. It's the natural consequence of developing the other seven traits that we mentioned and vice versa.

HSMAI Marketing Review, Fall 1987.

INDUSTRY COMMUNIQUE

SELLING IN THE '90S

William T. Brooks

What one-syllable word will redefine the very essence of professional selling in the coming decade? That all-powerful word is "change." The very same phenomenon that will forge the tone of politics, technology, and every phase of the world's structure well into the next century will also prove to be the major driving force behind the new face of professional selling.

As a result of permeating change, there will be a new set of increasing and all-encompassing needs that will appear in the marketplace. Sales professionals will be forced to anticipate and adapt to a series of events that will dictate their ability to meet the unique demands of a newly forged economy.

What are some of these changes? Economic trends finding their way to the marketplace more quickly and in full force almost immediately; customer preferences for design, quality, flexibility, style, technical superiority, and purchasing terms becoming more important and changing on an unpredictable, irregular, and more frequent basis; more prospects and customers speaking with purchase orders and vendor changes rather than accepting or fighting poor customer service, treatment, or dissatisfaction; and trends in the global economy affecting corporate- and consumer-spending patterns and behaviors in more direct and immediate ways than ever before are just a few possibilities.

Increasingly, day-to-day selling activities will be dictated by the power of mass communications, macro and micro economic realities, global affairs, consumer issues, politics, value shifts, and more. For example, several traditional sales philosophies and points of view will finally prove themselves to be totally outdated in the next decade; "I don't need to prospect—I work strictly off of repeat and referral business," "Everybody buys price," "I own this market," "I don't need to automate my territory," and "Selling is nothing more than selling yourself' are a few of the dead or dying.

The simple truth is that the future will belong to those sales organizations and salespeople who are flexible and nontraditional in their thinking. Those willing to adapt their thoughts, feelings, and actions to the new marketplace will rule the economy of the coming decade. The graveyard of business is crowded with those who didn't, couldn't, or wouldn't adapt. Each and every one of them became extinct: door-to-door sales, manual typewriters, Osborne Computers, and American Motors, to name a few.

Other traditional selling approaches will also become economic dinosaurs: selling without considering the wants and needs of the customer; canned or trite phrases, closes, and selling techniques; scripted sales presentations; selling pure price, not value; adversarial selling; complicated and confusing selling "systems"; not prospecting for new business; selling without servicing; salespeople not understanding the role of marketing; and marketing departments not addressing or understanding the needs of the sales force.

Let's consider several concepts that will work in this new environment. Here are five that will help catapult any sales professional into the decade of the '90s with an inside track for success:

Ultimate success will depend on a salesperson's ability to be in front of qualified buyers when the buyer wants to buy—not when the sales professional needs to make a sale. In the new environment, buyers are confused by a vast array of available products and services. This "blurring of the marketplace" will dictate a greater need for proactive prospecting and the carrying of a "message to the market" by individual sales professionals. There is, and will be, an ever-growing need to empower salespeople to personally bridge the gaps among marketing, prospecting, and selling.

More selling will occur in the "needs analysis" phase of the sales cycle. Needs analysis simply defined is understanding and selling to the buyer's needs rather than selling a product or service to meet a quota. This will result in a better positioning of the product or service in the marketplace. Conversely, more reliance on traditional closing techniques will result in more poorly positioned products. Traditionally strong, aggressive, and insensitive closing tactics will inevitably lead to more closed doors rather than to more opened accounts.

Not only must a product or service be well positioned, but the professional must also be positioned to sell in a relationship-based, need-focused way. This is, by the way, more than "coffee and doughnut" selling. It is a mutually beneficial business relationship based on trust, shared respect, and a sense of positive bonding.

All values and products will be considered equal by buyers until someone points out the differences. Because of "me-too" marketing, confusion in marketplace, and overcrowding in the minds of buyers, every product or service is perceived as being relatively equal. The role of the salesperson is to find what buyers value most, then to point out the significant differential advantages of his or her particular product or service in terms of that perceived value. This will result in more sales at a higher margin.

The more focus placed on a customer's needs rather than on the needs of the salesperson or sales organization, the more successful sales performances will be. The most fatal flaw in selling occurs when salespeople are so focused on what they or their parent organization want out of a sales relationship that they lose sight of what the prospect wants from it. This will lose more sales more quickly than ever before. The '90s will continue to be a "buyer's market."

Keep your head up. This is not only in terms of attitude, but it is also in order to stay in front of the changes that will occur quickly and sporadically in a progressively dynamic marketplace.

The decade of the '90s will be the most demanding, fast-moving era in history for sales professionals. It will also present the most opportunity. The secret to seizing this opportunity will be to understand the concept of change, a concept that winning sales professionals and companies must be able to use to their advantage.

USAir Magazine, October 1990.

Because most of the travel product is purchased through travel agencies and because travel agents are the purest example of salespeople in the travel and tourism industry, we will concentrate our discussion of sales techniques on that segment. The same sales techniques and concepts apply to any salespeople within the travel industry (and, in fact, within any sales industry).

Most supplier marketing efforts and advertising campaigns support both direct sales and sales through agents. Because travel agent sales ultimately benefit the supplier of the travel service, many suppliers recognize the need to keep direct competition to a minimum. The 33,000 agency offices eliminate the need for a multiplicity of airline, hotel, and other supplier offices throughout the country. The use of travel agents as the prime distribution network for sales to consumers makes economic sense as well. The operation of a ticket office is a fixed expense to the carrier, no matter how small the sales volume. Travel agent commissions are based on a percentage of sales, so suppliers incur costs only when actual sales are made. Further, no money is spent by the supplier until sales are made. The travel agency assumes all operational expenses, collection costs, and business risks.

The sales function essentially, is the culmination of the marketing process. Through personal communication techniques the transfer of services (or at least the promise of services) from seller to buyer is accomplished. Through the efforts of sales personnel, the traveler receives an airline ticket, hotel confirmation, cruise ticket, or other benefit. The marketing process has been completed—almost. The services must now be provided as promised for the buyer to be satisfied and want to buy again. As emphasized earlier, successful travel and tourism marketing depends heavily on repeat business for profitability.

INSIDE AND OUTSIDE SALES

Travel industry sales includes two different types of positions—inside and outside sales assignments. Some jobs include both functions, but most are either one or the other.

Inside Sales

Inside sales is the most basic of the positions. The inside salesperson answers telephone calls and responds to inquiries from potential customers coming into the office. Other marketing functions including advertising, sales promotion, and outside sales efforts generate inquiries. The inside salesperson takes over at the time of the call or visit.

Inside positions may deal with travel agents, tour wholesalers, the general public, or any combination of these. Airline reservation offices as well as city ticket offices and airport ticket counters are staffed by inside salespersons. Hotel reservation and banquet offices and car rental reservation facilities and rental offices require inside sales skills as well.

Most travel agency positions are of the inside sales type. The primary characteristic of the position is the fact that the potential purchaser made a decision to take action before the contact with the inside salesperson was made. The action decision may be to actually purchase or just to seek information, but a decision was made before the sales contact. The contact was initiated by the potential purchaser, not generated by the salesperson. The salesperson reacts to and handles the transaction after contact. Thus, the inside salesperson is dealing with an already interested, motivated party.

Selling vs Taking Orders

Does the person performing inside sales truly sell—or just take orders? Unfortunately, too many are really order takers, not salespeople. Their activities are limited to that of a fulfillment clerk who provides what is asked for—no more and no less. They are providing service, not selling. There is, however, ample opportunity for the use of professional sales skills in the inside position. It is

"Madame Zenobia, can you tell me if I'll enjoy my tour?"

"I sell the land, the sea, and the sky for a living...what do you do?"

essential that the inside salesperson understand customer needs and how to meet them. The sales techniques described in the next chapter should be understood and mastered by both inside and outside personnel. The challenge of helping a potential customer identify and meet needs is just as strong in both types of positions. Unfortunately, it is easier for the inside person to become lazy and not truly try to identify customer needs. The Industry Communique details how inside salespeople can be trained to sell, rather than just service, potential customers.

INDUSTRY COMMUNIQUE

A NEW WAY TO LOOK AT THE BUSINESS OF SELLING VACATION TRAVEL

Robert H. Dickinson
Senior Vice President, Sales & Marketing
Carnival Cruise Lines

The purpose of this article is to discuss ways wherein travel agencies can become more effective in selling discretionary vacation items such as tour packages, cruises and FIT programs. These suggestions for a new direction result from basic market research we conducted among travel agents during 1990.

In a nutshell, the research indicated that:

1. Agency owners and managers tend to "blur" the two components of leisure sales, and

2. Travel counselors convert a very low percentage of discretionary vacation prospects.

Over the years there have been a number of studies which have indicated that the typical or average travel agent in the United States splits his business roughly 50/50 between commercial and leisure travel. What is generally not considered, however, is that the main aim of this "leisure" travel component is point to point travel, visiting friends and relatives (VFR).

Given the dramatic projected growth for discretionary income in the United States during the decade of the 90s, the prudent agency owner or manager should look at his business as 80% servicing (commercial and VFR) and 20% selling (cruises and tours).

This new view of the business allows the agency's principal resources (people) to be deployed, educated, motivated and compensated in ways which best serve each objective. To compete effectively with realtors, car dealers, jewelry stores, et al. for the discretionary dollar, travel counselors devoted to selling cruises and tours need to be:

1. Trained as salespeople,
2. Dedicated to selling rather than servicing,
3. Have good product knowledge of a select number of preferred cruise and tour suppliers,
4. Compensated largely on the basis of sales performance.

A small but growing number of agencies are doing this. As a result, their cruise and tour sales are increasing dramatically. Their counselors are making excellent commission and the owners and managers are making far more than the 20,000 per year which a recent national study suggested was the norm.

When travel agents, in our market research, reported to us that they were only able to close sales on 3%-15% of their call-in and walk-in vacation prospects, the obvious question we asked was, "Why?" Their replies were as follows:

1. Lack of formal sales training,
2. The fear of rejection by the client motivated many agents to avoid selling or recommending.
3. The pressure of servicing commercial and VFR business distracted them from discretionary sales,
4. No financial motivation to close the sale (the agents receive virtually all of their compensation in base salary),

Yet we queried specific, successful agencies and found that they closed the sale 45-60% of the time. We asked how they did it, and they reported:

1. All their sales agents are fully trained in selling techniques,
2. In their jobs, they weren't expected to handle any commercial accounts or VFR servicing—these functions were turned over to others in the organization.
3. They had in-depth product knowledge of a manageable number of preferred cruise and tour suppliers,

4. The majority (if not all) of the sales agents' compensation is in commission, not base salary,

What does all this mean? It means a "typical" agency doing $1,500,000 per year in sales can easily become a $2.1-2.7 million agency. At a $1.5 million total volume, the cruise and tour sales would approximate $300,000 (20%). If the sales conversion could be improved from 10% to 30%, vacation sales would improve to $900,000 and the overall business would increase to $2.1 million. If the sales conversion could improve to 50%, the cruise and tour sales would increase by $1.2 million resulting in a $2.7 million total agency volume.

Importantly, not only would the volume increase, so would the agent profits—because it's simply far more profitable to sell cruises and tours than to service commercial and VFR business.

In the example of improving the sales conversion from 10% to 30% you should view the incremental $600,000 of cruise and tour sales as bringing in an additional $87,000 of gross profit (based on a 14.5% average commission) without spending an additional penny to increase traffic into your store! This would represent roughly 200 additional cruise bookings at $2000 per booking of two people and 200 additional tour package bookings at $1000 per booking of two people. If you are open six days a week it means only one and one-third additional cruise or tour sales per day! If you paid your sales counselor(s) $50 per cruise booking and $25 per tour booking—over and above their existing salary and fringe benefit package—this would provide $22,500 of additional compensation. Logically, this higher level of compensation will attract and reward the best possible sales people while still leaving $64,500 available to compensate the owner and manager.

An effective way to measure your agency's sales conversion is to measure each counselors sales productivity. Create a "contact sheet" and have each counselor fill it out daily. Record the number of vacation prospects that either call in or walk into your agency. Then record the sales, if any, that the counselor was able to close against the total amount of prospects received that day. (At the same time, remember to record the prospect's name, address and phone number.) At the end of the week, tally the counselor's contact sheets to get the total amount of sales versus the total amount of prospects received. You now have a tool to determine your most effective sales counselors (in addition to a new mailing list)!

Fundamental to the whole process, of course, is sales training. it is so critical that we have incurred great expense to train each of our 76 sales people so that they may, in turn, provide this sales training to your agencies around the country. By appointment, your Carnival rep will be most pleased to provide sales training in your agency either before or after working hours. We'll even toss in the coffee and doughnuts in the morning, or the pizza in the evening! These selling techniques are proven to be effective and work equally well selling cruises, tours, or anything else for that matter. I recommend you take advantage of this opportunity on a timely basis.

I realize that this analysis deals with average agencies—the numbers may not be appropriate for your particular agency. Nonetheless, this analysis should serve to point out, directionally at least, the opportunities for expanding discretionary vacation travel. If you have a different set of specifics and would like to know how this process could work for your agency, I invite you to call me or write, and I'll be happy to discuss your particular situation with you.

Reprinted with permission from Carnival Cruise Lines from a speech to travel agents.

Outside Sales

An outside sales job involves public contact work outside the employer's office. Rather than waiting for a prospect to make contact, the outside salesperson seeks prospects with sales techniques and personal contact. A full knowledge of selling skills and techniques is required for outside sales, as well as the ability to identify potentially interested parties. Some outside sales positions follow up "qualified leads"—potentially interested parties attracted by advertising and other marketing processes. Other positions require "cold calling," where the salesperson canvasses all offices in a given area, or all people on a certain list.

Outside salespeople with travel and tourism suppliers generally work with wholesalers and retail travel agents. Only the largest potential users within the general public (business accounts, government agencies, and associations) receive the attention of an outside representative. The position title "sales representative" or "account executive" is often associated with such positions in the airline industry. Hotel chains, car rental companies, and cruise lines, all of which have substantially fewer positions, often give the title "sales manager" or "district sales manager" to such positions. Most airlines use the title "sales manager" to signify personnel responsible for managing sales representatives. These sales managers do little if any selling, but usually have come from a sales background.

Travel agencies are using outside salespersons more and more as the years go by. Fifteen years ago, few agencies used such salespeople except in certain geographical areas such as Long Island, New York. However, today, many agencies make effective use of such positions in both the corporate and leisure areas. The practice of using outside salespeople is expected to continue to grow into the next century.

THE MARKETING PLAN AND THE SALES PRESENTATION

The effectiveness of a sales effort can be heavily influenced by the placement of sales within the overall marketing plan of an organization. While it might be said that if you do not know where you are going, any road will get you there, this philosophy has no place in marketing and sales.

The marketing plan should be a road map leading the way to a final goal of bringing product or service and buyer together. Target markets should be identified and the mix of products and services, distribution methods, communications techniques, and alternative terms of sale should be planned. Assuming that outside sales contact is part of the overall plan, attention should be given to a planned presentation that helps ensure the success of an outside sales call.

Specific Objectives

Every contact initiated by a sales representative should have a specific objective and a plan to achieve that objective. Depending on the situation, the objective may be to complete a sale based upon previously identified needs or merely to identify potential needs—but the objective must be determined in advance. The sales representative should prepare a logical, step-by-step action plan to achieve the objective. A simple yet effective strategy is the following:

- *Introduction (A brief overview describing what you are going to develop in detail).*
- *Presentation (Provide the detail to support your objective using appropriate sales techniques).*
- *Summary (Restate what you have said in a concise manner and summarize points of agreement and difference).*

"Let me give you an idea of what your tour to Britain will include..."

Written Sales Proposals

When the sales objective includes a complex program or set of services, a written sales proposal should be prepared. Often, when two or more organizations are competing for the business, the written sales proposal is a requirement. The proposal clarifies the concepts being covered orally, and also serves as a basis for comparing services. A sales proposal should be clear and concise and follow the basic presentation strategy. The ability of the organization to meet the needs of the prospect and the benefits to the prospect of accepting the proposal should be emphasized. The proposal should be neatly typed (or word processed) and the original (not a photocopy) should be given to the decision maker at the time of the sales presentation. A professionally prepared proposal is especially important when several people, such as a board of directors or a selection committee, are involved in the decision making process or when much time will elapse between sales presentation and decision making.

CONCLUSION

The sales function is a vital part of the broader process of marketing, and sales efforts will be most effective when they are planned and executed as part of a total marketing plan.

SUMMARY

The sales function in travel and tourism marketing is most effective when understood as part of an overall marketing plan that takes into account the dual distribution system present in the travel and tourism industry.

Dual distribution means, for example, that an airline ticket may be purchased directly from the airline or through a travel agent. However the costs of operating ticket offices makes it more efficient for retail travel agents to serve as the prime distribution network for the travel product.

Travel industry sales are handled by two positions—inside and outside sales. The inside salesperson responds to telephone calls or visits from prospective clients, whereas the outside salesperson seeks out prospects by phone or personal visit. Selling should not be confused with simple order taking, and whether in an inside or outside sales position, the travel professional will use personal experience as a consumer to enhance selling skills.

The marketing plan gives direction to the sales function, and ultimately to a sales presentation, which may be oral or written. In either case, the sales presentation must have an objective, and a strategy to achieve that objective. The strategy may be as simple as deciding on an introduction, a presentation, and a summary.

Written sales proposals are usually employed to present a complex program, and should always be carefully and neatly prepared.

QUESTIONS FOR THOUGHT AND DISCUSSION

1. Define dual distribution and explain its existence in the travel industry.
2. What is the difference between inside sales and outside sales positions?
3. List the eight qualities of a professional sales person and discuss why each is important.
4. Create a written sales presentation relating to travel. Describe who your client is and what you are trying to sell.

13

Sales Techniques

face-to-face sales
follow-up
identifying needs
prospecting
solving problems
telemarketing

As a lawyer logically develops a case...as an engineer plans a project...as a doctor diagnoses sickness...similarly, a sales representative in the travel and tourism industry is a skilled professional who diagnoses client needs and shows how specific travel services will meet those needs.

When you sell a service to a first-time client, you are really selling two services. First, you must sell your own and your company's ability to provide the required service. Then, you must convince the client that the specific service or product you are recommending will meet the client's needs.

APPEARANCE AND ATTITUDE

Before you can sell anything, you must sell yourself. In a face-to-face sales situation, a client's first impression of you will probably be of your physical appearance. You may be judged on such points as:

- *Clothes clean, pressed, and appropriate for a business setting?*
- *Hair combed and neatly cut?*
- *Cosmetics appropriately used?*

Chewing gum or a dangling cigarette gives a negative impression. (In fact, smoking at all during the sales process is probably not acceptable.) The successful sales representative conforms to accepted standards of dress and behavior. Overdressing is almost as bad as underdressing. Neither the dandy nor the unkempt person starts on the right foot. Your general appearance must be pleasing, but not striking. Practice a good posture and display a warm, friendly smile.

That smile can be your greatest sales tool. It has tremendous positive value. Friendliness and a warm smile perform miracles. Your smile radiates warmth to your prospect and that warmth is reflected back to you. A friendly smile sets the perfect sales climate. If you are moody or unhappy, it will reflect on your prospect and the opportunity for a successful sale will be lessened. When dealing with complaints or the difficult client, don't forget the smile. You may want to scream or argue—but don't. Finish your conversation with a warm friendly smile. You will get startling results.

THE SALES PROCESS

To many people the word "selling" means a glib-talking peddler with his foot in the door, hypnotically inducing people to buy a product they don't want with money they can't afford to spend. Professional sales people do not operate in that way. Ethics aside, in the long run, it would do more harm than good.

The sales activity does not exist in a vacuum. It is an integral part of the overall marketing process. It is part of the communication mix—the submix within the overall marketing mix that contains the tools used to bring prospective buyer and product together. To many people, sales is the most important part of the communications mix.

THE IMPORTANCE OF COMMUNICATING

Communication skills are critical to the sales process. Personal selling, where buyer and seller engage in face-to-face or telephone discussions, is the only part of the communications mix that is not one-way in nature, like an advertisement in the newspaper or a direct mail letter. Two-way communications, where salesperson and client can provide direct feedback to each other through verbal and nonverbal techniques, is, indeed, the most effective method of imparting information and securing commitment. The Industry Communique examines in depth how persuasive communication functions in the sales process.

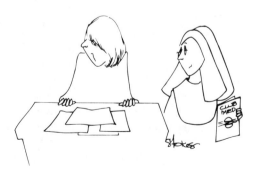

"All right! Who suggested Club Med to Sister Mary Agnes?"

As part of the overall customer-oriented philosophy of marketing, professional selling should also be customer oriented. The entire process is devoted to identifying the customers' needs and providing the right service to meet a specific need. In a nutshell, a professional salesperson is one who finds a need and fills it.

INDUSTRY COMMUNIQUE

WHAT YOU NEED TO KNOW
ABOUT PERSUASIVE COMMUNICATION

Julia G. Crystler and Richard V. Farace

WHAT IS PERSUASIVE COMMUNICATION?

Simply defined, the main goal of persuasive communication is to get someone to do something they wouldn't have done if you hadn't directed your message to them. Specifically, there are *three* goals a persuasive message addresses—getting someone to:

- *Do* what *you want*
- When *you want it*
- How *you want it*

So, the three basic objectives in developing a persuasive message in a sales situation are to get people to:

- *Do* what *you want (buy your products and services)*
- When *you want it (today, not next month or next year)*
- How *you want it (by paying a certain amount of money).*

WHY IS PERSUASIVE COMMUNICATION IMPORTANT TO SALES SUCCESS?

To succeed at sales, you have to succeed at the *process* of persuasive communication. A prospect is usually aware of your product and its potential benefits. He or she is searching for a solution to a specific set of needs. It is your job as a salesperson to persuade the prospect that you and your hotel can fulfill the prospect's needs better than anyone else. Persuasive communication between the buyer and seller is the key to this selling process. Persuasive communication skills provide the means by which salespeople can expertly assist clients in identifying the hotel services that will meet their needs.

WHAT ARE THE FACTORS THAT INFLUENCE PERSUASIVE COMMUNICATION?

Each situation where you hope to be persuasive has four basic parts:

1. The *sender* of the persuasive message (that's you)
2. The *receiver* of the persuasive message (the prospect)
3. The *persuasive message* (your job is to put this together and deliver it to the prospect)
4. The *channel* through which the message is sent (will it be via face-to-face contact, over the telephone, or by letter?)

HOW DO I PRESENT MYSELF AS A CREDIBLE SOURCE?

People's responses to persuasive messages are partly determined by what they think of the *source*—what they think of you as a person. If they see you as competent, truthful, and energetic—as someone they can relate to on a personal level—then they will be more receptive to what you have to say. If, in their mind, you *lack* these qualities, you face a tougher situation.

What happens if they don't know much about you, which is often the case? Then, people tend to make judgments on the first small pieces of evidence they see. Are you tired the first time you meet a prospect? They may see you as somewhat slow. If your handshake is limp—and that bothers a lot of people—they may not want to trust you with their business. If you don't get to the point quickly, they may believe you aren't prepared. It may be a cliché, but there's still a lot of truth to the statement, "First impressions count!"

Overall, then, one of the main elements determining your persuasiveness is the *credibility* you have in your prospect's eyes. The more credibly you can present yourself, the more persuasive effect you can achieve.

There are five basic rules to follow if you want to be viewed as a credible source by your client—are you:

1. "Expert" on the products and services you are selling—or if not expert, then at least *well-informed?*
2. On time for appointments, someone who delivers what you promise and consistently tells the truth?
3. Alert, active, and participative during a conversation?
4. Open-minded and impartial?
5. Interested in the receiver's personal welfare?

HOW DO I GET THE RECEIVER'S ATTENTION?

The next element in the persuasive communication process is the *receiver*, the target of your persuasive effort—your prospective client. Here, the ability to analyze your receiver is critical. The results of your analysis fuel your overall approach, or strategy, for communicating persuasively with your receiver.

There are three issues to cover in your analysis—how to:

1. Get the receiver's *attention*
2. Looks for points that *motivate* the person
3. Organize the message for maximum impact.

In any sales situation, your first and foremost task is to get *your receiver's attention—and hold it!*

There are two general ways to get someone's attention—do something *unexpected*...or something *pleasing.*

Do Something A Little Unexpected—People pay attention to the unexpected. So think of ways to make your message stand out from the run-of-the-mill. Send prospects a telegram, instead of a normal business letter. Use a videotape to demonstrate your facility, instead of a written brochure. Use a colorful, eye-catching flyer to describe your products and services, instead of many words in small, hard-to-read type. Arouse a prospect's curiosity by telling him or her a story about a famous person who stayed in your hotel.

Do Something That Is Pleasing—Another way to get people's attention is to do something they find *pleasing.* Meet in a restaurant they enjoy. Offer to go out of your way to get together. Show them examples of your facilities and services that highlight your property's strong points—and meet their needs. Show them in the letters you write how you can fulfill their needs and save them money at the same time—for example, by early booking, they qualify for special reduced rates.

Give some thought about the receiver before you select an attention-getting approach. If the person is conservative, careful, and not likely to respond favorably to a "different" approach, then be cautious. If you think the person needs to be stimulated into paying attention to you then be more creative in your approach.

HOW DO I FIND WAYS TO MOTIVATE THE RECEIVER?

Let's assume you have the prospect's attention. You've gotten him or her to put aside all the other distractions in life and pay attention to you—at least for the moment. Now you need to follow up with some statements that begin to respond to that person's specific needs.

This is a common-sense notion, but it's easy to overlook. Just keep in mind that it's your prospect's needs that are important, not yours. Figure out your prospect's needs and match them with the products and services you have to offer. (If you succeed in meeting his or her needs, you'll end up meeting your needs, too—right?)

There are many theories about people's needs. One of the most widely known and respected was put forward over 35 years ago by Abraham Maslow. He argued that people do things in response to five basic needs:

1. *Survival needs*—food, sleep, air
2. *Safety and security needs*—personal security (e.g., safe home) and financial security
3. *Belonging needs*—to be included by other people in their activities, to receive affection from others
4. *Esteem and status needs*—to feel self-respect and to receive respect from others
5. *Self-actualization needs*—to feel fulfillment in your work or hobby.

To use these needs to formulate your message, decide which one is most relevant to your prospect and then indicate how your products and services respond to those needs. For example, if *safety and security* are important, then describe how security services in your hotel and safety features in the guest rooms are designed to make guests secure. If the need is for *esteem and status*, then indicate how your facility gets "five star ratings" and is frequently the favored choice of well-known political and social figures.

HOW CAN I APPEAL TO MY PROSPECT'S NEEDS?

Once the prospect's needs are identified, there are two types of *appeals* you can use to respond to someone's needs—*emotional* appeals and *logical* appeals. Emotional appeals play on someone's *feelings*, while logical appeals play to the *intellect*.

Emotional appeals touch the things in life that people *want*—to belong, have friends, enjoy themselves, look and feel good, be proud, patriotic, respected. Logical appeals are directed to the thinking, factual side of a person—knowledge, control, impact. An emotional appeal for booking a meeting might focus on how good you can make the prospect look with his or her boss. A logical appeal might emphasize your ability to check guests into and out of the hotel with a minimum of inconvenience. Logical appeals are frequently effective in business situations, where statements about consistency or completeness of service, or about cost reductions and time savings, have high impact.

Either—or both appeals—can be used in a message.

HOW DO I CREATE A PERSUASIVE MESSAGE?

The next element in the persuasive communication process is the message itself. The message is built around three basic ingredients:

1. An *attention* element
2. A *need* element
3. And an *action* element

To construct an effective message, first get the prospect's *attention*, then arouse his or her interest by highlighting one (or more) of their *needs*, and finally describe an *action* step that indicates the behaviors that will fulfill those needs. Also, typically, arrange the message in this same sequence—*attention, need and action*.

Monroe's Motivated Sequence is a frequently used formula for constructing messages. It has five parts and expands on the "Attention-Need-Action" formula.

1. Attention. Use the unexpected or the pleasing to gain the receiver's attention. *Example*: "Did you know that President Reagan was a guest recently in our hotel?"
2. Need. identify the receiver's need and create a desire to fulfill that need. *Example*: "I understand that you've been put in charge of planning your company's next senior executive meeting. Is it true that your meeting budget is lower this year?"
3. Satisfaction. Provide a solution that meets the need. *Example*: "Let me show you how I can save you $5,000 if you book here."
4. Visualization. Picture the outcome for the receiver so that it is clear how the need will be met. *Example*: "We've just re-furbished our facilities and want our regular guests to experience them. Your group can enjoy our luxurious Grand Ballroom at a special reduced rate."
5. Action. Describe what the person must do to implement the solution. *Example*: "All I need from you to ensure your group gets the Grand Ballroom at a discount is a definite booking by the end of this month."

HOW DO I CHOOSE A PERSUASIVE COMMUNICATION CHANNEL?

There are several different *channels* available to communicate with your prospect. Some channels emphasize oral communication, while others use *mediated* communication. *Oral* communication included face-to-face situations, small group meetings and presentations, and telephone conversations. In mediated communication, the message is put into a written, audio or video format. Business letters, brochures, radio spots, and television ads are examples of mediated communication.

Each channel offers special advantages. Here are some points to consider in deciding which channel to use:

1. Do you want **immediate feedback**? If you need to know the receiver's response right away, oral communication provides the opportunity for feedback faster than mediated communication. In this case, you should use the telephone or visit with the client or prospect personally, rather than rely on a letter.

2. Do you anticipate **significant resistance** by the receiver? If so, then oral communication allows you to be flexible in your approach—to switch to different themes, or to change emphasis. For example, if you think a prospect might be reluctant you will probably want to meet with him or her face-to-face for maximum communication effectiveness. You can make full use of all the nonverbal and verbal channels to gather information about how the prospect is feeling and what he or she is thinking and tailor your message accordingly.

3. Do you need to **verify the message**? Often it is important to have evidence of certain aspects of a message, such as the date and time of an event, the food items to be provided, the costs and the payment schedule. Where you need this type of verification, such as when you are providing your client with a booking contract, mediated communication—usually written—is preferable to oral communication which is not generally recorded for later reference.

4. Do you need to convey **complex choices** or procedures? If your message involves many choices—such as the master menu for a banquet—or complicated procedures—such as check-in arrangements, then mediated communication is a better choice than oral to provide a record for reference and clarification of agreements.

HOW DO I BECOME A MORE PERSUASIVE COMMUNICATOR?

Taken together, these elements in the persuasive communication process provide the basic ingredients for constructing messages that bring sales successes. To illustrate this point, let's look at how the persuasive communication process parallels the process of making a sale—prospecting, relating your hotel's features and benefits, overcoming your prospect's objections, and closing the sale.

1. *Prospecting*—This step of the sales process is devoted primarily to getting the attention of the potential client, establishing your credibility, and gathering information about the prospect's needs. Remember that persuasive communication in a sales situation depends largely on your ability to match the services your hotel can deliver with what the prospect needs.

How well you succeed in this step will influence how well you do with the others. Use your *Active Listening* and your *Nonverbal Communication* skills to help you get all the information you can about what your prospect wants and what will satisfy him or her, and to establish an empathetic and trusting relationship. Probe for the reasons and possible costs of the prospect's problem or situation to help you develop a mutual understanding of the prospect's need and intensify the prospect's interest.

2. *Relating Features and Benefits*—What you tell the prospect about your hotel and its services and how they can satisfy the prospect's needs is the next step. Salespeople who gear their presentations to the specific needs of the meeting planner make it hard for the client to turn away. Both logical and emotional appeals are important here. People buy products and services for both reasons. You need to include both kinds of appeals in your persuasive communication.

     For example, if your prospect says when you ask about the purpose of his or her meeting, "My objective is to train a group of sales engineers to process orders in the field with portable computer terminals," you know that your client needs sophisticated technical assistance. You can explain the kinds of service you can perform in response to this specific objective: "Ms. Client," you can say, "here at the Hotel Excel we have one of the cleverest electricians in the business. He can set up your meeting room with a separate dedicated line for your computer and make sure you get constant line voltage."

     That kind of presentation is persuasive because it turns to how you can serve the meeting planner rather than what you charge for rooms and when guarantees are required for meal functions. You are a persuasive communicator when you can target your messages to specific client needs and avoid turning your prospect away by running on about hotel services the client doesn't need or want.

3. *Overcoming Objections*—Even though you may have done a great job of establishing a trusting relationship, finding out about client needs and presenting the sales story in an appropriate manner, human nature makes it likely that the prospect will still hesitate when asked to "sign on the dotted line." Success at overcoming objections requires that you use your *Active Listening* and *Nonverbal Communication* skills again to determine the specific reasons for the objection, and then build messages in your presentation that will directly address these reasons.

     "Selling" at this step of the sales process is a lot like counseling. Helping people through the emotional trauma of making a buying decision is predicated on trust, questioning, listening, and the appropriate presenting skills. For instance, you may see hesitancy in the prospect's nonverbal behavior that will lead you to question the prospect. You could discover that the prospect is new to the job of meeting planner and has never been in a position of making the kind of financial commitment a booking requires. You can then tailor your presentation to the client's need for reassurance.

4. *The Close*—If you have done your job well in the previous steps, the close should follow easily. In this step you present the prospect with the specific actions you want him or her to take to finalize the sale. The close is best handled in a face-to-face situation, preferably when you have the prospect with you at the property where you can more readily handle any last minute questions and where you are in greater control of the situation.

The persuasive messages you build to get the close should be as specific as possible and the action easy for the client to take. For example, having all documents and copies prepared in advance and providing the client with a comfortable and private place to conduct the final review, will help the client say yes when you ask for the signature and the check.

WHAT ARE THE MAIN POINTS TO REMEMBER ABOUT PERSUASIVE COMMUNICATION?

To become more capable at persuasive communication, you need to remember the following key points:

- *Persuasive communication refers to communication with the specific intent to direct the behavior of others.*
- *Persuasive communication is critical to success in hotel sales because it is the main link between a potential client's needs and the services your hotel offers. The better you are at persuasive communication, the more likely it is that you will bridge the gap between needs and services.*
- *The main components of persuasive communication are: the credibility of the message source; the attention-getting aspect of the message; the message themes we use to shape the message; the way we organize the message, and the channels we use to send the message.*
- *Persuasive communication plays a key role in the sales process at every step along the way—from prospecting to close. The skills of active listening and nonverbal communication are significant contributors to your overall persuasive communication effectiveness. Persuasive communication works best when it centers on the prospect's needs to have his or her problem understood—and his or her needs met. In so doing, the hotel salesperson will fulfill his or her need to close the sale.*

HSMAI Marketing Review, Spring, 1988.

Prospecting for New Business

An outside salesperson must be able to prospect for new business. The most profitable and dependable customer is the repeat or referral customer since these customers already trust the salesperson and the company. They have already been satisfied or know of a friend who has been well served.

The best prospecting is to actively request referrals from current clientele. Remind them to refer their friends and acquaintances to your services. Don't depend on their doing it automatically.

For new business not referred by current customers, the salesperson must actively prospect. This means keeping up with new potential sources of business that open or move into the area and calling on them. One call usually doesn't result in a sale. It is necessary to regularly be in touch with the prospect and remind them of your services and desire to help them. Eventually, when they either become unhappy with their current source or discover a need for your services for some other reason, the will be more likely to think of you.

Prospecting, of course is done by the promotional methods already discussed, such as advertising, direct mail, trade shows, and so forth. However, it is usually necessary to supplement these impersonal methods with personal "cold calling." This means phoning or visiting potential customers, determining who is the decision maker and meeting with that person. In Chapter 14, you will find a full discussion of the sales interview process once you have been able to arrange a meeting with a potential customer.

These potential customers can be found through research in the library, newspaper articles about new business in the area, and membership and attendance at meetings and organizations where potential customers tend to go.

IDENTIFYING AND FILLING NEEDS

In many situations in the travel industry, helping clients identify their needs and providing services to meet them is the core of the process. A travel agent helps a client find the right vacation at the right place, the right time and at the right price for the client's need. An airline cargo sales representative shows how the additional speed of air freight offsets the extra cost of the service. A hotel sales representative shows how one hotel is good for business meetings while another is best for rest and relaxation. The needs orientation is clearly the basis of operations. See the Industry Communique for more on the basics of the sales process in the hotel industry.

IDENTIFYING AND SOLVING PROBLEMS

In more complex situations, needs orientation is not enough. In these cases the salesperson must act virtually as a member of the prospective client's executive

INDUSTRY COMMUNIQUE

Edmund Sansovini, CHSE, CHA

Here is a refresher course in the fundamentals of sales, adapted from a speech presented by the author at the HSMAI Education Conference '87 in Orlando, Florida.

During the last several years the hotel industry has become very sophisticated. The computer and other state-of-the-art systems are now an integral part of the industry. This is both healthy and necessary. However, hoteliers must be careful that they do not become so sophisticated that they lose sight of some of the basics of their profession. Hoteliers are in the people business. They are people helping people; working with people.

COMPETITION

The hotel industry always has been extremely competitive, but nothing like it is today. The growth of hotels and resorts has been phenomenal.

The overbuilding and growth of hotels and resorts has created a negative effect on both occupancy and profits. While some hotels enjoy a good return on investment, the majority are hurting. Many properties are changing hands, and not necessarily for reasons of profit. Hotel salespeople are working harder now to make a profit. In other words, it's a "buyer's market" today and hoteliers can't afford to be complacent. They must be aggressive and innovative.

On the positive side, these new hotels have created over 50,000 new jobs. Experienced people are in demand, especially in operations and sales and marketing. The opportunities are most encouraging.

Why then is there a need to get "back to the basics?" There are several reasons:

- *The competition is keen and will increase as supply continues to be greater than demand.*
- *Goals and objectives only can be achieved through more sales.*
- *Customer relations must continually be improved.*
- *The "basics" help enhance a hotel's image in the marketplace.*
- *Selling is the most important aspect of a hotel salesperson's job. As someone once said, "Nothing happens until somebody sells something."*

Now to the crux of the matter. What are the basics?

ATTITUDE

The first basic is attitude. It's of paramount importance to effective hotel sales. It isn't possible to maximize productivity without a positive mental attitude. It is vital to have a positive attitude concerning the property. In order to sell it, salespeople must be sold on it themselves. They must believe it's the best product for the client.

How is the right attitude developed? There are three ways.

1. By commitment—Hoteliers must commit themselves to the task of promoting and selling their properties. They must dismiss the negatives and concentrate on the positives.
2. By knowledge—Hoteliers must have knowledge of selling, knowledge of the property, knowledge of the markets, and knowledge of the client's needs.
3. By being enthusiastic—It's contagious. If the salesperson is excited about the property, then the client and everyone else will get excited too.

AGGRESSIVENESS

Being aggressive doesn't mean being obnoxious. It means being a person with a driving force; one who has initiative; one who is above average and willing to cast aside obstacles to accomplish a task.

Hotel salespeople need to be more aggressive especially in light of the competition they face. Being aggressive will lead to more sales.

RESPONSIVENESS

A major complaint from planners is a frequent lack of response to their telephone calls and correspondence. The consequences can be serious for the hotelier. One meeting planner, for example, never makes more than one call to a property regarding a meeting. If the call isn't returned in 48 hours, he moves on to another property. He uses the same principle when sending a letter. He allows one week for the letter to be acknowledged. If it isn't, he assumes the hotel is not interested, and he eliminates that destination from his agenda.

Every phone call should be returned within 48 hours; 24 hours if possible. Correspondence should be answered within three working days. If it can't be answered in full, a telephone call should be made informing the client that the correspondence was received and is in the process of being answered.

Being responsive shows interest. The customer appreciates it and understands that the hotel needs and wants the business.

CREATIVITY

In today's market, sales executives must be creative to succeed. It doesn't take genius or a Ph.D. And, there are many ways to be creative. There are countless examples of creative selling techniques, or creative food and beverage presentations. What the salesperson needs is enthusiasm for the property, and an understanding of the needs of the clients, and a willingness to make the extra effort.

Being creative takes some thought and desire but it pays big dividends.

COLD CALLS

The most difficult call today is the "cold call." It is easy to call someone back or to call someone who is familiar. It is always difficult, however, for salespeople to pick up the phone and call someone they don't know to solicit business, or to be on the street knocking on doors and not knowing what's on the other side. It's fear of the unknown. But cold calling is a necessary part of any sales program. Cold calling will do four things for sales executives:

1. Keep them disciplined.
2. Keep them razor-sharp.
3. Build their confidence.
4. Develop new leads and business.

GOALS

Goals must be established. Trying to operate without goals is like being in a rowboat with one oar; you go around in circles.

Goals should be set both individually and collectively. For example, the annual marketing plan should include collective monthly and annual room night goals. The collective goals should then be broken down into individual goals.

Individual goals should be used as a barometer in determining the productivity and value of a salesperson. They also serve as a target for salespeople to achieve. It lets them know exactly what is expected of them.

These individual goals should be discussed on a one-to-one basis with the salesperson, and that person should be totally in accord with the goals set. Goals should never be determined arbitrarily be senior sales or management.

A balance must be struck in setting goals. They must be realistic and attainable. However, they should also be set high enough so that they are not easily achieved but at a level where it takes that "extra effort" to achieve them.

ORGANIZATION

A recent survey showed that 60 percent of executives are not organized. A successful hotel sales executive is one who is in the other 40 percent.

Organized people have a program for the day. Their desk calendars are prepared with "things to do and appointments for the day." The list includes priority items—possibly marked in red to identify them.

Organized people in charge of a sales meeting prepare the agenda. They don't go to the meeting unprepared and ask what should be discussed. It is a sign of being disorganized.

The same principle applies to a sales trip. Homework must be done, calls must be screened, and appointments set. The client interview in the office or on the phone should be organized. All the facts must be known beforehand so that the salesperson can talk intelligently.

PROSPECTING

The old adage, "prospect or die," is very true. Hoteliers must constantly prospect for new customers and new markets. Repeat business is not enough to achieve sales goals and objectives. An influx of new business is needed. How to get it? By prospecting.

It can be done in several ways. One of the best is direct mail. To be successful, direct mail must be specialized and creative. The normal response to a mass mailing is between two and three percent. But it is possible to achieve a much higher average than this. How? By being creative and developing something unique.

Another prospecting technique is the sales blitz. The blitz simply consists of getting a team together, and then going into a market, spending several days knocking on doors to develop new leads. If the blitz is well planned it can produce a great deal of business.

Another excellent method to develop prospects is through telemarketing, formerly called the "boiler type operation." Regardless of the name, telemarketing is a worthwhile and proven way to produce good business.

And, of course, there is advertising. A well-planned program, unique in style, will be very effective in producing good prospects.

ATTENTIVENESS

A sales staff must be attentive to their customers. Sometimes sales executives tend to book a piece of business, file it away, and go on to other things. But a good salesperson is a good communicator, one who not only pursues new business but keeps in constant touch with business that is already booked.

There are two areas to consider. First, be attentive to clients by communicating on a regular basis. This can be done by telephone, personal call, a letter, special mailing or through a regional office. Clients need to be updated on major personnel changes in the hotel, remodeling programs, ownership, policy, and tariff changes, to give a few examples. It is the responsibility of the sales department to communicate this information to the market.

Second, it is necessary to be attentive to meeting planners when they are in the hotel for a site inspection or to finalize a program. A nice room or a suite with amenities is important, but is it only the norm. One must go beyond the norm. Some examples:

1. A letter of welcome waiting at the registration desk.
2. The room should be pre-assigned and pre-inspected.
3. The amenities should be in the room before the planner arrives.
4. At many properties, meeting planners are personally escorted to their rooms by the assistant manager or someone in sales. This is really VIP treatment. It can't always be done, but when it is, it creates a 5-star atmosphere.
5. Room service and dining rooms should be alerted so that they understand that the planner must receive VIP treatment.
6. Far too often meeting planners are left alone after the normal tour or office visit. They need to be shown attention. After all, they were invited to the hotel by sales and they should be treated as special guests. A major complaint from planners is that, aside from the office visit to go over the meeting, they never see the salesperson again. Salespeople must pay attention to their customers throughout their stay at the hotel.
7. The salesperson must be sure to visit the meeting planners before they leave the property. It is a way of thanking them for coming.

RESEARCH

Research is not only one of the most important aspects of selling, but also one of the most interesting.

Research involves many things. It could involve the exploration of a new market or a particular file before a sales call is made. Research provides all of the initial information to intelligently make a sales call. It should tell everything about a customer; past history, future meetings, meeting requirements, exhibits (if any), attendance at large functions, etc.

Research can involve considerable time, particularly if the proper information on a group is not available. Hotels unfortunately aren't too responsive to letters regarding the history of a group. But the search for information is almost always worthwhile.

CLOSING THE SALE

This aspect of sales is fundamental to the whole process. It might be the fear of asking, or the fear of rejection, but it is amazing how many salespeople will cover all the other basic items but never arrive at the point where they "ask for the business." If they don't ask, they probably won't get it.

SERVICE

The most important of all the basics is service. Someone once said that the secret to a hotel's success is threefold: location, location, location.

But while location of a property is important, survey after survey shows that the most important item in any hotel is service. Meeting planners put it at the top of the list.

A sales staff must be totally involved in the service aspect of the hotel. Complaints that come in should be handled immediately and corrective action should be taken. When a meeting planner informs a salesperson of a deficiency, it should be brought to the attention of management, and it should be a priority item. Sales executives should be concerned with every department to make sure that the ultimate in service is extended to the customer.

Management has the responsibility to support sales in providing the service needed. Sales, on the other hand, should be very vocal to management whenever the service is below the standards of the hotel.

Perhaps, then, the secret to a hotel's success is service, service, service. Those that provide it will be sure to prosper.

WHY THE BASICS

These, then are the basics. If they are made priorities, things will happen. Productivity will rise, repeat business will increase, profits will grow, and image will improve. Those hotel executives who take them to heart will be better salespeople, and better people, because of them.

Reprinted with permission from HSMAI Marketing Review, Summer 1987.

staff to help a group determine their meeting room needs and banquet require-ments. A sales representative for an airline manufacturer must help an airline identify the future needs of travelers on its routes and type of craft that will meet those needs.

Only after identifying the problem in detail, can the sales representative show how a company's product will best meet that need. Similarly, a travel agency sales representative approaching a large corporation or organization must first help identify the basic problems of the organization or company before showing how his or her agency can meet those needs. The basic needs of a corporation may be to save money or it may be to control traveling within the company. An organization's main problem may be to communicate with its members, and travel products such as a convention or series of regional meetings can only be recom-mended after identifying that basic communications problem. In these cases, the sales representatives must immerse themselves in the prospective client's compa-nies and become, in effect, consultants.

TELEPHONE SALES

The modern term is "telemarketing," but the techniques are not greatly different from the face-to-face sales situation. When planning or participating in telephone sale situations, the basic sales process is the same. It is still necessary to qualify the client (get the initial information and determine what the client really wants). Having determined the client's real needs, it is still necessary to sell your recom-mendations, overcome objections (if there are any) and most importantly, close the sale. Sound familiar? It should. It's the same basic process. See the Industry Communique for the fundamentals of successful telephone sales.

However, the communications process for telephone sales is somewhat dif-ferent from face-to-face sales. Some critical factors are missing. Telephone com-munications is purely verbal. You cannot see the face at the other end of the phone line. There is no body language and limited nonverbal communication.

Just as the physically blind have developed heightened senses of hearing, the "blind" telephone salesperson must listen very carefully. Tone and inflection replace body language as signs of the client's true mental state. An experienced telephone salesperson can determine if the customer is truly receptive to recom-mendations or if there are any hidden objections.

Beyond lack of visual clues, there is an additional complication in the tele-phone sales situation. It is much easier to terminate communications than in the in-person situation. A prospect can call and ask "What is the group rate at your hotel?" A simple, direct answer could easily result in the customer saying "Thank you," and hanging up. Any opportunity for developing and closing a sale is lost forever. It is your responsibility as a professional sales representative to gain con-trol of the conversation, find out the details of what the prospect really wants, make recommendations, and close the sale.

INDUSTRY COMMUNIQUE

There's no doubt that yellow pages are the most effective advertising medium for reaching ready-to-buy customers. Businesses that successfully turn telephone inquiries into telephone sales are the ones that receive the highest return on their yellow pages investment.

Automated Sales Training Company (North Hollywood, CA) conducted a nationwide survey of 5,000 yellow pages advertisers who were spending more than $200 a month in the yellow pages. All businesses were asked, "How much does it cost for the (product or service) offered in your ad?"

Out of 5,000 calls...

2%	said "We don't advertise in the Yellow Pages," and hung up.
34%	provided the price and then hung up.
42%	provided the price, mentioned other products or services, but did not attempt to ask for an order or set an appointment.
11%	didn't know the answer and asked the caller to call back when the boss was in.
78%	never even asked the name of the caller.
50%	took more than eight rings to answer.
8%	put the caller on hold for more than two minutes.

Only

8.4%	introduced themselves to the caller.
1.5%	asked for the caller's phone number.
2%	made professional, planned presentations, and made the caller feel they wanted to be of service.

The point of the story is that many businesses underestimate the power of their telephone...to generate sales, or to help lose them. Customers are given special attention when met face-to-face, but how many businesses let current or potential customers slip away because they fail to treat each phone inquiry as a potential sale?

Remember, every time your phone rings, there's a potential buyer on the line. Effective telephone selling skills can turn more of your phone calls into sales.

Here are some easy steps that will help you and your employees increase the number of phone calls you turn into sales.

BE PREPARED

When the phone rings, collect your thoughts and be ready to enthusiastically handle all inquiries. You should have paper, pencils, price lists, product information and delivery schedules along with any other pertinent information on hand. The more information you have on hand, the quicker you will be able to respond to inquiries. This creates an immediate impression of a business that is competent and professional.

ANSWER PROMPTLY

Answer the phone by the second or third ring. This allows you enough time to channel your thoughts and energies on the customer needs. Your telephone is a doorway to your business. Open it promptly; don't keep your callers waiting. An unanswered phone gives the caller the impression of an unorganized, unprofessional business, incapable of handling their needs. If it does take a long time to answer the phone, don't apologize, thank the customer for being so persistent and continue on from there. By starting off on a positive note you can control the flow of conversation.

PROJECT A CONFIDENT AND ENTHUSIASTIC IMAGE

Your tone of voice and attitude project an image of you AND your company. Your initial comments will set the tone for your presentation.

- *Smile when you answer the phone, you'll notice it makes you sound pleasant and enthusiastic.*
- *Introduce your company and then yourself.*
- *When the customer gives you their name, write it down immediately and say it back to them to make sure you have proper pronunciation and spelling.*
- *Speak clearly and slowly. This will allow you to control the flow of the conversation and help you to emphasize key points.*

COMMUNICATE EFFECTIVELY

To satisfy the customer, you must be able to both send and receive information. A successful salesperson is able to positively convey information about their business and, most importantly, to listen and respond to the customers needs.

Listen. The key to effective communication and satisfying the customers' needs is listening. Focus your attention on the customers' needs. Encourage them to contribute information about themselves and their special needs.

Follow the points below to become a better listener.

- *Don't interrupt the customer when they are talking.*

- *Do interject with an occasional "yes," "I understand," "OK," etc., to let them know you are interested and understanding what they are saying.*
- *Don't jump to conclusions or make assumptions about what they are saying. A good listener will let the customer finish what they have to say and then ask questions to clarify things.*
- *Write down the customer's name immediately, and use it throughout the conversation. People are much more attentive when you personalize the conversation.*
- *Take notes. Don't rely on your memory to recall important points you have discussed. Write them down and read them back to prevent any mistakes.*
- *Listen to the way a customer says something and how they react to what you say. There is much to be learned about the callers preferences and needs by reading between the lines of the conversation. Truly hearing what they are saying will allow you to tailor your presentation to meet their needs.*

ASK QUESTIONS

Questioning is an excellent way of both discovering your customers needs and closing a sale. Questioning helps qualify the customer and lets them know you are genuinely interested in their needs. Moving from general to specific questions will allow you to easily pin-point their needs.

Open-ended questions help you to obtain information about the callers needs. Ask who, what, why, which, where and when questions to get the caller to provide the information that is important. For example:

- *"What model are you using now?"*
- *"Who currently provides this service for you?"*
- *"What features are you looking for?"*
- *"Which style do you generally prefer?"*

Close-ended questions generally require a yes or no answer. They force the customer to make a decision and are very effective in closing a sale. To close a sale, offer them a choice. For example:

- *"Mrs. Smith, we have the upholstery fabric you asked about. Would you like it in cream or taupe?"*
- *"Yes, we have the model in stock. Would you prefer pick-up or delivery?"*

USE SELLING SKILLS

- *Provide all the necessary product and price information.*

- *Avoid technical jargon. Use descriptive words and phrases that people outside your business can understand.*
- *Make positive statements. Your tone of voice as well as certain word connotations can present things in a positive or negative light. For example, the words on the right have a more positive connotation than the words to the left.*

Negative	Positive
cost	price/investment
buy	own
contract	agreement
signature	approval
deal	opportunity

- *Be prepared for objections. After you have made your recommendation, the customer will usually have some objections. Listen to what it is they are saying. Did you fail to address a need of theirs? Often you can anticipate possible objections and be prepared in advance to address them.*
- *Recommend additional products/services that will benefit the customer. Try suggesting:*

    Extra or related items
    Larger quantities
    Better grade
    Special offers

MAKE IT EASY TO BUY

- *When a caller hesitates to make a buying decisions often no attempt is made to help them to commit. Some people dislike making decisions and would prefer a gentle push.*
- *Reassure the customer that others have been very happy with the product, that you have had repeat orders, have received referrals from clients and offer a money back guarantee.*
- *Ask them WHICH rather than IF questions. Ask which color they want, cash or charge, pick-up, delivery, etc..*

LEAVE A GOOD IMPRESSION

- *Always thank the person for calling, whether they buy or not.*

- *Remember to repeat back important points to make sure you have them correct.*
- *Be sure to follow-up on the things you discussed.*
- *Let the caller hang up first; that way there can be no chance of you cutting the caller off by mistake.*

Reprinted from a brochure distributed by C & P Telephone Company.

IMPORTANCE OF TELEPHONE SALES

The total sales process for many types of travel services can be completed on the telephone without the necessity of personal visits. The availability of facsimile (fax) transmission to send and receive written material increases the importance of telephone sales. The sale of hotel reservations and airline reservations and tickets is normally completed over the telephone. The traveler may call the airline or hotel directly or make arrangements through a travel agency. An experienced travel agent can handle even complex, multisegment travel arrangements on the telephone without ever seeing the client. Many long-lasting client-agent relationships continue without either person ever seeing the other.

Very often, however, the telephone is only part of the sales process. The sales representative receives a request for information about the strong potential use of a travel product. The conversation becomes the basis for qualifying the client and setting up an appointment to continue the sales process on a face to face basis. The telephone is also a time and money saving method for the sales representative to make direct contacts with potential buyers to determine if there is the potential for a meeting or sales presentation. Complex transactions such as meetings and conventions or the handling of an entire commercial account may take many face-to-face meetings and many telephone calls before finalization.

Whether receiving calls or making outbound calls to determine client potential, your objective is to sell travel. See the Industry Communique for a discussion of telephone sales techniques. You want to close the sale with prospects who telephone just as you would with those whom you meet face to face. Their money is just as good, and their potential may be as great or greater than that of those who contact you in person. If you are receiving an incoming call, once you determine that there is any potential sale, be sure to get contact information (name, address and telephone number) so that you can follow up. Be sure to do this early in the call in case you are disconnected and to avoid forgetting to get the information. Too many salespeople have spent a long time on the phone with a prospective client only to realize after hanging up that they don't know who they were helping. This makes it impossible to follow up if the prospect doesn't call back. If a client requests literature on your service, send or fax it quickly. If you believe there is potential for a sale, make sure that you always follow up the mailing with a letter or phone call.

INDUSTRY COMMUNIQUE

THE TELEPHONE—FRIEND OR FOE?

Bruce Witwer

Many dollars are spent developing customer interest through advertising and publicity, yet a hotel's image can be quickly destroyed by communicating poorly on the telephone.

All callers should be treated as friends who stop to visit at your home. Make callers feel welcome even if they sound upset or irate.

Customers need to hear these signals from you.

- *I will not waste your time*
- *I care about you*
- *I am well organized*
- *I can be trusted*
- *I know what I'm talking about*
- *I'm proud of my hotel and myself*

Develop a telephone personality that reflects a smile. Others do "see" you on the phone. They can easily tell if you are alert, enthusiastic, tired, or bored. Most of all they will know if you care.

Here are a few suggestions for improving your telephone technique:

1. *Answer no later than the fourth ring.* There's nothing more frustrating than calling a hotel sales office and waiting forever for someone to answer. It always makes people wonder whether you are still in business. People become upset and customers will lost patience. If people have to wait too long when calling your office, you may need more employees, more phones, or a different system. If one person has the primary responsibility for answering the majority of your calls, always provide back-up coverage.

2. *Calls shouldn't be a surprise.* Have paper and pencil ready to receive calls. Smart hotel sales executives develop their own checklist form for transcribing pertinent information. There are also quite a few good "incoming message" forms available through office supply dealers.

3. *Let them know who you are.* "Good morning, ABC Hotel sales office. This is Jane Doe," or "This is convention services, Pat speaking." The approach saves time and confusion.

4. *Request, don't demand.* If you answer and they want to speak to someone else, say "May I tell her who is calling?" Another turnoff: "What do you want to speak to him about?"

5. *Listen actively.* Take notes. This increases your comprehension level dramatically. If in doubt ask callers to spell their names; repeat the name in your conversation. Everyone likes the sound of his own name, especially if it's pronounced correctly. If the name is hard to pronounce, write it phonetically. If the caller asks a question, indicate a willingness to help. Obtain information by asking questions that begin with what, who, when, where, why, and how. "What do you think?" secures far more information for you than "Do you like this?"

   Remember, too, that the caller is probably not a very good listener since few people are skilled in this vital communication tool. Don't be afraid to repeat yourself. Telling someone something doesn't mean you will be understood. How many listen when the flight attendant gives safety instructions or the waitress spells out the nightly specials? Good listeners can react quickly.

   Listening is not hearing and listening is not a passive function. It takes work. We must learn to listen actively. When we do, people feel recognized and "stroked." Like cats, "stroked" people purr!

   The importance of listening can be summed up by something Dale Carnegie said years ago: "The chronic kicker, even the most violent critic, will frequently soften and be subdued in the presence of a patient, sympathetic listener—a listener who will be silent while the irate fault finder dilates like King Cobra and spews the poison out of his system."

   When speaking, choose your words carefully. Certain words convey a negative, uninspiring connotation. How do you feel about words such as fault, rude, shirk, and blame? Most people dislike them. However, we respond positively to words like these: achieve, cheer, ease, valuable, cooperate, and the most powerful word of all: you.

6. *Maximum hold 15 seconds.* Have you ever placed a call where someone answers and says "Please hold a moment," and you sit there for what seems like hours, before anything happens? You don't like it, do you? Neither does your caller.

   Ask if the caller wishes to be put on hold and don't make it terminal. If the wait will be long, suggest it might be better if you get back to them and then be specific. "We'll call back by noon." Then do it.

7. *Courtesy, courtesy, courtesy.* Be tactful. Saying the right thing, at the right time, to the right person, in the right manner, will usually produce desired results. Be polite when you answer, throughout the conversation, and

especially when the call is terminated. "Thanks for calling," or "I regret we can't get it out today." Always let them hang up first.

The most difficult type of call to handle is a complaint. The customer is angry but most of the time it's not really at you. Something went wrong and you are going to hear about it. Show that you are sympathetic by not interrupting. Don't argue. Don't judge. Listen. Let complainers get it off their chest. Put yourself in their shoes. What are they trying to accomplish?

They have a problem. It might not seem like much to you but to them it's very important. Even though you might not entirely agree with their point of view, listen anyway. Request more information when you do not fully comprehend. They are looking for understanding, not sympathy. After you've listened and it's time for you to talk, speak slowly and softly. Paraphrase to assure the callers that you understand.

Determine defensiveness. Learning to anticipate defensiveness before you communicate can help you win a person over through reason and logic. Do not become emotional when you hear others use emotionally toned words. Refrain from interrupting and watch out for mental arguments. Stay alert. Don't daydream. (This is a danger when we've heard the complaint many times before.)

Before offering a "solution" find out what they truly want you to do. One good way to do that is to ask for suggestions: "What would you like us to do?" Don't lose your cool. Keep your temper under control. You are not out to win the battle and lose the war. The goal is to win for you and the caller.

Good telephone communication is basically common sense. Don't let a poor telephone personality ruin your business. Shop yourself! Ask a friend to call and pretend to be a customer. Find out how he or she is treated.

An ad by United Technologies Corporation states, "The telephone is one of life's miracles. With a little thoughtfulness we could make it one of life's blessings."

Have everyone in your sales office work on their phone skills. Tape record your end of several calls. It will help determine what you did right and what you did wrong. Then practice improving. You'll be amazed at the results.

Reprinted with permission from HSMAI Marketing Review, Fall 1987.

Using Your Voice

Generally speaking your voice is 50% of your personality as judged on first contact in face-to-face situations. On the telephone, it is 100% of your personality—the only means of practicing salesmanship. Not many of us have the trained voices of singers and speakers, but there are some effective methods of improving speech abilities. All too often, our lips don't move, our jaws are stiff and our tongues just hang. We have no expression in our voices. We have what are known as "lazy articulaters."

Here are a few suggestions which may help:

- *Use your articulators (facial muscles) and make a conscious effort to improve your diction.*
- *Speak with enthusiasm. Put expression into your voice so that you sound warm and friendly.*
- *Your voice should be heard as a smile is seen. Put a smile on your face while you are on the telephone and the smile will be heard by your client.*
- *Avoid a monotone. Attempt to vary the pitch of your voice.*
- *Relieve the strain from your voice by speaking at your normal pitch. Lower pitched tones carry best over the telephone. You will sound more relaxed.*
- *Speak slowly. Don't run on like a slow record at a fast speed. Don't let your words be lost.*

It is even more important to pace your conversation on the telephone than it is when selling face to face. After you've made your recommendations and asked for the business, pause. Say nothing. Let the prospect say the next word, no matter how long it takes. Don't lose the sale by talking too much or too soon and giving the prospect an opportunity to back out.

Enthusiasm for the product and the challenge of serving the prospect is an essential ingredient for an effective sales representative. Most travel and tourism products are quite exciting and interesting, and therefore enthusiasm is easy to generate. Enthusiasm is contagious. Your prospect will be enthusiastic about your recommendations if you show your own enthusiasm through friendliness: a personal interest in the prospect and in providing service, and a thorough knowledge of what you are selling. Again a word of caution, however—do not overdo your enthusiasm to the point of appearing insincere or ridiculous. Your prospect may never return.

"The next person who walks in here asking for the cheapest fare gets these!"

Don't confuse enthusiasm with doing all the talking. Let your prospect talk. Unless customers have the opportunity to let you know the many things they have on their mind, you will never really know what is wanted. You can easily jump to the wrong conclusion and waste time on an irrelevant detail. Do not dominate and overpower your prospect with conversation. Ask questions and control the conversation at all times, but let prospects have adequate opportunity to share their desires and concerns.

CONCLUSION

There are specific techniques which will improve your ability to practice effective selling. You must remember that you are always selling yourself and your company as well as your product or services. If you understand your client's needs, selling can be pleasant and profitable for both you and your client.

SUMMARY

A sales representative shows his or her professionalism in appearance, actions and the way the sales process is handled. A sincere smile and interest in understanding the customer's needs are essential tools for a successful salesperson.

It is necessary to prospect for clients and to identify their needs. Once you have done that, you move on to helping them solve their problems by using their products or services.

The telephone is a very common and effective selling method when used properly. It is important to remember, however, that you lose the dimension of visual aids when on the telephone. Therefore, you must be more careful of your tone of voice and of any other signals you are giving along with the words you use.

QUESTIONS FOR THOUGHT AND DISCUSSION

1. Discuss at least three ways in which you might prospect for new customers.
2. Give three examples of appearance or actions that might "turn off" a customer.
3. Discuss the similarities and differences between telephone sales and face-to-face sales.
4. Discuss the three basic ingredients around which a persuasive communication message is built.
5. Discuss at least three of the "basics" to selling in the Industry Communique by Edmund Sansovini and tell why each is important.

14

The Sales Interview

benefits
closing
assumptive close
alternate choice close
commitment
features
objection
probing
qualifying
sales interview

The personal sales process, where buyer and seller are in direct communication, is essentially an interview process. The salesperson is the interviewer and the client, the interviewee. In the most successful situations, the salesperson controls the interview. It should be noted that control is not domination but rather direction. The salesperson has one or more objectives clearly in mind at all times.

The interview should be structured. Overall, the general goal is to find out what the customer needs, recommend products or services to fill those needs, and persuade the customer to accept the recommendations and buy the travel product.

Obviously no two salespersons are exactly alike and no two prospective clients are exactly alike. Yet, there is a pattern that will work to generate sales. Certain elements should be found in all successful sales conversations. Keeping the elements in mind as a guide during the conversation will help to decide where you've been, where you are now, and what ground you must cover to complete the process.

STEPS IN THE SALES INTERVIEW

It is somewhat misleading to pull apart a sales conversation into separate pieces, because the actual conversation is a flow rather than separate steps. However, knowledge of the elements is necessary to be sure you cover everything which must be covered. The steps in this process were identified by Porter Henry in 1970 for the American Society of Travel Agents. These steps are as valid today as when they were originally identified. The major elements in the sales process are:

1. Getting the Initial Information

There are certain basic pieces of information that a sales representative needs in the beginning. When planning a sales call, this information is gathered ahead of time. However, when a prospective client comes to you, it is necessary to get this information right away. This information is the basic who, when, where, and how many. A lot of time can be wasted and inappropriate advice can be given if these basic questions are not answered early in the sales encounter.

It is critical to know who is going and how many. Is it only the person with whom the salesperson is talking or is a spouse (perhaps even an entire family) going? Is it one couple or two? Is it a group?

When are they going? The appropriate prices and packages might not even be known yet for the time they want to go. If the salesperson assumes the people want to travel soon, incorrect prices and availability can be given. This can greatly increase the work later in the process.

Where do they want to go? Sometimes, people know exactly where they want to go and sometimes they are only vaguely aware of what they want. People may ask to go "someplace warm," or to some other equally vague destination. Even when they request a specific destination, it is necessary to make sure the salesperson and the client are thinking of the same place. For example, when someone asks to go to Portland, do they mean Portland, Oregon, or Portland, Maine? The difference is virtually the width of the United States.

2. Finding Out What the Customer Really Wants

After the initial who, when, and where, it is necessary to dig deeper to identify the real needs of clients. Will the traveler's destination request really meet needs? Is the budget realistic? Can this hotel handle these needs?

Getting the initial information and finding out what the customer really wants are, together, the "qualification" phase of the sales conversation. It is essential to qualify a customer in order to determine product or service recommendations and to decide on the amount of time and effort you can afford to devote to the prospective sale. A professional sales representative will devote substantial amounts of time only to substantial prospects.

3. Selling Your Recommendation

Once you have qualified the client and know what is really needed, you should recommend the product or service that will provide the maximum satisfaction within the client's allotted budget. You sell your recommendation by convincing clients that you understand their wants and needs and that the product or service you recommend is the best way to meet those needs.

4. Handling Objections

Often the customer will accept your recommendation immediately. However, many times he or she will not. If you really believe your recommendation will meet the customer's needs, you must analyze the objections or concerns and overcome them.

5. Getting the Commitment

Traditionally this is called "closing the sale." Essentially, it is asking for the business. The salesperson who hands a purchaser a set of brochures or other sales aids and says "Call me when you've decided what you want," has not closed the sale. A professional salesperson will gain as much of a commitment as possible to close the sale, or at least get the commitment to talk again. It is better for the salesperson to say "I'll call you Wednesday to see what you have decided or if you have some questions," rather than "Call me when you decide." The latter leaves no chance for a follow-up without intruding, whereas the former approach leaves the way open without offense to continue the sales process with a follow-up effort. Of course, if there is no reasonable possibility of closing the sale in the future, no future commitment should be requested and the sales conversation should be terminated as quickly and graciously as possible. See the Industry Communique for specifics on this.

"How much breathless, exotic living on a romantic South Sea island can I swing for $39.50?"

INDUSTRY COMMUNIQUE

HOW TO ELIMINATE SHOPPERS WHO DON'T BUY

Lawrence J. Frommer, CTC

When is a customer not a customer? Frequently. The fact that a lot of people knock on our doors may be good for the ego but not necessarily for the pocket. Of every 10 people who phone or visit our offices, eight do not book—some because we don't do an effective job of selling, but most because they really aren't potential customers anyway.

Try this experiment that our agency conducted several years ago: In a given week, record the names of anyone other than established customers who phone your office or walk in requesting information and collecting brochures. Then, in 60 days check the list to ascertain how many actually booked. You may be amazed at how few.

When you get right down it, only a small portion of a travel agent's day is actually productive because it is monopolized by comparison shoppers, curiosity-seekers, armchair travelers, impulse callers, boredom-breakers, habitual reservation-cancelers and various other time-wasters. Yet we devote as much time—if not more—to the pseudo-prospects as we do to actual customers.

Incredible, isn't it, how much we give for so little?

To be sure, all businesses have their "non-customers" who flit in and out of their offices or stores without buying. But unlike most businesses, a travel agency's basic products are time and expertise. Thus, in our business, the non-customer virtually devours the merchandise:

IDENTIFYING THE NON-CUSTOMER

The question is, what can we do about them? What methods and strategies can we employ to gracefully filter them out so that we can get on with more profitable transactions?

There are no simple solutions. Instinct, ingenuity, diplomacy, discipline and a substantial amount of chutzpah are needed to make successful sales. But first we must recognize that not everyone who knocks on our doors is a potential customer. For if we are to effectively ferret out and deal with the profit-losers we must admit that such people exist.

Then we must learn how to identify the typical non-customer, to recognize the tell-tale signs, the characteristics and peculiarities that distinguish this individual from the authentic customer.

One obvious indication that a prospect lacks serious purpose is his reluctance to offer a name. Nothing is more tentative than a person who begins a conversation with, "You don't know who I am, but I'd like to get the roundtrip APEX fare to Barcelona." Shoppers and other casual inquirers do not like to be identified because they are a long way from making any kind of commitment and prefer to play games under a cloak of anonymity.

Another clue is when a caller seems to possess a wealth of information, indicating that he has tested the waters extensively before contacting your office. As I pointed out in an earlier article "...he has already digested the prices and knows that a specific hotel is sold out for the dates he wants..."You can bet that he is using you either for comparison shopping or to reconfirm information he has already.

There is the terribly indecisive prospect, the one who phones you five or six times, engages you in lengthy conversations but remains unbooked. He may come around eventually but experience has demonstrated that he usually decides not to go at all.

Needless to say, prospects who hold duplicate reservations on airlines, steamships and/or hotels from other sources should not be taken too seriously. In most cases they are protecting themselves by playing the field.

Also be suspicious of the caller who is unusually impatient, who demands to know everything immediately, who can't wait until the person who can answer his queries with greater authority returns from lunch and who threatens to book with another agency if you can't help him pronto. I have found this type of caller very unreliable. His impatience usually stems from either compulsion or impulse that often evaporates as quickly as it surfaces. I've discovered that the most impetuous are the ones I had to phone the most frequently for decisions, and in most cases, they didn't go.

There is the former customer, the one you haven't heard from in at least five years although you have reason to believe he has traveled. Out of the blue he contacts you, invariably when space is tight, prefacing his requests with a guilt-tinged disclaimer such as, "I haven't really traveled anywhere for a long time, which is why you haven't heard from me." Chances are he is using you—you're just one of several cards up his sleeve, and if reservations were not so scarce it is unlikely that you would have heard from him at all.

Be skeptical of the caller who inquires about one destination and suddenly shifts to others that are totally unrelated. I conversed with one of these armchair globetrotters recently who initially requested data on Bermuda; before the conversation was terminated I had helped her research Chile, Pakistan, Haiti, Biloxi and Alaska. Total time of conversation: 50 minutes.

Among the callers not to be taken seriously is the one who starts the conversation by criticizing another travel agency. Often this person's request will be just as difficult for you to fulfill as it was for your competitor, but he goes from agency to agency to find one with a "special magic." How many times have you heard such callers remark, "The other agency is not doing anything for me." Perhaps "not doing anything" means being unable to book a very popular Caribbean hotel in mid-February.

Learn to deal effectively with prospects who frequently book but never go. There are many well-intentioned people with hangups of one kind or another about travel who cancel when the moment to act arrives. I've had prospects who have booked as many as five consecutive trips but each time have come down with psychosomatic illnesses just a few days prior to departure. They are more to be pitied than scorned, yet we must recognize their patterns.

Be very leery of the person who phones you two days before he plans to travel, asking you to book hard-to-get flights and hotel reservations. In some cases this may be a legitimate last-minute booking, but far too often it is a case of someone who has frantically searched around without success or a caller who has a sudden whim.

Another potential profit-drainer is the person who confuses a travel agency with a government tourist office. He has little conception of how an agency operates and regards it primarily as a source of information, brochures and other travel data. I know at least four people who regularly visit our office to collect brochures and ask questions, but have yet to book a reservation in four years. We suspect that they are either vicarious travelers or are building a brochure library for their youngsters' school projects.

HOW TO DEAL WITH THEM

Having identified the profit-drainers, it becomes much easier to deal with them. Naturally you just can't come out and bluntly accuse someone of wasting your time and suggest that he take his foolishness elsewhere. But there are polite and subtle methods that can be employed to get the non-customer out of your hair more rapidly.

Travel industry consultant John Dalton of Columbus, Ohio suggests that when a customer doesn't offer a name, the agent should try to establish intent by saying something to the effect of: "Good morning. Let me introduce myself; John Dalton is my name. May I have yours?"

Dalton contends that the capricious caller has no interest in being identified and that the proffering of a name is too much of a commitment for him. "By asking for his name the chances are likely that it will be a short conversation," he adds.

A Washington, DC agency owner discloses that when a caller asks why the agency wants to know his name she replies, "When you ask me to send you brochures or are ready to book the reservation I won't have to bother you about it."

When a caller seems to have too much information, ask him if he has already tried to get what he wants and, if he has been unsuccessful, would he buy alternatives? Why go through a fruitless repeat performance for someone who has already contacted other agencies?

If an unfamiliar prospect phones a day or two before his trip, asking you to book flights or hotel reservations, insist that he come down to your office and put down a deposit before you can make arrangements. His reaction to this will indicate whether he is serious or just impulsive.

Concerning the prospect who holds duplicate reservations on carriers and in hotels, firmly insist that he make an immediate decision as to which set of reservations he plans to use.

The person who is disgruntled with another travel agency should be questioned immediately as to why he is dissatisfied. It may well be that you can't do any more for him than the other travel agency.

To the person who books elsewhere but consults you for supplementary information, you might politely suggest that he obtain that information from the booking firm.

For the constant canceler it might be helpful to establish a system of cancellation fees. The prospect might become piqued at the suggestion, but what do you have to lose?

For the person to whom "money is no object," it might be a good idea to give him an approximate price quotation early in the game. If he is going to defect let him do so before you have spent too much time with him.

To the person who pumps you for information on the street, suggest that he phone you at the office where you have all of your data on hand. If he doesn't, you know he really wasn't serious.

THE INDECISIVE PROSPECT

With the indecisive prospect who has already stolen much of your time, you simply have no alternative but to pin him down by: 1. asking for a deposit to cover any reservations to be made; 2. writing up an order in the presence of the person; 3. asking specific questions such as, "Should we inquire if space is available?" "If we can get this for you is this what you want?" "Do you prefer a morning or an afternoon flight?" "How do you wish to pay for this trip—credit card, cash, etc.?"

The former customer must be handled a little more gingerly than most profit-drainers. After all, he's been on your books before and you may reason that if you do a good job for him you might win him back. Unfortunately, it doesn't usually work that way. For one reason or another he hasn't seen fit to book through you for five years or more, and when his current booking crisis is history he is likely to return to his normal sources. You might give him a chance, but don't lose too much sleep over him if you can't get what he wants.

Now you might ask: isn't there an inherent danger in systematically trying to eliminate people no matter how politely it is done? Yes, fellow agents, I'm fully aware that once in a while you're going to blow one: the person who already has a lot of information may still let you book his reservation; the duplicate booker may release his space to your agency; the impatient caller might sincerely desire to go somewhere at the last minute; and the indecisive prospect may eventually make a decision.

But for every legitimate customer who gets away, you'll be discouraging a countless coterie of frivolous and unreliable people from wasting your time and energies. And in an age of escalating costs and marginal profits, that's a requisite to survival.

Reprinted with permission of ASTA Travel News, April 15, 1980.

QUALIFYING THE CLIENT

In the description of the sales process above, steps one and two were described as being part of the qualification process. Every professional sales representative develops a system for qualifying the prospect. You need to know if the person inquiring about a travel service is truly serious. If you are calling on a prospect, you need to determine whether that prospect has any real potential to use your services.

Getting the initial information should be accomplished in the first minute or so of the session with a prospect. In a travel agency setting for example, where a traveler has come in for the first time, a good set of basic questions to ask, if the destination is given initially, is as follows:

- *When do you plan to go?*
- *How long will you stay?*
- *How many people will be traveling?*
- *Have you ever been there before?*
- *Do you prefer to travel independently or in a group?*

Possibly ask about basic budgetary considerations at this point. A hotel sales representative might ask the first two questions above and then add:

- *How many rooms do you estimate?*
- *How many nights?*
- *Do you need meeting rooms, exhibit space, or meal functions?*

An air cargo representative might ask:

- *What kind of material do you ship?*
- *How frequently?*
- *Is special handling required?*

These questions will give the basic parameters from which to work. If the prospective customer is hedging about answering the above, the salesperson can't be sure the prospect is "real."

If the prospective traveler is not sure about destination, the agent needs to get the rest of the initial information and then start qualifying the person to find out likes and dislikes. Questions such as the following might be asked:

- *What do you like to do?*
- *When did you take your last vacation?*
- *Where did you go?*
- *What hotel did you stay in?*
- *What did you like or dislike most about it?*
- *What activities do you like?*

Prospects' answers will show preferences for types of activities such as beaches, pools, sightseeing, or nightlife. If a family stayed at deluxe hotels before, they won't be happy with tourist class this time. Questions about a previous vacation give a good indication of a client's available budget. The more the agent knows about a client the more intelligent the recommendations will be.

PROBING FOR INFORMATION

The agent must probe deeply (almost like a psychologist) when advising a first-time client about a trip. Before making recommendations, the agent must be sure what the client really wants. When a couple comes to the office and says "We

"I'm sorry, but none of these brochures has exactly the trip I've been looking for."

want to go to San Juan," the salesperson needs to probe further to see if this is the destination that will meet their needs. While the easiest thing to do would be to pull out a brochure on San Juan, quote the air fare and discuss hotels, this could be a mistake. Do the clients like the hustle and bustle of a large city? Upon probing, it may be found that the client really prefers a quiet hotel with a good beach and nothing more than a combo in the evening. This couple's reason for asking for San Juan (or any other destination) could be because a relative or friend recommended it. Further questioning could show that the likes and dislikes of the person recommending the destination were totally different from the likes and dislikes of the prospective travelers. A salesperson performs a major service to clients by helping them identify their real needs.

The travel professional must also be careful not to take the easy way out, even if that is what the client seems to want. For instance, extensive advertising and promotion has given the general public the impression that tour packages generally are bargains providing more for the travel dollar. Many vacationers often ask their travel agent: "Do you a have a package to …?" Package tours are not automatically bargains or even the best value. Many are priced at exactly the sum of the individual parts if purchased separately. Thus, if a couple bought a Caribbean Island package with hotel, ground transportation, and sightseeing tour, priced at the sum of the individual components, and they did not really want the sightseeing tour, they would not be getting the best value for their money or needs.

Often, packages represent good values because of the volume purchasing power of the tour operator or special airfares available only through tour operators. Sometimes, however, packages cost more than the sum of the parts. Special event packages such as the Super Bowl or the Rose Bowl or Mardi Gras have large

"You and your bargain tours!
Anything to save a buck!"

profit mark-ups but sell well due to the demand to attend. Other programs include "development" or "operations" costs. The existence of such costs is usually noted in the small print in the package brochure—but few customers ever read the small print.

Travel marketers should be aware of the tour package and its potential usefulness. However, those dealing with the traveler directly should be careful to select those packages that meet the travelers' needs and are good values—not just the easiest to sell with the highest profits.

In another example, a hotel sales manager, talking to a leader of a prospective meeting group, might ask:

- *How many people will be coming?*
- *Will you need single or double rooms?*
- *What meal functions would you like to include?*
- *What audiovisual equipment will you need?*
- *How would you like to have the room set up—theater or classroom style?*

The same process continues, to make the sale, as that described above for the travel agent. The sales process is the same regardless of which segment of travel is being sold.

Qualifying prospects is rarely an automatic procedure. Simple questions and direct answers are not always the case. People are often indefinite concerning dates, destinations, lengths of stay and other key information. They may, for instance, be unwilling to let the salesperson know their financial situation.

A serious mistake that travel salespeople make, in contrast, is giving too much information at one time. The client says "Thank you," and leaves in confusion. It is easy to let the client control the conversation. When this happens, the salesperson is rarely qualifying and much time is wasted.

For example, a prospect may call and ask what the round trip fare to London is. If you automatically decide that the client wants the lowest fare and answer the question by saying "The lowest fare is $450.00" the prospect could easily just say "Thank you" and leave or hang up the telephone. There is a better way to do it. Give some information, by stating that there are a number of different fares that depend upon such things as time of travel, length of stay. Then add, "When would you like to go?" This brings your client right into the qualification process. By doing this, you differentiate the real traveler from the student completing a school project. You can continue to pin down the prospect and find out what is really wanted with minimum time wasted.

CONTROLLING THE CONVERSATION

In the qualification process, it is better to ask broad, open-ended questions that allow customers to give full information about their desires than to ask a simple "yes or no" type questions. Instead of asking "Do you like Las Vegas review shows?" ask "What type of entertainment do you like?" or "What type of evening activities do you enjoy?" With the open-ended question, the salesperson has a future avenue of discussion regardless of the answer given. With a closed "yes/no" question, the discussion can effectively be ended if the response is not the one expected. When that happens, the salesperson must back up and virtually start over. The flow of the conversation is stopped and the salesperson has lost control. An open-ended response allows the salesperson to continue controlling the conversation and to lead the customer down the path toward a recommendation that will satisfy the needs and result in a sale.

It is essential for the salesperson to control the conversation. Do not let the customer take off on time-consuming, unrelated tangents. For example, if a client who is purchasing an airline ticket to attend her son's wedding starts to talk about how her son met his fiancee or how she does or does not like her future daughter-in-law, the salesperson must bring the conversation back to the business at hand. The salesperson might say something such as: "By the way, did you say you wanted to leave on the earlier or the later flight?" The agent knows exactly which one was preferred, but it brings the client back to relevant conversation.

LISTENING EFFECTIVELY

Chapter Eight on communications discussed how important listening is in the communication process. Effective, active listening is also essential in the sales process—especially during the qualification phase. Every person wears an invisible sign. The sign says "I want to be important!" The best way to make someone feel important is to listen attentively and show that you care.

Several years ago the *Minneapolis Star* did a survey that shows dramatically the results of ineffective listening in a business situation. The objective of the survey was to find out why people did not return to a retail department store after shopping there at least once. The survey revealed the following information:

- *1% died*
- *3% moved*
- *9% shopped elsewhere for convenience or because of friends' recommendations*
- *10% were chronic complainers*
- *68% said "the salespersons were indifferent…they didn't seem to listen"*

The customer-oriented sales strategy is totally nullified when a salesperson forgets that the customer is the center of activity. Keep your eyes and ears on the prospect. Eye contact develops relationships. Even if you are listening intently while looking away from the client, you will give the impression that you are not concerned about that person. The more effective you are in analyzing the real needs of clients, the more successful your sales will be.

Industry sales trainer Porter Henry provides the following hints for the needs analysis phase:

- *Do not do all the talking—allow the client time to voice needs and wishes*
- *Help clients discuss their travel plans—this is the primary purpose of counseling*
- *Let the clients know you respect them and that you sincerely care*
- *Give clients some positive feedback that relates to their comments*
- *Frequently paraphrase what the clients have said—let them know whether you understand correctly what is being said.*

PRODUCT KNOWLEDGE

As well as listening to your client, you must know what you are selling. In travel and tourism this means that you must know both the product and service you are providing and the methods by which your company will provide the service. Because tourism is such an intangible, the prospective customer is buying you and your company as much as the product or service that you are providing. For example, if you are representing a hotel or chain of hotels, you should thoroughly understand the facilities of your properties (rooms, banquet facilities, recreation activities, amenities) and the way your company does business (credit terms, promotional support activities, type and quality of staffing for the projected event).

ACKNOWLEDGE THE CLIENT'S NEEDS

When making recommendations, refer to your prospect's needs and show that your recommendation will fit the needs. One very effective technique is to refer to your prospect's statements or preferences. Stating "As you said a moment ago," automatically puts you in the client's frame of reference. Saying, "You will like this hotel because you said you like small, intimate places with luxurious facilities" proves you have been listening to your prospect's request. Paint word pictures using colorful language to conjure images to put your prospect in your hotel...on your tour...or on your airline. Do not be dishonest and describe something that doesn't exist; rather emphasize the comforts and amenities that are really there.

Sell the Benefits, Not the Features

Since your job is to fill a need, a most important technique is to sell the benefits of a travel product, not just the features. You must convey to your prospect the real value of your product or service in a way that will appeal to the prospect's emotions. For example, if you are a travel agent or a tour operator selling an escorted tour, one important feature is that the tour is fully escorted. However, you must talk about more than "a fully escorted tour." You must stress the benefits of the escort—being advised of places to eat and sites worth seeing, as well as being provided with direct transportation and baggage handling (no worry about how much to tip porters, for example.)

A major feature of a cruise is that the price is all-inclusive. What is the benefit? Budgeting is easier and your prospect need not carry as much cash or travelers checks. There is no right side of the menu with prices and the choice of food can be made without considering individual item cost. The list goes on and on.

As the previous examples show, the **feature** is a noun, a name for something. The **benefit** is its personalized value to the buyer. The same feature may provide a different benefit to different clients, depending on their needs and desires. Communicating benefits must be more than the transmission of words or facts—it is the transmission of ideas that are understood by the listener, who interprets them according to experiences and purpose. Knowing the benefit will help the prospect feel that wants are being met. In contrast, features have no direct emotional value. See Table 14-1 for example of how the same features can provide different benefits to different customers.

TABLE 14-1

FEATURES VS BENEFITS

Feature	Benefit for Affluent Widow	Benefit for Family with Teens
All meals included in dining room	companionship; needn't decide where to eat	costs are contained; no fights on where
Full entertainment program	not alone; safe; convenient	together but separate; each can do own thing

Using Your Own Experience

Porter Henry suggests three other techniques for selling your recommendations. First, refer to your own experiences when you have had an experience and your client has not. Referring to your own experience can often be reassuring. This is particularly useful if the prospective client is slightly worried about something. Your personal experience can often allay the fear. Be careful, however. Some clients are know-it-alls. They are experts in everything. Recounting personal experiences will not help with this small percentage of prospects.

Using a Third Party

Referring to a third party is another helpful technique. A satisfied client's reference can be helpful in selling a new client. If the XYZ Company has problems similar to ABC Company, showing how your service helps XYZ can help sell ABC. Two words of caution are necessary with respect to references to a third party, however. First, the "third party" should know and approve of your using them as a reference. Secondly, don't overdo it. Some prospects, especially those with well-developed marketing plans, resent salespeople who stress how their product or service helped another company and do not seem to give enough evidence on how the product or service can help the present prospect. They resent that the sales-person considers them all the same rather than unique people with unique needs. Know your customer first and then decide whether a third-party reference will help you or backlash and hurt your potential sale.

Reassurance

Reassuring your prospect can also help in the sales process. For example, travel agents should recognize that prospective travelers are often unsure about a prospective trip. Rather than salesmanship, they need just plain reassurance. Stating "You're going to have a wonderful time," can be helpful. Reassurance about how details are handled as benefits rather than features is also helpful. One warning at this point, however—Don't oversell! No travel experience can be absolute perfection. Be realistic in your promises.

OVERCOMING OBJECTIONS

You have qualified your client and recommended travel services. Now the client says "No." What do you do?

The above situation is certainly not typical. Rarely will a client say "No" without further comments. normally, a response would be:

- *"No, it costs too much"*
- *"I want to think it over"*
- *"I want to go at a different time."*

Objections are a normal part of the sales cycle. Some sales people live in fear of the "no." Professional sales representatives, on the other hand, expect objections and are prepared for them. Many see the challenge of salesmanship as overcoming customer objections.

INDUSTRY COMMUNIQUE

MEMO TO: TRAVEL AGENCY STAFF
FROM: MANAGER
RE: SELLING

Lawrence J. Frommer, CTC

You and your customers are different people. One of you in the office took a cruise recently. You loved it. You're excited about selling cruises to as many people as possible, and heaven knows I would be the last person to dampen your enthusiasm. But make certain that your next customer is the "cruise type" before you try to persuade him. Another of you spent a few days last month at one of those charming cottage colonies in Bermuda. You fell in love with the place. But is your next Bermuda customer the cottage-colony type or the high-rise-hotel type? Remember, it's not what you like; it's what your customer likes.

Never bluff. If you're fuzzy about the answer to a customer inquiry, don't bluff it. It's far better to say, "May I check this for accuracy and get back to you?" or "Someone in the office is more current on this than I am; would you mind if I talked with her for a moment?"

Recognition is the "game of the name." There's a lot of truth in that old cliché that nothing sounds sweeter to a person than the sound of his own name. And there's nothing deadlier, no greater put-down than not being recognized. Think of the times you have phoned a place of business and identified yourself, only to be greeted with a dead silence or a rather bored "yes." Kind of took the stuffing out of you, didn't it?

So put yourself in the customer's shoes. If, for instance, a Mrs. Smith visits your office, greet her with a "Yes, Mrs. Smith" or "Hello, Mrs. Smith." It's flattering. It's friendly. It's the sweet sound of her own name. During the course of the conversation, re-identify her. Repeat her name several times.

And try this on for size: Instead of the usual greeting—"May I help you, Mrs. Smith?"—how about "*How* may I help you, Mrs. Smith?" Obviously you can help her. That's why she's talking to you. By going a step further and asking how you can help her, you get into the selling posture much quicker, and it's much friendlier and more personal.

Don't let customers play the waiting game. It's not good business to keep a prospective customer waiting. First of all, don't let incoming phone calls ring more than four times without answering. Protracted ringing suggests operational sloppiness and the caller begins to get nervous. If you must put a customer on hold, try to get back within 60 seconds. Otherwise, it poses uncertainties in his mind. Have you forgotten him? Is he still connected? Should he call back and start all over again? Should he just forget it and call someone else? If you're going to be busy for a while, explain the delay and ask if you can call back.

But let the customer know approximately when you will be calling. Most customers expect an immediate call back. If this is not possible, you or someone else in the office should indicate so at the time, something to the effect: "You know, Mrs. Williams, it looks like I'll be tied up anywhere from 30 to 45 minutes. May I phone you as soon as I'm free, or is there another time more convenient for you?" This gives the caller the option of waiting for your call back or doing other things. Above all, the caller will know what to expect.

What are the alternatives? By its very nature, our industry demands more alternatives than most others. A person may want a particular brand of vacuum cleaner or make of automobile, but the chances are he can wait a few weeks for delivery if it's not immediately available. He doesn't have to have the product on a specific day. In travel, it is just the opposite. The customer is programmed to travel on a specific date. He's made arrangements to go then. In most cases, he has little leeway.

Boost certain customers up the ladder. Price is the most overworked word in today's travel vernacular, and "bargain travel" has become a household phrase. But there are clients whose lifestyle is inappropriate to bargain travel and who would be unhappy booking a package with less-than-deluxe hotels or a cruise ship that is below their usual standards. You will do this type of a client a service by suggesting an upgrade and a disservice if you don't. In this case, you're not trying to get the customer to spend more money per se, but rather to maintain his lifestyle. So next time such a customer says he's interested in some bargain he's read about in the newspapers, you might say to him: "You're accustomed to traveling better than this, Mr. Holmes. Why do you like this particular package?" or "Please keep in mind, Mrs. Johnston, that the ship you're interested in is not nearly as elegant as the one on which you cruised last year."

A toughie is the unspoken objection, the one you don't hear or feel. That's the one at work when the customer says, "I'll think about it" or "Let me go home and talk it over with my wife" or "I don't know if I can afford it." This kind of remark usually means that you haven't overcome all of the client's objections, that there are still a couple lurking that must be gotten out on the table. Certainly, at that point, a question such as "Do you need additional information?" or "Is there still a question in your mind that we haven't answered yet?" would be timely and appropriate.

The toughest type of sales resistance is when you get seemingly unrelated objections that don't ring true. No sooner do you answer one objection than you get another, totally unconnected to what has gone before, almost as if the customer is trying to throw as many roadblocks in your way as possible. This pattern often indicates that it is both painful and difficult for the prospect to make a decision and this is his way of postponing it. Sometimes this can be handled with a sense of urgency on your part, that is, by persuading the prospect that if he doesn't act now, it could work against him later. A comment like "This package is very much in demand and if we don't book it very soon it will likely be sold out" reflects this approach.

As you might have ascertained by now, we are in a perfectly illogical business, a business in which income is disproportionate to the amount of work invested. Pushing our products and services requires an extraordinary amount of time and talent. There are constant barrages of questions and answers, incessant changes, busywork, long conversations. There's rarely a quick transaction. There's always a lot happening with nearly every prospect we talk to.

Yet nothing really happens...until we close the sale.

Reprinted with permission from ASTA Travel News, December 1982.

For the most part, objections are actually requests for more information. Many objections indicate that the client has not been totally qualified, and you need to obtain more information on the client's real needs. Then you can determine whether to modify your recommendation or provide additional explanations on why your recommendation is the best for the client's needs.

It is essential to prepare for objections. You must anticipate them. A prospect will not generally accept everything you propose. Modifications are a way of life. The give and take during discussions of objections really helps point out what the client is looking for. Listen effectively and be prepared with alternatives. Most important, isolate the objection, discuss it fully with your client, and don't let that objection negatively affect agreements already made. When handling a client's objection, you must make an important decision. Almost on split-second notice, you need to determine whether to accept the client's objection and modify your proposal, or to bring the client around to your way of thinking. If you really believe the client would be better off by accepting your recommendation, take that split second of thought and then make a polite, diplomatic, low-pressure effort to resell your recommendation. Restate the benefits of your suggestion, noting that perhaps you had not explained the alternative adequately. Make the prospect your partner—not your adversary.

Porter Henry describes a well-known one-two-three method for convincing your clients to accept a suggestion they have just objected to:

- *If you're not sure what's behind the customer's objection, ask about it. If the customer just says "That doesn't sound too good to me," you need to know more about why the client feels that way before you can respond adequately. Don't hesitate if the objection is vague. Ask the client to explain it.*

- *Meet the customer part way. Never say "No, you're wrong." Avoid arguing—you want the sale. Empathize with the client and agree that he is reasonable. For example, say:*

"Yes, some people do feel that way, but...."
"Yes, that is an important point, however...."
"Yes, it may appear that way at first, but..."

- *Having met your prospect halfway, explain the reason for your recommendation. You're really going back to the phase of selling your recommendation to the client's interest. Another technique is to admit that an objection is valid, but offset it with other benefits. For example you could say "Yes, the hotel is a very large one, but it has more recreation facilities and a greater choice of restaurants than any other." Sometimes a disadvantage can even be turned into an advantage. When a client objects to a high deposit, you can say "Yes, the deposit is high, but it should be easier to pay the balance when it is due."*

It is very dangerous to discredit your competitors when selling your service. Few people like to hear one person discredit another. This particularly applies with regard to one's competitor. You do not prove your own worth by degrading someone else.

When a prospect brings up your competitor's name, you are on safe ground by not being critical of that company. Instead explain the advantages of the services you provide. Knocking the competition can weaken your own company and yourself.

CLOSING THE SALE

Getting the client's commitment to purchase goods or services should be the goal of every professional sales representative. Without the commitment, all the time and effort invested in qualifying the client, selling your recommendations and overcoming objections was for nothing. No commitment—no sale—no money—no job—no company!

"It's your wife. Shall I go ahead and tell her that you've decided against taking her to Hawaii?"

Closing the sale refers to specific techniques that the professional sales person uses to get the client's commitment. All efforts from the initial stages of the sales conversation must be directed towards the close. The initiative for closing the sale is clearly the responsibility of the salesperson. Too often salespeople avoid or evade this responsibility. Research indicates that

- *the salesperson closes only 20% of the time*
- *the customer closes 20% of the time*
- *and no one closes 60% of the time*

When no one closes, there is no sale.

Asking for the Business

Closing the sale is asking for the business. Salespeople ask for the business only 20% of the time because they fear rejection—they fear the client will say "No." The time at which you ask for the business is important. The method by which you ask for the business is even more important.

When do you ask for the business? It is effective to ask for the business whenever the prospects have given you a clue that they are ready to buy. Normally the initial close begins when you have qualified the prospects and know what their needs are. If they are not ready, they will raise an objection—by asking a question or indicating a lack of certainty. At this point you overcome the objection (to their satisfaction, of course). It is time to attempt to close again. Objections are often stated when the salesperson attempts to close the sale and the customer is not ready. More qualifying or recommending is needed before the close can be effective. Another good time to begin closing techniques is when you have described a benefit of your service and you have seen that the client reacts favorably.

Although the anatomy of the sale process separates the closing phase of sales from the overcoming-objection phase, the two phases are totally intertwined. It is through understanding a client's objections and responding to them that the professional salesperson identifies those clues which lead to a successful close.

Closing represents the natural end of the flow of the sales conversation. Closing techniques can be soft and subtle, applied on almost a trial basis to determine if the client is ready to buy. Closing the sale does not require high pressure. Rather, it requires sensitivity to each one of the client's reactions.

Kinds of Closing

"Let's see if there is space available." Known as the assumptive close, this is the lowest pressure close of all. You are not asking the clients for anything—not for money, not even for formal concurrence. If the clients are not ready, they will let you know—with an objection. You must then overcome the objection and try again.

There is another way to move into this type of assumptive close. That method is to say "That seems to cover everything. I'll go ahead and start looking…"

A slightly stronger form of close, requiring at least an acknowledgment from the client, is to offer to make a reservation. In this kind of close, a travel agent might say "That's the height of the season and I know that space will be hard to get. Let me make the reservation for you now." A hotel representative might say "Group space is tight in October. Let me make a tentative reservation." There's always a reason you can use—"The best rooms are reserved early;" "The ship cabins in the price range you are looking for are in the biggest demand;" and so on.

Even when a deposit is required, the assumptive close technique can be effective. You can state "Fine, I'm glad you like that idea. We'll go ahead with the reservations—we'll need a deposit of …;" or "We want to be sure that these (hotel rooms, staterooms, charter seats, and so forth) are held for you so we will need a deposit of $____." If the clients are not ready they will let you know.

Another soft, low-pressure method of closing is to offer alternate choices. Does the client want A or B? This is another form of the assumptive close, known as the "alternate choice" close. Note that there is an assumption that the client wants something—therefore the term "assumptive close." The following examples of alternate choices can apply to almost any travel service:

- *"Will this be cash or on a credit card?"*
- *"Do you wish to depart from JFK or LaGuardia?"*
- *"Do you want to leave in the morning or the afternoon?"*
- *"Do you want a sit-down banquet or a buffet?"*
- *"We've narrowed it down to plan A and plan B. Which do you prefer?"*
- *"If space is not available on these dates, will those dates be okay?"*

Again, if you have misjudged the timing and the clients are not ready, they will let you know.

Another type of close is based on your knowledge of the travel product you are selling as well as your understanding of client needs. You can make a statement such as, "From what you have told me, I know you will be happier with…" And move into the reservation phase. You can also say "The XYZ organization had a similar convention in our hotel, very successfully. They really enjoyed the Caribbean dinner. Which day shall we set it up for…? The client's reaction will tell you where to go from there.

WHEN NOT TO TALK

Too many sales are lost because the salesperson talks too much. This is especially true during the closing phase of the sale. There is one very critical procedure which must be mastered by the professional salesperson—after you have asked the closing question, wait for the client to respond. This powerful pause may be difficult. When you ask a closing question ("Shall I make the reservation?"), you have thrown the ball to your client. Wait for an answer; do not add more information. Do not confuse the client. If the client has a problem, you'll know about it soon enough.

There are many times when you try to get a "Yes" with the above techniques and the client for some reason doesn't want to make a decision. If you still believe that your results from qualifying the client are correct and there is a reasonable chance for a sale, you do not have to give up at this point. Offer to do something that will be of interest to the prospect—develop an estimate, get a specific piece of information, or do something else of importance for the client. At least get the client's agreement for a follow-up contact. Then you can try again. Remember, the more complex the situation, the greater number of contacts are necessary to develop the sale.

FOLLOW-UP

Many sales can be concluded or saved with proper follow-up techniques. If the only commitment you get from the client is an agreement to let you call back in several days, you must call back. Do not delay and do not forget. Make a note on your calendar or appointment book. Get the information you promised and call back. A good percentage of callbacks convert into sales. If you were unable to get the promised information on time, call anyway to let the customer know the status and reassure them you didn't forget them. If they have to call you before you call them, they will never believe that you were really working on your promise to them, but if you call to tell them, they will have much greater trust in you. People are very forgiving and patient when they are kept informed.

CONCLUSION

If you follow the tested pattern of the sales interview process, you can successfully reach a close. There is a structured process. Focussing on this structure will be efficient and effective. With practice it becomes quite natural.

SUMMARY

During the sales interview, the salesperson must control the conversation and listen carefully so that the necessary information can be developed. The sales process progresses in these stages:

- *Qualifying the client*
- *Probing for information to discover what the client really wants*
- *Selling the recommendation based on this information*
- *Handling any objections*
- *Closing the sale*

In the selling portion of the interview, the professional will attempt to sell benefits—what the product will do for the client—rather than features of the product. He or she will use such tools as personal experience, third party references, and reassurance. The professional will also be prepared to meet objections by understanding them, acknowledging them, and then explaining the recommendation once again.

Closing the sale—asking for the business—is essential to the selling process. it should be done as soon as the salesperson has a clue that the prospect is willing to buy. Closing need not be high-pressure to be effective. Techniques can vary from the very soft-sell assumptive close to stronger approaches. Even if the client does not respond to attempts to close the sale, the professional will offer to provide other services, such as getting an estimate or providing more information. And if no definite response can be evoked, the professional will plan on a follow-up call, knowing that such calls often result in sales.

QUESTIONS FOR THOUGHT AND DISCUSSION

1. What are the five steps in the sales process? List and describe.
2. What is meant by "effective listening"?
3. Give three examples of possible closing statements or questions.
4. Explain the advice, "Sell the benefits, not the features."
5. You have two clients, both interested in taking a cruise. One is Mrs. Brown, an elderly widow traveling by herself for the first time. She is financially well off but is somewhat insecure about traveling alone. The second client is a family of four, the Smiths. There is a father and mother as well as two teenage daughters. They want a nice vacation together but must watch their expenses. Translate the following features from the cruise brochure into benefits for each of these clients:
   a. All meals included
   b. Nightly entertainment on board
   c. A full choice of shore excursions
6. Give three examples of possible objections a customer might give to a proposal, and how you might overcome them.

15

Service—The Most Important Marketing Tool

accessibility
consistency
courtesy
empathy
expectation
first impression
job knowledge
perception
personal attitude
satisfaction
service
teamwork

In our highly competitive world, service becomes the most important marketing tool. As Robert Hazard from Choice Hotels stated in a speech to his firm's franchisees: "Successful companies will examine their operations and get back to basics. They will work harder to create a happy guest. The secret is to keep our focus on serving our 92 million customers. To be successful, we must focus on our customers—and not on our competition…The business of business is to create and serve a customer. We have to earn the right to do business with each one of our 92 million customers, and earn that right every day."

WHAT IS SERVICE?

Service—or the perception of it—can make the difference between an initial sale or the loss of it as well as directly affect profitable repeat business. Although the term "quality service" has become a modern-day cliché, it is essential to understand the principles of service and how they can be used in the marketing process.

It is also essential to avoid spoiling an otherwise excellent service product through inattention or unprofessional behavior.

THE "SEVEN DEADLY SINS" OF SERVICE

"Seven Deadly Sins" can spoil an otherwise excellent service product. Travel professionals must work to avoid these service "Sins":

1. Leaving someone expecting a reply. While this may seem obvious, it is the most frequently committed service sin. Too many travel industry sales people fail to return or follow up on phone calls adequately. When you tell someone you will call or send something, you must follow through and do it. If the customer calls again to check it, you have lost. The service level is down. Even if customers appear not to mind, they do. A bad impression will be difficult to overcome. Customers expect callbacks. Even if you do not have the answer to the customer's question, let him or her know you have not forgotten. Contact breeds satisfaction.

2. Arguing with a customer. Even when you know a customer is wrong, you gain nothing by proving it. Speaking with an argumentative tone when dealing with a customer is a losing proposition from the start. The personal satisfaction of being right is no compensation for the consequences of watching valued customers take their business and their money elsewhere.

3. Presenting a dirty or unprofessional look. Dirty facilities or unprofessional-looking employees undermine the overall credibility of a service organization. In food service it specifically undermines the appeal of the product and may also violate laws or regulations. Many companies require uniforms to enhance the visual appearance of staff. Others have at least some form of dress code.

At Disney theme parks, the entertainment model forms the base for appearance and conduct. Employees are "cast members" who wear "costumes" (not uniforms) and perform in a "role" (not merely job function). The result is a large group of young, highly-motivated employees providing high levels of service.

4. Giving conflicting or incorrect information. Nothing is more frustrating to a customer than receiving two conflicting pieces of information from two different people in the same organization. Most customers do not understand that perfect communication within a company is impossible. They expect perfection. They expect each person within an organization to be perfectly up-to-date and knowledgeable about almost everything about their services.

In the event that you do not know something or are not sure of your accuracy, you should advise your customer tactfully and promise to get the information and call back. Do make sure to call back or you will commit sin number one as well as giving the appearance that you do not care. It is far better to admit lack of information than to guess and give incorrect information.

5. Arguing with a fellow worker in front of the customer. Nothing undermines professionalism more quickly than an internal squabble in front of a customer. There is no disgrace in disagreeing with staff members, but arguing while the customer is present is disgraceful. If a confrontation is needed to solve an internal problem, wait until the customer leaves. If something must be solved immediately, excuse yourselves and go to a back room. Then go back and work with the customer.

6. Implying that a customer's needs are unimportant or trivial. Clients and customers expect to feel that they are important and that their needs are unique. They may be the fiftieth couple requesting the same service today, but to them this is the first time they have needed it. You cannot trivialize their request or act as if they are imposing on you.

7. Passing the buck. It would be nice to be able to answer every question and solve every problem without seeking higher level approval or bringing in another member of the organization to assist. However, this is neither practical nor possible. But if someone else must participate, or if the customer's needs can be met only by others, don't frustrate them by sending them through a maze of red tape. Your customer is already tense because of a problem and you must avoid creating further frustration. Minimize the bureaucracy. Know who can really help and bring that person to the scene as quickly as possible. If you must turn your customer over to another, do so in as friendly and informative a way as possible.

THE COMPONENTS OF GOOD SERVICE

Service is defined as anything of value, other than physical goods, which one person or organization provides to another person or organization in exchange for something. Thus, virtually all travel and tourism activities short of selling guide books falls within the service concept.

The best way to analyze service is through the eyes of the customer. There are three laws of service, plus one important corollary, which help explain service as a job that adds value, a highly subjective variable, for the customer.

THE FIRST LAW OF SERVICE

The first law of service is:

Satisfaction equals perception minus expectation.

$$S = P - E$$

Both of the variables in this equation—perception and expectation—are psychological phenomena. Thus, they are quite subjective and may have little relationship to reality. Providers of service cannot judge performance or customer expectations based upon what they feel the customer should be thinking rather than what the customer actually thinks. The service provider must show empathy and think as the customer thinks.

INDUSTRY COMMUNIQUE

THE SECRET INGREDIENT: ANTICIPATING NEEDS

Frank Storione is in the service life.

His lifetime hitch is in restaurant, not military, service, and the 28-year old waiter's orders come from customers at Philadelphia's Old Original Bookbinder's. He serves them well by imagining he's one of them.

"I picture myself sitting at the table and think, "'What would I want? Is there anything that should be replenished?' And then I do it myself, I don't ask the busboy," he says.

Storione began his career at Bookbinder's 10 years ago and wants to stay there "for the rest of my life...I'm studying to be a sommelier; I hope to be a banquet manager and eventually general manager."

His keys to good service:

- *Don't try to take care of too many tables.* "The further away from the kitchen, the fewer tables (a waiter) should have."
- *Timing.* "Make sure everybody gets their food at the same time."
- *Stay a step ahead.* "Anticipate the next item to be put on the table. If they're going to have soup, have the soup spoons out. If they've ordered crab, have the (shell) crackers there. Give it to them before they ask for it."

Diners are different, and service must adapt accordingly, he says. "You gotta feel every table out," he says.

That the waiter may be rattled by performance pressure may not occur to diners, but it can affect service. Storione's advice to a shaky waiter: "Customers are meeting him for the first time, too, and they're not nervous, so why should he be?"

Most valuable is pride in the job, he says. "I do whatever I have to do to get the restaurant through. You've gotta care about the place where you work."

Reprinted from USA Today, July 22, 1992.

The formula of the First Law of Service states that a customer expects a certain level of service when participating in a service transaction. If the customer perceives that the service provided was equal to or higher than that which was expected, **satisfaction** results. If, however, the customer perceives that less service was provided than was expected, dissatisfaction results.

Thus service providers must both deliver high quality service and manage customer expectations. An excellent example of managing expectations is the restaurant maitre d' or hostess who advises diners that the waiting time for a table is slightly longer than it actually will be. As a result, they will not experience a longer wait than they expect. Almost all the diners will be very happy when their wait is shorter than anticipated. Contrast this with their feelings when the waiting period for a table is longer than promised.

Another not-so-excellent example of managing expectations is the airlines' notorious use of the "rolling delay." In this situation, passengers are informed of a "slight delay," which keeps growing. As time goes by, and they keep expecting the flight to board and depart, they lose the chance to change to other carriers' flights and get angrier and angrier. If they are told right at the beginning of the true expected delay (or even slightly longer than expected), they will be satisfied when they finally depart. People can handle almost any situation as long as they are kept informed and they believe the supplier cares about them as people.

INDUSTRY COMMUNIQUE

SERVICE MAY BE COMING BACK IN STYLE

David Brezing

Joan Champie of Austin, Texas, was 10 minutes into her pizza dinner when all conversation was obscured by the roar of a vacuum cleaner.

"We all looked at our watches to see if it was closing time," she says. The Italian restaurant outside Cleveland "usually has good service. This was such a flagrant disregard for the customers," she says.

Complaints about restaurant service are starting to boil over, according to industry observers. Though restaurants have generally improved the quality and selection of food over the last decade, the quality of service hasn't always kept pace.

Recent surveys indicate the pretention and status that accompanied dining out in the '80s are being overshadowed by a desire for basic personal satisfaction. Service, says Barbara Caplan of the trend-tracking *Yankelovich Monitor*, "is an enormous issue. Consumers want a restaurant to relieve stress, not create it."

Nowadays, 80% of customer gripes "turn out to be people problems not food problems," says Tim Zagat, co-publisher of nationwide *Zagat Surveys* restaurant guides drawn from diners' critiques.

Part of the problem is that culinary schools have been turning out first-rate chefs, but "waiter or maitre d' still is not considered a serious career path," Zagat says.

Danny Meyer, owner of New York's award-winning Union Square Cafe, agrees: "Our country has an attitude of service being servitude, whereas in Europe and Asia service is an honored profession."

Wages are a factor. While servers in top restaurants can earn $40,000 or more a year, most, working for minimum wage, earn half that or less.

Another problem is the lack of thoughtful training, says Elaine Tait, restaurant critic for the *Philadelphia Inquirer.* Many mid-range restaurants employ "revolving-door" staffs of college students who may be eager and attractive but inexperienced.

And inexperience can lead to negligence of simple details—the things customers say turn them off the most.

"My biggest complaint is when they don't listen to your special orders," says David DeLuca, 27, of Falls Church, Va., who relies on restaurants during his job-related travels.

"For example, I may ask them not to put butter on my potato, and it comes with butter anyway. That's annoying when you're trying to reduce the fat in your diet," he says.

How a restaurant handles children is important, too, says administrative supervisor Marty Unger, 44, of Pasadena, Calif. The mother of two young boys dines out with her family two to three times a week, and appreciates speedy service.

"Bored children are miserable for *everybody* in a restaurant, not just the parents, she observes.

But in-house training and food- and wine-service seminars appear to be on the rise, says Art Siemering, publisher of *The Food Channel,* an industry trend letter.

One example is Fullers restaurant in Seattle, consistently highly rated for service by customers. It has succeeded by cross-educating its employees, says spokesman Louis Richmond.

"The servers know the food—many have cooked on the line—and the chefs have served in the dining room to help them understand the needs of the diner," he says.

Restaurants that skimp on service pay a heavy price, says Siemering, who notes that 7 out of 10 customers who don't return to a restaurant cite bad service.

"The real offenders get what's coming to them," he says. "The customers educate them the hard way—by voting with their feet."

Reprinted from USA Today, July 22, 1992.

Expectations

Customer **expectations** fall into seven categories:

1. Accessibility
2. Courtesy
3. Personal attention
4. Empathy
5. Job knowledge
6. Consistency
7. Teamwork

Service providers who understand their clients' expectations in each category can ensure that their efforts will provide high levels of satisfaction.

Accessibility

Customers expect prompt and efficient service. Service providers must help meet their needs and answer their needs as soon as possible. As marketers, they must have both the authority and the responsibility to handle all but the most complex problems without having to seek approval at a higher level. See the Industry Communique for specifics on how this question of authority and responsibility is handled by Hampton Inns.

Courtesy

Clients expect to be treated in a professional manner. Kind words are essential, even when saying "no" or providing an answer that the client does not want to hear.

"Travel agents are not mere mortals! We're expected to find fares that don't exist! Lost luggage, seats on overbooked flights and last minute reservations...Predict the weather and flight delays...So, I'm dressed for the part...40% magician and 60% psychic!"

"We will now circle JFK for the next three hours, at no extra charge to you."

INDUSTRY COMMUNIQUE

THE CUSTOMER IS ALWAYS RIGHT

Remember the good old days when the hottest thing in slogans was a company's "money-back" policy on its product? It was a no-questions-asked kind of guarantee that worked because, in those days, the customer was always right.

The folks who run Hampton Inns remember, and they're doing something about it. In what could be considered the ultimate awards program, this company is offering a "100% Satisfaction Guarantee" that the guest will always experience "high-quality accommodations, friendly and efficient service, and clean, comfortable surroundings." Or your money back.

How has the response of cynical modern America been to this quaintly old-fashioned approach? "So good it's almost scary," laughs Ray Schultz, president of Hampton Inns and the creator of this program. "The beauty is that it works on two levels—it's great for guests, of course, but great for our employees too. Nobody wants his or her performance to be the reason a customer demands his money back."

The process is simple: if a guest encounters a problem (leaky faucet, something not quite clean enough, a rude desk clerk) he reports it, setting off an immediate full-court press to right the wrong. If the guest still isn't happy, the room rate is refunded on the spot.

Some 25,000 people check into Hampton Inns every night—there are 208 of them in 36 states across the country (with 100 Embassy Suites and 25 Harwood Suites joining the program soon). Surely there have been one or two guests who've taken advantage of this generous offer? "Of course," admits Schultz, "We're not so naive as to believe there aren't cheaters out there." But, he adds, "We're fully automated, so we can run a complete profile every time anyone invokes the guarantee. We're onto the cheaters pretty fast."

Perhaps the best aspect of all is that the company has empowered every employee to honor the guarantee. The "I'll have to check with my supervisor" delay is eliminated, and there are no other time-consuming procedures before the money changes hands. That may be the best award of all.

Courtesy Frequent Flyer magazine, May 1990.

Personal Attention

Customers want to be treated as unique individuals, not as just another name on a long list. They want to know that the service provider cares about them as individuals as well as for the business they are providing.

"Just how many HOURS is a 'slight delay'?"

Empathy

Empathy is the ability to see and feel things from another person's view. A hotel front desk manager, for example, must understand how a guest with a reservation feels when he or she arrives and no room is available. Empathy is the essence of a "customer-oriented" philosophy.

Job Knowledge

Customers expect employees to know all pertinent facts about their job and their company. They expect honest answers. Except for complex special requests, customers expect service providers to give answers without seeking information or permission from higher level personnel.

Consistency

Customers expect to get the same answer, no matter who they talk to. Nothing hurts service levels more than receiving different answers from different people in the same organization. If everyone meets job knowledge expectations, there is no reason for two employees to give conflicting answers. Customers also expect consistent treatment as well as the same level of treatment as other customers in similar circumstances. Variable treatment is acceptable when there is a clear understanding of the reasons for it—for example, a special check-in counter for first-class passengers or an express check-in for airline passengers who already have their tickets and need only to check their baggage.

"He's not a member of our Frequent Flyer Program."

Teamwork

A company may be composed of many different departments with different goals and methods of operation, but to the customer it is one single entity. Customers expect different departments to work together as a team. They do not expect to be affected by internal turf battles or to be passed from one department to another for answers to basic questions.

Perceptions

After determining the expectations of clients and customers, the goal becomes the delivery of a level of service that will result in perceptions which exceed their expectations. Thus, they will perceive that they received value for their dollars. All facets of their experience must meet or exceed the standards our clients expected.

Unfortunately, the cliche, "one bad apple spoils the bunch" has great meaning with respect to the provision of service. Just one or two things going wrong will result in the perception of poor service even though many things went right.

The higher a customer's expectations, the easier it is for one small mishap to ruin everything. Thus, a blip in service will be more acceptable at a Holiday Inn or on a Carnival cruise ship, because both companies are in the mass market price and service range, than at a Ritz Carlton or on the *Seabourn Pride*, both of which position themselves by price and by image as being "above the crowd."

THE SECOND LAW OF SERVICE

It is because of the importance of perceptions that the Second Law of Service gains its own importance:

First impressions are the most important.

It can also be stated as, "First impressions are the most lasting," or as "You never get a second chance to make a first impression." From the point of view of providing service, a few things done right at the beginning will create positive goodwill. From the reverse standpoint, early errors are the hardest to correct. They also create concerned customers who may be looking for future problems even though none exist.

The look and feel of the physical facilities where customer contact is made, together with personnel trained to deal with the public in a friendly manner, aid in creating a great first impression—and the basis for long-lasting relationships.

Just because first impressions are the most important, however, does not mean that service providers can stop there. First impressions alone do not guarantee satisfied customers. Those impressions must be followed with good service as well. But a good first impression will give us the advantage of a customer on our side. A poor first impression will not.

THIRD LAW OF SERVICE

The First and Second Laws of Service focus on the interrelationships between customer contact personnel and customers. It is, of course, impossible to deliver quality service without a customer-oriented philosophy. The third law suggests that philosophy and interrelationships are not enough:

A service-oriented attitude alone will not assure good service.

Even though you are service-oriented and motivated to provide high levels of service, attitude alone is not enough. A company's systems must be developed to provide products and services that meet the customer's needs rather than the company's own internal needs. See the Industry Communique for a discussion of how attempts to contain costs have led to increased attention to customer's needs.

INDUSTRY COMMUNIQUE

HOTELS TRIM GUEST PERKS, GIRD FOR '90S

Doug Carroll

The frill is gone. In the 1980s, hotels cluttered bathroom counters with more soaps, shampoos, conditioners and mouthwashes than their guests used at home. No more. In the 1990s, extravagance is out and frugality is in. Hotels, many of them struggling, are getting in tune with the times:

- *"We are guilty of turning our bathrooms into mini-apothecaries. We need to re-examine what guests want," says Jonathan Tisch, president of Loews Hotels.*
- *"The product we developed in the '80s is not a product the customer is willing to buy in the '90s," says Hyatt Hotels President Darryl Hartley-Leonard. "You are going to see some of the amenity lunacy of the 1980s disappear."*

Hotel restaurants that don't make money are being closed. Middle-management jobs are being combined or eliminated. Guest rooms are being stocked with smaller bottles of shampoo and soap bars. Some hotels have stopped putting sewing kits in bathrooms and are providing them only when asked.

"Wherever they can cut—no matter how small—they're doing that," says hotel consultant Saul Leonard. "Hotels are rethinking how they operate. They will focus more on what guests want and eliminate frills that don't produce customers."

In fact, hotel executives are starting to ask customers what they want. They're finding guests don't necessarily want all the conveniences of home or office in their room as long as they know the hotel can provide them if needed.

Hilton Hotels President Carl Mottek says hotels must adapt their services for guests paying a wide range of rates. While Hilton provides room service for guests in the luxury sections of many of its business-center hotels, it also sets up coffee and doughnut bars for budget-conscious guests who consider breakfast in hotel restaurants too expensive.

Change is long overdue. Hotels are fighting for survival after a decade in which the number of hotel rooms grew faster than the number of travelers. About 60% of all hotels will lose money this year, and their losses will average $1,200 a room, says hotel analyst Bjorn Hanson of Coopers & Lybrand.

The problem is that hotel rates—flat for the past four years—don't come close to covering most hotels' costs. Average rates at first-class hotels are half what they need to be for them to break even, says William Hulett, president of Stouffer Hotels. "You can get a first-class hotel room for $80 a night," he says. "You can't get a first-class room in other parts of the world for $80 a night. We're entirely out of whack."

Hotel executives blame themselves. "In the '80s, we did a wonderful job of spoiling our guests, and now the realities of the '90s may not allow that to continue," says Tisch.

Industry executives insist they're only cutting things guests don't really care about. "When you serve a Bloody Mary, do you need a bloody vegetable garden on top?" says Hartley-Leonard. "You don't have to have an entire fruit salad with your breakfast on the side of the plate.

"The customer has changed," he says. "It is virtually immoral in this country to order a $120 bottle of champagne. And is it not true that traveling around in a full-stretch limousine is just a little decadent today?"

Hyatt's 39 limousines are for sale and will be replaced by Lincoln Town Cars. Bathrooms once stocked with three washcloths and three hand towels now get two each, saving Hyatt $3 million a year. Its restaurants are no longer garnishing plates with fresh strawberries, saving $1 million a year.

Hartley-Leonard, observing companies increasingly clamping down on travel and entertainment expenses, has instructed hotel chefs to plan more entrees that can be sold for $12.95 instead of $22.94. Lafitte-Rothschild, which sells for upwards of $195 a bottle, has been stricken from every wine list.

Hotels are making cuts in ways that are visible and invisible to guests. The Smithtown, N.Y., Sheraton, which is in receivership, converted its luxury dining room to a meeting room, says Stephen Brener, whose consulting firm manages the hotel. In addition, "we cut back on the number of road signs because we didn't think it would produce the amount of business it did four or five years ago," Brener says.

Some hotels are eliminating whole layers of assistant managers and combining departments. Hyatt recently cut 1,000 middle-management jobs. Loews has reduced its staff 5% this year. Marriott has a hotel restaurant in Fort Lauderdale, Fla., with no managers—the employees manage themselves.

Aside from saving money, hotel executives say their larger objective is to please customers. More hotels are giving employees on the front lines the authority to solve guests' problems instead of running off to ask their bosses what to do. "You don't need a manager to tell you your meal wasn't right," says Marriott Hotels President William Tiefel.

Hotels also are looking to technology such as voice mail to help them save money. Voice mail frees operators from taking messages and bellmen from delivering them.

Automated check-in and check-out creates labor savings, too. Starting February 1, Hyatt's toll-free telephone number for early check-in—now offered only to members of its frequent-guest program—will be available to every customer.

In the long run, the changes hotels are making now will help them earn higher prices later. Once some of the older hotels are closed and demand catches up with supply, higher rates are inevitable. But not right away. Hartley-Leonard believes It will be another four years before the hotel industry sees the growth it enjoyed in the 1980s. "I believe the let's-make-a-deal mentality will continue," says Hartley-Leonard. His slogan: "Survive 'til '95."

USA Today, International Edition, December 4, 1991.

Quality service requires management support at all levels to encourage customer service. In addition, all customer contact personnel must receive training in the technical skills and psychological knowledge needed to be truly service oriented. Management support and careful training can help customer contact personnel avoid spoiling an otherwise excellent service product.

Marketing and sales personnel in all areas of travel and tourism are often the source of first impressions for travelers and potential travelers. We must develop the relationships necessary for providing high quality service. We also must have enough knowledge of how our own organizations operate to be effective problem solvers and get things done for our clients.

Our company knowledge should include all areas of importance to our clients. We must understand not only the products and services themselves, but reservations procedures and potential post-travel problems. One often forgotten area is accounting. If our clients return with payment or improper charges problems, we must be able to facilitate solutions, in order to keep our clients' confidence in our ability to meet their needs. The Industry Communique discusses how the hotel industry is attempting to meet customers' needs.

INDUSTRY COMMUNIQUE

DECADE OF THE GUEST

Brenda Fine

Browning held that "All service ranks the same with God." Perhaps. But most hoteliers feel that business travelers are a good deal more finicky. If the past decade has been chaotic in the skies, it's been something of a scramble on the ground, too, with hotels squaring off in heated combat. It seems every possible enticement has been used to woo the business traveler: all-suite hotels, airport hotels, hotels with waterfall lobbies, hotels within hotels, and, of course, frequent stayer programs.

But after all the trumpets and trumpery had subsided, it turned out that what the guests wanted was that old standby: service.

"There is probably no issue more important to the travel industry today than service," observes Darryl Hartley-Leonard, president of Hyatt Hotels Corporation. "Anybody can build a first-class hotel—there's really no trick to getting the best rooms, the best decorator, the best facilities, and all the rest. The real trick is being able to present the very best in service."

It seems everyone, from the CEO to the hotelier to the concierge, agrees: service is the key. The unfortunate rub, though, is that no one agrees on just what service is. Indeed, it's a tricky problem, since service, like a great work of art, seems to be all things to all people.

In the last ten years or so, hotels have been a lot more successful at ferreting out just exactly what guests don't like: they hate long lines when checking in, and they don't want to waste time with elaborate checkouts. They can't stand unreliable wake-up calls and are even more irritated by garbled messages from the front desk. They resent feeling cramped, crowded, rushed, or dismissed.

Still, the question remains: what do they want? Turn-down chocolates, valets, high-tech efficiency? And what is service, anyway?

As difficult as it may be to formulate a precise definition, every hotelier is nonetheless quick to assert that whatever service is, his hotel has it.

"A customer may forget his luggage, or his manners—but he'll never forget how he was treated," declares Jonathan Tisch, president and CEO of Loews

Hotels. Loews's seventeen disparate hotels are each focused on being recognized as the leading property in its market. Tisch, in full agreement with the theory of "guest expectation," argues that guests as his posh Regency Hotel in New York City, paying a $200 room rate, receive the same service as those staying at the Summit, another Loews Hotel just ten blocks away, where the room rate is only $125. The difference, Tisch explains, lies in the physical plant: more elaborate rooms, real crystal, linen, silver, upscale restaurants. Says Tisch, "We've done a great job of spoiling the customer. We've successfully raised his expectation level—now we have to keep on meeting and exceeding it."

At Four Seasons, the emphasis is on employee training. Their policy, according to the chairman, president, and CEO Isadore Sharp, is to train every employee to think through a problem and act on it quickly, to never pass the buck. A guest won't ever hear the old "It's not my job" excuse. In return, employees are secure in the knowledge that they will always be backed up by their superiors for taking the initiative. As Sharp explains, "If they make a wrong decision, that's something that can be corrected later. At least they acted in good faith. This is part of our commitment. We can risk losing money—that can always be regained. But not our integrity, our credibility. Once that is lost, it can never be regained."

What about the traditional wisdom that says the typical American worker is sort of a blue collar-snob who feels that a job in the service industry is beneath him? Nonsense, declares Hyatt's Hartley-Leonard: "The problem is not that people don't want to do the work; the problem is management. Show me an example of poor service and I'll show you a manager who's a jackass."

Horst Schulze, president and CEO of the Ritz-Carlton Hotel Company, agrees. "Service is the business we're in. But we're not servants. We're ladies and gentlemen serving ladies and gentlemen." In fact, not only he, but every employee at each Ritz-Carlton hotel carries a laminated card that spells out the company's credo of the ideal hotel-guest relationship in his or her pocket. The credo consists of three basic Steps of Service, written by Schulze more than ten years ago: 1. warm and sincere greeting. 2. Anticipation and compliance with guest needs. 3. A fond farewell.

And the credo works. Schulze recounts the story of the Ritz-Carlton guest who walked out of his room carrying an empty ice bucket. A maintenance man was kneeling nearby, fixing the hall carpeting. When the guest asked him for directions to the ice machine, the employee jumped to his feet, saying, "Let me get the ice for you, sir."

Schulze's point: "That guest really didn't want directions. He wanted ice. And that's exactly what that maintenance man gave him."

Stan Bromley couldn't agree more. For Bromley, who is a regional vice president of Four Seasons Hotels as well as general manager of the Washington, D.C. property, "The ultimate high is hearing from a guest that one of your employees has done something wonderful—all on his own, and just because he wanted to."

Bromley, acknowledged by his peers as responsible for some of the best-run hotels in the business (he was general manager of the Four Seasons Clift in San Francisco before moving to D.C.), believes in treating his employees as well as he expects them to treat the guests. His list of "fundamental dignities" to which they're entitled includes top-quality food, uniforms that are attractive and well-fitted, and clean and pleasant locker rooms.

The "happy guest" experience seems to hinge on this employee initiative. After all, it is the bellman, the doorman, or some other "front line" employee who really creates the lasting impression of any hotel.

J.W. Marriott, the second-generation chairman of the board and president of the Marriott Corporation, believes it's no longer enough just to please the customer—"you must delight the customer." And, Marriott believes, the logical way to do this is to find out exactly what it is that the customer really wants. A man of his word, Marriott even designed an entire hotel segment—Courtyards by Marriott—based on what business travelers had told him they wanted. They didn't pine after fancy restaurants or a choice of workout equipment, but instead the basics: clean, well-designed rooms; a simple restaurant; a generic health club. In short, a no-frills environment that would be administered by caring personnel.

Back in the eighties, hotels delivered the services they thought the guests would or should want. Finally, somebody got a bright idea of asking the guests. Today, millions of dollars are spent on research determining exactly what appeals to guests.

Those guest comment cards, for instance, are invaluable tools to hotel managers. The average guest, idly checking off items on the card while eating breakfast and watching "Today," has no idea of the impact his casual comments will have, how carefully his every word of praise or criticism will be scrutinized and analyzed. Most hoteliers hold weekly meetings at which every card is discussed, its contents tracked and researched. Employees who have been cited favorably are rewarded; heads may roll over unfavorable comments. And policies are set.

What are the things today's guests hate the most? Telephone surcharges top most lists. The fervor of guest protests over these outrageous charges led Stouffer's president William Hulett, to eliminate them altogether. "We want our level of service to be memorable—not our bills," quips Hulett, who figures that, although this move cost his company about $3 million in revenues, it was worth it for the goodwill it has generated. "The ultimate challenge," says Hulett, "is achieving consistent customer satisfaction—an important part of which is not to nickel-and-dime them to death." Toward this end, Hulett has eliminated another loathsome charge: the per-page charge for incoming faxes. He reasons that people don't have the option to refuse these things. He also has established a hot line that puts Stouffer's guests in direct contact with the general manager twenty-four hours a day.

In seeking answers, hotels have made good use of advisory boards, panels of frequent travelers, loyal guests, and other experts eager to give their input. In addition to designing the Courtyards concept, Marriott's customer forums have resulted in a series of service guarantees to the guest that promises delivery of breakfast at Marriott restaurants in five minutes (or it's free), a similar promise of fifteen-minute room service breakfast, and a guarantee against overbooking. The expert panels of Hyatt's Travel Futures Project helped to identify the "love-hate" relationship most business travelers have with being on the road, which, in turn, prompted Hyatt to install more homelike touches, such as twenty-four-hour room service, better reading lights, and television remote controls.

The advisory board of Swissotel, composed of a revolving membership of frequent travelers and industry executives, pooled its knowledge to determine details of the Swissotel Atlanta before it was built. They vetoed bidets and voted for hairdryers, opposed in-room safes and favored several phones with multiple lines. Amid the flurry of details that dominated the discussion at a recent meeting—how big the room should be, the size of the soap, the number of towels—emerged the main theme: a guest wants to be made to feel important from the minute he walks through the door. "VIP-ness boils down to service," concluded the Swissotel Advisory Board. "This is the bottom line in hotel excellence: treat them like gods for the day."

But not all traveling gods are so well-treated, according to figures recently released by Opinion Research Corporation. This Princeton, N.J.-based marketing research firm recently polled 400 executives from Fortune 500 and Fortune Service 500 and Dun & Bradstreet's Million Dollar Directory to find out their priorities when they travel. (These are people who travel on business an average of forty-five days a year, with about thirty-four nights spent in hotels, thirty-four plane trips, and twenty rental car days.) Of the three industries covered—hotels, rental cars, and airlines—hotels scored highest in demonstrating that their personnel care about customers. (Other major hotel considerations of those polled included billing accuracy, efficient check-in, and reliable message services.) Westin Hotels emerged the winner, ranking first in overall customer satisfaction, with 71 percent of the 400 executives giving them high marks.

"I'm not surprised. Pleased—but not surprised," responded Westin's president and CEO, Larry Magnan, when told of the results. Westin relies heavily on its Guest Satisfaction Service, a random sampling of some 250 to 300 guests each night, systemwide. This is a lengthy questionnaire, far more detailed than the usual in-room comment card; Westin rewards each person who fills out a completed form with a $5 token thank you.

One outstanding result of these questionnaires was Westin's installation of an electronic voice mail system. "Our guests told us in no uncertain terms that they wanted—indeed, demanded—accurate messages. So we went with the best, a system that allows callers to leave spoken messages—in their own language. No mix-ups, no confusion. Everybody's happy," says Magnan. So successful was this system that Westin now uses it throughout its corporate offices as well.

There are some who believe American-style service is the wave of the future. Hyatt's Darryl Hartley-Leonard believes that America's folksy, friendly attitude uniquely positions the U.S. to set global standards for hotel service in the future. "In Asia, the style is slightly subservient. In Europe, employees are expected to 'know their place,'" he explains. "Neither of those attitudes washes here in the States. I believe the rest of the world is evolving to where we are now. Our style of service is appropriate to the world today."

In the final analysis, service isn't about outrageous pampering (although that's wonderful sometimes)." It's about offering a genuine welcome, about consistently delivering a level of comfort that provides a buffer against the hassles of travel.

This is, after all, what hospitality is all about.

Frequent Flyer, September, 1990.

An interesting corollary can be derived from the Third Law of Service:

Eliminate the need for service and you are giving good service.

Remember the Maytag repairman? He is so lonely because no one ever calls him to repair a Maytag—Maytag products are so reliable. By eliminating the need for service, Maytag developed a reputation for excellence. Many companies have developed reputations for high-quality service by following this corollary alone.

Eliminating the need for service is very possible within the tourism industry. Simplification and elimination of services is especially effective in the "mass" services sectors such as airlines, car rental firms, and even hotels. Travelers seek hassle-free experiences, and the fewer direct encounters with personnel, the less chance of delay or hassle.

Advance seat reservations and boarding passes are a must for frequent flyers. Airline clubs provide special check-in facilities to reduce waiting time. Curbside baggage checking and direct passage to the gate eliminate the need to stop at the ticket counter.

Car rental companies allow regular users to bypass both the airport counter and office at the lot. Some even have the trunk open and the motor running. Portable computer terminals provide return check-in as renters leave their cars.

Hotel chains provide special check-in facilities for regular customers. Express check-out is a regular feature for credit card guests, and television billing review and check-out is becoming more popular.

CONCLUSION

The provision of quality service is essential for the profitability of businesses in the travel and tourism industry. By recognizing and understanding the laws and corollaries of service and how they can be used in the marketing process, we can assure our capability of meeting or exceeding customer expectations and thus be providing quality service.

SUMMARY

There are seven deadly sins which can spoil an otherwise excellent service product:

1. Leaving someone expecting a reply.
2. Arguing with a customer.
3. Presenting a dirty or unprofessional look.
4. Giving conflicting or incorrect information.
5. Arguing with a fellow worker in front of a customer.
6. Implying that a customer's needs are unimportant or trivial.
7. Passing the buck.

There are three laws of service plus one important corollary that help explain service as job which adds value for the customer. The First Law of Service is:

Satisfaction = Perception – Expectation.

Customer expectations fall into seven categories:

1. Accessibility
2. Courtesy
3. Personal Attention
4. Empathy
5. Job Knowledge
6. Consistency
7. Teamwork

The Second Law of Service emphasizes the importance of perceptions:

First Impressions are the most important.

The Third Law of Service suggests that philosophy and inter-relationships are not enough:

A service-oriented attitude alone will not assure good service.

An important corollary states:

Eliminate the need for service and you are giving good service.

QUESTIONS FOR DISCUSSION AND THOUGHT

1. How do perceptions and expectations affect customer satisfaction?
2. Describe the categories of customer expectations.
3. What are the seven deadly sins of service and why are they important?
4. Why are first impressions most important?
5. Why won't a service-oriented attitude alone assure provision of good service?
6. Describe travel and tourism situations where the elimination of the need for service improved service.

16

Technology and Marketing

computer reservations system (CRS)
database
desktop publishing
facsimile transmission (fax)
functionality
personal computer (PC)
spreadsheet
videotape
WATS service
word processing

The development of technology over the past 25 years has had a profound effect on marketing processes. It has, for the most part, been a positive effect, with the products of technology enabling marketers to develop and strengthen relationships and communicate more effectively. Computers, electronic telephone systems, videotape equipment, and facsimile transmission (fax) equipment have become important tools for the marketing process.

COMPUTERS

Just as they have affected almost all phases of our lives, computerization has made major contributions to the sales and marketing of virtually all aspects of travel and tourism. Computerization in the travel and tourism industry has taken place in two waves. The first wave was the implementation of reservation services, primarily for air seats, hotel rooms, and rental cars. The second wave was the development and use of the personal computer (PC) by businesses large and small.

Computer Reservations Systems (CRS)

The earliest **computer reservations systems** were developed by individual airlines in the 1960s to manage the growing inventory of airline seats available to the traveling public both on a direct basis and through travel agencies. Before computers came into use, reservations were controlled with big boards and cards at many reservations centers. When a passenger in New York wanted a seat from Los Angeles, it often could not be confirmed until the New York airline reservation agent called or telexed the Los Angeles reservations office to release the seat—a painfully slow and inefficient method.

CRS data storage and processing is handled by large main-frame computers in central locations. The computers are connected, primarily by dedicated telephone lines, with remote terminals. Thousands of terminals can be connected to the system. Today's CRS central sites can process 15,000 to 25,000 messages or more per second.

Early CRS systems transmitted data to electric typewriter terminals that printed all information in hard copy form. The move to cathode ray tube (CRT) screens greatly decreased data transmission time. Continuing improvements in telephone data transmission lines have now made it possible to transmit information almost instantaneously throughout the world.

During the 1960s and 1970s terminals were located in airports, airline reservations centers, and airline ticket offices. By the end of the 1970s, airlines began installing CRS terminals in large numbers of travel agencies. Within 10 years more than 98% of the nation's travel agencies had CRS terminals in their offices.

As CRS development progressed, their functionality increased. Hotel and car rental reservations were a natural addition. Automatic fare calculation eliminated the need for maintenance of airline tariff books. Computer-generated tickets replaced both hand-written tickets and teleticketing machines. Seat selection capability was soon followed by issuance of boarding passes for most domestic flights. See the Industry Communiques for latest developments in automated ticket/boarding passes.

INDUSTRY COMMUNIQUE

LEARNING YOUR ATBs

Jim Glab

When it comes to better tickets and easier boarding procedures, Japan has the edge: travelers simply insert a boarding pass into a machine when boarding a plane. The machine reads a magnetic stripe on the back of the pass encoded with data about seating, baggage, and passenger preferences.

That technology will soon be available to travelers in the U.S., along with new kinds of ticket delivery options—two developments that should reduce the time spent waiting in line at airport counters.

Frequent flyers may have noticed that some airlines have already replaced the traditional ticket and boarding pass with a single piece of stiff paper, resembling a punch-in computer card. The document is known as an automated ticket/boarding pass, or ATB. What's new is the magnetic stripe that has begun to appear on the back of some ATBs (called ATB2s).

Actually, magnetic-stripe technology has been within the reach of the airlines for years. Both United and Continental employ "magstripes" on their ATBs. "We've been using it for almost two years," said Greg Zarelli, director of technology planning at Continental Airlines. According to Zarelli, the magnetic stripes on Continental's ATBs are being used to track passenger names, seating information, the ticket's sequence number, and certain security applications. "Basically, everything that's on the face of the ticket is encoded on the stripe," he said.

United's magnetic boarding pass includes the passenger's name, the flight, date, seat data, and frequent flyer number as well as the level they're at in that program, and any special customer identification such as unaccompanied minors or military.

The problem is, no U.S. carriers have yet deployed the readers—the devices at the gate that "read" the magnetic data. Resistance from some airlines, notably American, has held things up. The carrier has questioned whether installation of the readers is worth the expense. Recently, however, American has had a change of heart; the airline has agreed to put mag-stripe technology in place by April 1996. Says Terry Jones, a product development specialist with American's Sabre computer division: "The acceptance of ATBs is going up rapidly, and more and more travelers like it—they don't get red carbons on their shirts."

American's decision has enabled the industry to move ahead. Last summer, U.S. and international carriers finally agreed on a common format for encoding data in the stripe, which will enable one airline's readers to decode another airline's—and hence make installation of the readers worthwhile.

Continental is all set to go. "At Newark's Terminal C, all the gates and jetway are already wired," said Zarelli. "We're going to start doing some testing with a new reader in about a month, and we've given our specs [for readers] to a lot of different companies."

Once the readers are in place the benefits to the airlines will be manifold. For starters, they will be able to check the fare data on the mag-stripe to make sure the passenger has been charged the correct price for the flight. And if he hasn't?

According to Renee Martocchio, an executive in United Airlines's customer service planning department, "If we find that the customer is due a refund after the fact, especially if it's [charged to] a credit card, we'll do everything possible to get a refund back to the customer." If it's an undercharge, "the customer just gets a cheaper ride." If a travel agent issued the ticket, "we're still not going to penalize the customer," she said. "We'd go back to the travel agent."

The mag-stripe technology also will enable the airlines to detect stolen tickets—of which there are tens of thousands a year. "If the reader identifies a stolen ticket, the procedure might be to let the passenger on and do something at the other end—alert security when the aircraft arrives," said Zarelli.

Other functions of the mag-stripe ATBs are speeding up data entry and quickly matching up the boarded passengers with reservations lists. But what's in all this for the business traveler?

"I think you'll see a lot of improvements in passenger service," said Zarelli. "Currently it's very difficult, with the last-minute rush, to property process the passenger and do all the things we'd like to do for him, such as make sure there are no seat duplications and that people are on the right aircraft. I've seen instances where the plane pulled back from the gate and there was a passenger on the wrong aircraft, going to the wrong city. It's very tough to verify all the things that need to be verified at the last minute."

When the system is tied into existing baggage tag scanner devices and new scanners that will check baggage being loaded, "we can verify that baggage is on the right aircraft," Zarelli said. The frequent flyer who misses his flight and tries to catch the next one out on another airline shouldn't have any problems with the new ATBs, since they will encode data in a format that can be instantly deciphered by other airlines' readers.

"If anything, it might even help in that situation," Zarelli said. "You can read the information off the stripe and compare it with a data file that tells you, 'Yes, this type of fare basis can be accepted without any questions, it doesn't need to be endorsed.' You can do a lot more electronically, which really helps the agent and the customer."

Zarelli predicts that airlines will also use the technology to butter up their best customers: "I think you'll see the customer treated more personally. What we're intending to do is have the reader display the customer's name, so our gate agents can greet him. If the passenger is one of the Elite members of our frequent flyer program, we'll do something special for him—such as find out what the customer's preferences are for meal service or drink service, so we can put it on a flight attendant printout and be able to serve that customer a little more quickly."

Another application of new ATB technology—deployment of so-called "satellite ticket printers"—means that travelers away from home who need a new ticket issued, or an existing ticket reissued quickly due to an itinerary change, won't have to wait in line at the airport ticket counter. Whenever the business traveler needs his ticket reissued, he simply contacts his corporate travel agency, and the agency can electronically order the ticket printed out at a location that could be as close as the lobby of the traveler's hotel.

Some of these remote ATB printers, which are distributed by firms such as Hoteleticket, National Ticketing Network, and QDAT (Quick Delivery Airline Tickets), are already in place in hotels. Although those firms had to obtain airline accreditation as travel agencies in order to handle ATB stock, the airlines recently agreed to rule changes that will permit vendors to operate networks of printers without going through the agency accreditation process. This means that many new printers will soon be available to the traveler.

One of the new printers is located in the lobby of the Novotel New York. Michael Kirschenbaum, the hotel's front desk manager, said the hotel acquired the printer because "there was no cost to us, and it enables us to provide our guests with a valuable travel service." He added that "there's very little for us to do: the guest makes his own arrangements with the travel agency through a special toll-free number and then goes over to the printer and picks up his ticket."

The latest generation of printers will have the capability to issue not only the new mag-stripe ATBs, but also "almost any negotiable instrument," said Robert Danoff, vice president of marketing for Dallas-based QDAT. His firm's printers issue ATBs as well as itinerary summaries with graphic symbols representing air, hotel, and rental car segments, and can even print maps and issue traveler's checks.

QDAT has printers in some 200 hotels now, and the company expects to move into Canada and Europe before the end of this year, said Danoff, who was formerly an executive with American's Sabre computer subsidiary. Ultimately, he said, QDAT expects to have about 1,600 printers in the field—in hotels, in courier offices for hand delivery, in office parks that serve several companies, and in airports.

Some airline planners contend that there's no longer a need for travelers to carry any kind of ticket or boarding pass; some form of personal ID to match identity with the passenger's computer-stored records is all that's really required for check-in. But Danoff said he doesn't think travelers are ready for "ticketless travel."

"There's a security factor," he said. "Travelers are nervous if they go to the airport without a ticket. When you tell them, 'This little plastic thing has a chip in it, don't worry, it's all in there,' they still worry."

Who wouldn't?

Frequent Flyer, October, 1990.

INDUSTRY COMMUNIQUE

END TO LOST-LUGGAGE BLUES

Megan Mackenzie

Standing in front of the baggage claim carousel, you watch countless pieces of luggage go by. People surround you from all sides, staring apprehensively at the ramp from which the luggage emerges out of a black hole, hoping it will produce the one thing that will make or break this traveling experience: their luggage. You watch the relief and joy of fellow travelers as they reunite with their luggage.

You look at them with a longing glance only for a short, envying moment, for fear that if you take your eyes off the black hole for a split second too long, you might miss your luggage.

Turning back to the carousel, you hope that your suitcase will be the next one down, having made it through the adventure of air travel.

This apprehension is what many travelers habitually encounter when they fly, in rain, sleet, snow or even sunny weather. The dilemma of lost luggage seems to be a hopeless one, as travelers across the nation have learned the hard way. Lost luggage can ruin a trip for even the most prepared and experienced traveler. Anxiety begins from the moment a traveler checks his or her bags in at the ticketing counter.

To help relieve this anxiety, Northwest Airlines has developed a program that demonstrates its dedication to improving luggage handling and awareness. According to Joe Leonard, Executive Vice President of Customer Service, the program, named "The Future is in Your Hands," is part of Northwest's 1992 "Year of the Customer" declaration. "Now that Northwest has accomplished its goal of being the on-time airline, the best way to follow up such a challenge is to become number one in luggage handling as well," says Leonard. He adds that by listening to both customers' and luggage handlers' ideas, Northwest has taken the first steps in implementing programs that will ensure a feeling of security for the Northwest traveler.

"We aim to be the number one airline with the fewest complaints in luggage handling."

One program that Northwest has emphasized is the improvement of bag checking using a new automated system. Luggage tags are automatically printed for the passenger from the Passenger Name Record (PNR). When the passenger, flight number and number of bags are input, the computer prints out tags that specify the luggage's destination. These tags help cut back on simple human errors; for example, the destination MQT (Marquette, Michigan) being misread as MOT (Minot, North Dakota), and the luggage then sent to the wrong destination. "This basic change reduced mischecked luggage by 3.3 percent in indoor checking stations last year," says Leonard.

The notable improvements with the indoor automated luggage system have led to experimentation with outdoor curb-side check-in stations. An estimated 20 percent of all luggage is checked at the curb by sky caps and is often a prime spot for luggage mix-ups. In January, the outdoor systems were tested in two extreme weather airports, Tampa and Minneapolis/St. Paul. The stations upheld the outdoor test with few adjustments, but had yet to face the final and telling assessment from the sky caps. The sky caps approved of the stations despite the extra step it took them to type in passenger information. The predicted 33 percent reduction in mischecks is worth the extra step, and will reduce passenger stress as well. Since April 1992, outdoor checking stations have been installed at all airports across the country that have such a service available.

Other Northwest "The Future is in Your Hands" programs being implemented to put customers' minds at ease include elimination of human error to the greatest extent possible in luggage handling. Better communication lines are being opened between the luggage handlers and the terminals, making baggage changes, transfers, loading and unloading easier and more efficient. Additional training classes and recognition of outstanding performances by workers are being incorporated into Northwest's employee programs. Employees are being encouraged to look at things from the passenger's point of view, considering the importance of the luggage to the traveler and the success of their traveling experience.

In addition to these improvements, Northwest has also been noted for its new Priority Pet program for customers traveling with animals.

To supplement new programs going into effect, Northwest has placed great emphasis on educating passengers as to luggage transport. It is up to passengers as well as check-in employees to specify and double-check luggage tags. Passengers late for a flight must understand that in this situation, their luggage may not make it on the flight. When passengers are aware of these facts, then there is less misunderstanding and confusion in the long run.

With the knowledge of Northwest's extra efforts to improve luggage handling, passengers will be able to rest a little easier at baggage check-in. They might even relax as they wait at baggage claim, knowing that their bags will be there. "This change is just one of the ways Northwest is working to let customers know they are valued," says Leonard. "The airline is committed to maintaining customer loyalty and to making flying an enjoyable and relaxing experience."

Reprinted from Northwest Airlines World Magazine, August 1992.

CRS systems provided major productivity gains to both airlines and travel agencies. It was truly serendipitous that the development of CRS systems for travel agencies accompanied deregulation. It would have been impossible for travel agencies to help their clients secure the lowest fares without assistance from sophisticated CRS systems.

The same systems allowed airlines to develop complex yield management techniques to control the number of seats sold at different fare levels on each flight each day. For example, since Monday morning and Friday afternoon flights are popular with business travelers, yield management will limit the number of seats available at the lowest excursion fares on those days. Airlines set parameters for the yield for every flight. Adjustments can be made either adding or reducing seats at specific fare levels as the date of the flight approaches. Management personnel use previous flight history (same day last year, day of the week demand, etc.) and information on other market conditions to set parameters and actual sales results to modify them.

The demise of World Airways and PeopleExpress, two low-fare airlines that both grew and died during the height of deregulation, can be directly attributed, at least partially, to the lack of sophisticated computer technology. World set low fares, but could not practice effective yield management. PeopleExpress also lacked the sophisticated systems of its competitors. "Technology is a powerful competitive tool," stated former PeopleExpress President Donald Burr at a 1992 information technology symposium sponsored by IBM.

Hotels and car rental companies also developed their own computer reservations systems, which connected terminals in hotels and car rental sales offices (primarily at airports) with central reservations computers. Linkage of hotel and car rental computers with airline CRS systems made one-stop shopping for air, hotel, and car rentals a reality, especially through travel agencies. Clearly, CRS functionality was a major force during the 1980s in the growth of the travel agency as the primary distribution system for business and commercial travel.

From a marketing standpoint, CRS systems enable all segments of the industry to develop the personalization clearly required for successful relationship marketing. Client profiles assure travel agents that the seat, meal, and other special needs of regular clients will always be included in reservation requests. Car rental companies can track the size and even the make and model preferences of frequent renters. Hotel chains can store guest preference information and have it available for the front desk agent when guests arrive. Follow-up letters of thanks can be generated automatically.

Future CRS functionality will benefit leisure segments of the travel and tourism industry in the 1990s as the functionality of the 1980s benefited commercial segments. Access to cruise reservations by travel agencies exists on a limited basis today; it should be universal within a few years. Direct bookings of

"I am surrounded by the world's greatest automation and...I miss WALK-INS!"

independent, hosted, and escorted tours is also growing. Allowing computer access to leisure products will increase the productivity (and thus, the profitability) of leisure-oriented travel agencies and their suppliers as well.

The Personal Computer (PC)

Airline, hotel, and car rental reservations are now accessible to anyone with a PC and modem through public computer networks such as Prodigy and Compuserve. American Airlines' Easy Sabre permits public access to the Sabre CRS with user-friendly inputs. Tickets can be picked up at an American Airlines office or a travel agency. Corporate versions of Apollo, Sabre, and other CRS systems permit companies and business travelers to make their own reservations on a home or office PC with their reservation automatically sent to their travel agency for ticketing. In this manner, the PC operates almost as if it were a CRS terminal in the agency.

Although the PC can be used as a CRS terminal, it has become a far more useful marketing tool in all segments of the travel and tourism industry. Word processing, database management, spreadsheets, communication, and desktop publishing have become powerful PC functions for businesses of all sizes.

Word Processing

The word processing program has replaced the typewriter in many offices. With word processing, form letters can be saved on disk and used as the basis for personalized, individually printed letters, giving, with little additional effort, a more professional appearance than a duplicated form. Operations and training manuals can be stored through word processing, printed as needed, and easily amended without having to retype an entire manual or chapter.

Database Management

With database management, client or traveler histories of all types can be stored. Personalized sales letters can be sent to any or all of those on the database. Depending on the message to be sent, selections from the database can be made based on demographic background or client/traveler interests as indicated in their files. In addition to producing personalized letters, the database can easily be used to print mailing labels for the envelopes.

A hotel or tour operator, for example, could send personalized sales letters to all travel agencies in its database, to those in a specific geographic area, or to agents who have expressed interest in the hotel's meeting facilities or in a specific destination served by the tour operator. A travel agency could send a letter to all clients or just to those interested in cruising, family travel, or both.

Databases can be used to keep track of the preferences, predilections, and characteristics of customers to customize service and encourage repeat business.

Ritz Carlton Hotels, for example, keeping track of favorite rooms, foods, and reading material of nearly 500,000 frequent guests.

A number of specialized database management programs have been developed for tracking the sales process. Prospect lists can be maintained, including records of sales calls, comments on account potentials, and schedules of follow-up visits. A sales calendar with reminders of things to do is an integral part of these programs. Weekly and monthly sales reports can also be generated.

Spreadsheets

The spreadsheet function makes number crunching and "what if" games easy. The spreadsheet will automatically calculate the effects of changing one or more numbers on all the other numbers that are affected by them. For example, how different rates of sales affect the profitability of a cruise or tour could be determined using a spreadsheet.

Other aspects of the marketing planning process are analyzable as well. Hotels can determine break-even points in terms of occupancy rates and room pricing assumptions. Travel agencies can develop group pricing models to assure that all contingencies are covered as well as proper calculation of potential profit.

Communication Programs

Communication programs enable PCs to link with other computer systems in remote locations, using a modem and telephone lines. Cruisematch 2000, for example, is Royal Caribbean Cruise Lines' (RCCL) reservations system. Cruise-only and other travel agencies can use the PC to access RCCL's system.

Airline and other travel industry sales representatives use communication software with their PCs (often portable laptop models) to send and receive information and reports from their regional or national offices, thus having up-to-the-minute sales information at their fingertips. The light laptop PC provides full PC power and functionality anywhere in the world. Sales representatives can literally bring their office systems to their client's or prospect's location.

Desktop Publishing

Desktop publishing is a major marketing benefit available through the PC. By using appropriate software and an ink jet or laser printer, professional, camera-ready brochures, flyers, advertisements, and so forth can be produced quickly and inexpensively in-house. Add a scanner and virtually any drawing can be stored for later use in a printed document. A small hotel or tour operator can now design and develop its own brochures. A local airline district sales office can develop its own promotional materials and maintain the image set by headquarters. Cruise lines now produce their daily activity sheets on-board, using desktop publishing.

Travel agencies can produce newsletters and flyers quickly and inexpensively to maintain high levels of communication with their clients.

The desktop publishing function eliminates the need for either using an outside typesetting firm or maintaining expensive photocomposition equipment. Speed and flexibility are added benefits. Deadlines can be met more easily as well as last minute needs fulfilled. Of course, it does require some time for workers to develop proficiency in the use of these programs.

TELEPHONE SYSTEMS

Just as computer system developments have brought the power of computerization to the smallest firms in travel and tourism, computer technology has brought great improvements in both telephone systems and telephone communication. Modern, multifunction telephones are available to both small and large organizations. Inbound and outbound "Wide Area Telephone Service" (WATS) lines, along with competitive long-distance service companies, have brought long-distance telephone costs to their lowest levels ever.

Electronic telephone systems for small companies provide many of the features previously only available on big systems. Transfer and intercom capability has been available for many years. However, "Station Message Detail Reports (SMDR)" are relatively new on smaller systems. SMDRs record call-by-call usage (number called, time, length of call, and so forth) of each telephone station for total management control of telephone communications. Voice mail programs are also available for small systems.

Reservations centers and large commercial travel agencies can purchase or lease communication control equipment that handles many incoming lines and automatically directs calls to available reservations agents. Management reports on systems usage, length of waiting time, lost calls (customer hung up before being connected to an agent) and length of call time are automatically compiled and printed as needed. These systems are, in reality, combined computer/telephone systems.

WATS Lines

Inbound WATS lines allow businesses to extend their communications capability nationwide. Customers either within a specific geographic area or from all over the country can call a toll-free 800 number and be connected to the business that subscribed to it. Small companies can use "800 Ready-Line," a toll-free service that does not require a separate phone line and still provides inbound service to their customers at modest cost.

Outbound WATS service is designed for heavy users of outbound calls. It provides a high degree of cost control, taking advantage of competition in the phone service field.

Telemarketing has become a force in the travel and tourism field. Because of the high cost of sales calls, many travel suppliers have established formal telemarketing programs to maintain contact with and provide information to both travel agencies and corporate clients. Airlines, cruise lines, hotels, rental car companies, and tour operators all use telemarketing to some extent. Some have formally categorized their accounts and provide differing levels of service to different accounts.

Unfortunately, telephone sales of travel products to the general public has been badly tainted by scam operations that use high pressure sales techniques to gain sales and often do not provide the products promised. Some scam artists do provide some travel services, but they are provided at substantially inflated prices. As a result, telemarketing of travel by legitimate companies has been made more difficult.

VIDEOTAPE

Twenty years ago, if an airline or travel agency wanted to show a film of a destination or travel service to a group, the only medium was 16 mm. film. If the office or agency did not own an expensive projector, they would have to have rented one. Usually, they would have to secure the film from a film library or airline or tourist office headquarters. The process was time-consuming, expensive, and often fraught with technical difficulties (film breaks, projector problems, and so forth). In those days, there was no way a prospective client could view the film at home.

The availability of both commercial and home videotape has changed the above scene completely. Videotapes are small, inexpensive to duplicate, and easy to play. The half-inch VHS format has become the standard for home and general office use. Equipment is available at virtually all hotel meeting facilities, using either a television set as a monitor for small groups or a video projector for large groups.

Travel lends itself easily to videotape. Many travel suppliers and tourist offices have developed videotapes of varying quality describing their services. Many travel agencies maintain videotape libraries, using the videos they receive either free or at very low cost from suppliers both for staff training and to lend to clients for home viewing. A few agencies have video viewing rooms for their clients, but most believe that viewing videos at the agency slows the sales process. Although a good videotape is an effective marketing support tool, it does not substitute for sales ability. See the Industry Communique for information on how the availability of videos has affected marketing in the cruise industry.

FACSIMILE TRANSMISSION (FAX)

Facsimile transmission is not new. The Associated Press and many newspaper wire services have transmitted photographs and other material over telephone lines

INDUSTRY COMMUNIQUE

REMARKS AT THE SEATRADE CRUISE SHIPPING '90 CONFERENCE

Kirk Lanterman

...The industry has observed that a significant percentage of North Americans, Europeans and Asians own home VCRs. The use of product videos also has seen considerable growth in the 1980s as cruise lines discover their considerable advantages as a sales tool. The video industry estimates that 66 percent of U.S. households owned at least one video cassette recorder in 1987. That number is expected to climb to nearly 92 percent by 1991. In addition, it is estimated that 80 percent of the travel agencies selling leisure travel are now using video—up from 30 percent in 1988 and only one percent in 1985. And a recent survey reports that 97 percent of the agents using video said it helped them close sales more effectively.

Remarks at the Seatrade Cruise Shipping '90 Conference in Miami, Fl, March 21, 1990, by Kirk Lanterman, President and CEO, Holland America Line-Westours, Inc., and Chairman, Cruise Lines International Association.

since the 1930s. The fax explosion, however, took place during the late 1980s as a result of the development of Group III fax equipment and improved communications software coupled with low-cost, mass-produced fax machines. Fax boards can also be added to office and laptop computers, providing dual functionality.

No machine has done as much to improve business communications in as short a time as the fax machine. Just a few short years ago, the question was: "Do you have a fax machine?" Today's question is: "What is your fax number?" Home faxes are as prevalent as home computers and small, portable fax machines are gaining in popularity.

The fax machine permits virtually instantaneous transmission of documents from one fax machine or computer to another over normal telephone lines. Transmission is so inexpensive that a one or two page fax can be sent almost anywhere in the United States for less than a first class postage stamp. International faxes are considerably less expensive and easier to send than telex messages.

Many travel suppliers are now using fax transmission to advise travel agencies of last minute sales of charters, tours, cruises, or other products at reduced rates. Faxes are also used frequently to present new flights, rates, routes, rules, and so forth. Travel agencies can provide commercial clients with fast, written confirmation of travel plans. In short, the fax is another marketing tool within the communications area of the marketing mix.

There is no doubt that the tools of technology have increased the productivity of operations personnel throughout the travel and tourism industry. We must realize, however, that the tools of technology have also increased the productivity of marketing personnel.

CONCLUSION

The growth of technology has had a positive effect on the marketing process. Computer reservations systems, personal computers, electronic telephone systems, videotape equipment, and facsimile transmission are all important tools that can increase marketing effectiveness if used properly.

SUMMARY

Computer reservations systems (CRS) produced the first wave of automation in many segments of the travel industry. Started for internal use by airlines in the early 1970s, CRS systems were installed in virtually all travel agencies during the 1980s.

As CRS systems developed, their functionality increased. Hotel and car reservations were natural service additions. These same systems allowed airlines to develop complex yield management techniques to maximize sales and revenue

"I wish I could fax myself to Tahiti!"

production. CRS systems or the lack of them helped strengthen strong carriers and weaken weak ones.

CRS systems are permitting all segments of the industry to develop the personalization needed for successful relationship marketing. Future developments will assist leisure travel as past developments have assisted commercial travel.

The personal computer (PC) has brought the power of technology to even the smallest of businesses in the industry. Word processing, database management, spreadsheet analysis, and desktop publishing have become management and marketing tools available to all.

Modern, multifunctional telephone systems have improved the communications capability of all segments of the industry. Both inbound and outbound WATS (wide area telephone service) services have helped control costs. Call director systems have improved the service levels of large reservations offices.

Videotape has replaced motion picture film to show destinations and travel in action. Videos are far less expensive to produce and duplicate as well as to use.

The facsimile transmission (FAX) device has revolutionized paper communications. Letters, reports, and proposals can be faxed throughout the world instantaneously, making management decisions easy, fast, and more accurate.

QUESTIONS FOR DISCUSSION AND THOUGHT

1. How have CRS systems affected the marketing process in the travel and tourism industry?
2. What are the primary functions of the personal computer?
3. How can desktop publishing be used in the marketing process?
4. How do travel agencies use videotapes effectively?
5. What is facsimile transmission and how is it used in marketing?

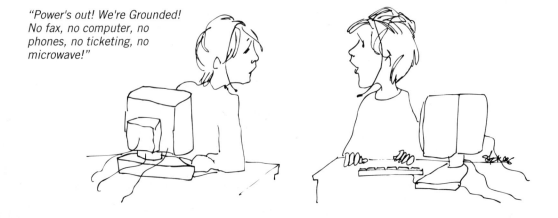

"Power's out! We're Grounded! No fax, no computer, no phones, no ticketing, no microwave!"

17

Marketing in Travel and Tourism—Present and Future

back office
code sharing
consolidation
consortium
franchise
front office
globalization
market share
merger
network
teleconferencing

As we have seen throughout this study of marketing in the travel and tourism industry, every action taken by a business affects the marketing effort. It is hard to say which part of the marketing process is most important, but it is easy to point out that all parts must work together. Cooperation and integration of all aspects of the process are necessary to obtain the final objectives of any marketing effort—the successful sale of the product or service, and the creation of a repeat clientele. Because all these parts of the marketing process are so important, they will be reviewed here.

LOOKING BACK—THE MARKETING PROCESS

The first step in the process is determining just what product is being sold. Management must look at the potential product mix and pull from it the products and services it wishes to sell. Then the manager must examine the potential market and determine what the needs are and how the company can meet these needs. The product must be tailored, if necessary, to meet these needs. Proper research must be done and a determination made of what will motivate the market to actually buy the product. The marketing mix concept should be used to guarantee a planned approach to the overall market plan.

After these decisions have been made, management must make sure that the proper image is developed for this particular market segment. Personnel must be trained to promote this image on the front line. Advertising is usually necessary to inform the potential consumers of the existence of the product and to persuade them to consider purchase. Advertising will develop leads for the business. The sales techniques discussed in Chapters Thirteen and Fourteen must then be used to actually close the sale. After the sale is made, management must make sure that what was sold is actually delivered. This will ensure satisfied customers and a continuation of the marketing cycle. Satisfied customers will help maintain a positive image for the company, and ensure the long life of the business.

LOOKING TO THE FUTURE

A discussion of marketing would not be complete without a look into the future. Many things happening now may have a considerable impact on the marketing of the travel product in the future. Some of these happenings are in the province of government and regulation; still others are sociological in nature.

"Which airline is still flying?"

After-Effects of Deregulation

When the United States Congress passed the Airline Deregulation Act of 1978, it laid down the framework for deregulating the airline industry by the end of 1984. After its passage, this law, as it was phased in, resulted in the creation and operation of many new, small airlines that operated with lower costs (newer personnel, no unions, and fewer services) and marketed primarily on the basis of price differences. The influx of these new carriers made the public much more price conscious in regard to travel, particularly air travel, than they had been previously. By the early 1990s, few of these airlines had survived, but they left the legacy of very price-conscious consumers.

Established carriers had to meet this marketing challenge. One of the methods they used successfully was the various frequent flyer programs, which reward travelers who fly regularly on the particular carrier.

These programs developed brand loyalty, a customer characteristic that had eluded the airlines in the past. Hotels and car rental companies imitated the airlines with various gift and incentive programs for the frequent customer. This is a marketing policy that will continue in the future.

Technological Changes

The advance of technology is another feature of modern life that has influenced the travel industry. The airlines created extremely sophisticated computer systems that allowed them to practice "yield management" of their fares. By allowing only a certain number of seats on any flight to be sold at low fares, airlines have been able to maximize the average fare used. Without the computer, this would not have been possible. Unfortunately, in the early 1990s, airlines suffered record losses in spite of their ability to manage their yield. As several airlines fell into serious financial trouble, they tended to create major sales, through drastically reduced air fares, to gain immediate cash flow. The stronger airlines matched the weaker ones to avoid losing "market share," the percentage of the traffic they were used to carrying.

In addition to the airlines' greatly enhanced automation capability, travel agencies also benefited from enhanced technological capability. This was true in both their front office (reservations and ticketing capability), and in the back office (accounting, management, and marketing functions).

Several hotel properties in major cities have been equipped for teleconferencing. Teleconferencing allows a group of people to see and speak through a TV hookup with others located in another place. Many forecasters believe that teleconferencing will reduce the need for travel. Others believe that rather than reducing the need for travel, teleconferencing will just change some of the methods currently used. All the members of a conference might not come to the same place, but instead might gather in four or five different cities. Each location would give the members a regional conference, and each region would be in contact with the other regions through teleconferencing. This would reduce the cost of air travel, because members could travel shorter distances.

The disadvantage of this form of meeting is, of course, the lack of the personal meetings and discussions that take place (and the business that is often accomplished) when all members are physically together. A TV or movie screen can only do so much. For this reason, many disagree on the degree to which this technology will change the nature of travel.

As their automation became more sophisticated, hotels followed the airlines with yield management. They introduced advance purchase rates and nonrefundable rates as well as a complex mix of special rates (such as a variety of levels of corporate rates). See the Industry Communique for more on technology and pricing in the future of the hotel industry.

INDUSTRY COMMUNIQUE

TRENDS

Prepared by Michael D. Olsen and Katherine Merna

For the 1990s and beyond, broad trends such as changing demographics and global political reform will continue to affect hotel consumers' buying behavior. Increasing cultural diversity will provide new marketing opportunities.

Political reforms and the move to market economies have resulted in increasing numbers of international arrivals to the United States, and this will continue. Growing interest in environmental issues and concern for healthy lifestyles also will affect buying decisions.

Responding to these trends and turning around the industry's present situation will be no easy task. The brand proliferation of the last decade will yield brand stagnation in the 1990s. While product tiering provided the necessary growth vehicle of the 1980s, deciding what to do with a national inventory of aging rooms will be the marketing challenge of this decade. This challenge will be met by firms' returning to core products and reducing the dilution of management energy and capital resulting from portfolios of hotel brands. Refocusing on the core brand will result in a greater number of more defined competitive methods used by firms as they seek to strengthen their niche.

One of the biggest challenges will result from the increasing power of the buyer, who is more price conscious. Whether it's corporate travel or dealing with megareservation systems, the buyer will be more in control. With government employees at stable or even reduced per diems and corporate managers enforcing stiffer travel policies, the focus of marketing efforts will have to shift from amenity creep to effective pricing.

Pricing will become even more of a challenge when it becomes time to refurbish tired room inventory. With a shortage of capital for this purpose and the continuing use of creative financing to accomplish desperately needed upgrading, marketing and finance activities will have to be blended more completely.

The pricing problem will be compounded by the continuing decline in the average life cycle of today's hotels. This will become a serious problem over the next 10 years.

On a more positive note, communications technology will provide outstanding marketing opportunities for both product innovation for the customer and distribution of the product to the customer. For example, with the possibilities presented by such technologies as hypermedia, the guest will be allowed to look inside the property, listen to the manager explain its competitive attributes, and make reservations, without leaving the home or office. Marketing managers must begin to look into how best to blend this fast-moving technology into current distribution systems and future marketing strategies.

In addition, the business traveler will come to expect increasing sophistication in communications technology in the hotel room itself. High-tech rooms, like non-smoking rooms, will represent an important component of differentiation. While this is not new to the astute marketing manager, it will be important to stay on top of technology to satisfy tomorrow's traveler.

Reprinted from Frequent Flyer, October 1992.

Another technological advance that might affect the marketing of the travel product has been the development and advance of the home computer system. Many forecasters feel that this will radically change the manner in which the public buys its airline tickets and makes its hotel reservations. They believe that purchasing will be done from the comfort of the living room over a two-way TV or computer system. Others believe that although a certain amount of travel will be sold in this manner, most travelers will continue to need the personal service they have come to expect. Up to the early 1990s, the home computer was more of a novelty than a basic tool for purchasing travel.

It is debatable if the home computer will ever be a major factor in the travel and tourism industry. With the present complexity of air fares and hotel rates, it is hard enough for a travel agent, working 40 hours a week on travel planning, to be sure of the "best" fare. It is almost impossible for occasional users on a home computer to be sure they are getting the "best deal." Confusion over air fares and schedules, questions about the location of hotels, sightseeing opportunities, and the need for help with travel decisions should make the travel agent distribution method necessary well into the future.

Sociological Changes

Other trends that have occurred over recent history and that should continue to occur are sociological in nature. Travel to distant places for pleasure was once the privilege of the wealthy, who took long, expensive trips. Today, travel is available to the mass public, and vacations have become shorter in length. The 2-week, 3-week or longer cruise has become less popular than the 1-week cruise, although longer cruises still fill a niche in the industry. Three and 4-day cruises are growing rapidly in popularity, with new ships being assigned to this market. Even vacations to Europe, which used to be at least 2 weeks long, are now frequently 1 week or less.

This does not mean, however, that vacations from work are still the automatic 2 weeks of the past. Workers with seniority frequently earn vacation time of 20 or more days a year. They frequently choose to spread these days through the year, thereby enjoying more than one vacation period. This trend to several shorter trips a year will probably continue into the future.

Travel by the middle class will also continue to grow as more young people become more sophisticated about the world outside their own community. In contrast to the class trip to the state capital, or perhaps all the way to Washington DC, that was common in the past, high school students today take class trips to exotic places. Often their parents may not yet have visited these destinations. Once they have tasted travel, these young people will usually continue to make travel a priority item in their budgets as they get older.

Cruises have become the fastest growing segment of the travel industry and it looks as though this should continue for at least several more years. New deluxe ships in all sizes and price ranges have been introduced since the late 1980s, and, although the number of new ships due out in the mid-1990s is somewhat less than in previous years, there will still be a growing desire for the value that a cruise represents. See the Industry Communique for a detailed look at the future of the cruise segment of the travel industry.

INDUSTRY COMMUNIQUE

SEATRADE CRUISE SHIPPING '90 CONFERENCE

Kirk Lanterman

...I'm only 100 percent certain that the cruise industry is going to continue full speed ahead in the 1990s.

Although capacity expansion was modest in 1989, in the immediate future capacity will take another huge leap upward. CLIA figures show that nearly

30,000 new berths—and 33 new ships—will be coming on line between now and 1994, including three from Holland America. In 1990 alone, 14 new ships—and 11,000 new berths—will enter service, for a 16 percent increase in capacity. When you add the ships that are planned and announced, but not yet contracted, the total number of new berths between now and the end of 1994 could rise by 36,000—or a nearly 50 percent increase in capacity in just five years.

The rate of capacity growth will slow after 1992, according to CLIA. Just two newbuilds are contracted for delivery in 1993 and one for 1994.

While the largest cruise lines won't stop building, the slowdown in construction will likely occur among the smaller lines. This, in turn, could lead to further consolidations, as the smaller lines seek to ally themselves with bigger partners with deeper pockets and deeper penetration into the distribution system.

Additional mergers will take place as some of the new niche players—and a few of the older, smaller lines—find that they are not economically viable as stand-alone companies and must align themselves with larger operators to stay in business.

By the end of the decade it's likely we will see the number of cruise lines shrink to perhaps five or six megalines, which will have several different and distinct product "brands"—much like the auto industry. CLIA figures show that by 1994, the four largest cruise companies will own 57 percent of the berths in the North American market.

Still, the attempted development of niche players, such as Renaissance, Club Med, Seabourn and Crystal, will continue through the '90s. These lines will offer products that appeal to certain, select market segments. Careful marketing and successful differentiation of their products will be key to their success.

A larger trend, however, will be the "cradle to grave" concept—the large cruise company that offers something for everyone of every age. Probably the clearest example of this is the partnership of Carnival Cruise Lines, Holland America Line and Windstar Sail Cruises. The Carnival family of companies offers products to appeal to all age groups and income levels—from the first-time cruisers who want to "get their feet wet" with a three-day Carnival cruise to the Bahamas...to the professional couple who want an exotic South Seas trip on a Windstar super-yacht...to the experienced cruiser who wants a longer world-class cruise vacation on a Holland America luxury liner. And, cross-marketing among the companies will keep our passengers "in the family."

We've recently seen the development of another interesting trend involving short cruises. The three- and four-day market traditionally was the "elephant graveyard" where elderly, fuel-guzzling ships went to pasture. But no more. The short cruise market has become a valid, viable market in response to today's trend toward short vacations of five days or less that appeal to today's dual-income couples on hectic schedules. The short cruises have always been an excellent way to sample cruising—but now those passengers are getting superb ships to sample as well.

As more and more new, modern ships are introduced in the Caribbean—still the dominant market with nearly 47 percent market share—older, smaller ships will be redeployed. The European market is becoming increasingly attractive to the major cruise lines, several of which have already based ships in Europe. The Mediterranean cruise market is rebounding to its pre-1986 levels. In addition, not only will the easing of trade restrictions in 1992 help to reduce air fares to port cities, but it is projected to raise the standard of living for Europeans, who will then have more money for travel. The cruise industry stands to benefit from this in Europe, but also from more European travelers coming to the U.S.

Along with the European expansion, cruise lines are looking at other new destinations as they seek to expand their offerings beyond the traditional seven-day Caribbean itineraries from Florida. South America and the Far East have shown the greatest percentage of growth, according to CLIA. And more lines are featuring cruises to the Southern or "deep" Caribbean. This growth is further encouraged by the development of new home ports such as Trinidad.

The probable slowdown in newbuilds, the demise of older ships, coupled with the projected growth in demand will mean higher utilization of existing capacity. This, in turn, will mean higher yields and less emphasis on discounting. While discounting will probably always be with us in one form or another, its nature will change. As the cruise lines become more sophisticated about marketing, pricing will come to reflect more accurately the quality of the product as well as the seasonal demand for that product. Product differentiation and consistency of product will help cruise lines to maintain price stability—especially for the quality cruise products.

We'll also be seeing more emphasis by cruise lines on service and value, as opposed to low price. Increasingly in the industry, the marketing message will be "you get what you pay for" and lines will be less inclined to give product away.

As the industry's passenger base expands through the '90s, our marketing messages will be reaching ever-larger audiences. And more members of these large audiences will be within the prime target range of the cruise industry—40 to 65. In the next decade the 77 million Baby Boomers will be turning 35, 40 and 50....These people will be in their peak earning years. According to another study, by 1995, one in four Baby Boom households will earn more than $50,000 a year. By the year 2000, one in 10 Baby Boom households will make $75,000. By the year 2000, Baby Boomers alone will spend an estimated $280 BILLION more annually than they do today.

The Baby Boomers are also healthier than their parents and will live longer, on average. A third will live to be 85—and a million will live to be 100. This generation will continue to be a strong market for the cruise industry well into the 21st century.

We cannot assume, however, that the Baby Boomers will necessarily be the proverbial geese laying the golden eggs for the cruise industry. They will expect and demand quality, value and service. In addition, there is and will continue to be heavy competition for their discretionary dollars.

The cruise industry already offers a high degree of quality, value and service—it's why cruising has the highest satisfaction rate of any segment of the travel industry. We in the cruise industry must guard that satisfaction level, ensure that standards remain high and get the message out about the all-inclusive value of a cruise. We're not just marketing cruise vacations—we're marketing VACATIONS. And we are competing with every other vacation vendor out there, as well as consumer goods like big-screen TVs and designer jewelry.

In the 1990s, the retail travel agent community—which is expected to grow to at least 50,000 outlets from today's 35,000—will become increasingly more sophisticated. Since time and convenience will be paramount with busy, dual-income couples, the successful agents will be those who provide the service and value that travelers of the '90s will expect. Retailers also will become more knowledgeable and professional, using such tools as user-friendly travel stores, videos and improved sales training to sell the client.

Preferred supplier relationships will become increasingly more important in the '90s. Cruise lines will court and reward the travel agents who can produce. Agents need to establish these arrangements so they can gain a competitive advantage—and because they cannot become expert on 25 to 30 cruise lines. Agents will be providing better service to their clients by being knowledgeable and having an excellent working relationship with a few preferred suppliers that can supply across-the-board products.

To summarize the expected trends for the 1990s:

- *The early '90s will see many of the trends of the late '80s, including another surge in capacity growth and continued growth in passenger carryings.*
- *We'll continue to see a lot of turbulence in the cruise marketplace—such as more new products, additional consolidations, fluctuating cost of fuel, and the retail community scrambling for volume.*
- *We'll see a clear positioning of the cruise vacation vs. other vacations or retail challengers.*
- *We'll see the impact of improved retail technology—with worldwide computer linkups.*
- *And if the economy holds up, we just may see the predicted 10 million annual passengers by the year 2000.*

Remarks at the Seatrade Cruise Shipping '90 Conference, Miami, Fl, March 21, 1990, by Kirk Lanterman, President and CEO, Holland America Line-Westours, Inc., and Chairman, Cruise Lines International Association.

Many families have two incomes. A growing number of professional two-income families have developed. These families are frequently unable to obtain 2 weeks at the same time for a family vacation. Therefore, they are taking more shorter vacations. Parents are also taking their children on vacation with them more often, because they don't spend as much time together at home as they used to. This phenomenon has led to the development of good children's programs on cruises and at hotels. Hyatt Hotels has developed Camp Hyatt at all their resort properties. Most cruise lines provide counselors and programs for a variety of age groups. This allows parents and children to vacation together, but without too much togetherness.

As the population of the United States is growing older with better health and vigor, companies are marketing travel opportunities for the elderly, who have the time and frequently the money to travel in style for longer periods of time. There has also been a growth in vacation packages aimed at grandparents traveling with one or more grandchildren.

The future will involve more niche markets. There will be cruises, tours, and even travel agencies aimed at a variety of special interests. See the Industry Communique. Travel is considered a right rather than a privilege within the United States, and companies are filling the voids for virtually any type of special interest they can think of.

Another sociological change that is affecting travel is the growing concern of the world about protecting the environment for the future. Some popular tourist sites, such as Stonehenge in England, are now protected from the onslaught of human contact that has been wearing them down. They must now be viewed from a distance.

Cruise lines are very careful not to dump trash into the ocean and most of them request passengers to sort trash into one of several well marked containers for recycling. Travel destinations, airlines, hotels and other suppliers make concerted efforts to market an image of environmental concern. Many of them take part, both through membership of their executives on committees and by financial contribution, in environmentally active organizations. There are a number of awards presented by organizations such as the Society of American Travel Writers and the American Society of Travel Agents to travel suppliers that have demonstrated concern for the environment.

A number of tour operators have even started marketing tours directed at people concerned about the environment. These tours usually visit historic and/or scenic sites that are environmentally fragile. Care is taken not to disturb the environment while allowing the visitors to enjoy the experience.

CONSOLIDATIONS AND MARKETING RELATIONSHIPS

During the 1980s, the airline industry was a focus of mergers and consolidations. The hotel and travel agency industries also saw great changes in the business relationships they needed. Franchising and joint marketing organizations grew by leaps and bounds. Hotel chains such as Choice Hotels, Radisson, and Best Western expanded their operations by aggressively seeking new franchisees and, in the case of Choice Hotels, purchasing existing smaller franchise groups (Rodeway, Econolodge, and Friendship Hotels) to gain economies of scale. For several years, Radisson added new franchisees at the rate of one every 5 days.

Travel agency group marketing organizations have enjoyed great growth since the early 1980s. Uniglobe, a franchise organization based in Canada, established hundreds of agency locations throughout the United States. The Carlson organization purchased Ask Mr. Foster, a large hundred-year-old travel agency organization, and added both company-owned agencies and hundreds of independent franchisees as associate agencies.

Other group marketing organizations, known as consortiums and cooperatives, gathered thousands of affiliates desiring to increase their clout and profitability. By joining together, they are able to increase their marketing power with suppliers. In addition, by working closely with their members, they are able to enhance the suppliers' ability to reach independent travel agencies throughout the country more economically and efficiently. See the Industry Communique for a discussion of consolidation in the travel industry.

INDUSTRY COMMUNIQUE

SPEECH TO FRANCHISEES, SEPTEMBER, 1991

Robert C. Hazard, Jr., President and CEO, Choice Hotels

CONSOLIDATION

Come together. Consolidate. Become more efficient. Recessions are a grim reminder that there is no law that says businesses will remain in business forever.

In this recession, unlike others, the service industries—airlines, banks, computers and hotels—got clobbered. The airlines, the banking industry and the computer industry are already in the midst of major consolidations.

Strong U.S. air carriers have shrunk from 22 to three—United, Delta and American. In August [1991], third place Delta catapulted past arch-rivals American and United when Delta purchased most of Pan Am for $1.4 billion.

The number of U.S. carriers continues to shrink. Gone are such well-known names as Eastern, National, Allegheny, Frontier, Western, Republic, Air Florida,

People Express, Ozark, Texas International, Piedmont, Hughes Air West, North Central, Air California, and PSA. All have been merged or disappeared. 150 carriers have gone out of business during the last 12 years.

Talk about industry consolidation! The stakes are huge—control of the world's skies. When you see 22 strong airlines shrinking to three—or possibly five U.S. carriers—it's a prelude to the future. You begin to see the probable shape of the U.S. lodging industry in the decade ahead.

The urge to merge is no less strong in the banking industry—which has also been gripped by mergia-mania.

In a merger of California giants, the number two U.S. bank, BankAmerica, has agreed to swallow the nation's number five bank, Security Pacific, confirming BankAmerica's status as the most powerful bank in the West. Now the pressure is on for Wells Fargo and First Interstate to become the nation's next banking mega-merger.

In the East, New York's Chemical Bank has agreed to merge with Manufacturers Hanover to better compete with super-giant Citicorp. In the Southeast, C&S/Sovran has accepted a takeover bid from NCNB and will be renamed NationsBank.

In the computer industry, arch-rivals IBM and Apple have formed a new joint venture to better compete with Bill Gates' Microsoft in the development of personal computer software.

The urge to merge trend is global because the driving forces are greater efficiency, increased competitiveness and global survival. The process is irreversible. In the '90s, every hotel company will have to decide whether it intends to become an acquiror or an acquiree.

Reprinted from a speech to franchisees, September 1991.

GLOBALIZATION

In addition to the networking described above, all segments of the industry have become more global. Airlines have worked out code-sharing agreements that let a passenger from many cities in the United States get on a plane in their home town and change at a gateway city to an international carrier with minimum hassle. In some cases, in fact, the flights go by the same flight number and use a single carrier code. Although this has been quite confusing to many travelers, this code-sharing has increased the marketing strength of many carriers.

The United States has gone through deregulation and is looked at as a role model for much of the world. The nations of Western Europe plan to deregulate their aviation industry during the 1990s in much the same manner as the United States.

Computer reservation systems have increased their global influence. Galileo and Amadeus, the two largest international CRS systems, are each owned by a number of international airlines. Both systems have installations in a variety of countries.

Hotel chains have all gone global. With the increase in travelers from foreign countries into the United States, hotels need to be known around the world so that foreign travelers will be comfortable booking well-known hotels in the United States.

Travel agency groups, especially the large ones and the franchise organizations, have purchased or franchised companies throughout the world. This has become especially necessary for major commercial agencies, because corporations now are multinational and need consistency from businesses that service them.

Travel agency leisure marketing still remains heavily oriented toward local community needs. The reputation of the local agency and even of its individual agents continues to be a critical factor. "Branding" (the use of a nationally known name) has had little impact on the consumer's choice of leisure travel agents. See the Industry Communique for a discussion of some ways in which leisure travel agents can use consortiums and the importance of diversification to the future of forward-looking travel agencies.

INDUSTRY COMMUNIQUE

MARKETING FOR THE TRAVEL AGENCY

Phil and Doris Davidoff

SELECTIVE SELLING BREEDS STRONG RELATIONSHIPS

Travel agents are finding that both service levels and profits benefit from an established, preferred supplier and product policy. Concentrating selling efforts on specific products and suppliers helps agents develop relationships with travel suppliers that will both help solve problems when they occur and bring important recognition to the agency and its clients.

Developing a preferred supplier list gives a travel agency manager control over what is being sold in the agency. The staff is less confused because they know the operators and programs with which they are expected to be thoroughly familiar. Since the agents know certain products more thoroughly, they can match products to clients' needs more effectively. Thus the clients benefit as well. Of course, the choice of preferred supplies must be based upon a full analysis of the travel needs of target market segments.

Concentrating sales as much as is reasonable within a preferred suppliers list can often provide substantial override commission income. When standard product commission is 10 percent, earning 12 percent or 14 percent commission is actually a 20 percent or 40 percent increase in income on a transaction without additional sales effort.

Many small- and medium-size travel agencies have joined consortiums and cooperatives. These organizations have negotiated override commissions for their members from certain suppliers. Other operators will provide overrides directly to individual agencies based upon sales volume or number of passengers booked, usually on a yearly basis. Through consortiums, overrides are often paid from the first booking.

The marketing question today for the smaller travel agency is not whether to join a consortium, but which consortium is best for the agency. An analysis of suppliers participating in the consortium judged against the clientele and target markets of the agency is required for a sound decision.

Recognition and clout are among the most important reasons for dealing with preferred suppliers as much as possible. By concentrating bookings with fewer operators, volume increases with the chosen suppliers. As volume grows, recognition from the operators should increase as well. Sales support for special promotions or groups becomes more readily available. Agents who concentrate their business are more likely to be invited to special seminars, familiarization trips, and other special recognition functions.

Problem solving will also be easier. Accumulated clout, used judiciously, will help clear wait-listed space when other agents cannot. Clients from agencies with clout will be the last to be walked when a preferred supplier hotel is oversold. If a client does have a problem or if an agency employee receives poor treatment from a preferred supplier's reservationist, the agency will have achieved the recognition with supplier management to assure satisfactory solutions.

Relationship marketing, while not in fact new, is one of the most modern marketing concepts. The crux of the concept is that, given relatively equal situations, buyers will purchase from the companies with which they have developed the strongest relationship and which they believe will provide the highest support levels.

Nowhere is this theory more true than in travel agency sales situations—both between agent and supplier and agent and client. Travel service is clearly an intangible. The agent is in the middle, bringing supplier and traveler together. The agent secures from the supplier a confirmation of services to be provided to the traveler. Often the confirmation is only verbal. Most often it is an electronic message received via computer terminal. The traveler pays large sums of money to the travel agency and receives only paper (for example, tickets and vouchers) in return. Strong relationships among the three parties are clearly critical to successful operations.

DIVERSIFICATION VERSUS SPECIALIZATION

The decision to diversify or specialize has always been a difficult one to make in any business. Should an agency handle a broad range of products or specialize in just a few? Should it become known as a commercial, vacation, or group specialist, or does it develop expertise in all facets of the industry? Should the agency specialize in one or two destinations or should it sell the world?

For some strange reason marketing comparisons are often made between travel agencies and inventory-based businesses such as dress and grocery stores. How many times has the question "Do you want to be a supermarket or a boutique?" been asked?

The deck is automatically stacked if the travel agency is viewed as either a supermarket handling a broad variety of products or a boutique specializing in just a few. Everyone knows the vast financial and human resources needed for the successful operation of supermarkets. There have also been successful low-budget boutiques. As a result, as basically small businesses, travel agencies often opt for the boutique approach.

The comparison of boutique versus supermarket is not valid in the travel agency industry. Grocery stores and dress shops depend on prepurchased inventories. The amount of money (or credit) and space required to purchase and house inventory for a supermarket or department store is vastly different from that required for a convenience store or boutique.

Certainly the staff skills and knowledge required for a broad-based travel agency are more varied than for a specialized agency. However, since the travel agency is not in an inventory business, there are no goods to prepurchase or store.

A travel agency is affected by many factors outside its control. Perceptions of terrorism and the effects of a declining dollar damaged the European market in 1986. Declining domestic airfares directly affected travel agency commission income as well.

The more an agency depends upon a single type of business, the more it will be hurt by negative forces affecting its chosen specialty. Conversely, an agency with a broad product and service base will not be hurt as much by declines in any one product or service. There is some truth to the old cliché, "Don't put all your eggs in one basket."

Most agencies are suffering from an overdependence on the air travel product. The double whammy of lower domestic fares plus the loss of the European market had a major effect on profit. Those agencies with a strong cruise market were in better shape in 1986 than those who concentrated almost solely on air tickets or Europe.

An agency that specializes in a single destination can claim to be an expert in that area. However, can that agency make needed marketing changes when destination popularity abruptly shifts?

The great growth of commercial business since deregulation has created many agencies totally dependent on this market segment. Small agencies handling local branches of national accounts have lost large portions of their business, through no fault of their own, when these accounts centralized their travel.

Diversification is the best method of protection a travel agency can develop. While specialization may provide higher short-term profits, the diversified travel agency will be stronger over the long haul. The pitfalls of specialization are highly unpredictable.

A final thought on this issue. When determining the value of a travel agency, most experts will give additional credit for a diversified business mix. Thus, a diversified agency has a higher sales value than a specialized agency of equivalent size, age, and profitability.

A WORD ABOUT THE FUTURE

The future is bright for the travel agency industry. In contrast to the predictions of many so-called experts, the industry will not be dominated by a few mega-agencies. The travel industry is driven by client needs and different marketing strategies meet differing client needs, thus assuring the future of virtually all types of agencies.

Any travel agency that defines its market or markets clearly and serves it or them well will survive. Those that are well-managed, properly apply marketing concepts, and are flexible to meet market changes can prosper.

The Complete Travel Marketing Handbook, 1988, ed. Andrew Vladimir, NTC Business Books, Lincolnwood, Illinois.

CONCLUSION

It is, of course, impossible to predict with certainty what the future holds. All we can say is that as with all things, there will be changes. However, it is highly probable that travel will continue to grow in the future. As it grows and changes, thorough knowledge of marketing techniques will be even more necessary to meet the challenge of tomorrow's travel and tourism industry. Our final Travel Communique sums up the changes that lie ahead for the travel and tourism industry as a whole.

INDUSTRY COMMUNIQUE

THE INDUSTRY OF THE FUTURE

Robert C. Hazard, Jr.
President and CEO, Choice Hotels

Five key trends will shape the travel industry over the next decade.

1. Accelerated industry consolidation. Look for a rash of new mergers, joint ventures and acquisitions in every sector of the travel industry. Expect the pace of consolidation to quicken as a handful of industry mega-giants emerge to dominate the travel landscape.

Today, the top 25 hotel companies control more than 50% of the room supply. Already, six air carriers control 90% of domestic air traffic. By the year 2000, analysts predict that as few as 20 giant global airlines will dominate the international market. Right now, there are 20 to 30 major travel agency companies and consortia. Over the next two decades, two or three major international players will emerge from the pack.

Expect new partnerships to provide integrated marketing and reservations networks across the world. Dick Ferris' dream of a single Allegis integrated travel company (UAL, Hertz and Westin) was not totally wrong; only the timing and methods were flawed. We'll see more strategic alliances linking hotels, rental cars, airlines and travel agencies.

In the hotel industry, look for Holiday Corporation to sell its core Holiday Inn brand. Hilton Hotels may go on the block and Ramada is up for bids. More foreign investment in U.S. hotels will follow in the wake of foreign ownership and off-shore investment in Westin, InterContinental, Hilton International and Omni.

2. Greater Globalization. Spurred by a booming international travel market, the once stagnant U.S. travel industry will become one of the hottest growth industries of the '90s. In 1988, international airline arrivals to the U.S. rose a dramatic 20%. We congratulate ourselves because 33 million international visitors came to the U.S. in 1988—half of those from Canada. But, with 400 million travelers in the international marketplace, the potential for increased inbound business is enormous.

We need to market the U.S. properly overseas, build better airports, fund a stronger government tourism promotion program with higher passport fees, and watch inbound visitors really take off. Last year, international travelers spent $2 trillion or 12% of the world's GNP. Consider the favorable potential impact of a boom in inbound tourism on the trade balance and the U.S. deficit.

3. More segmentation and niche marketing. Just when you thought every possible travel product had been invented, more will appear as travel companies

seek a competitive advantage. Within the hotel industry, Marriott, Holiday and Quality International alone market a total of twenty brands of hotels. Segmentation and niche marketing will accelerate in the years ahead. Witness the emergence of the individual incentive package, the non-smoking hotel room, the Trump shuttle and the budget air carrier.

4. Technological change. Travel marketing automation is still in its infancy. What next? Laser disk imaging, better guest recognition systems, a new generation of more accurate, more efficient global reservation systems. New industry partnerships will improve the quality and flow of information to the travel agent and the traveling public; yield management systems will drive rates and fares on a minute by minute, space-available basis. From video test displays to automated satellite ticketing outlets, the consumer will become more directly involved in the process of buying travel products. But who will control these new networks? Travel agent consortia? The airlines? Massive travel companies?

5. The quest for service. The travel industry's future lies not with bonus type frequent travel programs or rate discounting, but in offering superior service to the customer. Worldwide, travelers are growing increasingly frustrated with rude, inept, uninformed, insensitive, unpleasant service. Companies that unlock their employees' potential, not through empty slogans or smile buttons, but through professional recruitment, massive retraining and innovative incentive motivation programs, will emerge as the market leaders. With the "baby bust" years upon us, the competitive battle for good people will become an all out war. Winning travel companies will find, train, motivate and promote the best people to provide the best service to tomorrow's traveler.

Lodging Hospitality, February, 1989.

SUMMARY

Our society is in a fast-paced transition from the so-called industrial age to the "information" age. The travel industry, which is dependent on the exchange of information of all types, is in the forefront of this transition.

Deregulation of the United States' airline industry has taken place. The rest of the world is beginning its attempts at deregulation as well. It is too soon to tell what the final result will be, but most analysts foresee a globalization of airline companies instead of the highly nationalistic companies that have existed in the past.

Technology is becoming ever more important to all industries. With the vast amount of information to be shared in the travel and tourism industry, technology will continue to expand, both in volume and in capabilities.

Interest in protecting the environment and the pressure on families for leisure time will also be factors that will help shape travel in the future. Aging of the population and the growth of long-distance travel by the middle class will continue to make the travel industry one of the largest and fastest growing industries in the world. Travel and tourism, more than any other industry, transcends national borders and brings people of all countries into personal contact with other cultures.

QUESTIONS FOR DISCUSSION AND THOUGHT

1. Choose two segments of the travel and tourism industry and discuss your view of the future changes that might happen by the end of the century.
2. What effects has the growth of technology had on the travel industry (discuss at least two)?
3. Choose two articles from a current newspaper or magazine that discuss potential future changes within some segment of the travel industry.
4. Describe two changes that you would like to see within the travel industry (these should be from two different segments of the industry).

Index